BLUE BOX BOY

A MEMOIR OF DOCTOR WHO IN FOUR EPISODES

MATTHEW WATERHOUSE

Having grown up a Doctor Who fan, Matthew Waterhouse found himself – at the age of 18 – catapulted into the regular cast, alongside Tom Baker and Peter Davison. This memoir covers all aspects of Matthew's involvement with Doctor Who, from his childhood of collecting books swapping Weetabix cards and producing his own comics, through his two year working on the programme, his occasional contributions to DVD commentaries and his appearances at fan conventions which continue to this day.

Matthew Waterhouse has worked extensively as an actor, in theatre and for the BBC. He is the author of two novels, Fates, Flowers and Vanitas. He lives in New Haven, CT, visiting Europe frequently.

By the same author
Fates, Flowers: A Comedy of New York
Vanitas: A Comedy of New York
Precious Liars
Sugar: A Quartet of Stories

BLUE BOX BOY

A MEMOIR OF DOCTOR WHO
IN FOUR EPISODES

MATTHEW WATERHOUSE

HEADMUSIC

Text © Matthew Waterhouse 2010.

First published in the UK in 2010 by Hirst Publishing. Reprinted five times.

Reissued with minor amendments and a new introduction in 2013 by
What Noise Productions,
Third Floor,
207 Regent Street,
London,
W1B 3HH

www.whatnoise.co.uk

'Head Music' is an imprint of What Noise Productions.
Design and layout by David Darlington & Daniel Latimer.
Proofread by Robert Dick.
Edited by David Darlington.
Typset using Adobe Garamond Pro and Trajan Pro.

Printed and bound in the UK by Imprint Digital.

The moral right of the author has been asserted.
A CIP catalogue record for this book is available from the British Library.

ISBN 978-0-9568539-7-4

All rights reserved. No part of this book may be reproduced or transmitted by any person or entity, including internet search engines or retailers, in any form or by any means, electronic or mechanical, including photocopying, recording, scanning or by any information storage and retrieval system without the prior written permission of the publisher. This book is sold subject to the condition that it shall not, by way of trade or otherwise, be lent, resold, hired out, or otherwise circulated without the publisher's prior consent in any form of binding or cover other than that in which it is published and without a similar condition including this condition being imposed on the subsequent purchaser.

3rd impression 2016

Note: **The Changing Titles of Doctor Who**
Stories are sometimes referred to in this book by the titles favoured by their authors, when these are known. So the story called *The Wasting* in rehearsal, and broadcast as *State of Decay*, is here called *The Vampire Lords*. The story broadcast as *Full Circle* is here *The Planet That Slept*.

BLUE BOX BOY

A MEMOIR OF DOCTOR WHO IN FOUR EPISODES

MATTHEW WATERHOUSE

The general effect produced by all this is sinister and at the same time slightly phony. What really introduces the sinister element is that the dramatic trappings are somehow unconvincing. The massive walls might quite possibly be made of paper; the whole place might taper off into a flimsy tangle of wires and screens just out of eyeshot.

Anna Kavan, **Sleep Has His House**

All these moments will be lost in time, like tears in rain.

Blade Runner

Matthew Waterhouse

Introduction to the 50th Anniversary Edition

I found myself in a small hotel in Montreal in January 2009. Large parts of Montreal are built underground so that the city can function during its freezing winters. The pavements covered in ice, there is a lively arts scene under the streets and this is why I was there. People pushed past my hotel window in thick boots and scarves and mufflers. Was the man in the flat cap and suit looking elegant and humming in a gravelly voice Leonard Cohen? I took out my notebook and began writing notes for what would become *Blue Box Boy*. Why then? I had always wanted to write about *Doctor Who*, and, now, I don't know why, but out of the blue I felt the right time had come to try. 2009 is a long way from 1984, when I last appeared on the programme. It's a third of even a long lifetime, but intense experiences remain in the memory.

It was not the first time I had tried to formulate some thoughts about *Doctor Who*. Ten year earlier, in London, on the cusp of moving to the USA – for personal, not professional, reasons – I was staying at a friend's house for a couple of days. He had a computer. I had never so much as touched a computer, except fantasy ones in episodes of *Doctor Who*. While my friend was out I began, virtually automatically, in the way of the surrealists, to type passages – scenes of description and dialogue – for a potential *Doctor Who* novel in which the Doctor and Adric landed in a strange red desert landscape which owed something to De Chirico, where the Doctor's memories were sucked out of him, objectified but distorted: he and Adric were walking through corrupt versions of the doctor's past. There was a marketplace like the one in *Doctor Who and the Crusaders*. It smelt of spices but was abandoned and decaying. There was the broken shell of a Dalek. One picture I remember was a distant sandy mountain range in the shape of a dead Cyberman, like those hills which suggest a sleeping human being. I managed to write around six thousand words in two mornings, without the slightest idea where the story was going. I do remember that it was very dark: as his memories were drawn from him, the Doctor began to die. What is anybody made up of but memory?

This piece was more in the style of the new series than the old, being fairly plotless, mainly about image and heightened moments. A skeletal alien army stole the TARDIS and then marched through the doctor's landscaped memories. The memories flaked and burnt and turned to ashes. I do not remember what the aliens' motive was. Perhaps I never knew. Perhaps they did not have one, because the landscape turned out not to have any material existence. The Doctor and Adric had been sucked from reality into the dream of a sleeping alien. They were dying because they had literally ceased to exist – once the alien awoke they would be extinguished – and their only hope was to escape the trap of the dream and re-enter the real universe. God knows how they were to achieve this.

When I left London, I forgot about those six thousand playful words. Whatever happened to them? Are they still on a disc somewhere?

So, in Montreal, I went back to the idea of a book of memory. This would not be a novel but it would not be an autobiography either: it would use devices from theatre and film and fiction.

At first it was a plod to work on. It would not come alive. This is because it was splattered with the word 'I' and was inevitably becoming about me. I did not want to write about myself. I wanted to write about *Doctor Who* and the impressions it left on me, first as a boy viewer and then as an actor. I wanted the 'I' to be only a character among other characters. I suppose it would be possible for me to write a book about myself but this wasn't supposed to be it.

The piece only began to fizz when I stopped writing in the first person and transferred to the third. I'd read several memoirs written in the third person and had found their air of coolness, of detachment, to my taste. One of these books, which I have read more than once, know well and regard as something of an influence on *Blue Box Boy*, is *Christopher and his Kind* by Christopher Isherwood, which is now, weirdly, associated with *Doctor Who* because in a recent BBC TV movie version the current Doctor, Matt Smith, played Isherwood. (One could go on making these sorts of connections forever. In the seventies Isherwood turned out a screenplay for a Frankenstein film in which Tom Baker had a part. Things link up in strange ways).

Writing in the third person, the element of fictionalising, always implicit in memoirs, becomes explicit. Anecdotes are never actually true, even though they spring from a remembered event. Once shaped into a story, with a structure and a punch-line or a sting, they have the quality of fiction. They are not lies but they should not be believed. All memoirs are a form of gossip.

Most of all, *Blue Box Boy* is a book of description. I try and say something nice about each of the stories because, well, why not? – and because I do like them all in different ways. But otherwise I avoid mere opinion. The hope is that the reader becomes a present observer as rehearsals and recordings unfold. I do not make simple judgements about people because these are always banal and false and journalistic. Unfortunately in our culture you can shove a microphone under the mouth of any fool on the planet and ask his opinion about anything you like and his jaw will start clacking up and down like a ventriloquists' dummy. I do not claim to see anyone clearly. I see people only partially, caught in fleeting moments, like a camera. "I am a camera," said Christopher Isherwood.

It was important for me to trust what I remembered: I did not watch any old episodes. I don't have copies of them, in fact, not even the ones I'm in. It is a common complaint from *Doctor Who* actors that the stories are rather samey and all blur into each other. Perhaps because I was so young and because I liked the series and because the whole experience was so strange and intense, I have not found this to be the case. There has not been a moment in the years since when I could not have named every story I was in. They all seemed very different. One could not mistake *The Keeper of Traken* for *The Visitation*, any more than one could mistake *Dinosaurs on a Spaceship* for *Asylum of the Daleks*.

It was a matter of sitting in a quiet room for a few hours each day and seeing what came to me. Sometimes not much, sometimes a particular remembered moment would set off a chain reaction and a thousand words would arrive painlessly. I used my favourite writer Graham Greene's trick of stopping the day's work with a half-completed sentence so there would always be something to write the next day.

Blue Box Boy is essentially a book of praise: for an old TV series that still has the power to charm and delight, and a modern version which has captured the imagination of a whole new generation. Some of these new watchers have dipped into the past episodes and this is great because *Doctor Who* is one vast piece really, one vast 50-year piece of British pop art. How cool it is and how cool to be a part of it.

Writing this book was an exciting and enjoyable trip. Believe me, if it had not been enjoyable to make *Blue Box Boy* I would not have made it.

This is what I wrote.

PROLOGUE

Jane Judge, secretary to the producer of *Doctor Who*, tall, slim, blonde, with an appealing, narrow face and a friendly smile, appeared in the reception of Threshold House in her long skirt and sensible shoes. Threshold House overlooked Shepherd's Bush Green. A few hundred yards to its left was the Bush Theatre, where BBC variety shows were recorded.

Jane said hello to Matthew with her glowing, encouraging smile and she took him up to her office, which was attached to the main *Doctor Who* office.

Matthew expected to find a crowd of boyish actors waiting, all looking a little bit like him, but there weren't any. This was a relief. The last thing he wanted was to see the competition and perhaps to have to make light chatter with them. But he supposed that beyond Jane's desk, behind the door in the wall on the left, a lad was reading his socks off for John Nathan-Turner. He wished the boy all the bad luck in the galaxy.

Jane handed him a two-page scene to study. It was a dialogue between The Doctor and Adric. He read the lines of Adric through and through under his breath in cockney. The character had been described in the breakdown as an artful dodger, so cockney was obviously *de rigueur*.

One chunk of this scene remained in Matthew's memory ever after, though this particular passage of dialogue belonged almost wholly to the Doctor, Adric having only to express wonder. The Doctor talked about Bombay Duck. Bombay Duck was symbolic in this little scene because it was not duck but fish.

"Things are not what they appear to be!" exclaimed the Doctor. "Like Bombay Duck!" What's Bombay Duck, asked the boy.

Matthew loved the scene. The door in the wall opened and John Nathan-Turner emerged. He was younger than Matthew had expected, scarcely into his mid-thirties. (Thirty-three, in fact). He had a neat beard, and black curly hair only slightly disorganised, and a circular face which was not fat. When he smiled his cheeks puffed upward. He shook Matthew's hand and said hello warmly. His voice was light, the vowels drawn-out, especially the last vowel of each word, giving a mildly camp effect. Matthew clutched the script so tightly that it crinkled at the edges. He followed John into the main office, which was long and narrow. On one wall was a board, plastered with countless dozens of photographs from the series. If he had had time to look at them, Matthew could probably have told John which episodes they were from, but it did not seem like a good idea to draw attention to his absurd knowledge. There was also a white board with dates and titles and names in blue and red ink. At the other end another door led to the landing. At the window end, near the door off Jane's office, was a desk. Matthew was offered the chair facing the window.

Matthew was all ready to burst into cockney. John said,

"This character is an artful dodger type."

"Okay," said Matthew, as if he didn't know. He pretended to reflect. "Okay. Yes." He was all ready to stun John with his Londonisms. *Oy, Doctor 'Oo, we goin' to earf or wot?*

"But we don't want cockney dialect."

Matthew was so relieved he let the cockney accent fly away from his mind like a freed dove. "No, we want you to speak in your ordinary accent."

So, Doctor, are we going to Earth by any chance?

And they read. Matthew read Adric and John read The Doctor. Halfway through Matthew tripped over a sentence and asked if he could start again. The second time he felt he was doing okay, the scene took on the right rhythmic shape. John made a couple of directorial suggestions, to which Matthew responded. It seemed to be going quite well.

Too soon it was over. As John stood up and went to a filing cabinet he said,

"See you soon."

Matthew smiled sweetly and said he hoped so.

See you soon! Was this a hint to Matthew that the job was in the bag? Or at least that a recall was? Matthew analysed this comment as the tube rattled through tunnels. Did he *mean* it? Or was it something he said to everyone, like *see ya*, the sort of thing that might be said to someone he would never see again? Perhaps it was a deliberate act of meanness, to create false excitement? *See you soon.* He turned the phrase in his head. He filtered every possible meaning – more than might be supposed, if you really made an effort to find them. He tried to remember the exact sound of John's voice. Then he began to think that John had winked at him as he'd said it, and he became more and more certain he had seen the wink until he became more and more certain that there had *not* been a wink.

He was perhaps at the edge of a stunning change in his life. He might now find himself a cast member in the TV entertainment which had most impressed itself on his imagination, from his earliest memories and throughout his teenage years. How weird would that be? Of course, he might not. What then? He would see. But what if...? What if he was? How would it feel? Fated? Ridiculous to think so, but young people, innate supernaturalists, see the hand of fate in everything.

From the day he first saw *Doctor Who*, he had missed scarcely an episode of this vastly creepy and strange series with its eccentric and changing central character, its monsters, its screaming girls, its cliffhangers, its flimsy sets, its inexplicable magic.

And its blue box, which was perhaps the masterpiece of the series, the symbol of escape, and also of security, though God knew outside it there was menace.

The programmes came on BBC 1 on Autumn and Winter and Spring Saturdays, always around the same time, 5:15, 5:30, 6:00, each in a slot not of half an hour but of the unconventional length of twenty-five minutes, (why?) and they were exciting and atmospheric and terrifying but when the closing credits ran each episode was gone forever. There was permanence in the books and comic strips: the first book he had fallen in love with which had not been only a colourful picture book had been a *Doctor Who* book.

And there was his own vivid imagination.

Sometimes he had obscurely felt that he *was* Doctor Who...

EPISODE ONE
AN UNEARTHLY CHILD

21 February 1943
At this moment I have just come to the Irish part in Siegfried Sassoon's Sherston's Progress. This is a queer book, full of dullness in the active war parts and then penetrating when he writes of peace and leisure and thinking. Perhaps it proves that one should never keep a diary if one wants to write a book about one's past. If he had had no diary, could he remember all those things which bore one so? Wouldn't just the bare essentials of his experience emerge? (Not necessarily facts at all).

The Journals of Denton Welch

1

Matthew lay in bed and prayed to God. His room at night was very dark because his deep green curtains were thick and heavy. It was dark enough to believe in ghosts and demons and God and Jesus, so dark that it would have been impossible not to. He asked God to send one of his angels to Earth with a *Doctor Who* book.

He pictured the angel with its halo glowing orange, hovering in the blackness of his room, holding the book out to him. It was a thick, musty, cobwebby, gold-bound volume a thousand years old. It was lit by the heavenly light. The pages were browned and curled and whispery like an old bible, profusely illustrated in the style of old biblical paintings with dramatic highlights from the television episodes, only a few of which Matthew had seen. He squeezed his eyes tightly together in this act of prayer.

He did not really expect the angel to appear to him like this, but rather to come while he was asleep and leave the book at the end of his bed like Father Christmas. He promised God that in exchange for the book he would worship him and maybe become a monk. He fell asleep, fully believing.

The next morning sunlight seeped under his curtains and the world was objective and realistic, the one in which angels brought books to the feet of a child's bed had vanished with the gone night. Still, he opened his eyes beneath the sheets slowly, just as much to prepare himself for the shock of the heavy book at his feet as for the disappointment of finding it was not there. He meant to throw back the sheets and look to the bottom of the bed, but instead kept his head under the blankets and stared down into the dark. He pushed one foot to the left corner of the bed, feeling for the weight of an object that he did not find. He pushed his other foot to the right side, where the sheet was icily cold, and there was no large alien text to be felt there either. He refused to be disappointed at so ridiculous an unanswered prayer and yet he was, just a tiny bit: that small feeling of let-down.

A few weeks later he was on a Summer holiday with his family in Devon and they wandered, after a day on the beach, into the Dawlish branch of

Woolworth's. His father went to get some chocolates and Matthew looked in a box of cut-price books.

There, a few volumes in, was a hardcover book in a yellow jacket. It caught his eye as he flicked past it, and he flicked back to it and pulled it out.

It was a *Doctor Who* book!! It was called *Doctor Who and the Crusaders*. It was by a man called David Whitaker. On the jacket, a crested warrior wielded a sword. To his left in a separate image was the familiar, endlessly promising and mysterious blue police box which could take you anywhere, anywhen. The word 'Who' of *Doctor Who* was printed in big letters, sliced horizontally several times to create a shimmering effect, reminiscent of the pulsing lines of the programme's opening credits. The book was priced at a special low price of one shilling and sixpence.

He gave up building sandcastles, he hardly ate any lunch. He ignored the trains rumbling along the cliff side behind. He sat on the beach in his shorts and his aertex shirt and he didn't do anything but read until he had got to the last word. Then he started again.

It was a very exciting tale. In the few drawings in which he was represented, Doctor Who did not look at all like the skipping, bow-tied brown-haired clown, weird but reassuring, potty but comforting, known to Matthew from the TV programme. Here he was a much older man, with long silver hair drawn back at the ears. This Doctor was slightly moody, and not above stealing things: he nicked some clothes from a market stall.

He was absent from much of the story. The action scenes involved instead a heroic fellow called Ian, who was Doctor Who's male companion. There was also a female companion called Barbara. Like Ian she was a school teacher. There was another female companion too, young enough to be called a girl. Her name was Vicki and she didn't do much in the story but act as a sort of nurse to the ancient Doctor.

The novel was stewed in Eastern exotica which to Matthew was acutely vivid. Characters entered rooms through bead curtains. Everyone wore those Arabian Nights slippers which curl up at the toes. A prince in a domed palace fell in love with Barbara, and lots of lovey-dovey, kissy scenes took place. There were never any scenes like this on the programme, which was blessedly free of kissing, but Matthew didn't mind them in the book. They were in the mould of exotic silent films with torrid love scenes in desert encampments. There were lots of formal Eastern courtesies, kissings of hands and long-winded pledges of love, and expressions of amazement at Barbara's beauty. When Matthew countless years later saw an old episode with Barbara in it, he noticed that she was impressively statuesque, but she had a mildly disaffected look, as if she was under the weather.

There was a horrible villain called El Akir, every bit as creepy as

Matthew would later find the man with the gammy eye who sat in an office tower communicating with Cybermen. El Akir had no access to futuristic devices. For this the planet Earth must be grateful. Instead he used ancient Eastern tortures, or what pop fiction writers passed off as ancient Eastern tortures.

Towards the end, Ian was buried up to his neck in sand by El Akir and his henchmen. His face was brushed with honey to attract insects and scorpions and he was left to die in the scorching heat of the desert sun. Though the *Doctor Who* programmes were scary and exciting, they did not contain scenes quite so creepily sadistic.

The book was both like and unlike the TV programme and this made it doubly intriguing. Why *did* Doctor Who look different? Why was his temperament different? And why was he a vivid but oddly marginal presence? On the *Doctor Who* programme, scarcely a scene went by without the Doctor in it but this old waspish silver-haired man hovered at the edge of events. Oh, and who were these travellers who were not called Jamie or Zoë or Ben?

Best of all in the book was the one heavily science fiction scene, the one scene in which Doctor Who was the prominent character. It was an opening chapter with a one-word title which Matthew did not understand. He read the word as 'prologula'. It sounded impressively solemn. The Doctor explained to his companions the science of time travel in a way that seemed to Matthew complicated and incomprehensible and at the same time clear and convincing. It proved beyond doubt the credibility of it, as to a child a conjurer's sleight of hand is proof of mystical realities.

The Doctor explained that time travellers could not change history because whatever had already happened could not be undone. As an example, he gave Napoleon: Napoleon could not be made to win at Waterloo because, once he had lost, the eternal fact was that he had lost. Matthew discovered the name of Napoleon in this chapter. Eventually, when he read *War and Peace*, he would think of Napoleon as a name first discovered in a conversation with *Doctor Who*. *War and Peace* was quite exciting, but not as exciting as *Doctor Who and the Crusaders*.

This 'prologula' was so alive to Matthew that he felt he was sitting in the TARDIS with the Doctor and Ian and Barbara and Vicki, not a reader but an auditor. It was a beautifully intimate scene. Even though the Doctor did most of the talking, it seemed like a real exchange of conversation, as happens over a meal or drinks.

Often he reread the whole novel, but hundreds of times he reread this opening sequence. It stood by itself. To him it was the most magical passage in books and the most mysterious Somewhere in this novel – it might have been a clause from the very first sentence?-there was a phrase which

Matthew would always afterwards remember. It said that the TARDIS flitted around the universe, appearing and disappearing, 'as swiftly and silently as a shadow'.

As swiftly and silently as a shadow. That was just how Matthew wanted to travel through the universe. This line was the first conscious experience in his life of what might be called a 'poetic' effect. Lying in bed one night pawing the book, Matthew remembered his prayer to God and his angels. He looked at the book and compared it to the book he had imagined. The one under his hand was not thousands of years old, but it had been printed in 1965 so it was very ancient to Matthew's way of thinking. It was not bound in gold exactly, but the yellow of the dust jacket had a rare and exquisite glow. When he put it on his bookshelf, among the Beatrix Potters and the Amatole books and *Bleep and Booster* and the Railway Series and Ant and Bee, it stood out from them. It always drew his eye.

He decided he had learned here a lesson about the mysterious ways of God and his angels: God ensured that everything you wanted came to you and that all your dreams came true, *but only when you least expected it*. And like the gifts of a pagan trickster, there might be a price exacted for those dreams. In this case the price was one shilling and sixpence. He was a tricky one, God, but essentially nice. Matthew wondered whether he should now take steps to become a monk, or at least a vicar, but he decided that, as the book had not appeared at the foot of his bed in a halo of light but in the stark strip light of a seaside Woolworth's, he could quietly forget his vow without the risk of going to hell.

Doctor Who and the Crusaders was published by Frederick Muller. Matthew was curious about Frederick Muller and wondered what he was like. A name, like a voice on the telephone, had its own powers of suggestion. He pictured him as a grey-haired eminence in a dusty Dickensian office. Frederick Muller sat in an upright chair all day, surrounded by books. He was not really of the twentieth century, not of the outside world of The Beatles and *Thunderbirds* and *Pogles' Wood* and Mary Quant and Aston Martins. He was Victorian. He had long sideburns and wore a black suit. He was stern but kindly. He was not ever, ever called Fred. He liked to send *Doctor Who* books out into the world, to the panting boys. This was his purpose. He sat in his chair waiting for David Whitaker to send in chapters of another novel. This is mainly how Matthew pictured Frederick Muller: just sitting there, waiting, like a Beckett character.

What would Matthew make of *Doctor Who and the Crusaders* forty-plus years later? He is certain he could still enjoy it. It was, he supposes, a simplified variation on the thigh-slapping historical romances of Walter

Scott or Conan Doyle, in which knights say "avaunt!" and "By my hilt!" and "win" pretty ladies though they never make love to them, and bearded kings in animal skins "sup" at feasts on whole legs of beef and huge overflowing flagons of wine and beer, – "bring me ale, wench!" – while commanding their jesters to "entertain me, varlet!"

This style of historical fiction, out-moded by the nineteen eighties, was, if not exactly alive and well, at least lingering on, courtesy of Terence Dudley, on the *Doctor Who* programme. Matthew was delighted to see a story with the superb title of *The King's Demons*, in which a brutish King roared and over-acted in just the right way, and the Doctor himself participated in a sword fight with the Master reminiscent of old swashbucklers, though the *Doctor Who* sword-fight must have been the slowest ever recorded. The cast had clearly decided that they were not willing to spill blood for an episode of *Doctor Who*.

A couple of years after he found and read (and reread and reread) *Doctor Who and the Crusaders*, Matthew uncovered another *Doctor Who* book, also sent into the world by Mr. Frederick Muller and Mr. David Whitaker, not a new book but in fact older than *Doctor Who and the Crusaders*. It was in the children's section of a second hand bookshop in Brighton. It cost more than *Doctor Who and the Crusaders* but it was not being sold as a collector's item, which was just as well because Matthew's pocket money did not run to collector's items. The book was not too badly bashed up. It was called just *Doctor Who*, the letters of *Who* on the jacket sliced horizontally as on *The Crusaders* jacket. It was tantalizingly subtitled '*in an exciting adventure with the Daleks*'. Below the title was a charcoal drawing (or what looked to Matthew like charcoal) of the long-haired Doctor of *Doctor Who and the Crusaders* under a futuristic curved archway, looking downward, thoughtful and a bit sad, an arm, invisible beyond the arch, seeming to rest against a post or perhaps against the door of the TARDIS.

In an unusual design choice this book, though plainly a novel for boys, was presented in a jacket of bracing pink, as if in brilliant prediction of *Doctor Who* becoming synonymous with camp. Someone at the office of Frederick Muller must have had second thoughts because when the book was reprinted the jacket, identical in terms of the drawing and lettering, was now blue, not clear hard TARDIS blue but a very strange variety of blue, with undertones of green and grey, like an underwater dream. Maybe it was ultramarine. Matthew was never sure what exact shade ultramarine was.

Matthew was every bit as pleased by this discovery as by *The Crusaders*. In fact the story was better in a way, it was more like the programme he knew because it was set in the future on a distant planet, with metallic doors that rose and fell, shiny but soulless corridors, a domed city, nuclear war, a group of outsiders called Thals who were all blond and handsome and lived in a cave beyond the city. There was plenty of action and not a single kiss in the entire story.

The book was thoroughly gripping and he loved it, though it did not contain anything as fascinating as the opening scene of *The Crusaders*, which his mother told him was called a prologue. It was narrated, in plain adventure story sentences, by the character Ian, so though the story was tremendously exciting it was not quite as mysterious. The Daleks took a good while to appear, not rearing their tin heads until chapter four, which felt a long way off when Matthew was on chapter two. Even before he got to chapter four, he knew this was when they were to appear, because the contents page said the chapter was called *The Daleks*.

This excellent thriller was accompanied by a large quantity of line drawings, done like the cover in what Matthew took to be charcoal. These wonderfully warm, fuzzy illustrations were at odds with the clean metallic lines of the Dalek city. The Doctor played a much bigger part in the story than he'd done in *The Crusaders*, fussily looking for mercury to make his TARDIS work. But it was still Ian who did the heroic fights. Barbara stood about a lot. Vicki was not in *Doctor Who in an exciting Adventure with the Daleks* at all, but instead, here was Doctor Who's grand-daughter Susan. Ian's wild adventure with the Doctor started under banal circumstances: a foggy night on Barnes Common, where his car broke down. Ian stumbled into a police box to call for help, and of course it wasn't a police box at all.

Lindfield Common, which was near Matthew's house and was the only Common he knew, substituted for Barnes Common in his imagination, though he had never walked across it on a dark foggy night. It was fun to think of the TARDIS landing on Lindfield Common, which was so ordinary, so far from aliens and adventures and time travel: schoolboy footballers and mothers with prams, a cricket pitch, the lazy green descent to a circle of houses below, and the curve of the upper road with the duck pond opposite, on which floated two swans and some cygnets, and round the corner the White Horse pub and the Church hall.

Sometimes a fair came to the village with roundabouts and a coconut shy and wheezy music, and there was also the November bonfire, with vans selling hot dogs, candy floss, toffee apples. On Bonfire Night, the one night of the year Matthew saw the Common in the depths of the evening, it was possible to imagine (even with the loud children and the hot fire and the exploding fireworks), still and silent and unseen behind a tree at the edge, away from the heat, where the air was cold and breath made clouds, the TARDIS materialising and taking him away.

Matthew later got to know Barnes. He lived on and off in West London, for a while in Hammersmith, for a while in Putney, and his Aunt Liz lived nearby in Mortlake, just beyond the brewery and the level crossing. He visited Barnes often, because he and his partner liked the pubs and restaurants of the High Street. A pub called the Bull had a good jazz room. He would make the short train journey from Putney, emerging at twilight from Barnes station with its old Victorian frontage, onto the Common, which didn't resemble Lindfield Common, tennis courts and benches and a neatly mown lawn, at all. Barnes Common was huge and thickly wooded and quite wild. It smelt of ferns. It was seamed with roads which could be heard but not seen. The sound of cars and the train moving off broke the silence, but the Common was always very still, no-one else about. It was easy to see how Ian could get lost in a fog here. Matthew could never make the walk over the common, which was sometimes actually foggy, without thinking of the TARDIS, somewhere just out of sight.

Every so often a van from the local public library would back into the playground at Matthew's junior school and from this stock the children were encouraged, by which is meant compelled, to choose a book. The selection was predictable: westerns, almost always with 'gun' or 'bullet' in the title, Biggles, a ton of Enid Blytons, adventure stories set in historical periods, almost always with 'sword' in the title, girly horse stories, Lewis Carroll, C. S. Lewis's *Narnia* series, Ladybird books: about Jesus, policemen and nurses. Worthy classics: *The Prince and the Pauper*, *Black Beauty*. One girl called Alice went home with an Agatha Christie, and liked it so much that ever after she spent her lunch breaks sitting on a step reading one Agatha Christie after another.

Once Matthew walked into this van with a gaggle of other children and his eye was drawn to those words to which his eye was always drawn, *DOCTOR WHO*, the same eerily shivery sliced lettering of the first novel and *Doctor Who and the Crusaders*. This cover was not police box blue but telephone box red. Rarely has a child crossed a floor so fast.

The jacket had been glued to the book's boards which gave it a cheap, shiny, fingered look. The page edges were dusty, with the library odour of sweating paper. The cover illustration was of an interplanetary mountainscape with a perfect disc of a moon in the sky, the silver-haired Doctor Who to the right, behind him a giant ant with awful pincers. Doctor Who was turning his head to this ant, as if to engage it in conversation.

It was called *Doctor Who and the Zarbi*. Weirdly, it was not by David Whitaker but by a man called Bill Strutton. *Bill Strutton.* Say it aloud. This was an exceptionally masculine name, the sort which belongs to a person who builds bridges or works on oil derricks.

Doctor Who and the Zarbi was about not the one evil giant ant on the cover but a whole hoard of giant ants, in combat with nice semi-humanoid butterflies.

Suspicious glass tubes dropped from above, presumably to wipe the minds of Doctor Who and his friends. Bill Strutton had the distinctive quirk of saying who was speaking before they spoke, filling his book with "Doctor Who said…" as opposed to the usual "… said Doctor Who." In the end the evil ants became nice. Little of *Doctor Who and the Zarbi* remained in Matthew's memory. He liked the drawings. They were more *Doctor Who*-ey than the others. The main reason he remembered the descending tube was because there was a drawing of it, dropping over the Doctor's face. The Doctor looked disconcerted but contained. The episodes from which it was drawn must have been very striking to the kiddies who watched them in 1965, and indeed the producers had hopes that the Zarbi would be a phenomenon to equal the Daleks, leading to sequels and to toys and comics. This shows how little they knew of the minds of the horrid post-war children of the nuclear age, who liked their scary toys to be slick and shiny and pushable and robotic and phallic. What peculiar child would want to play with toy ants, however wicked? The Zarbi did not take off as hoped.

In another sense, both the ants and the butterflies took off. There was a great deal of flying all over the place in this story.

Matthew read it and read it over the three weeks he was allowed to keep it. He decided, wickedly, that he would not ever, ever, ever give it back to the library. It was *his* now. *His*. So, on the day everyone was supposed to bring their books back, he 'forgot' *Doctor Who and the Zarbi*. No-one mentioned his 'mistake' and he was *sure* he had it permanently in his clutches. Ha ha! Now he could read at his leisure about alien butterflies!! But the next day his teacher announced to the class that one of the borrowed books had not been returned.

"It is a *Doctor Who* book, "said his teacher accusingly. She was a battle-axe with a bun.

"Oh," said Matthew, "but I'm sure I handed it in." He made a show of searching his memory. "Yes, I brought it back yesterday."

"Well," said his teacher, acid as a hanging judge, "maybe you can bring it in tomorrow."

And the next day he forgot it again, and the next. Each day it was brought up and the teacher, who was not a smiley person, grew less warm. Matthew had a vague suspicion that if he said he had lost it he would have to give the library loads of money and he didn't have any money to speak of. His pocket money ran to a comic and a packet of spangles. He might be in debt to the library for years. He might have to go to debtor's prison.

And this is why he later remembered the book less well than the others in that early trilogy: for many years he did not have a copy. Until the Target Books reissue of the early seventies, he lived with the bitter knowledge that he had two *Doctor Who* novels on his sweetly organized shelves but that out there in the ether was a third.

In 1982 he came across a copy of the first edition, at the collector's price of fifteen pounds. He certainly wasn't paying fifteen pounds for it. Besides, he was now sophisticated and read proper books by proper writers. No, he would not buy it...

Back at his flat, he read it and it was very good fun...

And now it sits nestled on a narrow old oak bookcase next to the other two, among material with which it is sympathetic, a Sherlock Holmes collected edition and the Professor Challenger stories and English translations of Leo Perutz. It is half a world away from where he lives.

When the original TV episodes, called *The Web Planet*, surfaced on video in the late eighties Matthew borrowed the tape and was impressed to see that the butterflies which had flown about all over the book were to be seen flying all over the set with reckless abandon, assisted by extremely visible harnesses. Matthew was informed that the director had tried to remedy this by greasing the cameras, which was why all the flying scenes looked as though they had been shot through a coat of clarified butter. Matthew was quite impressed by the episodes, the lo-fi solution to the problem appealing to him. Also, the blur leant a dreamy sheen to all the goings on, reducing by a hair's breadth their ridiculousness. The butterflies had black rings around their eyes so they looked as if they were wearing amusing spectacles.

2

Matthew lived in a large house which had been built in the nineteen thirties, though it was pretending to be older. It had four eaves cupboards in it, little triangular storage spaces the shape of Toblerone boxes, formed where the roof sloped at a steep angle between the wall of the room and the outer wall. Each of the upstairs bedrooms had its own eaves cupboard. They were places of dark suggestiveness to him.

Even as a small child he could not go far into one without bending, and though he carried a torch he would get spider's webs in his hair. Over the years the eaves cupboard off his own bedroom became all sorts of imaginary escapes. When he was nine, it was a Batcave, complete with a superhero costume made from old black curtains. He would sit in it for hours, reading American comics by torch light, wearing nothing but underpants and curtains, like Batman.

When naughtiness got him into trouble, he would go and hide in it. This was completely irrational, because it was such an obvious hideout. Once, he and his sister decided it would be nice to paint their parents' car, which was a green Armstrong-Sidley, though Matthew told his friends at school that it was a Rolls Royce. It was a huge car and any huge car was a Rolls Royce. It smelt of leather and petrol. It had two orange arm signals, one on the driver's side, one on the passenger side. They dropped down from slots between the front and back doors. He and his sister found some silver spray paint. Silver was a much more exciting colour than green. The car would look like a cyber-spaceship. So they sprayed a line just above the running board, starting at the driver's door, and all around the car. Matthew was nonplussed to find that his parents were undelighted. He hid in his eaves cupboard but was soon found.

All sorts of things could be discovered in these webby spaces: toys, cushions, a stool, boxes. In their mystery, they were like those attics in movies where trunks can be found, full of sepia photographs and disused passports and old clothes of the long dead.

Other families threw things away, but in this house unwanted stuff disappeared into these cupboards or into the loft, where they were forgotten. This was merely habit: preservation had nothing to do with it. Even after Matthew had not lived in the house for thirty years, it was still owned by his family and the eaves cupboards were still overflowing with stuff, now probably tacky with damp and grime: old magazines and books, broken toys, almost certainly old annuals, perhaps even a script from *Doctor Who*.

Once Matthew was exploring the eaves cupboard off one of his older brothers' bedrooms. He pulled out a cardboard box, and uncovered a handful of old weekly comic papers. Among them were several copies of the *Eagle* with Dan Dare strips on the cover. *Dan Dare: Pilot of the Future*, was the first science fiction comic strip hero of post-war England. He had adventures on planets like Mars and Venus. He was a square-jawed military man with a jagged eyebrow. He had a trusty Northern sidekick who was called Digby and was part loyal help meet, part buffoon, part clever chap in his own right. Dan called him his batman, though he did not resemble the caped crusader. He said things like "ee, by gum" a lot.

This bundle also included some issues of *TV21*, which was devoted mainly to the Gerry Anderson puppet adventure series, *Thunderbirds*, *Stingray*, and, later, *Captain Scarlet*. Matthew loved all these programmes.

Blue Box Boy: A Memoir of Doctor Who in Four Episodes

TV21 was excellently printed on glossy paper. Thrillingly, on the back page was a gorgeously painted series called, simply, *The Daleks*, in which Daleks flew around on jet-propelled platforms. Doctor Who himself played no part in this strip, which was credited to Terry Nation.

TV21 revolved around a terrific concept: it was presented like a futuristic newspaper, each issue dated a hundred years hence, 2064, 2065, 2066. The front pages were blazoned with eye-catching headlines: "Stingray in trouble in the North Sea!" or "Thunderbird Three Trapped in Space!"

There followed a report in breathless journalese, referring the reader to an inner page, where the drama unfolded in outstandingly well illustrated comic strips.

But these were not the peak of Matthew's excitement that winter morning. He found also a single issue of a weekly called, imaginatively, *TV Comic*, which was a kind of *Beano* for goggle-box kiddies, a collation of one and two page strips, most based on telly programmes. It was in every objective way an inferior publication, in a smaller format and with a more knockabout tone, the drawings scratchy. Even the colour pages were less spectacular. But…

Among the unpretentious gathering of one-page slapstick comedies, broken up by the odd adventure serial, was a discovery of, to him, vast importance: a full-colour strip about *Doctor Who*!

This was the old man of *Doctor Who and the Crusaders*. He was tall and wiry in this strip, his face thin, distinguished, his hair goldish. He was less bad tempered than the Doctor of *The Crusaders*, solicitous in a grandfatherly way of the welfare of his two companions, who were younger than the TV characters, little children of a Janet and John type. The final panel had a terrifying ending: a wall with knives in it, moving towards the heroic trio, the Doctor's hands, palms open and outward, at a level with his chin, as if to ward off evil: Matthew would later come to recognize this as the artist's formula representation of fear.

Would Doctor Who make it out alive???

This issue of *TV Comic* was the sole survivor. Forever, that lethal wall would roll towards *Doctor Who* and the children.

Finders keepers. Matthew took all these comics from his brother's eaves cupboard and put them in his own. On top of the pile was the *TV Comic*, which he read often. He placed an order.

So, for many years he went down to Gase newsagent and bought the crisp new issue, his name written in pencil on the right above the title banner: Matthew Waterhouse or M Waterhouse. Sometimes just Waterhouse. The anticipation every Saturday morning was scarcely less intense than the one he felt at 5:14 in the afternoon. At the end of each strip was a gasped query: 'Will Doctor Who Survive? See Next Week!'

When a brand new *Doctor Who* comic serial was to begin, an announcement ran above the banner on the cover: "An incredible new *Doctor Who* story begins this week!" He liked the dramatic thud of the word. Incredible! *Incredible!* INCREDIBLE!

There were other melodramatic words: thrilling, gripping, terrifying, action-packed. ACTION-PACKED! "An action-packed new *Doctor Who* story starts this week!"

For a while, *Doctor Who* was the flagship strip: three pages, including a full colour page on the cover. Then it moved to the middle pages, in full colour, until, disappointingly, it was downgraded to the inner back pages, where it was black and white. Sometimes the strip was titled *Dr Who and the Daleks*, even when the Daleks were not in the story. The *TV Comic* creators came up with a recurring monster of their own, called the Trods, who were robotic in nature, with legs like slinkies. The Cybermen landed on a planet and were destroyed by the smell of fragrant flowers. The artist, who Matthew was later informed was called John Canning, somehow got the very essence of the Second Doctor's character, though his drawings did not much resemble Patrick Troughton feature by feature. In the strips, with his compressed, playful grin, his head a little flattened, the cheeks wide and humorous, a finger held up in an 'aha!' moment, Canning caught not the Second Doctor's literal likeness but his spirit. Of course, the Second Doctor was an overtly characterful incarnation, even cartoony, in a good way.

There was a brilliant regeneration story. The Time Lords sent scarecrows to capture Doctor Who. Echoes upon echoes: this reminds Matthew both of *Worzel Gummidge*, Jon Pertwee's hit series about a scarecrow, and of the ghostly figure that stalked the Doctor and Adric in the last Tom Baker story.

Mr. Canning's Jon Pertwee was less characterful than his Patrick, though extremely elongated, like a character in a drawing by Phiz for Dickens. Canning was very good at drawing the Doctor's ruffled sleeves. The Doctor stopped a wicked boy with round glasses who fed a drug to the animals at the zoo which changed normally sedate creatures into vicious killers. A professor built a rocket to Venus.

Canning did not get much time to hone his Pertwee representation, because after a few months of the Third Doctor's reign, the *Doctor Who* strip was snatched away from him and from *TV Comic* entirely.

For a couple of years, *TV Comic* had a companion paper for slightly older readers called *Countdown*. The page numbers, in the spirit of the title, counted down. The front cover was page twenty-four and the back cover was page one. In *Countdown*, the Third Doctor was not Canning's lengthened cartoon figure, but a more careful representation of Pertwee himself.

In what may have been a first for British weeklies, the comic strip artists in *Countdown* were credited. *Doctor Who* was drawn first by Harry Lindfield, then by Gerry Haylock, who may have been Harry Lindfield under another name, and sometimes Frank Langford. With these names and their art styles came invented faces and personalities, as had happened with Mr Muller: Frank Langford plump and rather delicate, Gerry Haylock, humorous and airy but also deep-thinking and – reminiscent of the creator of *Thunderbirds* – certainly bald.

Harry Lindfield, or a man calling himself Harry Lindfield, was the first *Doctor Who* artist. He drew the strip for only the first dozen issues but Matthew would never forget his name: the village adjoining his town was called Lindfield, with its Common, the one he thought of when the TARDIS landed on Barnes Common.

In the first issue it was revealed that Doctor Who was renting a cottage, where he was trying to repair his TARDIS. Unfortunately there was no sign of Doctor Shaw or Jo Grant. A robber crouched in the garden outside and waited for him to switch the lights off and go to bed so he could break in. The robber thought, doesn't he ever sleep? Here was a rich and stimulating piece of information: The Doctor scarcely ever slept. He was up all night, doing mysterious things. In this first strip, though *Doctor Who* failed to get the TARDIS to function properly, he did succeed in making a short hop, ending up in the arid Australian desert, near the skull of a dead animal half covered with sand. Matthew knew less about Australia than he knew about Skaro.

Long before the same twist occurred on the programme itself, Matthew was fascinated by a strip featuring Herbert George Wells as a protagonist. In this, an evil supercomputer was lodged in St. Paul's Cathedral. In another, thin withered narrow-headed aliens with long moustaches and tiny, bony legs sat on hovering discs (a close variation on the Mekon from *Dan Dare*, but Matthew did not know this), and in another an artful dodger on the streets of Victorian London was swept by the TARDIS to the Wild West, and there was another with Daleks on sleds in the arctic. Interestingly, the presence of Daleks in the arctic was revealed not in the final panel of the first episode, but, completely unexpectedly, at the end of the second.

Countdown got one important *Doctor Who* fact wrong for months. Their Doctor drove round in a yellow roadster identical in every way to Bessie (WHO 1) of the programme, except that she was called Betsy. This was inexplicable.

After a year, *Countdown* changed its name to *TV Action*. Daleks invaded a rain forest planet. The Post Office Tower was nearly destroyed. Sometimes there was a bumper complete story: five whole pages of *Doctor*

Who. In one of these long stories, the Third Doctor had to solve a series of dangerous puzzles, which would have spelt his end if he got the answers wrong. This, of course, was later a key element of that marvellous special called *The Five Doctors*.

The comic held a competition to design a monster which would be used in the *Doctor Who* strip. Matthew had entered competitions before, but had never won a prize. Once, *TV Comic* had held a colouring competition, giving away fifty Basil Brush glove puppets, and Matthew had not won a glove puppet, though he had coloured and coloured and coloured that picture of Basil Brush until it was sticky with layers of crayon. But he was sure the *Doctor Who* monster competition would be a cinch. He entered a design called the Paasifaal, so terrifying and gruesome it should surely have won, though he was willing to admit his drawing did not do justice to the monster he had envisioned. Instead, the winner was a wretched boy who invented a monster much inferior to Matthew's called the Ugraak. The Ugraak had a high bald head and a long face and tusks, as amateur monsters are wont to. *Well, if all they want is tusks and an ill-tempered expression, they can have it,* fumed Matthew. In the serial, the Ugraaks were closely related to toadstools. A little photograph of the winner appeared above the first instalment, looking like a generic boy, bleached of all individuality.

No good idea goes unrepeated. Matthew, on a flying visit to London, saw on a hotel TV in 2009 a portion of a Saturday night variety show, of the kind which makes viewers complain about the decline of the BBC. ("We pay our licence fee for *this??* Bring back Mr. Blobby!")Among the highlights of this disheartening entertainment was a *Doctor Who* design-a-monster competition, to be voted for by the viewers. It was not a matter only of drawing a picture of a monster, but of making a full-blown costume and wearing it on TV. A woman walked around covered in shiny foil, a man had a dirty sock pulled over his face. In interviews, always on the verge of tears as is the way of reality shows, the contestants said, "to be a monster on *Doctor Who* will be my dream come true!" On the old *Doctor Who*, none of the performers under monster make-up had led Matthew to believe he was witness to a dream come true. The only dream come true was his own, which was as it should be. Russell T. Davies was filmed in Wales, frantically flapping his hands, begging the viewers to make the right choice. "The reputation of *Doctor Who* is in your hands!"

Matthew never found out who won, but supposed it was not the woman in foil nor the man in the sock. There was nothing as good as an Ugraak and certainly nothing as good as a Paasifaal.

*   *   *

TV Action breathed its last with issue 123. The next week it merged with *TV Comic*, becoming *TV Comic and TV Action*. *Doctor Who* returned to its traditional place on the last double-page spread. Gerry Haylock continued to be the artist.

Matthew looked younger than his age but there came a time, as the Third Doctor turned into the Fourth, (who began with an exciting adventure featuring a character in Invisible Man-style bandages and also the lovely Sarah Jane Smith, one of the rare occasions the publishers used a TV companion), when it became embarrassing to buy *TV Comic* every week. He cancelled his order, though often he covertly read *Doctor Who* in the newsagent or at the bookstall on Brighton station, next to signs saying *Buy Brighton Rock*. By this time the strip had gone full circle, and was back in the hands of John Canning, Tom in Canning's drawings as characterfully barmy as could be hoped for, his hat floppier than ever.

The strip ran in *TV Comic* unbroken until the late seventies, when Marvel Comics snapped up the rights to *Doctor Who*.

So then, finally, there was *Doctor Who Weekly*. This emerged in 1979. Matthew was one of its most excited readers, and dashed off a slightly pompous letter in his nearly unreadable hand-writing, which was published, to his subsequent embarrassment. When the comic came out, the best thing about it was the photographs from old episodes, of which there were many which Matthew had never seen.

The strips, to Matthew, were strangely schizophrenic. They laboured to reproduce the amusing tone of the latest episodes. *Doctor Who* made arch comments all the time and had a silly grin on his face. For a while he had a comedy alien animal as a companion. A gifted writer called Pat had been poached from *2000AD*, which was a sort of *Eagle* for punk rockers, and the artist was Dave Gibbons, who eventually became a comic book legend as the collaborator with Alan Moore on *Watchmen*. The first story was an inventive tale about a sort of robotic Roman Empire called *The Iron Legion*. But here was the problem: for all the Doctor's fake Tom-style amusing remarks, the strip did not *feel* like *Doctor Who*, it felt like a *2000AD* strip with the Doctor dropped into it.

The strip's writer Pat had a story outline sitting around in the *Doctor Who* office, which the producer Graham Williams had seriously considered. It was called *Song of the Space Whale*, apparently a kind of *Doctor Who* version of *Moby Dick*.

Long before the Marvel comic, Matthew produced the infinitely superior *Doctor Who Comics Monthly*, named after *Spider-Man Comics Weekly*. His *Doctor Who* comic was supposed to be a Weekly too, but he could not draw fast enough. It covered twelve foolscap sheets of paper, stapled together. It included three thrilling, incredible, action-packed serials each issue, as well as piquant facts drawn from *The Making of Doctor Who*. One strip featured the First Doctor, another the Second Doctor, the last the Third Doctor.

In a fantastic cliffhanger, the Third Doctor watched in horror as his TARDIS dematerialised, stolen by the Daleks. The Paasifaal became a regular monster. The Cybermen and Ice Warriors appeared a lot. The Ugraaks appeared once. Matthew's capacity for invention was high, but he was not good at drawing and relied on traced images from Messrs Canning and Haylock and the annuals. His backgrounds were rudimentary on paper though not in his head. Whole pages consisted of little but faces talking to each other, showing suitable expressions of terror or thoughtfulness, with perhaps a futuristic doorway in the background or a couple of TARDIS discs or a tree. He drew quite good trees of a twisty, Tolkienesque kind.

Doctor Who Comics Monthly was a lot less boring than a fanzine, though it only ever had one reader, and he was also the writer. It ran for two superb years, until its publisher, Kroton Komics Ltd., lost interest in it.

The shops in November were clogged with large hardback annuals for children produced for the Christmas market.

Every programme with the slightest appeal to children had its own annual, from police programmes like *Z-Cars* to infants' puppet entertainments like *Camberwick Green* to cartoons like *Tom and Jerry*. Even the soap opera *Compact* had an annual. Matthew never saw *Compact*, which was about a magazine, but John Nathan-Turner's big dream as a producer was to revive it, and he proposed this to the BBC in nineteen eighty-one. John loved *Dallas* and wanted to turn *Compact* into a British glamour soap of a similar kind. The idea was rejected in favour of the dowdy *EastEnders*, endlessly confronting ishoos.

From Christmas 1964 onward, every year but one, right into the nineteen eighties, a *Dr. Who Annual* (as it was called) came forth. Because the old *Doctor Who* ran for so many years, a complete set of *Dr. Who Annual*s would now take up an entire bookshelf.

The first of these fabulous books Matthew read had a terrific cover painting of the Doctor grinning loudly, creases around the eyes, with his companion Liz Shaw peering over his shoulder at the reader, and the Brigadier smaller and much further to the back. A UNIT helicopter hovered over their heads. Again an outlandish design decision had been made for a book whose readers would, presumably, be boys, because the characters were backgrounded by a bright pink wash, and the spine of the book was the same ice cream pink. It made you want to lick it. At the lower left, near the Doctor's shoulder, was an important statement: 'Based on the popular BBC series starring Jon Pertwee as Dr. Who and Caroline John as

Liz Shaw'. Somehow having the names of the actors on the cover gave the impression they had approved the contents, making it more legitimate, more official. Approval by the BBC was abstract, approval by Jon Pertwee was concrete. "Yes, old chap," Jon Pertwee seemed to be saying, "this is an excellent read."

Matthew wondered if Nicholas Courtney was a little offended at not being asked for his approval too. Maybe he had withheld it. He wondered if Caroline John was proud to see her name on the cover, perhaps showing the book to her friends and bragging a bit, which was only human. The stories were all set on Earth in the style of that year's TV season. One magnificently peculiar story was called *The Mind Extractors*, in which bald aliens sat in the backs of country buses smoking long thin cigarettes which emptied the minds of the other passengers.

The talented but anonymous author had a memorable stylistic kink. He dropped all pronouns. I, we, you. A character did not say "I will meet you at the allotments." He said, "Will meet you at the allotments." So it continued: "In desperate trouble." "Don't understand you." "Need your help urgently." "Far too busy." Matthew thought this telegraphese sublimely like real life.

The book's spine tore and soon the whole thing fell apart. The pages dropped out. Next to Matthew's name in his spidery writing was the name of his school-friend George, stamped in ink. George got his own name stamp for Christmas and, when Matthew leant him the book, he decided to claim it. We can share it, he said. Matthew never leant him a book again.

But George must be credited with an act of generosity, for he gave Matthew a copy of the previous annual, which featured Patrick Troughton. The annual was wonderful. The cover photograph had Patrick with his lovely expression at once authoritative and flustered, leaning on the TARDIS console, which, strangely, was greenish rather than the familiar bone-white. The first story in this annual was about Dinosaurs. It was extraordinary how often a hack writer, required to turn out a quick story about Doctor Who, whether for an annual or a slide projector or the wrapper of a chocolate bar, fell back on dinosaurs, though on the programme itself dinosaurs were a rarity. There was also a comic strip about a robot in a nearly destroyed city of the future, with some very good drawings of Zoë, which Matthew traced when making his own *Doctor Who* comic.

A footnote regarding the pink annual: Matthew's schoolboy copy soon became defaced, as he has said. But the Monday after his first TV appearance, on a live programme called *Saturday Night at the Mill* – it was without question that very Monday – Matthew wandered into the second-hand bookshop at the bottom of his road, Murray Books. There, in the children's section, prominently displayed so that it virtually called to him, was a pristine copy. No greasy childish fingers had smeared it, no moustaches had been drawn on the astronauts, no ink-stamp-owning friends had tried to say it was *theirs*. It was ten years old, but it might have been shot through time fresh from the printers.

When Matthew was in *Doctor Who*, John Nathan-Turner gave him a copy of the newest annual. It turned out to be the best in many years, though it did not seem to contain anything as splendid as *The Mind Extractors*. (He never read the stories). He was impressed to see that he was a prominent feature in it. The first half of the book featured the Fourth Doctor, the second half featured the Fifth Doctor, though the Fifth had not appeared on TV yet and looked suspiciously like a young vet. Only Adric was present throughout the book, and Matthew was pleased to see that the magnificent and unpretentious artist had made him look quite sexy, as in real life. But Paul Darrow – Avon in *Blake's 7* – mentioned the generous fee paid to him for the use of his face in the *Blake's 7* annual. Matthew went to a newsagent and had a little look in the *Blake's 7* annual, which was covered in half-off stickers. He called his agent and asked why he had not been paid an enormous fee. Well, said his agent dryly, they don't have to pay you anything, and at least they gave you a copy…

3

In the early seventies, a man in a publishing house called W. H. Allen decided there might be a few easy pounds to be made by reissuing those novels published by Frederick Muller in paperback editions through their Target imprint. There had been the slightest possibility that the austere Mr. Muller had been slumming it by putting out *Doctor Who* novels. W H Allen had long been established as the tackiest book publisher in Britain. Yes. For W. H. Allen, *Doctor Who* novels were a move upmarket...

The reprints sold by the truckload, despite starring a Doctor unfamiliar to most of the young ones who bought them. There was a note about this on the first page, '*The Changing Face of Doctor Who*'.

Eager kiddies did not mind. Matthew did not mind. He was in at the beginning, buying all three of the novels in their new covers, representing William Hartnell's haggard and mysterious face, though he already had two on his bookshelves.

Why stop here, thought the fellow at Target Books, when there are

20,000 eager kiddies willing to send a chunk of their pocket money his way? And so he got in touch with Terrance Dicks, who was still labouring in the script-editing vineyard, and Malcolm Hulke, who was not.

One day, changing trains at Brighton station on his journey home from school, Matthew glanced at the wares of W. H. Smith, one of those railway bookstalls with a large counter tipped at a slight angle for papers and books and mainstream magazines and sweets, behind it a plump paper seller in a flat cap, and behind him along the back wall a series of narrow shelves for upright display of assorted other goodies: the 'naughty' magazines like Mayfair, out of the reach of curious adolescents, and some more paperback books, all held in place by a long wire. Matthew, looking up from an array of boring war comics and boring footer comics, glanced at the back rack. He was slightly short-sighted and too vain to wear glasses outside the classroom, so he had a habit of squinting.

He felt a little shiver in his brain at the words in black *DOCTOR WHO*. And next to it, again in black, *DOCTOR WHO*. For a second he thought these were copies of two of Target's Frederick Muller reissues. He could not make out the cover images clearly. There was something wrong with the colours: had not the Target versions of the Hartnell books been red and blue and yellow? But these were shades of green and brown...

"Sir, what are those books at the back? Those two books which seem to say, though perhaps they do not, *DOCTOR WHO?*"

"Oh, they *do* say *DOCTOR WHO*, young man." He pulled them over the wire. "They are two novels just arrived from the printers. One is called *Doctor Who and the Auton Invasion* and is scribed by a Mr. Terrance Dicks, and the other is called *Doctor Who and the Cave-Monsters* and is the work of a Mr. Malcolm Hulke."

Matthew knew instantly that these books were renditions in prose of *Spearhead From Space* and *Doctor Who and the Silurians*, the first and second stories of the third Doctor Who.

When he got off his second train he ran faster than the Whomobile to his house and gouged the money from his mother and raced back round the station and under the railway bridge and past the grounds where the Tuesday cattle market was held and up to Clark's Stationers, which had spinners of low-end paperbacks. Matthew had once found *Spock Must Die!*, a *Star Trek* novel, on the very spinner from which he now pulled *Doctor Who and the Auton Invasion* and *Doctor Who and the Cave-Monsters*.

The Doctor's face was drawn in speckly black and white and below him on one was a sort of octopus of a sickly brown colour and on the other the familiar figure of a Silurian, green and leathery and rather sad with his squashed nose and veins like a fan running up to the top of his head and a red disc like a third eye.

Matthew rushed home. Tea could wait. He opened *Doctor Who and the Auton Invasion*. The note about *The Changing Face of Doctor Who* was at the bottom of the first page, but everybody knew about *this* Doctor. Dotted about the book were pen-and-ink drawings, but these were hardly necessary. As he read, all of the imagery from the TV episodes came right back to him.

And these two novels were just a beginning! More titles were listed as 'in preparation'. From now on, there would be *Doctor Who* novels forever!! Matthew pictured himself as a little old man in the year 2047, sitting in his house with bookshelves full of *Doctor Who* paperbacks, reading the very latest in his high leather armchair with its wings and anti-macassar. This new novel was written, of course, by Terrance Dicks, who never grew old.

And so, throughout his teenage years, *Doctor Who* novels came out in a flood from Target Books. Soon it was hard to step over the threshold of W. H. Smith without seeing a new one. They were all extremely welcome in Matthew's house. The bulk were written by Terrance Dicks. Terrance was a wizard of productivity. It would be fair to say the publishers had spotted a lucrative market and leapt enthusiastically into it, clutching Terrance by the collar.

The first few Target Books emulated the style of the Frederick Muller trilogy by interspersing the text with a generous helping of line drawings, but these became fewer and soon vanished all together. And the first handful of new novels ran to a hundred and fifty or sixty pages, but speedily a formula was worked out: each four- or six-part serial was chiselled into a slim little document of a hundred and twenty-seven pages of fairly large print.

As Matthew himself approached fourteen and fifteen, he had one difficulty with these wonderful novels. He yearned for sensual information. He had smelt Eastern spices in *Doctor Who and the Crusaders*, had felt the magical vanishment as the TARDIS (sometimes called 'the Ship') moved from star to star, just as he had felt African heat and the dry red sands of Barsoom in Edgar Rice Burroughs. This kind of evocation was less strong in the many dozens of *Doctor Who* novels which emerged during the seventies. Matthew wanted to be told what it *felt* like to stand in the TARDIS. What did it smell like? Of bacon and eggs? Of petrol? Of plastic? Was it a little too hot or a little too cold? Could the temperature be adjusted? Was its hexagonal console warm to the touch? Did your tummy wobble when the TARDIS dematerialized? Where was the Doctor's bedroom? Where was Jo Grant's bedroom? Was there a library? A TV lounge? The characters could not spend every second of every day standing at that console. Did the Doctor and Jamie and Zoë and Jo watch BBC 1 on slow evenings between planets and adventures, laughing like Matthew and his friends at Dad's Army? (What came on TV at 5:15 on a Saturday afternoon in the *Doctor Who* universe? There was an old joke about *Coronation Street*: the least realistic aspect of the programme was that none of the characters watched *Coronation Street*).

The novels never described the *sensation* of being shot by a ray gun. In those last moments before you died, or if you were the Doctor or one of his travelling boys or girls, fell unconscious, how must it have felt to have the ray run through your guts: painful, burning? Or like an orgasm? Or pleasantly relaxing perhaps?

They might tell you that someone knocked his head against the bulkhead but… Did you get a headache? Did you feel ill? Did you bleed?

What, incidentally, *was* a bulkhead, he wondered? In action scenes, characters were always being thrown against bulkheads, by monsters or guards or meteor showers. Matthew was too lazy and incurious to look the word up. He decided the bulkhead was the horizontal bit of a doorframe, deducing this from the word 'head,' to suggest 'above'. This meant that, in the picture created in Matthew's mind, the Daleks or Cybermen had to *raise* a victim to slap him against the bulkhead, which was difficult to envision if they were some distance away. And if a spaceship rocked and threw a character against the bulkhead, which happened often, he had to be pictured near an open door, and somehow springing *upward* as well as backward. Matthew, being short, could not imagine his own skull hitting the bulkhead (as he saw it) even if his spaceship had been hit by a violent meteor storm.

Terrance was unarguably the King of novelisations, but other people occasionally pitched in an adaptation, including Ian Marter, the actor who had wonderfully played Harry Sullivan in Tom Baker's early run. Matthew had written to Ian and to Elisabeth Sladen for autographs as soon as they had appeared on air, and both had replied. (Lies had written a charming little note. Matthew had said in his letter something asinine like this: "I expect you are very like Sarah Jane." In her response, Lis had said, "Sometimes I am like Sarah Jane and I will leave you to guess when!" This awesomely puzzling reply threw up no meaning, however often Matthew mulled it over. He liked it so much that when appropriate he used it in replies to his own fan mail: "Sometimes I am like Adric and I will leave you to guess when!" He hoped that one day a *Doctor Who* fan might come up to him and say, "Are you aware that you and Elizabeth Sladen write identical letters?" This never happened). Anyway, Matthew thought very well of them both.

Ian's handful of books were more ambitious than Terrance's. He often augmented the scripts with his own ideas. This was inventive, but sometimes his adjustments blurred the focus. He adapted *Earthshock* into a novel, and while signing a copy Matthew had a peep at the final page. In Ian's version, at the last moment of Adric's life, the boy hugs himself. This movement struck Matthew as entirely wrong. "No, no, no!" thought Matthew, like Delius chastising Eric Fenby. "No, no, no!" The moment worked on TV – and for the audience of the day it did work – because it was absolutely still. By having the boy hug himself, Ian, to Matthew's mind, cluttered the moment and lost its delicacy.

The episodes were becoming books at an alarming rate, but not much had been written about the production of the programmes themselves. There was one book on the subject called *The Making of Doctor Who* – in fact, two editions of this, a few years apart – and there was a lovely *Radio Times* special to celebrate the tenth anniversary.

The Making of Doctor Who was a bible. Matthew carried his copy around in his school bag at all times so that he could refer to it as necessary. The first edition had appeared long before the people at W. H. Allen had built an industry out of adaptations. It had a cover photo of the Third Doctor looking as if he had been pinched on the bottom, with a Sea Devil behind him, which had perhaps done the pinching.

It contained plot summaries of every single *Doctor Who* story ever. These were of vital, unending interest. They were exciting in their own right. Matthew read them like prose poems. He was intrigued to find out that Ian had not stumbled across the TARDIS on a fog-filled Barnes Common at all, but had voluntarily visited it with Barbara, following the moody girl Susan to an old junkyard on the evocatively named Totter's Lane.

And he found out – up to a point – about people from history of whom he had never heard. Napoleon was one thing, but who on earth was Marco Polo? He found out about monsters of which he had never heard. He knew about the Mind of Evil, but what was a Mind Robber? Who was the Meddling Monk? Where was Galaxy 4? Who was Wyatt Earp?? Now he knew! Oh, and all those promising titles, *The Roof of the World* and *An Unearthly Child* and *The Tenth Planet* and *The Evil of the Daleks* and *The Tomb of the Cybermen* and *The Sensorites* and *The Macra Terror*. What in God's name was a Macra? Matthew seems to remember a photo of a giant crab. These thumbnails were the nearest to the real programmes anyone could hope to get.

Of equal importance was the clutch of photographs bound into the middle, including one of William Hartnell. William Hartnell! Matthew's mother knew of him from old movies, and he lived in Sussex an hour's drive from Matthew's house. Emotionally, this was like being able to say that *Doctor Who* lived next door but one. Here was the first photo of

Blue Box Boy: A Memoir of Doctor Who in Four Episodes

Hartnell Matthew saw. It was a tight close up, snapped from below so that he looked down to the viewer, eyes lidded, lips pursed, with all the imperiousness Matthew had gleaned from *Doctor Who and the Crusaders*. It was an archetypal Hartnell image. Matthew reread *Doctor Who and the Crusaders* with the photo to hand. Yes, one could believe that that face was irascible!

This glorious volume included script excerpts from *The Sea Devils* and descriptions of location filming and an intriguing section of Secret Files of the Time Lords. These secret files revealed that the Doctor's real name was a series of squiggles, inarticulable by the human tongue.

Matthew was fascinated by these Secret Files and decided to make some of his own. It was to work on these that he stopped producing *Doctor Who Comics Monthly*. If the files in the book were intriguing, they were as nothing compared to the many hundreds of pages of Secret Files which Matthew, in his guise as the Archivist of the Time Lords, wrote up. There were Secret Files about the Doctor and also Secret Files about his arch nemesis, the Master. There were files about the monsters, especially the Daleks, the monster most feared by the Time Lords. The drawings of the Daleks in the Secret Files bore a similarity to pictures from the Dalek annuals.

There was a timeline which suggested that nearly all important moments in human history – British history – had behind it the hands or claws or mechanical arms of a *Doctor Who* monster. There was scarcely a corner of the world – Britain – which did not conceal a few feet under its crust a *Doctor Who* monster. Often these were in places Matthew had visited, on a school trip or on summer holidays.

In the nineteenth century, The Sontarans had a hidden base under Sir John Soane's newly-built Bank of England. The Uffington Chalk Horse in Wiltshire was a dimension gateway developed by a now destroyed race of scientifically advanced witch-like druids (or druid-like witches). Under the steep cliffs of Devon along which the coastal railway line ran was submerged the tomb of an old Knight, part Lancelot, part Crusader, who the Master revived, with terrifying consequences.

Salisbury Cathedral was a spaceship. The residents of Shanklin were zombies under the control of the Krotons. The holiday makers at Butlins had had their frontal lobes removed by the Giant Spiders with their effeminate voices. The bespectacled boy who had drugged animals at London Zoo was now endowing domestic cats with the strength and viciousness of tigers. The people of Sandwich in Kent suddenly vanished utterly, kidnapped by the Trods from *TV Comic*, their pretty village nothing but an abandoned wasteland strewn with newspapers and the drooping heads of dying flowers.

The Nestenes took control of the plastic buckets children used at the beach, leaving a litter of suffocated little bodies, their buckets moulded to their faces. Marco Polo materialized in the Scottish highlands. The Master cunningly used the *Doctor Who* exhibition at Longleat to kidnap human specimens for his alien zoo. *The Mind Extractors* smoked in cinemas, emptying the heads of innocent movie goers as efficiently as George Lucas. A new clan of Silurians had caves under the Sussex Downs, not far from Brighton. Dinosaurs grazed on Dartmoor.

On rare occasions, the Time Lords reported something important from outside the United Kingdom. The Daleks had a base underneath Vesuvius. They were trying to harness the power of the volcano to turn the whole of Earth into a nuclear weapon. *Doctor Who* prevented this happening, but not before the Daleks caused the volcano to erupt.[1] The Master took the place of the real Gustav Eiffel, and tinkered with the newly constructed tower, making it emit alien radiation which drove the people of Paris to brutal violence. The Ice Warriors had a base at the North pole, and in the Gobi desert there lived giant intelligent gecko-like creatures, relatives of Silurians and Sea Devils.

The Archivist of the Time Lords did diligent research for many years, uncovering hundreds of wicked plots and schemes. It is better they are not revealed to the human race in detail. The human race is not ready for them.

While employed as the Archivist of the Time Lords, Matthew became increasingly certain that he *was* a Time Lord. Why did he know this only vaguely and intermittently? Because the Time Lords had wiped his memory! Which was only now seeping through! Yes! He was an exile of the Time Lords, banished to Earth like *Doctor Who*. On his journey from school every day, his train went past a scrap heap of old cars near Portslade, and Matthew became increasingly certain that somewhere in that scrap heap his TARDIS was concealed.

Worries about how he could square being an exile like *Doctor Who* and at the same time the most important Archivist of the Time Lords need not detain anyone: he did not try.

Matthew began to write TV scripts. These were not *Doctor Who* scripts, but they were modelled on the excerpts from *The Sea Devils* included in *The Making of Doctor Who*. His scripts were full of 'establishing shots'. This was because *The Sea Devils* excerpts were full of establishing shots. He did not know what an establishing shot was and assumed that it described just about any shot on TV. All shots, he intuited, established *something*, so they

---

[1] Apparently the new Doctor Who series includes a story about the destruction of Pompeii, which says something about great minds.

were all establishing shots.

Once for English homework he had to write a play and he had the ingenious idea of making it a TV play. This had a great benefit: TV scripts used only half the available space on a page, as *The Making of Doctor Who* showed, instructions consigned to one side and dialogue to the other, so by writing only ten pages' worth of material he could produce a massive twenty-page piece. Most children wrote essays of three or four pages in large handwriting. Twenty pages in his small spidery handwriting was truly epic. (He saved large handwriting for science essays).

Matthew conceived what he thought was a brilliant idea: a man with ESP predicts that someone will kill his girlfriend. He moves her to his flat for safety. In the depths of night a criminal breaks into the flat and the girl catches him by surprise and he shoots her. What a twist! If the man had not had ESP, he thinks, his girlfriend would have stayed in her own house and would not have died!??! What the man with ESP did not know was that another criminal broke in to his girlfriend's flat that very same night. *Whether she had stayed at home or moved to the flat of the man with ESP, his girlfriend would have been shot! How strange are the machineries of fate.* Wracked by guilt, the man with ESP decides to use his special powers to help others (hopefully with greater success) and agrees to work for an institution run by Colonel Letwin-Stone called WEIT, the Western European Intelligence Taskforce. Yes, this script was the pilot for a series. A TV classic, chock full of establishing shots. The rights are for sale to Russell T. Davies.

Once the series got underway, there was to be an evil enemy organisation called TREMOR, though Matthew never worked out what the letters stood for.

This thriller was highly praised by his teacher and friends for its dramatic content. Also admired was Matthew's business sense, because he put in a five minute commercial break, though his real motive for this was that it meant writing less material.

He was instructed by his teacher to read this script to the whole class and was miffed to find that his half-hour drama took only nine minutes to read, including directions. Even with five minutes of ads, it would have had to be performed at a freakishly slow pace to fill up half an hour.

Of course, there was also the BBC's weekly programme listing magazine, *Radio Times*, which, despite its title, included the TV stations BBC 1 and BBC 2 as well as the four BBC radio channels. You had to buy another magazine entirely to find out what was on ITV.

Most of Jon Pertwee's new seasons were heralded by a cover photograph, one of them by a thrilling but incomplete comic strip. To find out how it ended, you had to watch the programme. This strip was beautifully illustrated by a *Dan Dare* comic artist called Frank Bellamy, who for a while became the official *Doctor Who* artist at the *Radio Times*. On the Saturday listings page, below the title and above the episode plug (which was, *TV Comic*-like, always a question), was often a postage-stamp-sized illustration by Bellamy, of the Doctor himself or a monster, lit by a flash of lightning.

The first cover, for the week of *Spearhead From Space* episode one, was an iconic image: Jon Pertwee, photographed from the waist up, in his cloak with the burgundy lining and his shirt with ruffles at the cuffs and buttons, his eyes wide, hands held at roughly a level with his chest, his palms and fingers slightly curled as if he were touching the shell of some vast but fragile invisible egg. He looked directly at the camera. This was a dignified enactment of terror which Matthew would try to reproduce in front of a mirror. Normally, fright looked silly and humiliating, especially when played by girls. They pressed the tips of all ten fingers against their lips or their fingers and palms against their cheeks and they opened their mouths extremely wide and screamed and screamed and screamed. It could be seen that, though terror had gripped the Doctor for a second, his mind rushed with thoughts. Matthew decided that, if he should ever encounter abject terror – and he was certain that one day he would, being adventurous – he would hold his hands up exactly as Doctor Who held them, so the monster could see that he was smart and not to be toyed with. The key was to keep your arms tight in to your torso, your elbows pinned to your ribs, so that your hands were only a couple of inches in front of your nipples. If you flung your arms too far in front of you or, God help us, above your shoulders at your ears, you immediately looked like a complete idiot. Also, you had to avoid throwing your arms out to the sides of your body, because then you looked more like Jesus than Doctor Who.

Dignity was essential in all moments of stillness, including those of terror, but not in movement: the Second Doctor had an extremely silly way of running, with windmill arms. If you were going to be like Doctor Who, you had to cultivate distinctive, even eccentric, habits of movement.

In 1973, to celebrate the tenth anniversary of the series, the *Radio Times* produced a special magazine. This was infinitely more interesting than the *Radio Times* itself. It was full of fragrant facts and info. In one respect it was a bit of a cheat because it included plot summaries of the stories, but these were the same as in *The Making of Doctor Who*. They were, however, now accompanied by many more pictures, most in colour.

More interesting were the interviews. All of the regular cast members were interviewed. Many of them Matthew had never seen, some he had hardly heard of.

William Hartnell said that every child he met begged him to return to the series because it had not been any good since he'd left. This was odd, because most of the children watching *Doctor Who* in 1973 had never seen him. Matthew was amazed also to find out that Peter Purves, one of the famous presenters of the adored children's series *Blue Peter*, had, long before, been a *Doctor Who* boy. Even in the brief interview, Peter Purves made it clear that he was not overly fond of *Doctor Who*. He said that he had been unemployed after *Doctor Who* for two years, and in a fit of anger he had thrown away his last remaining souvenir of the series. A couple of weeks later he got another job and soon *Blue Peter* came along and made him a household name. Matthew later happened to be at the first *Doctor Who* convention Peter Purves ever came to, and he was a pleasant man, though time had not mellowed his view of *Doctor Who*. He was more interested in producing pantomimes, which he did with great financial success, and publishing a magazine about dogs. Yes, there was a magazine called *Peter Purves' World of Dogs*. Matthew never read it. Is it still running?

Deborah Watling described how she had been booted out of RADA and Caroline John said she had driven Doctor Who's car Bessie without a driver's licence. Sometimes at signings Matthew sat next to one of these wonderful women. He wanted to say to Caroline, *you drove Doctor Who's car without a licence, you naughty thing!* He wanted to say to Deborah, *booted out! A scandal!* There was an interview with the new *Doctor Who* girl, who had not yet appeared on TV. Her name was Elisabeth Sladen. She was to play a character called Sarah Jane Smith and she looked completely different from Katy Manning as Jo Grant, with her roundish face and dark hair, which had the severe, boyish cut of an early seventies secretary who was slightly fashion-conscious. In the photograph which accompanied her interview, Liz leaned against what looked like a castle wall and her face expressed, of course, abject terror. Sarah Jane was the latest attempt to do a *Doctor Who* girl for the liberated woman, being a journalist, strong-minded and independent, until she turned out to be a gibbering wreck like all the others.

The second half of the magazine was less appealing to Matthew. There was a long non-*Doctor Who* story about the Daleks, written by Terry Nation, or at any rate credited to him. Then there were detailed instructions about how to build your own life-size Dalek. This was a long way from the washing-up-liquid-bottle-and-sticky-back-plastic school of home-made toys promoted by Peter Purves and his pals on *Blue Peter*. This was the kind of craftsmanship which required saws and drills and screws and sandpaper and many, many hours of concentrated work. It was beyond Matthew. He was hardly alone. Most readers pored over the instructions and fantasized, before turning back to the episode summaries.

Matthew met at a convention a person who had tried to construct it. The directions had proved inaccurate and none of the pieces had fitted together. After much bending and stretching and twisting and pulling and sawing and hammering so that pieces which did not fit were damn well *forced* to fit, the Dalek looked a little misshapen and drunken, and curved in all the wrong places. it began to warp, becoming increasingly peculiar with each passing day…

Of course, a similar thing happened at the BBC when the familiar TARDIS console was put into mothballs and a wooden one without a time rotor took its place. This permanent change was found to be impermanent when, between seasons, the wooden console warped and the old one had to be hastily dusted down and polished.

4

More from the eaves cupboard:

A cardboard slide strip six inches long contained seven images, printed on plastic and inserted into the card, narrating a crudely drawn but not uninteresting *Doctor Who* story featuring the long-haired Doctor, now at once familiar and unknown to Matthew, and a couple of children battling a dinosaur. This strip had come with a projector and perhaps a host of other strips, to be projected onto the wall, a sort of home cinema system for the very young and impecunious. The projector had long gone and only one other slide strip could be found, featuring Whirlybirds, whatever that was, but only the *Doctor Who* strip excited Matthew's fascination. Because there was no projector he had to view it by holding it up to the light, which did not give the full effect, which would no doubt have been modest enough.

And there was a black plastic badge, cut in the shape of a Dalek, with the eye and arms and spots picked out in gold paint. It was a hopelessly inaccurate representation, because each vertical line had seven spots, not the correct four. Matthew wore it all the time. It was quite heavy and hung, tipped downward, against his left nipple where, more than eleven years later, his blue star badge would be. One day he forgot to put it on before going to school. He arrived home to find his mother upset and apologetic. He had left it on the cistern of the upstairs toilet, she said, and while cleaning she had accidentally knocked it into the bowl and it was gone forever. Matthew on another day might have been put out by this news but he took it with Christian calm and forgiveness. He supposed it would float about in the sewers for years, perhaps eventually to be found by a Cyberman, who would pick it up and look at it from all angles and try to attach it to his chest, only to find that the pin would not pierce his metal torso.

More spectacular was a large piece of thick cardboard, perhaps two and a half feet long and a foot high. On this cardboard was printed in garish colours a thrilling scene: a Dalek spaceship and various Daleks looking threatening in an arid landscape. About a third of the way from the rightward edge was a circular hole, representing the entrance to the Dalek spaceship. On the back, a gluey line indicated where once there had been a metal slide, angling down to the hole. Daleks were to be placed along this slide, the rightward one in the entrance. The metal slide was lost, and all but two of the Daleks which had slid down it. There had once been a rifle which fired, perhaps, ball-bearings, for shooting down each Dalek. Once one had been blown away, another slid into view.

Somebody must have had a good time with this toy. One of his older brothers? Presumably. Now the card was curled at the corners, where it was separating into thin grey layers. On the two remaining Daleks, (each printed in colourful reds and blues onto a black arched sheet of tin about the size of a playing card), were silver scratches. These scratches perhaps recorded successful hits with a ball bearing.

There was an old record player in Matthew's house, which played 78s as well as 33s and 45s. There were large numbers of 78s in a heavy box, including sixteen discs of John Gielgud and Edith Evans reciting poems through a heavy crackle. It was as if John and Edith were reading at the other end of a railway platform on a breezy spring day. There was a folk song called *The Foggy, Foggy Dew* in an arrangement by Benjamin Britten and sung by his boyfriend, Peter Pears.

There were modern records as well. Matthew's older brothers occasionally came home with an album or an EP, which soon lost its interest for them, the record itself becoming scratched and dusty and up for grabs. The Beatles, Pink Floyd's *Dark Side of the Moon*, and a curious album called *Brain Salad Surgery*, with a science fiction face on the sleeve. There was an album called *Bob Dylan's Greatest Hits*, on which a man strummed his guitar and sang incomprehensible lyrics in a nasal voice. Matthew's reaction to this was a fatal combination of bewilderment and eye-watering boredom which would slow down his appreciation of Dylan and it took him years to discover, suddenly, that he loved him.

A thousand times more appealing than Bob Dylan was Jon Pertwee. Jon Pertwee sang children's songs somewhat in the style of Archie Rice, jolly but oddly threatening, among them *The Runaway Train* ('The Runaway train ran down the track and she blew, she blew!') and *I Know An Old lady Who Swallowed A Fly*. In this song a woman gobbles up a whole menagerie of animals. ('I know an old lady who swallowed a fly / I don't know why she followed a fly / I guess she'll die / I know an old lady who swallowed a spider / that wriggled and tiggled and jiggled inside her./ She swallowed the spider to catch the fly/ but I don't know why she swallowed a fly. /I guess she'll die'. And so on, until : 'I know and old lady who swallowed a horse./ She's dead, of course'.)

A record label called *Music for Pleasure* specialized in low-price albums which were sold not in record shops but in unusual outlets like newsagents. The first album Matthew bought with his own pocket money was called *Children's TV Themes*, played by Cy Payne, whoever he was, and his orchestra.

On the front of *Children's TV Themes* were drawings of various characters and objects familiar from the telly, a Thunderbird and Rupert the Bear among them, and, most excitingly, a drawing of Jon Pertwee, looking just enough like himself to be recognized.

Children's TV Themes was a gem, though the renditions sounded only faintly like the proper versions. *Doctor Who* was played on an electric organ and did not sound outer space or frightening at all. It lacked atmosphere but it was rollicking. There was a very leisurely interpretation of the UFO theme and Matthew found that this sounded more like the TV version when played at 45.A woman sang *Rupert The Bear* with an audible grin. If the glorious work of imagination that was The *Magic Roundabout* had a limitation, it was that it was not notably erotic. Cy Payne and his Orchestra put in the missing piece. The theme tune on the programme was a tinkly music box jingle, but in Cy Payne's arrangement it took on a swaying, strip-joint rhythm. It was possible to picture bras and knickers flying across stages to Cy's version of the *Magic Roundabout* theme.

Children's TV Themes featured only the first of many renditions of the *Doctor Who* music issued over the next few years. Matthew acquired a splendidly odd interpretation in which the melody was played, believe it or not, on a trombone, with a sparse rhythmic accompaniment. This album also included a seven minute version of *The Pink Panther* theme, in which the familiar few bars were played without development over and over and over again. There was also *Skippy The Bush Kangaroo*, with lyrics that could have taken no more than a minute to write. ("Skippy, Skippy, Skippy the Bush Kangaroo,/ Skippy, Skippy, Skippy the friend ever true.") Skippy, like Kanga and Roo in *Winnie the Pooh*, led British children to think Kangaroos were extremely sweet, and it came as surprise to Matthew to discover years later that in Australia they are not much loved, because they gobble up farm crops. Kangaroos themselves are eaten with gusto: on a Perth menu Matthew found, but did not order, Smoked Baby Kangaroo. Peter Davison shared with relish the information, acquired God knows how, that the making of Skippy had been fatal for many kangaroos, and during filming a number of caged replacements were always kept to hand. When the current player of the role was killed in an accident, the cry would go up, "break out another Skippy!"

The best *Who* theme, of course, was the BBC 45 of the real version, which came in a blue sleeve with a picture of the TARDIS, but the most memorable was the one which accompanied a recitation by Jon Pertwee of a *Doctor Who* poem.

This was called *Who Is The Doctor*; no question mark. It was recited by Jon with a sonority which by comparison made Gielgud's poetry readings sound like Rolf Harris doing *Jake the Peg*. It was officially Matthew's favourite record for years and years. As a boy it never crossed his mind that, just possibly, *Who Is The Doctor* was a load of rubbish. From the ages of nine to thirteen he played *Who Is The Doctor* nearly every day, sometimes more than once. He could recite it word for word. He once recited it at school during an English class and got a round of applause. He said he had written it. This was the advantage of the single being a horrific flop and therefore unknown to his class mates.

Ever after, if he made an effort, Matthew could recall the lyrics pretty accurately. You will have to imagine the thrumming theme in the background:

> I cross the void beyond the mind,
> The empty space that circles time.
> I see where others stumble blind.
> I seek a truth they never find.
> Eternal wisdom is my guide.
> I am – *The Doctor!*

(When Jon Pertwee announced that he was the Doctor, an echoey effect made his voice weird and wobbly, whispery but declamatory).

> Through cosmic wastes the TARDIS flies
> To taste the secret source of life.
> A presence science can't deny exists,
> Within, outside, behind,
> The latitude of Human mind.
> I am – *The Doctor!*
> Then a bridge:

My voyage dissects the course of time.
Who knows, you say – but are you right?
Who searches deep to find the light
That glows so darkly in the night.
Towards that point I guide my flight.

(An exciting rushing sound accompanied the last line. Notice how the lyrics are becoming less science fictional, more mystical. Matthew hadn't a clue what 'dissecting time' was supposed to mean. Wouldn't 'bisecting time' have made slightly more sense? Robotic imagery follows, but mixed up with religion.)

As fingers move to end mankind,
Metallic teeth begin to grind.
With sword of truth I turn to fight
The satanic powers of the night.
Is your faith before your mind?
Know me – Am I – *The Doctor?*

(By the end, the Doctor seems to have become God. It is all very puzzling, isn't it? The line about faith is wonderful, pregnant with meaninglessness. Then came the fade, which went on for ages.)

This piece of spacey evocation was not a threat to Hawkwind but it was very lovely. It was backed with an earthbound song called *Pure Mystery*, sung in Jon's uniquely Pertweeian vocal style, a cross between Noel Coward and Worzel Gummidge, with just an edge of bad temper to add salt to the exuberance. The protagonist was an entertainer – "Pure Mystery, I've a talent to amuse" – who had seen dark times – "Pure misery, and yet I've a talent to amuse." Jon's voice slid and wobbled and deepened on the word misery, as if the tape had slowed for a second. Though in every way an inferior track to *Who Is The Doctor*, *Pure Mystery* had its own outlandish fascination.

The 45 came with a label of a livid purple, and indeed the company which put it out was called Purple Records. This may have been their only release. Over the years the purple faded to a shocking pink and matched the jacket of *Doctor Who in an exciting Adventure with the Daleks*.

Though *Who Is The Doctor* was very much its own entity it was not unique: other oddities were released to record shops featuring actors from science fiction. Matthew was informed that, even before *Who Is The Doctor*, Frazer Hines had released the similarly titled *Who Is Doctor Who?* which had also failed to make inroads into the charts. Matthew never heard this record, much to his regret. He sat next to Frazer at convention dinners once or twice. Perhaps he should have asked about it. Perhaps Frazer still remembers all the lyrics.

Matthew bought a couple of albums by Mr. Spock. Mr. Spock had a singing voice of limited range. It was dredged up from his boots. He sung his low-pitched versions of *Clouds* and *Gentle On my Mind*. He even attempted *Where is Love?* from *Oliver!*, normally sung be a young boy in the tones of an angelic chorister, here in a flat baritone. When Matthew was twelve, he auditioned for an amateur production of *Oliver!*. He did not have a singing teacher, so he learnt *Where is Love?* by singing along to Mr. Spock's version. He did not get the part.

Mr. Spock's records were appealing curiosities. Also a curiosity was Tom Baker's version of *Hello, Dolly!*. Tom Baker did not put out *Hello, Dolly!* as a single in its own right. This is a pity. He sung it, or at any rate a few bars of it, in a special *Doctor Who* drama never shown on TV and released only on vinyl. This was called *Doctor Who and the Pescatons*. It was written by a nice old queen called Victor Pemberton who had scripted for the programme in Patrick Troughton's day. He may even have been the script editor for a while. Matthew met him once. He was very pleasant, full of moans about the decline of the BBC since its heyday, which was the years he had worked for it.

Doctor Who and the Pescatons had a miniscule cast, only Tom Baker and Elisabeth Sladen and a fellow from Tom's world of Soho voice-over boozers as the Pescaton. There was nominally a whole race of Pescatons, but only one of them spoke.

If thinly peopled, *Doctor Who and the Pescatons* was thick, indeed oppressed, with atmosphere. It took place under the sea and someone in the studio had a lovely time making creaking noises and foghorns and splashes. One of its highlights was Doctor Who singing *Hello, Dolly!* to scare off the Pescatons, which worked.

Like earlier *Doctor Who* record releases, it found only a small number of buyers. This irritated Tom Baker. Tom complained to Matthew in the pub at Acton near the rehearsal rooms that, though *Doctor Who* was one of the most popular programmes on TV, it was impossible to get anyone to buy spin-offs.

"I did this thing, *Doctor Who and the Pescatons*, and you couldn't give the bloody thing away."

Matthew kept quiet.

The drawback of *Doctor Who and the Pescatons* for Matthew was that it was not very durable. If Matthew was going to buy a record it had to be one he would listen to a lot. He had only a small quantity of pocket money. He could listen to *Who Is The Doctor* many times, it only lasted three minutes, but *Doctor Who and the Pescatons* took forty concentrated minutes, lying on his bed with eyes closed. Also, once he had heard it a couple of times the suspense factor, always moderate, had drained away. Ah, if Tom had only recorded an orchestrated version of *Hello, Dolly!*. This undoubtedly would have had many happy spins on Matthew's record player.

The least pleasurable of all *Doctor Who* records was an official BBC release called *Doctor Who Sound Effects*. Nobody could say that its title failed to do it justice. It can't have sold in large numbers, but second-hand copies in mint condition must be easy to find, because few people would have played it more than once. It had a certain documentary value, maybe, but lying in bed pretending to be transported by its endless collection of zaps and judders and crashes and roars was beyond Matthew's powers. Perhaps some lad somewhere produced home-made *Doctor Who* movies and found that this album's thunks and squeaks, judiciously selected, added zest?

Strangely, there were to be found in grocers a number of *Doctor Who* foodstuffs, ensuring that *Doctor Who* fans, not on the whole the healthiest or sportiest of children, were in worse shape than they would otherwise have been.

For many years, there was a cereal called Sugar Smacks. This staggeringly unhealthy concoction of puffed wheat pieces dowsed in sugar must have kept many a dentist busy over the years. For a while Sugar Smacks was a *Star Trek* cereal, until its manufacturers saw the light and it became a *Doctor Who* cereal.

The box had a fairly crude illustration of *Doctor Who* sitting in front of circles which were perhaps meant to suggest outer spaciness but looked more like a gaily coloured dart board. *Doctor Who* held a bowl of the sticky cereal towards the purchaser. In wobbly letters near the bowl was the refrain, 'through time and space with *Doctor Who*'. The first time Matthew looked at the box, he was struck by a resemblance. "The Doctor looks like granny!" he said. It was true. He looked every bit as much like Matthew's grandmother as like Jon Pertwee.

Matthew never liked Sugar Smacks much. After a bowl, his teeth were coated with sugary tackiness. Secretly, he preferred Ricicles, which had a great rhyme on the box: 'Ricicles are twicicles as nicicles'. They were at least twicicles as nicicles as Sugar Smacks. But they were a *Magic Roundabout* cereal.

It was essential for him to eat Sugar Smacks for better reasons than the picture on the packet. Each box contained one of six *Doctor Who* badges. Nothing as simple as finding the cereal unpleasant would prevent him from amassing a complete set. The more Sugar Smacks he ate, the faster he emptied the box and another one could be delivered from VG Grocers.

Matthew ripped open the new box, his hand delving into the mountain of sticky pieces, pulling out the badge, a few bits of the cereal adhering to his fingers.

The artwork on the badges was extremely crude. It was just as well that the name of each character was supplied at the bottom in bright red and yellow letters. The least recognizable was Jo Grant, whose lips were gashed with a garish red. She could have been Mae West. The Brigadier was any bloke with a moustache and a beret. The Master and the car Bessie and Doctor Who, who was Dr. Who on the badge, were the best.

Matthew suspected that the wicked Sugar Smacks people had not manufactured equal numbers of these badges, because, though he doubled his intake of that horrendous cereal, he never found a UNIT badge, though he had six Jo Grants and four Masters and three Bessies. Jo Grants were no good for swapping because everyone else had six of them too.

The badges rusted after a couple of years. Wonderfully, one of the cameramen on *The Keeper of Traken* dug out his Sugar Smacks Master badge. It was ten years old and discoloured, the white background was urine yellow. He wore it on every *Traken* studio day. Matthew casually asked him if he had ever succeeded in getting a UNIT badge and he said he had not, but he had got a heap of Jo Grants. Matthew noticed that his teeth were not very good.

During the Jon Pertwee years, Nestlé put out a *Doctor Who* chocolate bar. If Matthew had doubts about Sugar Smacks, he had none about the chocolate bar, which was extremely scoffable and frequently scoffed by him. These bars had collector's appeal too, because on the back of the wrappers was a picture and three or four lines of narrative, making one episode of a fifteen-part serial featuring Doctor Who and the Master, who was bringing dinosaurs through time to menace the modern world. Fortunately, Nestlé could not conceal the episodes as Sugar Smacks could conceal its badges, so Matthew did not have to buy countless bars to gather together the complete, gripping saga, though he remained loyal to the chocolates even once he had collected all the episodes. He would eat a bar while pondering something about outer space, a small frown on his face, just like *Doctor Who* himself in thoughtful mode.

Sugar Smacks eventually dropped the *Doctor Who* connection – did it perhaps become once more a *Star Trek* cereal?- but when Tom Baker became the Fourth *Doctor Who*, his grinning face in his hat and scarf gazed from a corner of the yellow Weetabix box.

The Weetabix collectables were twenty-four cut-out card figures, and each box contained a wad of four. There were two *Doctor Who* figures in the collection, one of him standing, one of him running. There were two Sarah Janes. There were six Daleks, one in each pack. There were two Ice Warriors and two Cybermen. These figures could be pressed out from the oblongs on which they were laid, and by folding back a little flap at the foot they could be made to stand up. It would not have taken much of a breeze to blow them over. They were rather like miniscule versions of those paper dolls of historical personages, though the *Doctor Who* figures were already fully dressed. This is just as well: the sight of an Ice Warrior in his underwear would put any self-respecting adventurer off his Weetabix. On the back of the box was one of six dramatic backdrops for the exciting adventures these little figures might engage in if a fanciful child got his jam-smeared fingers on them. Among these backdrops was that perennial *Doctor Who* setting, the dank, dripping cave.

Matthew was now a teenager, just, and his pocket money had been increased to a more respectable sum. He could afford to buy Weetabix packets of his own.

He would not wrench open the new packet as he had once torn open Sugar Smacks. He was more sophisticated now. Like Charlie Bucket, he would savour the drama. He would take the box to the spinney behind his house. He would sit on the roots of an oak tree, next to the dry, leaf-filled pond. Cricket balls on bats could be heard from the recreation ground. He would pull up just a corner of the top flap. Then another corner. He could make this almost erotic unveiling last for minutes. Then:

Bloody effing bloody, it was one he already had! That flipping silver Dalek!

Or:

Yippee! The other Ice Warrior! The Zygon!! One of the Sarah Janes!! Wow!!!

Then the white shiny paper tube which enwrapped the stack of Weetabix would slide out of the box. He would open the tube and remove the Weetabix and put them in the dry pond and cover them over with leaves. But he kept the box with its scene on the back.

In this way, he found five of the six sets of figures, but now the moment of the UNIT badge crisis was upon him: only one to find, and how many Weetabix would have to be left to rot under leaf mould until that final set, with the second Sarah Jane Smith in it, would be his? He lay in the dark of his bedroom and worried about it. He dreamt of Weetabix. He dreamt of schoolfriends waving their Sarah Janes.

In the cold light of day, he asked a friend if he ate Weetabix and his friend said yes. Do you collect those rather awful and useless little *Doctor Who* cut-outs? asked Matthew in a laid back fashion. Oh no, they're rubbish, said his friend.

"Do you... do you by any chance have the, uh, Sarah Jane, the girl? Not the one of her running, the other one. Of course they're rubbish, I can hardly be bothered with them to tell you the truth."

"Oh, I think so," said his friend, "but I threw it away."

No!

"I think so. Or maybe I meant to throw it away. I will check at home tonight."

The next morning his friend came in. I didn't throw it away, he said, here it is. Lovely Sarah Jane!!

Doctor Who viewers grew plumper and plumper as a result of eating all these calorie-packed foods, but the Doctor himself showed no sign of having any appetite at all. Sometimes a guard brought a tray to a cell. The Third Doctor hastily ate a sandwich on an episode of *The Sea Devils*.

The Fourth Doctor's brown coat pocket concealed an edible which was, unsurprisingly, more for amusement than ingestion. He carried around a bag of jelly babies which was frequently plucked out and offered round, as if things were not arch enough already. It would seem strange to those who know only the über-capitalist twenty-first century that Bassett's, the makers of jelly babies, did not immediately plaster *Doctor Who*'s face all over their boxes. One of the first clues that America was a foreign country came when Matthew saw, at a convention in 1983, that enterprising profit seekers had imported tons of these boxes, which they were selling to 'fans' at the exorbitant price of three dollars. There was nothing more embarrassing than watching spotty boys and overweight girls in long scarves thrusting an open box under the nose of an unsuspecting victim, saying, with impossibly wide eyes in what they believed to be the manner of Tom Baker, "would you like a jelly baby?"

Just as Conan Doyle eliminated Holmes' cocaine addiction from the later stories, so the jelly babies ceased to be offered. Perhaps they had gone stale, sweating in that deep, deep pocket. Adric, in all his episodes with the Fourth Doctor, was never once offered a jelly baby.

Generous helpings of food floated around the Fifth Doctor. He wore celery on his lapel. Suddenly everyone was stuffing their faces. Adric brought a tray to a cell, he had supper with an android, he spent two episodes standing mere feet away from a smorgasbord at a country house. The Sixth Doctor met an interplanetary chef who had a taste for human flesh.

The Doctor suffocated him. "Your just desserts," he said.

*   *   *

Most of Matthew's friends were *Doctor Who* fans, albeit in a sane, small-scale way. His friends had all inherited one or another battered toy Dalek from some older sibling. The playrooms of Britain at Christmas nineteen sixty-five had been full of shiny new toy Daleks, freshly unboxed. By nineteen seventy all the storage cupboards of Britain were full of these same toy Daleks, scarred and bruised, their arms snapped off. Talking Daleks of nineteen sixty-five were silent Daleks in nineteen seventy. Daleks with flashing lights would never flash again.

Extremely susceptible to damage was a toy Dalek so cheap the average child could buy one with his pocket money and still have change for sweet cigarettes. It was about the size of a child's thumb. Under the Dalek's thin plastic shell was a ball-bearing, and with the flick of a finger the little Dalek rolled freely over floorboards. It moved more bumpily on carpets. Millions of these were sold. They were in such demand that they became an under-the-counter item. You had to hope your mother was having an affair with the man at the sweetshop.

Matthew had inherited three from his brothers but they all had arms or the eye stalk missing. One had a hole in its head. At school, Matthew asked his friends if any of them had a roller Dalek which was in pristine condition and none had, or if they had they were not admitting it to covetous little him.

It was the kind of programme much talked about on a Monday morning. (By boys, girls didn't like it much).This was especially true of outstandingly scary episodes: the Cybermen in the sewers – called Cidermen by many small children, who sometimes puzzled over what cider had to do with it – elicited hushed conversation one lunchtime in the junior school, as much later did the first appearance of a Sontaran, who had been pottering around in a threatening manner throughout his first episode wearing a helmet which looked both science fictional and medieval, until the last five seconds, when he removed the helmet to reveal a horrid fat blubbery face, with narrow lizard lips and tiny blinking eyes under long eyelashes and tiny holes instead of ears. He looked like a malicious baby gone wrong. He was seen in this first shot only from a distance and there had been barely time to take the visage in before the theme tune had pulsed across the shot and the credits ran. *Who was that horrible looking alien??* This question ran around Matthew's classroom like a refrain on Monday. It was one of those moments where no-one was quite sure what they'd seen.

There had been a similar reaction to the first appearance of the Daleks, at the end of the episode called *The Dead Planet*. A friend of Matthew's, old enough to have seen the episode when it was shown, said it was absolutely the weirdest thing he had ever seen and the most frightening:

Blue Box Boy: A Memoir of Doctor Who in Four Episodes

a momentary shot of something strange and metallic with an eye stalk, seen through trees, scarcely seen at all in fact, just suggested. The Doctor himself was much talked about. This would have thrilled Tom Baker, of course, who liked nothing more than to be discussed all over the country by worshipping kiddies, though kiddies in real life bored him.

Whenever Matthew was required to write the name John – in a story or a history lesson – he developed the habit of spelling it 'Jon'. Thus, King Jon, Jon Noakes, Little Jon, Janet and Jon. His teacher marked these 'errors' with red ink but Matthew persisted, until told that Jon was different from John, meaning Jonathan. The idea that the Third Doctor was played by a man called Jonathan Pertwee threw a whole new light on it.

Jon Pertwee made a great impression on everyone. He was called by one horrible boy at Matthew's school Doctor Danny la Rue. Matthew suspected this was an insult, though he had never heard of Danny la Rue, and it would be some years before he saw Danny on a TV show. Danny was the first female impersonator to become a big mainstream star in Britain. For a while Danny owned a bar on the edge of Soho across from the side entrance of Foyle's. Matthew sometimes had a drink there.

It was frequently said of the Third Doctor that he was a poof, by children who had no idea what a poof was. It was enough that Jon had a flouncy walk and wore a shirt with ruffled sleeves and sometimes a theatrical cloak. The question arose: what exactly *is* a poof? Matthew's friend George asked his mother and reported the next day that a poof was a person who ate a lot of chocolates. To George and Matthew and their friends this was a completely credible explanation, and it was not hard to picture the Third Doctor in his blossomy sleeves, lips pushed out, poring over a box of high-priced chocolates with the same care with which he approached a scientific problem, before picking out with his long, practical fingers the chocolatiest and nuttiest and swirliest selection.

Matthew did not take a particularly critical approach to the things he liked. He wanted to watch and read *Doctor Who*, not chat about it. When Kate Bush put out *Lionheart*, he wanted to listen to it rather than review it. Yet he became a kind of critic – a low-order, fanzine one – as regarded a cultural phenomenon of the time. On summer midnights, BBC2 would show horror double bills, usually a '30s Frankenstein movie with Boris Karloff followed by a '50s or '60s Hammer film with Christopher Lee and/or Peter Cushing. The Hammer ones were more appealing to Matthew because they were very bloody and the vampire brides showed their breasts a lot. They were also in colour, but the TV in Matthew's house was black and white.

* * *

When Matthew was sixteen, a fellow launched a Hammer film fanzine to which Matthew swiftly subscribed. There was already a commercial publication, *House of Hammer*, which contained comic strip versions of the movies (sometimes scripted by Alan Moore in what may have been his earliest publications) and photo-packed feature articles. Matthew loved it and one year he spent a lot of his birthday money on a set of back issues.

The fanzine was more modest: an unpretentious, photocopied journal the size of a funeral order of service. Matthew decided he would try and write for it. 'Decided' suggests reflection. There was none.

One evening he was leaning on his bed doing an eye-closing bit of homework. He always did his homework on his bed or on the train to school. This meant that his maps and his sketches of Bunsen burners and his isosceles triangles were wobbly and approximate. At their worst, when the train rattled over the points coming into Hove, they looked like they'd been drawn on a roller coaster. He tore a piece of paper out of his exercise book and began to scrawl a review of a Hammer film. He posted the ink-splattered sheet of paper off, and, his awful hand-writing notwithstanding, it was printed. They must have been desperate for contributions. So he began to turn out slightly camp reviews whenever homework got boring, sometimes of films he had never seen. All these reviews were written on his knees, his bed the writing desk.

Was he a harsh and damning critic, deluding himself that he had incredibly high standards while knowing nothing about anything? It would be impossible to find out now, but probably not. He was not so much reviewing as riffing on the subject. Yet there is no doubt that he mistook his opinions for thoughts. This was childish.

Matthew went to his only convention as a 'fan' on the strength of his admiration for Hammer films. The makers of the little photo-copied journal organized a weekend at a dowdy London hotel. This was not the glittering celebrity-packed event with which science fiction audiences are now all too familiar. Peter Cushing did not take the train from Whitstable to thrill his countless admirers and autograph their *House of Hammer* collections. Christopher Lee did not jet over from LA between rounds of golf. The convention was simply a hundred or so fans and a ton of movies. Oh, and David Prowse. David Prowse had been a Frankenstein monster in one of the lesser instalments. He was also the body, but not the voice, of Darth Vader, though Hammer fans cared nothing about that.

David Prowse did not do a panel. He was saved from questions: What is Peter Cushing like? What is Christopher Lee like? What is André Morell like? Is it hot in that Frankenstein make-up? What is it like being directed by a genius of the order of Terence Fisher? Terence Fisher was the director most acclaimed by Hammer fans. Matthew thought Terence Fisher was a genius because everybody said so. Ingrid Pitt was talked of as an actress of luminous brilliance, turning out performance after performance of seductive subtlety in various states of undress.

David Prowse stood silently at the back of the hall for half an hour, a figure of awe.

The real point of the convention was watching movie after movie in a darkened room. For two days Matthew sat on a plastic chair and watched *The Scars of Dracula* with Patrick Troughton as a sado-masochistic Renfield/Igor type, and *Taste the Blood of Dracula* and *The Evil of Frankenstein*.

Hammer films always had spiffing titles: *Dracula Has Risen From the Grave*, *Frankenstein and the Monster From Hell*, The *Curse of the Mummy's Tomb*, *The Plague of the Zombies*, *The Legend of the Seven Golden Vampires*, *Vampire Circus*: they all *sounded* terrific. Lalla Ward was in *Vampire Circus*.

This was the kind of film which even dedicated Hammer fans could not quite call a classic.

Matthew had a penchant for melodramatic titles: he loved the titles of *Doctor Who* stories. *Spearhead From Space* sounds great when you say it aloud, as does *The Talons of Weng-Chiang*. Later on, many of his favourite serious writers had a talent for good titles: who could resist *The Heart of Darkness*, *A Burnt-Out Case*, *The March of the Long Shadows*, *The Master of the Day of Judgment*? At the other end, trashy books were concealed under marvellous titles: *The Drums of Fu Manchu*, *The Black Path of Fear*.

Did he think watching Hammer Films all weekend was a good way to spend his time? He could not think of anything he'd rather do.

Matthew did not go to any *Doctor Who* conventions, but when he was still in primary school he went to a special *Doctor Who* event at the London Planetarium. He and his sister were allowed to take the day off school to go to London to attend. Friends disguised their jealousy with a show of disapproval.

"It's awful that you are allowed to *miss school* to go to something *frivolous* like *that!*" said snooty, envious Miles.

In the dark of the planetarium a panel of three scientists talked about the night sky. Matthew found this exciting but was too overcome with anticipation to take much of it in. He did, however, get to ask a question. Ex-*Doctor Who* boy Peter Purves, now reduced to *Blue Peter* presenter, walked through the audience with a microphone, fielding the questions. Earnest children who liked chemistry lessons made curlicued scientific queries. Boring! When Peter Purves was within spitting distance, Matthew shot his hand up, half standing to make it higher. Peter Purves came to him and asked him in a whisper what his question was. Matthew noticed that Peter had coffeeish breath. He invented a question.

"Some people say the moon was once part of the earth and some don't. Which is right?"

Peter Purves said into the microphone, "A rather more *abstract* question this time," and passed the mike to Matthew, whose voice rolled all over the London Planetarium. The scientists coughed and sniffed and pretended he had asked a very interesting question and gabbled vague answers, the gist of which was that they didn't know.

Then... the big event... The *Doctor Who* music began!! Mr. Barry Letts!! producer of *Doctor Who*!! came on stage!! and then a round spacey vehicle appeared!! at the corner of Matthew's eye!??!

Jon Pertwee!!! In his Whomobile!!!!

Jon sprang from the car to wild applause. He circled the audience, shaking the hands of all the children in the front row. He did not shake Matthew's hand, because Matthew was in the second row. But Matthew was not to be defeated. He sprang to his feet and said as loud as he could,

"*Doctor Who*'s my favourite programme!!"

Jon Pertwee smiled and looked extremely pleased, thankful even, and said,

"Glad to hear it, old chap!"

Glad to hear it, old chap. What a great phrase. Matthew used it afterwards on every appropriate occasion, and some inappropriate. ("That was a shoddy physics essay, Waterhouse." "Glad to hear it, old chap!")

Then Jon Pertwee went on stage and Peter Purves fielded more questions. Matthew was annoyed to have asked the moon question because he could tell by Peter Purves' body language that no-one was to get a second bite, thrust their arms up all they might. So dull boys asked dull questions and Matthew's fascinating question – many fascinating questions – were never heard. Still, a great day was had and it was much, much, much better than school.

5

When Matthew was six months old, his brother Richard - nearly two - toppled out of a high chair and cracked his head open. Matthew had two other brothers, much older, whose lives, it is possible, were ruined forever by this death and the tensions which must have followed it. Matthew, at six months, knew none of it, though many years afterwards he supposed his mother must have hugged and hugged and hugged him to her.

He knew a bit more come the next encroachment of real life at its darkest. During his sixteenth year, he was at a sports day at his school with his parents. He was not participating in any of the sports, he hated sports, but he was required to turn up and watch them. Hundreds of parents milled about, watching their lads throw googlies and sprint a hundred yards. It was a lovely day, that rare English spring day when the sun is out and the sky is blue and the breeze is fresh.

They went home at tea-time. Moments after entering the house the phone rang and Matthew picked up. It was Guy's hospital calling for Mr. Waterhouse. Matthew's brother Nicolas, at twenty-seven, apparently in a state of distress over a failed marriage proposal – at least, this was the immediate trigger for an action which could not be explained by it – went into a barn at the farm where he worked and drank a can of paraquat. Paraquat was an industrial weed killer.

Matthew's father took the train up to the hospital. For a week Nicholas, who Matthew scarcely knew, moved between certain death and hope of survival. Matthew did not go to Guy's and nor did his sister. After seven days of pumping Nicholas died. It was of tremendous importance to his mother that the coroner's verdict was death by misadventure rather than suicide. It left behind an emotional mess.

Matthew once spent an afternoon with Kurt Vonnegut, a writer he liked. Kurt Vonnegut's mother had committed suicide. Vonnegut believed that traumas of this kind, though awful to live through, do not do the same lasting damage as the slow accretion of small human meannesses.

Matthew's reaction at the time was unreadable to him. He turned more into himself, to his *Doctor Who* books and his comics and his records. Kate Bush was on his turntable nearly all the time, he fell asleep to *The Kick Inside* most nights. Sometimes he played an album called *Crusader* by the Irish songwriter Chris de Burgh. He bought it because it reminded him of *Doctor Who and the Crusaders*, and because it was produced by Kate Bush's producer Andrew Powell.

At this time, he would have loved all those unavailable *Doctor Who* videos. It is as well he could not get them.

One thing came from this: an affected but sincere sense that he had officially suffered, that he knew about life, was wise, was in a way a tragic and therefore interesting figure. Boys at school commented on how little he mentioned the incident: they had been told about it by a teacher to ensure they were kind to him. He did once burst into tears during an 'A' Level English class. Sometimes he felt religious, sometimes not. In his bedroom at night, in the far corner to the left of his bed, many times he saw the ghost of his brother, who he hardly knew. After an incident based in a stunning reality life became less real, less solid. Everything was intangible, insubstantial, misted over.

This death was full of suggestion and meaning, but Matthew had not the faintest idea what to make of it. It was like trying to read a hieroglyph.

For people who liked *Doctor Who* in the sixties and seventies, the programmes themselves were mere wisps, hence the importance of the books and the comics. Twenty-five minutes a week for six months, then a six month drought. The TV programme was the fount of the obsession but it was distant, elusive as a rare fish off Brighton Beach.

When Matthew found himself an actor on *Doctor Who* at the age of eighteen, the first episodes Tom Baker had appeared in, five or six years earlier – let alone Patrick's and William Hartnell's – with giant robots and arks in space, were as irrecoverable as dead pets. When you are a teenager five or six years is a third of a lifetime, ten is over half of one, they are other worlds.

Sometimes during the summer holidays one or two of the serials of the previous winter were edited into TV movies. Someone once told Matthew that these shortened versions were so ruthlessly abridged that they made no sense at all. Matthew did not notice this and would not have minded. He was glad to see *Genesis of the Daleks* or *The Sea Devils* a second time, even in butchered condition.

These repeats were an exception. Most stories were shown only once. Several of the black and white shows from the nineteen sixties, as everyone knows, were tossed away after broadcast and though every so often a 'lost' programme is uncovered, which may not be to its best advantage, a fair number look to be gone forever.

Matthew thought later that the (to all intents and purposes) non-existence of all these past episodes must have been, for him, a very good thing. It chilled him to think how awful his mid-teens would have been if, after Nicholas' suicide, he had been able to lock himself in his bedroom and watch episodes of *Doctor Who* over and over and over again.

Doctor Who programmes were not recycled but there were two *Doctor Who* stories which cropped up every so often. These were the *Doctor Who* movies, full-colour widescreen reworkings of the first two Dalek TV adventures.

These were produced by an American fellow called Milton, whose main cinematic pursuit was sub-Hammer cut-price horror films. There was apparently an insatiable demand in British cinemas in the 1960s for gothic horror films.

Matthew saw both *Doctor Who* movies all at once in 1969 on a special double bill for the school holidays at his local cinema, named the Perrymount, after the road it was on. It was only three minutes from his house. He didn't go to movies very often but sometimes to a Disney cartoon on a summer afternoon. He saw 2001 there at the age of seven, loving every moment, intoxicated by the planet shots, the colours, the strangeness, understanding not a word. The *Doctor Who* double bill was the last thing Matthew saw at the little flea-pit before it closed down, but it remained standing, empty and smelling of cigarettes and acetate and mice, for several years, with that sweet corrupted odour of rotting wood, the walls trickly with damp, the lobby carpet streaked, shattered glass underfoot, blackened ashes where a tramp had made a fire. For some months after it shut the seats were intact, the nests of rodents, and when they were taken out the metal uprights to which they had been fixed remained. A narrow rusty ladder ran up the brickwork outside.

In Matthew's childhood, derelict buildings stayed around for years and when they were thought to be dangerous they were fenced off with barbed wire. There were always gaps in the wire where someone had cut through. As far as the span of Matthew's own life was concerned, these buildings rotted and stank for many more years than they had been used, and were more inviting in their crumbling state. A cinema is a cinema, but an abandoned cinema is full of ghosts and mystery and danger. The Perrymount backed on to the land where his old infant school had been, which itself backed onto the spinney behind his house. The small wooden hut for the infant class had long before become derelict. He had only spent a year there before it closed down, but when he was ten the structure still stood, becoming stranger and stranger with each passing year as if it were underwater. Thick plants grew though the floor. It had caved to an angle like a frozen boat.

After seeing the *Doctor Who* films at the Perrymount shortly before it closed its doors forever, he saw them frequently on TV. This had some advantages. The problem with cinemas, then as now, was inattentive audiences who seemed to think they were in their living rooms and could squawk and yell and run about as they chose. During *Dr Who and the Daleks* at the Perrymount, a red-haired girl from Matthew's school called Hazel, who was a bit smelly and was called flea-bag by everyone, could not stop running back and forth throughout the films, buying sweets and huge bags of very bad popcorn, and slurping on Cokes and pinching her friends and gadding about and screeching. Hazel seemed incapable of manifesting the intellectual concentration it took to appreciate *Dr Who and the Daleks*. At least in his house Matthew could give the material the full attention it deserved.

Few years went by without these films getting a showing. While Matthew was in *Doctor Who*, he toyed with buying a pad in Brighton and was sent by an Estate Agent to look over a dusty basement flat on

St. James' Street. The flat was owned by a gay man in late middle age, the skin on his face red and dry and taut and veiny in the way of people who drink a lot. He wore a lime green pullover which rode up his wrists when he folded his arms, exposing reddish-yellow hairs. When Matthew went into this flat one Saturday morning, the small TV in the compact, darkish kitchen was playing *Dr Who and the Daleks*, which made the meeting rather embarrassing. The man leant on his kitchen counter and looked at Matthew in a curious way which may or may not have been recognition. Matthew looked at his shoes and then glanced hastily through the flat, which was so small that this was a matter only of craning the neck to the left to see into the bedroom and to the right to see into the living room, while Daleks made threatening noises from the TV and their lights flashed. Then he said thanks, he'd think about it, and ran up the outside steps and was relieved to be back in the fresh air. He did not put in an offer.

The *Doctor Who* movies starred the horror actor Peter Cushing, whose Doctor Who was a doddery eccentric scientist with a trim moustache and short white hair. He wore a neat brown jacket. Because Peter Cushing was younger than his Doctor, there was something in him of the lovable Corporal Jones from *Dad's Army*. He lived in a sweet little cottage with his granddaughter. In the first shot of the first film, he was seen reading *The Eagle*, exactly like the boys in the cinema for whom the film was made. This warm-hearted old fellow had built a time machine in his basement. On the outside it was a police box, on the inside it was a ginormous mess of wires and flashing lights, a bit like the inside of a television set.

In *Doctor Who and the Crusaders* Ian had been a lantern-jawed action man of little humour. In the first movie, he was played by Roy Castle as a broad comic buffoon. Many scenes strived for slapstick hilarity. Roy Castle was always comically tripping over things at otherwise dramatic moments, and in one scene caused the metal doors of the Dalek City to open and close repeatedly.

In the TV episodes Susan was approaching womanhood. (Did she not abandon her grandfather because of a boy?) In these films she was a round-faced apple-cheeked girl who might have been an Enid Blyton heroine, *The Naughtiest Girl is a Monitor*, perhaps.

Once this widescreen masterpiece had come and gone from the cinemas, as swiftly and as silently as a shadow, Milton, surprised by its commercial failure, brought out a sequel.

No need to worry whether *Daleks: Invasion Earth 2150AD* could possibly match the glorious first: it was much, much better. Between the movies, dear old Doctor Who had tidied up his TARDIS so now its interior was no longer a mess of wires but a sleek sixties-futuristic spaceship, though still

Blue Box Boy: A Memoir of Doctor Who in Four Episodes

a police box on the outside. The movie took place on a battered, invaded Earth, and there were lots of scenes of angry rebels in underground lairs, including a bitter man in a wheelchair who heroically sacrificed himself at the end. It was like a World War Two movie, with Daleks instead of Nazis.

Though Roy Castle was not in it, Bernard Cribbins played a similarly dopey companion, in his case a knockabout policeman. In a jokey scene where Bernard Cribbins was pretending to be a mindless Roboman, he had to eat a meal in a robotic fashion, which lead to much slapstick spilling of peas. A very similar scene appeared some years later, with more telling comic results, in Woody Allen's *Sleeper*, though it seems unlikely that Woody Allen was directly influenced by *The Dalek Invasion of Earth*...

A generation later, the fabulous Bernard Cribbins, now of advanced age, appeared in the new version of *Doctor Who*. Bernard Cribbins has much to be proud of. Let's hope he is not the bragging kind. He is the only *Doctor Who* companion to play, in a different role, the grandfather of another *Doctor Who* companion, and only the second to return to *Doctor Who* in an unrelated part, the first being the elegant Jacqueline Hill, who, fifteen years after Barbara, was a queenly alien in an episode in Matthew's first season, though, sadly, he never met her. Bernard Cribbins, delightful as a comic policeman, was also delightful as a soft-hearted old geezer, and the script was even better.

The TV programmes were in black and white with plain, shadowy, sparsely decorated flats for sets, from around which monsters came. The movies were artificially bright and techni-colourful, the Daleks, though scary, were luscious loud reds and blues, the colours of playpen bricks, of ice lollies, of Thunderbird rockets. (Vide-colourful, maybe). They looked all ready for packaging as merchandise.

The lights on their heads were not the small domes of the programmes but tubular, lending them a likable, doggy, K9 aspect. They flashed and flashed an appealing Fanta colour which, early subliminal advertising, brought on thirst, encouraging that dumb-bell Hazel to go back to the concession stand yet again. In the first movie, these tubes lit up willy-nilly, the film makers not having realised that they were supposed to flash only when the Dalek spoke. The random flashes gave them a partying, celebratory air.

Tom Baker himself wrote a screenplay and made strenuous efforts to finance it. It was called *Doctor Who Meets Scratchman*, Old Scratch being of course the devil. Was it hilarious? Was it packed with Bakerisms, a sort of infinite Baker rewrite without the basis of an original script on which to lay those pert remarks? "It's a Technocothaca!" That was a rewrite described by Terrance Dicks as "a line so bad only Tom could have written it." Matthew would love to have read *Doctor Who Meets Scratchman*. Was it stuffed from first page to last with lines so bad only Tom could have written them? It must have been a wondrous thing. In newspaper interviews Tom Baker boasted of securing a commitment from Vincent Price, to play presumably Old Scratch, though no-one would hand over any actual money. But hope sprang, if not eternal, then at least for several years: it was not quite officially dead when Matthew was in the TV series. It got mentioned every so often. Lalla Ward said she had read it but she expressed no view on its quality.

So Matthew saw most of the original programmes once only. What remained, sometimes stimulated by photographs and the Target adaptations, was memory. Memory does not hold on to plot details nor in any complex way to character, as far as there can be said to be character to hold on to in the old *Doctor Who*. What it holds on to are images, colours, moments. Many of these best moments were climactic. One of the magisterial charms of *Doctor Who* was the sensational *Perils of Pauline* episodic structure, with its wonderful cliffhangers. These cliffhangers saved it from one of science fiction's most depressing pitfalls, which was pretension.

Matthew's lasting sense of *Doctor Who* was made up of collections of these images like packs of cards.

The shots in countless first episodes of an unrevealed villain, seated, just an arm and a shoulder, a gloved hand, an armoured hand, a hand of metal, or clawed, suckered, reptilian, withered; hooded, helmeted, cloaked, watching the figure of the Doctor on a screen. Watching silently or with slippery laughter or a hiss or a tinny command. Matthew thought of these as Jack Kirby shots. Marvel villains were often seen in the same way.

He remembered the moment when a man walked into the upstairs room of the plastics factory, where the Autons were lined against a wall until, in a heart-stopping moment, one of the dummies moved and the music dropped over the moment, an aural curtain, and the credits rolled. What the Nestenes were trying to do on earth (apart from the general-purpose motive of invading it) was lost to him, but years after *Spearhead From Space* had been shown, the movement of that Auton was as vivid and chilling as it had been the day he saw it, but also, of course, transformed, memory not being a camera. Many moments remained from that unusually vivid story; the farmer finding the weirdly glowing meteorites, which he stored –idiot! – in his barn; the grunting materialisation of the TARDIS and the first shot of the Third Doctor as he emerged from it and staggered and toppled over, a scene Matthew enacted many times over during the weeks after he saw it; the Doctor in a wheelchair, spinning out of control downhill; looking in a mirror, critically reviewing his new face; the close-up shot of the Auton hand dropping down to reveal a gun; the yawn of Doctor Shaw after a long night's work; the smashing of the shop window by the well-dressed mannequins; the tentacles from the tank, strangling the Doctor.

Doctor Who was packed with these crystalline moments. The stertorous breathing of the Ice Warriors, the boxy Krotons in their dank unlit room, standing over a metal tray like a cow's trough, from which dry ice swirled; the Cybermen in the sewers and the man with the strange eye who sat huddled over a microphone in an office building not unlike the one in London where Matthew's father worked; the execution of Doctor Who: gunfire, the drop of his head; his spinning around faster and faster in a sort of washing machine as the Time Lords discussed exiling him to earth.

The Dalek beside an overgrown tunnel; the black chair which suffocated people; the Master at the altar of a church; the little winged stone demon; the white witch on her bicycle; the Brigadier on the telephone to the Prime Minster, who was 'madam'; the guerrilla in the minister's large room, with its French windows; the curly-moustached carnival barker with his miniaturised zoo, which included a Cyberman; the humanoid reptile emerging from the ocean with its long overall of blue netting; the beautiful golden man and the beautiful golden woman in their living spaceship; the hermaphrodite with its single green eye and the manner of a fussy housemaid; the Doctor, thrown onto his chest in a battle with a minotaur; chattery high-voiced spiders who sprang on the backs of their victims; Captain Yates, in an asylum.

The giant robot, growing huge thanks to chromakey; a long-shot image of the cripple in his wheelchair which was like the lower part of a Dalek casing, mechanical eye on his forehead like a red welt; the inward curve of the skull where eye sockets ought to be but weren't, only a stretch of putrefying skin; the long speech, threatening to crush a phial which would destroy millions, the nearest the old *Doctor Who* series ever came to a soliloquy; the curiously empty ark, the stiff, preserved corpses of giant insects; the knife-wielding oriental dummy; the hansom cab speeding off into the dark, to the sound of appalling laughter; witchy women in a cave, dancing around a fire, casting coloured powders into the flame; *Doctor Who* ejected into space in a sealed coffin; the robots with their impassive gold masks like Tutankhamen; the long clanging staircases which were a TARDIS interior; the enormous octopus overlooking tiny men; the floppy tentacles under the mask/head of Julian Glover.

And so on. Pick a card.

*   *   *

Once he discovered *Doctor Who*, Matthew made great efforts to ensure he never missed an episode. It meant rarely going far afield on a Saturday, and even holiday trips had to be planned so he would near a TV at the appointed hour. Once his family were at a fete at a school for children with physical disabilities in Chailey, and even here a TV had to be located so he could watch *Doctor Who*, in a sort of common room where disabled children laughed and screamed and frolicked in front of the screen. A friend reminded Matthew of a hitherto forgotten instance: once on a tour of Lincolnshire with his school choir, an event had to be put back by half an hour so Matthew could see *Doctor Who*, which he did (his friend told him) in a huge luxurious red armchair placed directly in front of a large TV. That Matthew's powers of persuasion were impressive enough to get his school to reschedule an event says something about his personal charm.

No episode missed, but one: the final episode of *The Curse of Peladon*. A bitter day. This he had missed because of a miner's strike, which had caused a blackout in his town. He lay on his bed that candlelit afternoon, furiously weeping as 5:15 became 5:30 and then six o'clock, and *Doctor Who* was long gone from the airwaves before the wretched TV flickered back to life. As a result he hated all miners and all strikers and it took him some years to get over it. He did not see the final episode of *The Curse of Peladon* until he was in *Doctor Who* himself, when someone with whom he had just done a profoundly awful interview leant him a tape with a shaky, washy copy, which was extremely nice of him.

The *Doctor Who* series always had one foot in near-nostalgia, in something that had gone away. The structure was drawn from old movie serials. The stories were drawn from thirties pulp: by the sixties, serious science fiction was all sex and avant-garde experimentation and drug dreams, the monsters and screaming girls a thing of the past.

And Doctor Who himself flew around in a time machine modelled on the kind of Police Box which had once been seen all over London but had ceased to exist by 1963. This was not a sixties vision of the future like a Thunderbird or an Enterprise, in the very lineaments of the TARDIS it was a vision of the past. The First and Second Doctors seemed Edwardian in their bow ties and checked trousers, the kind of clothes, it might be imagined, suited to an aging clock maker in a disorganised workshop down a narrow crooked lane. The choice of dress showed more élan when the Third Doctor Who threw his theatrical cloak over his shoulders, but this was the theatre of mid-century, of Noël Coward, not of John Osborne or Arnold Wesker. This Doctor drove an ancient yellow roadster. He hated computers. When he got a futuristic flying car it was one that could easily have been displayed at a Future Expo in the nineteen forties. He was called 'the Carnaby Street Doctor,' but the phenomenon of Carnaby Street was finished.

The eccentricity of the Fourth Doctor Who was the eccentricity of post-war bohemian London, of Fitzrovia, of Dylan Thomas, drunken poets, of Muriel Belcher's Colony Club. His toy was a yoyo, a favourite of wartime children. The Fifth dressed to say, cricket. The Doctor's cricket was old-fashioned, gentlemanly, W. G. Grace, mythical England. His long creamy coat with its red edging was modelled after the ones worn by cricketing public schoolboys in the nineteen twenties – they can be seen in the movie Another Country – though the schoolboys did not have the advantage of celery on their lapels.

Doctor Who had a machine which travelled, when it worked, through time and space. It spun down time corridors. The Doctor journeyed all over the universe. He knew about chrome walls, Daleks, Cybermen, computers, planet-smashing missiles, and he saved people from them.

Daleks, Cybermen: living entities merging obscenely with their technologies, like Jacob Epstein's 1913 sculpture Rock Drill, in which a robotic figure – among the first – is seen to become one with his machinery, a horror confirmed soon after by the First World War. The Doctor knew about the future, but he did not live in it and did not seem to recommend it.

6

School was out! Forever!

What now? Matthew wanted to try out for a drama school, but there was a long wait before the next cycle of auditions. Until then, what?

He had an Aunt called Liz, who worked at the BBC TV Centre. She had been an actress for a while during the fifties and also a stripper. It had been legal in Britain for a woman to take off all her clothes on a stage in a licensed club, but she could not make the slightest suggestive movement, no dancing, no swaying of the hips. Except for the plain act of removing clothes, she had to be like a statue. Nor could there be any music.

By the time she was thirty Liz had got herself into the Beeb, at the time the ultimate ambition of all actors unless they were finding extraordinary success in their performing careers. There was scarcely a single director or producer or anything else in BBC drama who had not been an actor. Matthew's Auntie Liz had worked for years as a Production Unit Manager on *Play For Today*, the 'serious drama' strand of one-off plays. Matthew fancied himself hanging around drama sets importantly. That was his world! He telephoned her.

"Well, I *couldn't*," she said in her smoky voice. "You have to be *extremely special* for the BBC! And anyway there are no *openings*. Unless perhaps, unless... some low-down clerkly position...a position where you will be little noticed...somewhere near the abattoir... hmmm..." She ended the call and the next morning got back to him. "There's a place, extremely junior, mind, in the *News Information* department," she drawled. "They are interviewing prospective candidates soon so get a modest begging letter off as fast as you can..." News? It might as well have been the abattoir itself, where cows were slaughtered for BBC restaurants! This was not what Matthew had imagined. He had scarcely remembered that the BBC had a marginal department somewhere that produced news. He had never fantasised about socialising with news readers...

But, a low-down clerkly position at the BBC, he reflected, fast coming around to a different perspective, is like a high-up clerkly position anywhere else. Just wait till I can say, pretending not to hear a question perhaps, Oh, what were you asking...? Who do I work for...? Oooh, nowhere special, just the BBC, you know...! Oh yes, in the drear bowels of the Television Centre (sigh) ... Oh, *Bruce,* well of course I *occasionally* meet him for lunch, with dishy Anthea...! Ah, Tom, yes, we're quite close actually, Tom and I, lovely man, rather shy, takes a bit of *bringing out of himself...* no ego... *Nonononono,* don't think it's all *glamour. Nononononono!* I am a mere toiler in the weeds of our beloved National Institution...

Matthew decided he didn't care how low-down or clerkly the job was, as long as he would be at glamorous TV Centre, spotting John Cleese at a distance and winking to Tom Baker at close quarters!! Yes, he would be so high-flown all his friends would *drop* him and he wouldn't *care* because he would be *so far out of their league,* their ordinary *suburban lives,* (shiver) they being mere *shop* workers, or bank clerks, or *parents* – holy Christ, the pram in the hall! – or, worse yet, *styoodents...* yukky grubby beery pasty-faced pastry-filled *styoodents...*

He wrote a letter in his neatest handwriting and soon he was called to a BBC outpost. Not TV Centre, but Broadcasting House, or Bee Aitch as it was known to BBC insiders, of which Matthew, he confidently predicted, was imminently to be one. Though he hoped to God he would not be working at Bee Aitch, where Tom Baker never came...

The good news was that Matthew was to work for BBC TV. The bad news was that he would not be at glamorous TV Centre, but at grey Lime Grove, twenty minutes away. Lime Grove was an old fortress of a building off the Goldhawk Road, near Shepherd's Bush market where Pakistani women sold ethnic clothes and white men sold vegetables and white women sold hideous little porcelain sculptures.

Lime Grove had once been used for BBC drama productions. The early episodes of *Doctor Who* had been taped there. Now it was dedicated to sports and news programmes, including the numbing six-hour-long Saturday sports programme *Grandstand*. Matthew did not watch *Grandstand* but knew its closing music very well because it meant that *Doctor Who* was about to start. The weekday six o'clock programme *Nationwide*, which followed the news, was also a Lime Grove production, with its 'human interest' stories and its tabloid-level 'knocking-on-the-doors-of-con-men' investigative journalism. The proper news, however, was at TV Centre.

What was Matthew employed to do? To cut up newspapers...

In the office on the third floor where Matthew 'worked' there were two large windows on one side with a forgettable view over other buildings, and between the windows a cork board on which announcements were pinned. On the other side a heavy dark wood-lined wall had pigeon holes set into it, where journals and books could be stored, though there weren't any. Sometimes a used coffee cup found its way into one. The carpet was pale brown and well worn.

In a room across the landing, by contrast bright and spacious and airy, senior news information staffers went through the daily papers marking articles to be clipped and specifying the file or files in which they were to be stored. Sometimes an article needed to be filed in several places, so two or three copies of each 'serious' paper were marked in this way. (The tabloids were hardly filed at all). 'Margaret Thatcher meets Coco the Clown in Micronesia' would be clipped out three times, a label like a post-it note with the date stamped on it was attached to the top of each clipping, and they were placed in Thatcher, Coco the Clown and Micronesia files. The filing cabinets were in a windowless room of their own, like a large walk-in closet. Matthew spent his mornings cutting out these articles and his afternoons putting them into allotted files. The work was a miracle of brainlessness.

Every building with a news department had its own news information archive, so at TV Centre, a twenty minute walk from where Matthew and his scissoring colleagues sat, the same articles were being clipped from the same papers and stored in similar cabinets by similar boys.

There was another full-time staffer cutting up newspapers for his living. Douglas was a year or two older than Matthew. He had one of those constricted, high voices which seem to be trapped in the larynx. He was irritated at still being a virgin at nineteen. Matthew said he wasn't a virgin, though it was plain that Douglas didn't believe him. Whenever a woman walked into the room Douglas became polite to the point of smarminess.

Matthew and Douglas were supported by two part-time women in their sixties. Sometimes one of them was there, sometimes the other, occasionally both. They were decent working class women, with the strengths and prejudices of their time. One was a Northerner who still had a thick Mancunian accent. She had recently been widowed. She had been very attractive as a young woman. Her face was still tight and well-shaped. She got her first telephone a week or so after Matthew joined the BBC. She spent all her evenings looking at it, she said, waiting for people to ring. She was a staunch member of the Labour Party, and yet a dedicated reader of the *Sunday Express*, which was extremely right-wing. She would quote approvingly the columns of the nutty *Express* editor, John Junor. Junor supported the apartheid regime in South Africa and thought Nelson Mandela should have been executed. He hated homosexuals. So did she. Matthew tried in a tame way to challenge her.

"Some gays are nice. Some are even religious."

"Well, *so they should be* because they've got something to *beg forgiveness* about."

Matthew was still living at home and he would sometimes whinge about what a pain it was getting up at seven to be at Lime Grove at nine. (He almost always rolled in five or ten minutes late).

"I'm tired all the time," he said.

She was having none of it.

"When I was your age," she said, "I would have to be up at *five* to be at the factory at *six* and I would be there until *six in the evening*." Matthew was chastened.

The other woman was plain, with tightly curled hair and little buck teeth and thick-lensed spectacles of the kind school secretaries wore in comedies, the frames curved upwards at the ends like Spiderman's eyes. She was very London. She expressed no views on queers, but she had reservations about black people. She had been living in a nearby council block for years. It had been *lovely,* she said, *lovely,* until these blacks moved in with their loud music and now it's horrible. She got tearful as she talked about this and shook her head. She loved TV commercials and liked to try any new product, "but I'm not as mad about it as my daughter. She loves to try new products. The minute there's an advert for something new, she's down the supermarket trying it."

She did not approve of donating money to foreign charities. When Matthew, with his generalised liberalism, said it was good to help starving Africans, she said, "No! Give to your *own* people! Get things right in *your own back yard! Charity begins at home!*" She spoke inordinately in clichés. Later in his life, Matthew noticed that this was a common habit among humans.

These women often went together to the taping of BBC sitcoms and chat shows, and when they were next gathered at the office they would discuss what they had seen with firm opinions. They felt entitled to be stern critics, but it was impossible to escape the sense that they didn't really enjoy anything. Or rather, they most enjoyed not enjoying, and discussing not enjoying later on. "Ooh, I was most disappointed in Dick Emery, hasn't he gone downhill...?"

One marked characteristic of the British has always been that, like the News Information ladies, they lack the Mediterranean appetite for vast pleasures, their real enjoyment narrowing into particular obsessions: Hornby trains, the greenhouse, the sky at night, the Church of England, CAMRA ales, football, charity coffee mornings, Cliff Richard, a collection of saucy seaside postcards.

Across the hall, among the senior News Information staffers, was a large man with very black curly hair, proud of his working class roots. He was an adviser to Bernard Levin, the journalist. There was another beefy man , with long blonde hair and a narrow moustache, who famously had a ton of girlfriends though he was a bit camp and Matthew would have sworn he was gay. He had a habit of leaving early, always using the same phrase: "I think I'll push the boat out." There was a very masculine red-haired football fan, and an efficient young woman in her twenties and Matthew's favourite, an extraordinary woman in her late forties with gypsyish locks and a Dietrich voice who smoked cigarillos one after the other and wore at all times, inside or out, hot or cold, a rather well-cut raincoat with the belt hanging down at the back.

The atmosphere was relaxed and unproductive. The hour allowed for lunch tended to expand into two. Beers were drunk and games of bar billiards were played. The Levin adviser was very good at bar billiards, and he and the fat blond guy would challenge Matthew and Douglas. Matthew was objectively useless at the game, but often won by sheer fluke, the ball whispering past a wooden mushroom, making it wobble without toppling over. After several beers, it was lucky that in the afternoon nothing had to be done except a bit of filing, which could be achieved without the mind's operating at full capacity. Everyone absconded at three thirty.

On each Monday a discussion of the previous weekend's episode of *Doctor Who* was forced on Douglas and anyone else who happened to be present. Matthew thought every episode was an excellent classic and, predictably, everyone else thought it was rubbish. This was outstandingly pleasurable, it was nice that everyone hated it except Matthew. It was like having some incredibly rarefied taste, beyond the grasp of the lower orders.

Oh, said Matthew, Tom Baker is so *witty*, so funny, he's a genius you know, an absolute *genius*, he's Oscar *Wilde,* and isn't Romana s*exy* and just as sparkly as a Christmas tree light? Bloody hell, said the Levin adviser, it's *rubbish,* Tom Baker is *awful.* Plus, *there are prettier girls in my block of flats than that bony Romana...* This sounded to Matthew like tone-deaf philistinism. And, he added, wasn't that brilliant when the Doctor gave K9 the kiss of life...? No, said Douglas, it was rubbish. *Oh, you!,* said Matthew.

Matthew must have been much more of a *Doctor Who* bore than he would subsequently admit, because after a few weeks in News Information he acquired the nickname of K9, though no-one gave him the kiss of life.

Pleasingly, many of Matthew's heroes were represented by News Information files. There was a cornucopia of papers under Bush, Kate, and clippings from 1963 announcing the start of a brand new series could be found under Hartnell, William, as well as a full-page article about the making of an episode set in the Wild West called *The Gunfighters*, which, William Hartnell assured the reporter, had been his idea and was the best story yet.

Meanwhile, ambitious Matthew had no intention of having a career in News Information. He had enterprisingly sniffed out the name of the BBC Casting Director, a woman called Jenny Jenkins. This was not as clever as it sounds. The information was easily acquired from the theatre listings annual Contacts.

So he sent off a letter. He did not have a CV, of course, nor even an actory photograph, so he attached to the letter with a paper clip a little passport photo...

...And, unbelievably, kind, heavy-drinking Jenny got back in touch with him... because by coincidence they were looking for boys for a drama serial about a public school... of his age and look...She summoned him to a building on the outskirts of Shepherd's Bush. She looked tired and frumpy but she was friendly. She had died blond hair. Yes, she said, looking him over. Yes, you might be useful for public school serials...

And then, fast, he was summoned again, to meet a man called Ronald Wilson, who was, gulp, a *director...* of a *public school serial...* which was in desperate need of lads who looked young and were posh... Matthew was given a script. He had to burst into tears in the scene. While reading the script to himself he tried to force tears into his eyes. He felt so very *saaad...* He wanted to be seen by Ronald Wilson to be a *genius* at sad scenes... the leading contender of his generation for sad scenes... He rubbed his eyes until they were red, but then he looked not sad but hung over... but at least he could make his voice crack... So white-haired, red-faced, slim Ronald Wilson, in his white pullover and slacks, came out and took him into the office and asked him to read and... how his voice cracked... there was more emotion in that room than in a month of *Crossroads*... How his voice cracked and how sad his downturned mouth...how the little innocent suffered...

The call came. They wanted him!!! Hurrah!!! This had all happened unexpectedly, completely out of the blue, as when someone on the dole becomes a lottery millionaire.

He had been hired by News Information on a three–month try-out, to be put on the permanent staff if he was passable. He met the cigarillo woman for his review.

"You don't seem to really *want* to be in News Information," she said, "but we like you, so you can stay."

"Well actually," said Matthew, with spacious happiness, "I'm off..."

But he had to work another month after his resignation, before swanning off to do his miniscule role in the public school serial, and who knew what else the future held...?

One afternoon the red-haired football fan of the News Information department came to Matthew with a copy of the just arrived *Evening News*. Look at this article, K9, said the red-haired guy, tossing the paper to him.

The new producer of *Doctor Who* (said the paper) was developing a different kind of *Doctor Who* companion, a boy, inspired by the artful dodger of Dickens! He would be called, in Matthew's reading, Aydric.

The artful dodger! Why, Matthew knew all about him, who didn't? *Consider yourself at home! Food, glorious food!* A broad cockney accent – like in Berwick Market: *Oy, mate! That'll be fifty pee, mate, free for a pahnd. Cor, cheers, mate, cheers, me old Dutch. Arf a mo,' gotta see me trouble 'n' strife. Finished at the barrer, off to the caff. It ain't arf 'ot, mum! Eel pie and mash. Maybe it's because I'm a Londoner that I love London town. My old man said follow the van and don't dilly-dally on the way.*

Matthew did not practice speaking in cockney, which would have been silly, but he began to *think* in it, he tried to believe he *was* cockney. *Oy, mate, lend me a tenner! Oy, Doctor 'Oo, mate, gotta new motor? Gor, bleedin' 'eck, 'ed better get on the blower to that old drunk castin' directuh, gor' blimey!* He was becoming so cockney it was as if he were born not only within the sound of Bow Bells but in the bell tower of Bow Church itself. He was the most authentic cockney in Sussex.

He called Jenny in casting. *Please* put me up for this, *pleeaazzz...* She already had, she said crisply, and there was nothing more she could do.

A couple of days later Jenny had not got back to him. He was going crazy! Gor' blimey, what's a bloke to do?? He did not want his cockney period to peak before he was asked to read.

He decided to phone the secretary at the *Doctor Who* office and ask if they had drawn up the list of people they were going to meet for the part. This did not seem unreasonable or exceptionally pushy: what were secretaries for but to answer queries like that? Still, his hand was shaking as he spun the dial. The secretary might be a terrifying old harridan, many of them were, as anyone who had ever watched a sitcom could vouch. Perhaps she had bunned hair and wore mountaineer boots and typed away all day with tight little purple lips and a frown.

It turned out the secretary was neither a harridan nor a woman, but a man with a youngish voice.

"Yars?"

Surprise! Matthew went all shy, as was his habit. He did not have time to think about trying to pass as a cockney lad before his own voice came out.

"Hello, I'm Matthew, I'm up for the Aydric, do you know if they've chosen people to meet yet?" The voice said,

"Ny-ooo." They were considering people now.

"I hope you will consider *me*," said Matthew, a shove in the voice.

"I will keep you in mind," said the man non-committally.

When he put down the phone, Matthew knew that he had spoken not to the secretary at all, but to the powerful and important figure of John Nathan-Turner. Gor blimey me old mate.

A few days later, Jenny called and said he was on the list for a meeting...

It was a very good thing that Matthew hadn't any time to sit around and obsess about his upcoming audition for *Doctor Who*. He was busy, busy, busy! He had to go to Poole in Dorset, to the crumbling old school where much of the little public school drama was to be filmed.

So he said goodbye to his pals at Lime Grove. They had a lovely farewell party for him. Work stopped for good at eleven that day. Then, it was beers all round until sundown. The Levin guy showed him the filing cabinet for 'W'. They had started a file for him, which was sweet. It cannot ever have become a very fat one.

On the first day of the public school drama, for the read-through, he was so scared of being late that he turned up at the rehearsal room an hour and a half early. He sat on a bench near the upright piano. The room was as long as a gym, which it resembled in some ways. Strips of tape on the floor marked out the shapes of the sets, tall white poles marked corners. Long windows looked over the unlovely sight of Acton and off towards White City.

In a corner under an end window he saw a piece of paper, balled up: just one page. He picked it up and unfolded it.

It was a title page. It said, *Doctor Who: The Leisure Hive*. In the top right corner was a single name, scrawled in pencil: Baker.

It was term-time and the school at Poole was awash with pupils, all males, the over-confident sons of brokers who would be the brokers of the future. They despised the paid young actors and whenever they passed one they told him to fuck off. During a scene shot in the school chapel where they had been roped in as extras, they spent most of the afternoon throwing tight little paper bullets at the cast. This passed the time amusingly enough, and Matthew threw them all back. No doubt they carried the Shirley Temple/pushy mother notion of child 'stars.' Ironically, these boys were a great deal more obnoxious than the actors, and would grow up to be bankers and to do a *great* deal more harm.

Among the cast was Nicholas Lyndhurst, already tall, with a long, bony, pale face holding a touch of melancholy in it, ideal for the sitcom characters he would become famous in Britain for playing as an adult. He was already a sitcom star, in fact, and Matthew was bursting to ask him about Michael Ripper, a regular in Hammer films, who had worked with Nicholas in the series *Butterflies*. Nicholas had absolutely nothing to say about him.

There was also Simon Gipps-Kent, who had been a child actor on television for years. Simon was strikingly handsome with his close-cut dark hair and dark eyes, shortish, compact, very fit and proud of his body. He was the first person Matthew knew who wore a jockstrap by habit.

They were both likable, Nicholas smart and clearly a good actor and not as wild as, in Simon's company at least, he pretended to be. Simon was already in danger of becoming lost as he grew out of his childhood career. This in the end happened spectacularly: he died in his mid-twenties of a drug overdose, having worked very little in his last few years. He had when Matthew worked with him a huge, unfocused energy which many found draining, though Matthew found it exciting and enlivening. His energy did not abate through all his waking hours, so he was just as exhausting at midnight as he had been at breakfast. He could be taken as the classic type of the spoilt child actor, but he was essentially decent; not entirely happy. He was fascinated by arcade games and could beat anyone at Space Invaders, which he played with great intensity, slapping the buttons and tugging at the levers so forcefully that the machine rocked. He boasted of a fantastic sex life, picking girls up on railway platforms, but Matthew did not buy this in all its details. There may, however, have been some truth to his claims: on the couple of occasions Matthew found himself on the tube with Nicholas and Simon, they were recognized by bright-eyed girls. Matthew did not want to talk to strangers on the tube, but Simon loved any attention, and he charmed them. He had shortly before been in *Doctor Who* in that memorable comic gem called *The Horns of Nimon*.

Simon had got his hands on some bottles of whisky which were consumed by the three of them on a free afternoon. Matthew had never drunk whisky and liked the burning feeling. This was the first time he had ever been really drunk. He slept through his call the next morning and missed the cast bus. He had to be driven to the location by the producer.

They drank throughout the weeks of filming. Well drunk, they found themselves after dark in a large shopping mall, shut for the night, where they were chased by an aging, puffing security guard. Matthew and Nicholas raced to the exit in a shopping trolley pushed by Simon, to the horror of the guard.

Hardly was he back from Poole than he had to go to his *Doctor Who* reading. He tried to calm himself on the train by reading a Jack Kirby comic but his brain wouldn't let him follow the story. He arrived at Shepherd's Bush station and walked up to Shepherd's Bush market, where the calls of the sellers were a distraction. What he felt as he sighed and wandered was a strange variety of self-pity. So he swallowed and breathed deeply and went round to the narrow post-war block of Threshold House overlooking the green, with its small glass door which led to the reception desk. A man in a uniform stood in a box beside the arm in front of the car park.

Matthew gave his name to the woman at the desk. She ran her eyes down a list and told him chirpily to take a seat while she called up to the office.

Sitting in the reception area, he watched the arrival of none other than Carol Chell. Carol Chell was famous as a presenter of *Play School*. Seeing Carol Chell reminded Matthew that he was in the heart of the most important institution in Britain, where legends went up to receptionists and said, as if they were ordinary, "Hello, I'm Carol Chell." The receptionist received this information with the same all-purpose chirpiness she had used on Matthew.

Then Jane Judge arrived and there was no time to think of anything but reading as well as he could, until the meeting was over and he was on the train home and wondering about the meaning of John's wink…

Matthew was not a regular reader of horoscopes, but while waiting to hear back from the BBC he took to reading any astrology he could get his hands on. The day after his meeting with John, Matthew read the horoscope in his mother's paper over and over and virtually memorized it.

The astrologer said, today is going to be an outstanding one for Sagittarians. Well, thought Matthew, there's the proof: that telephone is going to ring itself silly before the day is through and I will be called back to Threshold House urgently.

It was a very slow day, the sky was grey and the atmosphere close, so that by elevenses a headache had set in, right between Matthew's eyebrows. The phone did ring, frequently, and Matthew ran to it before anyone had a chance to get their mitts on it first. It was always a friend of his mother at the other end. This was infuriating in itself, but worse was that, while a long, slow conversation (deliberately slow to provoke him, Matthew contended) about coffee mornings or hospital charities took place, the BBC were surely being prevented from getting through to him! If they kept getting engaged signals, wouldn't they give up and go to the next person on the list? The day wore on and three o'clock came around. He set up camp at the hall table by the phone, with a *Doctor Who* novel for research purposes. He did not leave the table until six, when it was certain that the *Doctor Who* office had closed. He mooned about, all evening.

The problem, of course, was that if he did not get cast he would have to start *hating Doctor Who* and everything to do with it. This would be tough, but he supposed he could find a way. Or perhaps he could draw a line in the sand. He could start saying, *it went all wrong in nineteen-eighty, after that it was rubbish!!!* He could learn to drone on (even if only to himself) about the lost, 'classic' years, like a completely boring retard. And of course, that Adric, *what absolute rubbish he was!!!*

The next morning the horoscope was of an even more optimistic tenor. It was impossible for a day to be better for a Sagittarian than this one. But by lunchtime the BBC still had not rung. Matthew could not bear it. He felt quite unwell. There was only one cure: he would have to ring the production office himself and hurry them along. He spun the dial with fast-beating heart, like a crime victim calling Sexton Blake.

Fortunately, the voice at the other end was not John Nathan-Turner's, but a woman, that adorable Jane Judge. She exuded calm and intelligence at all times.

"Hello," she said.

"Hello," said Matthew shyly. "Do you know if any decisions have been made about Adric?"

"Oh yes, we were just about to call you. John wants to see you again. Would you be free tomorrow?"

Matthew pretended to check a calendar.

"Tomorrow? Hmmm... I think so... yeesss..."

*   *   *

The next day he arrived at Threshold House, in a quite different frame of mind from the first visit. Now he was calm. In the night he had been overcome with a Zen moment. He would let whatever happened happen, it hardly mattered what. It might be imagined that, the nearer he got to the part the more he would have evil designs on the competition. Yet he felt now as he waited in reception nothing but warmth and love for the boys he was competing with, however many or few there might be.

As he approached the *Doctor Who* office with Jane Judge, a boy walked past him in the other direction. He was about Matthew's height but slimmer, and much better looking, though at that moment he looked unhappy. Matthew said, brightly,

"Good luck!"

But of course this attractive boy had already made it or blown it: for him, it was too late for good wishes now. He did not look Matthew in the face but at his own shoes, and said,

"Thanks."

John sprang up as if they were old friends. He shook his hand. At that moment all the clarity of the morning's events vanished and things became, for Matthew, a blur. He was not nervous exactly (or he didn't think he was) but a floatiness came over him. He read the same scene again and not just for John Nathan-Turner this time but also for Christopher Hamilton Bidmead, the sprightly, self-confident script editor, and at least one other person. Was this Barry Letts? Barry Letts, legendary producer of the Third Doctor's run, was now the Executive Producer, a vague job involving little more than giving John a few tips. But many months later Peter Moffatt said that he too had been in the room. Matthew had no recollection of him.

Assuming Peter was right, and why would he not have been, either there had been three listeners at Matthew's second reading or four. He searched and searched his memory afterwards and remembered only three, and only John's face remained clear to him, behind his desk, friendly, his head seeming to spring out from a colourful bowl of flowers because was wearing an especially garish Hawaiian shirt. He remembered Christopher with certainty, as much on account of Christopher's swagger as his face. The Barry/Peter figure was blank as a Robot of Death. Perhaps a peculiar twist in Matthew's hearing had made the name Peter Moffatt sound like Barry Letts? Or perhaps he had *expected* Barry Letts and so did not listen properly to the introduction, laying 'Barry Letts' over the real name even before it had been pronounced?

He read the Bombay Duck scene again. Christopher, representing intellectual rigour, grilled Matthew as to the meaning of the scene.

"Well," said Matthew in a blurt of A level Eng. Lit. chatter, "The Doctor is saying that Bombay Duck is *called* duck but it is *not* duck, it is fish!! He is using it as a symbol of the way things are not always as they appear to be!!"

This was met by Christopher with a small smile and a nod.

Too soon it was over. John leaned back in his chair. He was not quite as friendly as before. There was no see you soon, no wink, but a plain statement: "Either way we'll let you know."

Matthew had nothing to do but wait.

EPISODE TWO
TECHNOCOTHACA!

Humour in Riseholme was apt to be a little unkind: if you mentioned the absurdities of your friends there was just a speck of malice in your wit. But with her there was none of that. She imitated Mrs Weston with the most ruthless fidelity, and yet it was kindly at the bottom.

E. F. Benson, **Queen Lucia**

1

The next afternoon, the telephone rang.

"Hello," said the voice at the other end. "It's John Nathan-Turner."

It was a very strange moment. Matthew supposed that John might he calling to say the part had been offered to someone else, because he had said he would call either way, but he knew by the brightness of the voice that it had not been. He knew too that he would have had to wait a day or so longer to get a no, while things were sorted out with another actor.

He knew that now, what he had most desired had come to him.

"We'd like to offer you the role of Adric."

Yes.

"Okay…" He supposed he should not shriek and run around the house and burst into tears and laughter. He should sound cool about the offer, professional.

"Okay. Great. Yes. Great."

Was he supposed now to start asking about contracts and stuff? But he didn't have to.

"The contracts office will be in touch in a day or two."

"Great. Yes. Okay, great."

"Excited?"

"Yes. Yes! Great. Great. Okay. See you soon. Great. Yes."

He put the receiver down and looked at it for a few seconds.

Then he ran around the house and burst into tears and laughter.

When Matthew began to receive scripts, he always looked for the Bombay Duck scene. It never appeared. Had it been in some early, rejected draft of *The Planet That Slept*, or had Christopher Bidmead written it solely for the audition?

And the boy in the corridor? He must have been relieved a year or two later not to have found himself in the salt mines of *Doctor Who*. He got a trendy hair cut and transformed himself into a pop singer called Limahl and had loads of hits and got rich and had glamorous lovers.

* * *

Matthew was about to enter a world so exclusive it had only thirty-five or so members: the actors who made up the continuing cast of *Doctor Who*. The non-continuing cast was slightly less exclusive, there being few actors in Equity who had not at some time donned a monster mask and roared a bit or hissed, or donned a military uniform as a walk-on in a UNIT scene or a costume meant to look other-planetary, though often with a lingering Romanesqueness.

But Matthew was not one of these here-today-gone-*Tomorrow People*, Matthew was going to be around for a while, so there. "Nice to hear it, old chap." Of course, this was not an entry in any way into the 'world of the arts'. The BBC was full of people in 'the arts' and they did not regard *Doctor Who* actors as of their kind, nor the writers nor the directors, though some of the directors had a certain arty manner – or arty-manqué – Peter Moffatt with his air of specifically Beeb camp, and Fiona Cumming who dressed in ponchos and had a pageboy haircut as if she were *kind* of bohemian, but not really.

What Quentin Crisp said of the job of artist's life model perfectly applies to the *Doctor Who* girl and boy: "It required no aptitude, no education, no references and no previous experience." By signing up for *Doctor Who*, Matthew was giving up hope of pursuing a 'serious' career as a character actor. He was entering the delightfully twilit, ego-mad demimonde of the z-grade actor, which has many attractions.

Having been cast, his fee was 'negotiated'. The negotiator, if that was what she was called, was very posh and did not brook any nonsense. Her voice down the phone line was brittle. She said, when she had announced the remarkably low offer of one hundred and thirty-five pounds an episode, "there is little room for negotiation." This was accurate.

The contract arrived. He scarcely read it. He did not mind about one hundred and thirty-five pounds an episode, he just wanted to get it signed and back in the post. He remembered something Tom Baker had said in a magazine interview: "I signed the contract before they could change their minds!" Only a few minutes after Matthew had torn open the envelope, he had scrawled his illegible signature all over the contract and put a first class stamp on it and dropped it into the letter box by the railway station. 'By return' can rarely have been taken so literally.

A friend said to him, has the contract arrived yet? Matthew said it had. He'd already sent it off, he said.

"I signed the contract before they could change their minds!"

John invited Matthew to lunch. There was a modest French restaurant at the corner of Wood Lane, just off Shepherd's Bush Green. TV Centre was a five minute walk further up.

Blue Box Boy: A Memoir of Doctor Who in Four Episodes

It was not the grandest restaurant on earth. There weren't all that many grand restaurants in London, foodiness not having taken off yet. The West End was all Pizza and pasta joints, with a couple of more exotic places in Soho. There were no grand restaurants in the vicinity of Shepherd's Bush Green. To Matthew, however, this one was as fabulous and exotic and chic as the Ritz. He had never been to a proper restaurant. He had been to the sort of restaurant which was the side room of a pub and he had eaten at chippies and Wimpey's and tea rooms, but this was different. Here was a menu *written in French*. Here was a menu *with snails on it*. He felt like Denton Welch must have felt, having lunch with Edith Sitwell.

This restaurant was the home-from-home for many BBC producers who wanted to give their guests something a notch better than the BBC canteen could offer. John took all his expense account lunches there and went there for dinner too. On one memorable occasion which he described to Matthew he made a misjudgement about which he ever after felt guilty.

He took the composer Dudley Simpson to lunch. Dudley Simpson was the Mozart of *Doctor Who* music. He had composed nearly all the incidental music for many years. One exception was an interesting score by Geoffrey Burgon, but otherwise it had been all Dudley nearly all the time for ten years or more – though he had not written the famous theme tune, which had been composed by a man called Ron Grainer. John did not much care for Dudley Simpson's music. He said Dudley Simpson was the only composer alive who could make a five-piece orchestra sound like a three-piece. In this John was mistaken, as anyone who has sat through avant-garde classical concerts can attest. There are avant-garde composers who can make fifteen players sound like a duo.

John had decided that *Doctor Who* should move to electronic incidental music. He invited Dudley Simpson to lunch to break the news. Dudley Simpson arrived at the restaurant and the first thing he said to John was this:

"I've been working on this programme for years and years and you are the first producer ever to take me to lunch! I'm *so* looking forward to sharing a lovely French meal with you! And we can perhaps discuss plans for next season!"

John had no choice but to break the bad news, which he had meant to save to the end. Matthew pictured this scene taking place over plates of fat escargot and melted butter, though in reality it had probably occurred before they started poring over the menus.

"I'm afraid I've brought you here to tell you we don't need you any more."

"?"

"I'm firing you."

"!"

Needless to say, the rest of the lunch was uncomfortable and silent. Matthew hoped that Dudley Simpson had ordered a huge, multi-course, extremely costly meal and the most expensive bottle of wine in the house.

So Matthew never got to meet Dudley Simpson, though Simpson was still sometimes to be seen at the BBC, turning out his drum rolls and parping horns for *Blake's 7*. Matthew did meet a couple of enthusiastic boys who were tinkering on keyboards to add colour to the newest episodes, creating all those synth-misty four-note lines. One of these composers had given up his law degree to concentrate on making background atmospheres for *Doctor Who*.

Matthew's own lunch was not a catastrophe of the spectacular order of John's lunch with Dudley Simpson. He had come on the train with a couple of American comic books to pass the time. He arrived at Shepherd's Bush very early and walked around, browsing in a record shop to keep his terror at bay. At five to twelve he went to the restaurant, with The Fantastic Four and The Eternals crushed into the pocket at his left buttock. Suddenly, at the door, he thought, maybe it is unsophisticated to arrive at a posh French restaurant carrying Marvel comics on one's person? He darted round the corner to a bin at the edge of the green and threw them in, not without regret.

Mild laughter ensued as John translated the menu for him.

"Well, of course you know escargot…"

But long before lunch ended, the conversation, such as it was, had become interlaced with long silences, while Matthew toyed with whatever French delicacy he was eating, which was certainly not escargot. After he has said thank you a few times, there's not much for a teenage boy to say to a producer in his thirties. He wished he had The Eternals with him. He could have read it again in the silences.

He asked a question of hopeless banality, one which would be asked of him thousands of times:

"What's Tom Baker like?"

John paused for a moment.

"Tom's alright," he said, and immediately repeated it as people do when they have doubts about what they are saying. "Tom's alright." He nodded. That was the end of the subject.

Matthew did not want to spoil things by telling John that he had read hundreds of *Doctor Who* novels and was something of a lover of the programme, but after a couple of glasses of wine and a long silence it wormed its way out.

Blue Box Boy: A Memoir of Doctor Who in Four Episodes

"Yes, I *really, really* like it. I think it's *really, really* good... I've read *all those books...* and I'm a real *fan...*"

A deadly moment passed.

"... You're not in the *Doctor Who* Appreciation Society??" asked John, as if it was a terrorist organization.

"Oh, nooo... not really. I mean, I did once send off the money but... I don't *like* it." This had the advantage of being true but it did not *sound* true. "I mean, I think they're a bit..." He didn't know what to say. He did not want to say they were *mad*. It was too obvious and predictable and it might imply that *he* was mad. "They're *not much fun,* are they?" He chewed some more food. "I mean, they just *slag everything off...*" This also was true. They had well slagged off the previous season. They had been like his mocking BBC friends, but without the fondness and humour. They had hated it in a fanatical, frowning way.

Matthew wished he had kept his mouth shut.

The purpose of the meeting was not only lunch. Afterwards, he was taken to Threshold House where he sat in John's office.

"I've something I want you to hear," said John. He pushed a cassette into a little player. A few seconds passed. Music started. It was the *Doctor Who* theme, but in a new arrangement. Matthew listened intently. It was jangly and spacy and very modern. There was an echoey effect like thunder. It was exciting to hear. it ended and the tape hissed on until John pressed the off switch.

"What do you think?"

"I love it. It's great." Matthew *did* love it, but he would have said the same thing if he had hated it. He felt he should say something more. "If the visuals can match that, it will be great."

"I think they do," he said. "I've long thought the old arrangement, basically unchanged all these years, has become stale."

"This is very fresh and new."

John looked at Matthew's short, neat haircut.

"That's no good," he said. "It will have to be long and unruly like an urchin."

"I'll let it grow."

"Not enough time. You will have to be fitted with a wig."

"A wig?"

Christopher Hamilton Bidmead ambled in. Christopher was even then a relentlessly chirpy man. He had been a regular actor in an early hospital soap called *Emergency – Ward 10* and even while script-editing *Doctor Who* he turned up occasionally as a reader of poetry on Radio Three. Matthew's mother heard Christopher reading and said she liked his voice. John said,

tipping a thumb towards Matthew like a hitchhiker,
"He's one of them."

Matthew was a little surprised that his homosexuality was so obvious and was also surprised that John, whom he had assumed to be gay from the moment he'd met him, would use quite that phrase. *One of us,* perhaps. Then he realized that sex had nothing to do with it.

"Oh, oh, well," he stammered, "not really."

Christopher talked to Matthew about auditions he had sat through for assorted one-off *Doctor Who* characters. "We had this girl in who was too terrified to read well and I put her at her ease. I said, don't panic, you can't be worse than the rest of us, we're all failed actors here!" This was true and admirably frank, though Matthew doubted that John Nathan-Turner would have been pleased to be described in these terms to a young woman trying to impress him.

The afternoon wore on and the production office could not revolve around Matthew's presence until doomsday. So he got ready to leave. John shook his hand and said a script would arrive soon.

At the office door, Chris Bidmead turned to him. In a whisper, he said, "*Watch out for Tom.*"

Watch out for Tom? Matthew puzzled over Christopher Bidmead's remark. *Watch out for Tom??* What did he mean? He thought it over and worried about it and rejected it as too vague to mean anything and then for a while he forgot it.

2

Matthew was officially a new star of *Doctor Who*. The ink was on the contract, a hefty script would soon fall through his letter box. He was ready to throw himself into it. But there was a long wait for the first day of rehearsal.

There were still a couple of studio days to be completed on the public school serial. In the BBC Club at lunchtime Matthew was at the bar with Nicholas and Simon, in the school uniforms which were their costumes, when he spotted John Nathan-Turner hunched in a corner with a woman. Matthew waved to John who waved back. The woman turned. It was Lalla Ward. She approached him.

"Hello," she said, "I'm Lalla Ward," friendly in a laid-back way, both warm and cool if such a thing is possible. She held out her hand. Matthew shook it.

"I'm Matthew," he said, and Lalla said hello again, before going back to John. Matthew made to Simon a little enamoured fainting gesture, back of hand to forehead, batting his eyelids together, as if he had just shaken the hand of the most exciting woman in the world. Lalla glanced back and saw him mid-faint and turned back to John.

Matthew had to be fitted with his wig. He partly dreaded this but was also intrigued. In amateur theatre he had seen people in wigs, and they always looked extremely silly, as if someone above had dropped the head of a mop or a bird had built a nest. What would it feel like to *wear* a wig?

He supposed he would meet with the costume designer, who was called Amy Roberts, but it turned out that wigs were the business of the make-up department. The make-up designer for *The Planet That Slept* was an attractive light-skinned black woman called Frances Needham. Though *The Vampire Lords* was to be made first, for some reason Frances rather than Norma Hill, the make-up designer for *The Vampire Lords*, who was entrusted with overseeing the design of the wig. She had made an appointment with a wig specialist in Soho.

"Here's the address," she said, handing him a piece of paper.

A few days later, he went to Soho for a five o'clock appointment. It was a grey day, always threatening rain and occasionally breaking into a light, chill shower. By four forty-five daylight was already fading into evening. Matthew clutched the piece of paper with the address. He stood under a lamp post and opened his London A-Z and looked it up in the index.

It wasn't there. There was no such street name anywhere in Soho, or anywhere in W1. The nearest was countless underground stops away in a suburb. What was he to do? Matthew felt the pavement shake under him.

Perhaps she had got the name wrong. He looked at the Soho page and tried to spy a street name which struck him as similar and there were none that were all *that* similar.

It began to drizzle. Matthew felt a wash of despair and fear. His *first job* after having been cast was to *get this wig fitted* and he *couldn't even find the place!* His despair turned to that teary sensation where the eyes water though tears do not fall, his fear to anger – she must have given him the wrong address! And there was no telephone number on the piece of paper.

He wondered around Soho in the drizzly rain. It was five ten, five fifteen. He asked friendly-looking people if they had heard of this street. Most of them rushed past, – "Too busy!" – one or two stopped and read the address and shook their heads and went away. Matthew felt like a Victorian pauper, wet through and lost.(Not the artful dodger, who would have known every nook and cranny, but Oliver Twist. "Please sir, can I have some more?")

He passed an alley off Wardour Street, with a name which no-one would have called similar to that on the piece of paper but which had a slight echo. But it was a Court, not a Street, and he walked on and around again and now it was five twenty-five and the rain was still falling and he came back to the alley and walked into it. Halfway up there was a glass door in a wall and something about hair on it and he pushed open the door and saw an iron spiral staircase which ran down to a basement and he heard a voice:

"I feel a bit guilty because I wrote the address down wrong…"

He ran down the staircase, which rattled, and he wanted to run into her arms but he didn't. It was twenty-five to six. He said,

"I'm sorry, I couldn't find it…" and pushed his fingers through his hair and wanted to cry but he did not. The wig man said it was alright and sat him in a barber's chair and began to put pins in his hair…

And a couple of weeks later he went back for the fitting and made sure he was at the mouth of the alley five minutes early and waited there looking at his watch so that he would arrive *exactly on time* and as he approached the staircase at four fifty-nine and forty seconds he heard the man below say in a slightly queeny way, "I hope he won't be late *this* time," and Matthew was annoyed because it had not been his fault at all.

The wig consultation took place even before Matthew had received a script, which duly dropped through the letter box at his house with an appalling thud. Four hundred pages, four separate scripts, one for each episode, on heavy pink paper, each held together by bronze clips which were squares with the corners cut off, disfigured octagonals.

He unwrapped the scripts and ran upstairs and read them. This was a tremendous experience.

The story went by the incomprehensible title of *The Wasting*, and it was written by that legend of *Doctor Who* productivity, Terrance Dicks. It was to be Matthew's first recording for *Doctor Who* but it was not to be his debut episode, which was to be made later. No-one told him why these programmes were made out of order. So in the script his character was already there, though not established exactly –the Doctor did not yet know he had sneaked aboard the TARDIS.

Matthew read it greedily, with the enormous pleasure of discovering some old, previously unknown *Doctor Who* adventure. For an actor who knew the series, there could have been no better starting script, because it was so much in the style and spirit of the familiar episodes. He found he was not reading to find his own scenes and lines, but for the overall piece.

It contained one of the great *Doctor Who* twists, in which a tower almost

Yeatsian topples, and is seen to have concealed a narrow old-fashioned space rocket. Matthew thought this was a brilliant and breath-taking idea, on the edge of the absurd in just the right way for *Doctor Who*, an idea which could as easily fail as succeed.

The Wasting was about vampires. It called for countless shots of bats. Matthew loved stories with bats in them and this was full of bats. It was essentially the *Doctor Who* variation on *Dracula*, just as *The Brain of Morbius* had been the *Doctor Who* version of *Frankenstein*. This had also been written by Terrance Dicks, but he had been so unhappy with the script editing, which had watered his story down, that he had put a pseudonymous name on it, the faintly damning Robin Bland. No-one could say the script for *The Wasting* was bland.

The Wasting was not a follow-up to *The Brain of Morbius*. In its early draft it had preceded it, but someone in the upper echelons of the BBC drama strand *Play For Today* got wind of it and objected. *Play For Today* was in the midst of making its own 'serious' version of *Dracula*, and a firm instruction was sent to the *Doctor Who* office that nothing likely to trivialize the subject should be produced. So *The Vampire Lords*, as it had been called at that time (the title Terrance Dicks always preferred) was abandoned until John Nathan-Turner plucked it off a shelf.

If *The Vampire Lords* was a brother of sorts to *The Brain of Morbius*, it was also the fourth in a quartet of scripts by Terrance which referred to old Hollywood horror movies and also, in the case of all but one, to literature. (A fifth film was also referred to, because the owner of Robbie the Robot in *Forbidden Planet* was called Morbius). The first ever story about the Fourth Doctor was Terrance's version of *King Kong*, this King Kong a robot that, thanks to gloriously ropy chromakey effects, grew and grew and grew and grew, and clutched Elisabeth Sladen in his mechanical claw just as Kong had carried poor Fay Wray in his palm. It was a story so adored by the kiddies who gobbled it up, among them Matthew, that soon after it was possible to buy an action figure of the Giant *Robot* himself. This must be the only time a toy ever appeared of a one-off *Doctor Who* monster – in fact, almost the only toy of any *Doctor Who* monster at all except Daleks, though the same range included a Cyberman.

A year or two after the *Robot* Kong, Sarah Jane gone from the TARDIS and the knife-wielding jungle girl Leela in her place, Terrance wrote a version of a fifties monster movie which had been drawn from a Ray Bradbury story. The Bradbury story had the pleasantly understated title *The Fog-Horn*. The movie was more coarsely named *The Beast From Twenty Thousand Fathoms*, but this was a masterpiece of subtlety compared to the *Doctor Who* version, which went by the purple title *Horror of Fang Rock*. This was one of Matthew's favourite ever *Doctor Who* titles, or indeed titles of any kind. Matthew had a shameless taste for melodrama. He liked titles with words like Horror in them, and Terror and Death and Monster and Curse and Evil and Tomb and Fear and Revenge and Doom,- *Doom!* -liking slightly less those words, subtler and more abstract, but with a glint of precocity, like Image and Destiny and Genesis and Remembrance, which were more suitable for *Star Trek*.

He suspected at the time it was shown that Terrance had achieved another *Doctor Who* first with *Horror of Fang Rock*, because it must be the only *Doctor Who* adventure in which every character except the Doctor and his companion ends up dead. *Horror of Fang Rock* was a corpse-ridden bloodbath.

And then, Morbius and his Brain, and the faces of *Doctor Who* staffers playing, in photographs, earlier incarnations of Morbius – not a glamorous crew -as the faces of Jon and Patrick and William represented earlier incarnations of the Doctor. Because Morbius was, yes, a Time Lord, of supreme, exquisite evil.

Then there was the costume fitting. Matthew was excited about this: he was curious to know what kind of strange, science-fictional costume he would wear in his first story. He hoped it would look quite futuristic. He had all sorts of ideas in his head, drawn from Dan Dare and International Rescue and *The Mind Robber* and *The Space Pirates*. Perhaps he could wear a cloak and ruffled sleeves. Or a space suit. Or a silky Elizabethan top like Buck Rogers, though this would have been no good on the moon, as a science feature in an old *Doctor Who* annual had pointed out to him. There was a picture of Buck next to this informative nugget, in his sheeny shirt with ray gun at his hip. Even Matthew could appreciate that, without a helmet as he was, Buck would have had problems in the moon's airless atmosphere. Matthew had not heard of Buck Rogers at the time of this article, nor for many years after, and when the 1930s Buster Crabbe serial was finally shown one summer holiday over a dozen mornings, Matthew found himself unable to stop repeating in his head, between all the numbingly action-packed sequences, the first thing he had ever known about Buck: that if he stepped onto the moon dressed like *that,* he would immediately die. But then, if Zoë had stepped onto the moon in her charming mini-skirt or Jamie in his kilt (with football shorts underneath, according to the Tenth Anniversary *Radio Times* Special) they would have been no better equipped.

Perhaps Adric would, Buck-like, carry a ray gun at his hip. There was a precedent for this, because the animal-skin-wearing, sexy jungle girl Leela had carried a knife. Anyway, Adric was contracted for five stories, so he would wear, supposed Matthew, five different costumes, like Lalla Ward.

Blue Box Boy: A Memoir of Doctor Who in Four Episodes

Adric could wear *all* of the costumes Matthew envisaged.

Amy came and measured him. Costume designers, having measured hundreds of people, develop the manner of the nurse who, nice but efficient, joshes while emptying bedpans. She whipped the tape around body parts and noted the information on a chart while chatting inconsequentially. Actors develop their own grin of good humour over their self-consciousness while the measurements are made, as though there is no more amusing activity. So the tape measure was wrapped around his collar and shoulders and waist and then his bottom, which made him giggly, and he had to hold one end at his crotch while she pulled the tape to his ankle, with a whispery sliding noise as it ran between her fingers. She did not ask which way he dresses. (Modestly to the left, as all viewers of *Castrovalva* know). Poor Amy had to design two costumes for Matthew for *The Vampire Lords*. She showed him the drawings. One was a rather lovely kind-of-Elizabethan outfit of a deep red, with stockings. It was not accompanied by a ray gun a la Buck Rogers but with a heavy, rusty knife, a la Leela. Cool! The other was a green and yellow set of what could only be called pyjamas, with green cloth boots and a star-shaped blue badge edged with gold paint. As this was the costume he was to wear in the opening scenes of *The Vampire Lords*, he supposed he would be wearing it in the previous story as well, which was to be recorded a few months later. Matthew thought his imagination had covered every variety of possible costume but he had not once thought of pyjamas.

Materials were scissored and rushed through sewing machines and soon he was wearing his pyjamas for the first time and looking in the mirror. Yes, he thought, mmm….

Still, there would be other stories, other costumes…

John *loved* promotional activities. It sometimes seemed that he enjoyed publicity more than the day-to-day grind of selecting stories and looking over budgets .

Shortly after he had been cast, Matthew, having nothing better to do, turned on *Blue Peter* and discovered a short feature about a *Doctor Who* exhibition, when who should step into shot, fists pressed into his jacket pockets, but John Nathan-Turner! Grinning like anything! A man in his element! Matthew's father was off work that day and Matthew called him.

"Come and see John Nathan-Turner! He's the producer of *Doctor Who*!" His father came in to the TV room.

The presenter asked John about the monsters for the new season. As much as promotion, John loved secrets. He loved promoting his programme without giving *anything* away. He was visibly *keeping things to his chest!*

"Flying creatures!" he said, a look of shrewd concealment under the smile. After completing his first season, Matthew remembered the phrase and wondered what on earth John had meant. *Flying creatures? What flying bloody creatures?* Then it clicked: Bats!

"He seems like a very nice man," said Matthew's father.

"Yes," said Matthew, "he is."

John's playfulness crept into his press releases. Early newspaper pieces about Adric said, as the original character breakdown had said, that he heralded from the planet Yerfillag. None of the journalists writing up their few dozen words caught the joke, and there was no particular reason why they should have. Nor, it must be said, did Matthew. Having read the script of *The Planet That Slept*, he said to John,

"I'm glad you changed the name of his planet to Alzarius. I thought Yerfillag was a bit silly-sounding."

John looked at him as if he was simple-minded.

"It's Gallifrey backwards!"

"Oh." Matthew swung the letters around in his head. "Oh yes!"

This humour leapt from press releases into the programmes themselves, when a nice old man called Tremas was destroyed by a very unpleasant Time Lord... The moment Matthew read that script he remembered Yerfillag and thought, that's not Johnny Byrne, that's Jay En Tee. It would be some time before Matthew found out that John Nathan-Turner was a stage name, adapted from the name on his birth certificate, which was Jonathan Turner.

So a little spurt of promotion was embarked upon. A man called from the *Daily Mail*. Matthew had been in local papers once or twice for outstandingly dreary reasons but had never before spoken to what he supposed was a proper journalist. The man asked what it was like to be the new *Doctor Who* assistant.

'Assistant' had always been the newspaper term for the *Doctor Who* companion. Matthew could see how it had come about: real scientists had assistants in white coats to carry test tubes and samples and to flick switches. But most of the girls and boys who travelled with Doctor Who did not *assist* him. Jo Grant was given to Doctor Who by UNIT *precisely* to assist him, but those schoolteachers and Jamie and Zoë and Vicki, and Sarah Jane and Leela – were they *assistants?* Matthew, working on *The Vampire Lords*, thought that whatever his character could be said to be doing, it was not *assisting...*

"Well," said Matthew to the *Daily Mail* voice, "it's very nice indeed to be the new *Doctor Who* assistant, but he's not really an *assistant* exactly. He doesn't *assist,* you see..."

"Then what is he?"

"Well, I suppose the word is companion. They're normally called companions, I think, because they don't really *assist,* do they? Not this one anyway."

The next day a short article appeared on page three, in which the word assistant was used multiple times. This caused hilarity in Matthew's house.

More important was a photo session outdoors with a handful of newspaper photographers, to be followed by a meeting, which was probably called a press conference, though it amounted to three journalists in a small, rather warm, room.

Matthew put on his wig and his *Doctor Who* costume with its blue badge and posed by a mossy brick wall. One of the photographers said would he mind climbing onto the wall and standing there, hands on hips like Superman, and he obliged. Then, would he shake his fists in the air like a triumphant wrestler, and he obliged. Would he mind jumping off. He obliged.

Then he took off his costume and put on his t-shirt and jeans. John took him to the 'press conference' and stood at the back of the room throughout.

One of the questioners at the interview was a chubby, unsmiling middle-aged woman from the *Daily Mirror*. With her tight, curly hair and her bulky frame and her circular face, she looked like the kind of professionally firm woman to be found in government offices, who turns down applications for grants.

"I saw you last weekend on *Saturday Night at the Mill*," she said. "I thought, *now there's a bright button!*"

Next to her was a woman from *The Sun*, a genuine grotesque. She may have been sixty, but she had peroxide blonde hair and a slash of lipstick running approximately over her lips. Her cheeks were creamed so thickly they shone, reflecting the light, like a headlamp on glass. She wore a short skirt. This fake youthfulness made her look tired and ancient, pickled in whisky and tobacco. Her legs were tucked under the chair, her right foot resting on her left ankle. She narrowed her eyes when she asked questions. She held her notebook like a weapon. Matthew felt she was trying to corner him, sniffing for the moment he'd let his guilt slip. She was looking for an *angle,* a *scoop,* a *story,* but there wasn't a story, beyond 'Boy on Telly'. She asked about his background. She asked about acting and how it felt to be on a TV serial. Matthew was nervous and cautious and referred to John before giving his answers. He felt *accused.*

She narrowed her eyes to slits. Her head sprang forward.

Did he not think perhaps there was an element of *luck?* She endowed this word with two syllables: luck*ah.*

Well, yes, he said, (what did she think he was going to say?), there's an element of luck in anything to do with acting, even an end of the pier job. It's all luck, really. And in the end it's all end of the pier. Plays, telly, movies: it's all end of the pier work really.

The meeting came to an end.

The *Mirror* had wangled an extra photo session, so on the next studio day, when shooting had finished, he posed by the TARDIS console with Lalla Ward behind him (like Dr. Liz Shaw peering with a broad grin over the shoulder of the Third Doctor on the pink annual cover).

The papers came out. The *Mirror* woman was quite nice about him. *The Sun* woman had got her angle. He was a brat, he was a *superbrat.* Because journalists 'write' their material mainly from cuttings files, exactly like those he had filed a few months earlier, it was a phrase that would repeat itself like burps of garlic.

Yet the Sun woman was on the phone to him only a few weeks later. She was *charming,* all compassion and warmth and concern. How *are* you, she asked, in the caring way of a wife dropping poison into her husband's drink. I'm fine, he said. Have you heard the latest rumour, she breathed, that K9, the beloved robot dog, is to be *axed?* This was the favourite word of tabloid hacks. No-one left a series, no contracts expired, people were *axed.* Ka-*thunk.* Even mechanical puppies were *axed.* Well, he said, he hadn't heard about it, how amazing, oh well, oh dear.

So *The Sun* launched a campaign to save K9. This was a campaign which Matthew supported, if you believed *The Sun*. He said K9 was a "great little character." This phrase Matthew would always recall, because it was so perfectly one he would never use, about anyone, about anything.

There were other publicity opportunities. John leapt on all of them. Even before the press conference, Matthew had made his first live TV appearance, which was his first time on the TV airwaves because, though he had done that public school serial before he was cast in *Doctor Who* it had not yet been shown.

This first appearance was on the late evening programme called *Saturday Night at the Mill.* It was for this appearance he had been praised by the *Mirror* woman as a 'bright button'.

Pebble Mill was the name of the BBC studio in Birmingham. God knows why: perhaps there had once been a cotton mill on the land. It was best known outside the region for a weekday lunchtime magazine show called *Pebble Mill at One*, which was packed with celebrity interviews and gardening tips, and sometimes a cookery spot presented by a Church of England canon. It usually ended with an unthreatening pop song. The programme entertained the housewives of England when housewives still existed in large numbers, and because it was live it had a tiny edge of danger. Sometimes a pop group failed to get the signal that their pre-recorded mime track was starting, so they stood there with egg on their faces while their hope-to-be-hit single blared to the viewers at home.

Matthew once met a woman who had had an affair with one of *Pebble Mill at One*'s boyish presenters. He was astounding in bed, she told him, but so boring out of it that she dumped him. Both these comments sounded believable.

Saturday Night at the Mill did not have the cookery or the gardening. It was more of an old-fashioned variety show, but like its daylight sister it went out live. Before the main guests were introduced, the presenter, Bob Langley, would pick out a couple of extremely minor celebrities who had been planted in the audience, for fifteen or twenty seconds of chat. Matthew was to be one of these not-quite-non-entities.

Bob Langley was no-one's idea of a boyish presenter. Middle-aged and extremely masculine, when not making Pebble Mill programmes he turned out excessively bloody paperback thrillers.

Matthew had never seen *Saturday Night at the Mill* so he was going into it blind.

After a morning rehearsal of *The Vampire Lords*, he leapt onto the first Birmingham-bound train. He arrived at about half past two and took a cab to the studio. He hoped he would arrive in time for the run-through.

This was a mistake. Except for a security guard and a woman at the desk, Pebble Mill had an air of abandonment. He went up to the woman at the desk and gave his name.

"You're a bit early," she said, with raised eyebrow. "You're not expected until six."

She phoned the producer, who was called Rod. He appeared from an inner sanctum. He wore a soft hat and looked like a racing tipster.

"We can give you a dressing room."

"That's fine. I've got a book with me."

He didn't have a book. He was too nervous to read.

So for several hours Matthew sat in an empty dressing room pretending he had a book. Eventually there was a rap on the door. The behatted Rod stood outside with the butch Bob Langley. Bob talked to Matthew as if he were extremely interested in him. Considering Matthew's contribution to the show was to be tiny, both he and Rod were tremendously solicitous of his welfare. Bob discussed how the interview would go.

"I will say, here is *Matthew Waterman* from… is it *Blue Peter?*"

"*Doctor Who*. And it's Waterhouse."

"Martin *Waterhouse* from *Doctor Who*. Then we'll talk a little about making the programmes."

"I can talk about how great Tom Baker is."

"Yes, that's excellent. So, Ladies and Gentlemen, Matthew Waterman from *Doctor Whooo!*"

"Yes. But its Waterhouse."

They went to the canteen and talked a bit more. Bob mentioned that he had once been at a party where Tom had been both present and absent.

"He sat in the corner the whole time reading a book," he said. "He never spoke a word to anyone."

Matthew wondered what the book was. It was certainly not one of Bob's torture-filled thrillers. Tom was a fan of Solzhenitsyn, so perhaps it was *The Gulag Archipelago*.

The proper guests began to appear and Bob left Matthew to himself. The proper guests included the Welsh actor Hywel Bennett and the show stopping music hall turn Two-Ton Tessie O'Shea. The show's regular band rolled in, Kenny Ball and his Jazzmen. Matthew had seen Kenny Ball on TV before. Like many jobbing musicians, Kenny Ball exuded the vibe of a man who wouldn't take any shit off anyone.

The broadcast got underway. Matthew sat surrounded by Midlands housewives and grandmothers, all clutching free tickets. They had placed their handbags on their knees. They sat there, acidly waiting to be entertained. Matthew wanted his little bit to be over.

Kenny blew his horn. Loud applause. Bob announced the guests for the evening. Ooohs and aaahs circulated from housewife to granny to housewife, up and down the rows, between the straps of cut-price handbags. But before the real excitement got underway:

"Ladies and Gentlemen, Matthew Waterman from *Doctor Whoooo*!!"

This was a talk show, but Matthew was speechless. Should he say, no, Bob, it's *Waterhouse?* It might even get a laugh. But he thought, no-one will notice, I'll just say something chatty. He felt frost in the corners of his brain. He talked about how terrific Tom Baker was but how hard it was to realize he was not actually *Doctor Who* but a person. Somehow Matthew managed to compare Tom to Noele Gordon. Noele Gordon was the star of a long-running five-day-a-week soap opera about a motel, called *Crossroads*, which was hugely popular but reputedly, despite having for a while a theme tune written and played by Paul McCartney, the worst programme on TV, at least among those who did not think *Doctor Who* was the worst programme on TV. (There was, in fact, a link to *Doctor Who*, because the creator of *Crossroads*, a man named Peter Ling, had written the *Doctor Who* story *The Mind Robber*). It was one of the very few programmes on which a *Doctor Who* actor could find himself and feel he had taken an artistic downturn, *Emmerdale Farm* being another. Matthew had never met Noele Gordon, but she had a reputation as a terrifying firebrand. She had a special chair in the *Crossroads* Green Room, and if a guest artist should happen to sit on it unawares, his life on *Crossroads* would ever after be a living hell. Tom Baker and Noele Gordon are *people* first, said Matthew wisely, enormous stars of TV second. Bob Langley twinkled approval.

Then his appearance was all over and Matthew could relax while Bob talked to Hywel Bennett, who discussed his career and plugged some new programme, between puffs of his cigarette. Once Hywel had finished, applause broke out. A pinch-faced Midlands grandmother in front of Matthew leant to her friend and said, even as she applauded, "I thought Hywel Bennett was *very dry!*"

No-one could accuse Two-Ton Tessie O'Shea of being dry. Even in old age, she was a glitter ball of showbiz energy, knocking out her saucy music hall tunes in a mountainous voice, with a swing of her hips and a shake of her maracas, her body as wide as it was high, the audience stamping along.

At the party afterwards, Matthew said to Bob,

"It's still Waterhouse!"

He had meant this in a jokey fashion, but Bob looked put out.

"Did I get it wrong?"

"I don't mind."

It was strange to Matthew that a short, shy teenager could make the author of sadistic, bloodcurdling CIA thrillers blanch.

Matthew was not comfortable at large parties. He liked to be in groups of three or four. He wondered away as the drink flowed and raucousness set in.

There was a little dining room off the party lounge and in a corner, by herself, sat Tessie O'Shea, eating a meal. She summoned him. He went to her table and she embarked on a sort of impromptu interview with him. She wanted to know all about him, she said. He didn't have a life worth talking about, but she acted like everything he said was fascinating. She would say to each of his answers, in her Northern accent, "Well, that's very interesting, I'm glad I asked that, I'm finding out more."

Do you like the Beatles, she asked.

Oh yes, said Matthew, I love them. This was not quite true. He was too young ever to have caught the full force of their music. His heroine was Kate Bush, with whose music he had a deep, intimate relationship. He was sure Tessie O'Shea wouldn't care about his love for Kate Bush.

Tessie talked at length about the Beatles, thinking Matthew would be interested, which he was. She talked about how she had been on the TV programme on which they had made their American debut. She talked about John, Paul, George and Ringo as if she were their mother, their discoverer, their manager and their best friend, all rolled into one. It was exciting to listen to.

Kenny Ball sidled over and sat with them. By this time Tessie was talking about her career.

"I was an enormous star. I could sell out huge theatres."

"But," said Kenny, turning his beer bottle in his hand, "you couldn't do that now."

"No," she said, looking down at her plate. "No, I couldn't do it now." That was the end of the conversation. Matthew was narked with Kenny. He didn't mind if Tessie O'Shea talked proudly of her success or had a large ego. He had liked listening to her.

In the corridor, several people waited for cabs to the hotel. Matthew said, lightly,

"I'm just going to empty my bladder."

Hywel spun to him and said, not loudly but with the vehemence of a very drunk man,

"For Christ's sake, you're going to *piss!* You're going to *have a piss!*"

Matthew's mother had a friend who worshipped Bob Langley. This lively if corpulent woman in her fifties with dyed black hair talked about Bob in much the way a teenager talks about a pop idol, with a semi-giggle bubbling under her speech. When she heard that Matthew had met him she wanted to know *everything* about him and, though Matthew had little of interest to impart, he said that Bob was very nice. She was pleased to hear this, she said.

She did not like his novels but, being a loyal fan, she read them all.

Many years later Matthew would find a bootleg video on a market stall in Camden Town of a TV special Kate Bush had made for the BBC in the late seventies. He had watched it when it was broadcast, but like most BBC material it did not get a second showing.

It was a delight to see it again, even with a picture which broke up and colour which kept fading into black and white. At the end, he read the credits. It had been made at Pebble Mill. The producer was Rod of the tipster's hat.

Matthew wished he'd known. He would have pumped poor Rod with so many questions about Kate Bush that his hat would have crumpled and his hair fallen out.

Doctor Who was famous, even among the many who detested it, for its extreme longevity. It may not have been much good, but by golly it went on. Another programme with a similar longevity was *Top of the Pops*. *Top of the Pops* was exactly what it sounded like: a chart show on which groups mimed their current hits. It was not half as cool as it pretended to be.

It showed the occasional pop video, but the pop video was still in its early stages. Instead, *Top of the Pops* had its own dance group. Every week they performed a simple dance to a hit whose artist was unable or unwilling to come into the studio. The name of this group changed every so often, but the choreographer remained the same, so Pan's People morphed into Legs & Co. without any discernable change in the style, which was literal. If a song lyric mentioned a dog the four or five girls of Legs & Co. would dance around a dog, perhaps wagging a finger at it. If a lyric mentioned a storm, someone off camera would turn on a wind machine. If it mentioned a little baby, one of Legs & Co. would curl up like a foetus. If it mentioned a horse they would make little galloping gestures. It would have been instructive to see them interpret *Tangled Up in Blue*. Matthew would see the girls of Legs & Co. sitting around in leotards in the café at the Acton rehearsal rooms. They were a bit snobby and very self-possessed. They never looked as if rehearsals had taken much out of them. Sarah Sutton had been a dance student and knew a girl from the group. She told the girl that she was now in *Doctor Who*.

"How nice for you," said the girl, "I *never* watch it."

The most remarkable thing about Legs & Co. was not that they were hopeless, but that nobody in Britain knew they were hopeless. Nobody said, did you see those ridiculous girls dancing round that dog? Whooor, said pimply male virgins on school buses the next morning, I wouldn't mind giving them one. In this, Legs & Co. were like *Doctor Who* girls. However ambitious *Doctor Who* writers sometimes wished to be, the bulk of the audience were farting boys who said, whooor, I wouldn't mind sticking my head between *her* knockers, her being Leela or Jo or Zoë or Romana. It should be said that Matthew was flattered when he met young gay men and also some girls who said they had often thought about him while masturbating. He was easily pleased.

Most of the many millions of viewers of *Top of the Pops* did not buy records. They watched while eating tea or ironing. When punk came along, suddenly the average ironing housewife found she hated the music and she switched off. This was why *Top of the Pops* was now, in 1980, in the doldrums. The latest idea to revitalize it was to have non-musical guests. Matthew secretly thought this was a rotten idea. John Nathan-Turner thought otherwise. *Matthew was to make an appearance.*

The programme was recorded on a Wednesday, and broadcast on the Thursday. Matthew turned up at the studio in the early evening. He felt a glimmer of envy when he saw that the floor manager, a man called

Nicholas, was wearing a Lene Lovich t-shirt. Matthew most loved Kate Bush, but Lene was a close second, her witchy, metaphysical new wave, all angels and telepathy and suspended animation and dead birds, was right up his street. He played her album Flex all the time. She had the most idiosyncratic dress sense in pop music: she wore what seemed to be old curtains, and she could make old curtains look goodish. The t-shirt had been given to the floor manager by Lene herself, he said. Matthew wanted to find out more but Nicholas had other things on his mind, saying only that she had been on the programme the previous week and was very nice, almost as nice as Toyah Wilcox who was super-nice.

"Let me introduce you to Dave," he said.

"Who's Dave?" asked Matthew.

"Dave Lee Travis," said Nicholas, with a slightly condescending inflection, the kind an opera fan will use to someone who asks who Wagner is. Matthew had in fact heard of Dave Lee Travis, who was widely known by the witty sobriquet the Hairy Cornflake, because he had a thick beard and presented the breakfast programme on Radio One (breakfast/cornflake, geddit?) as well as being one of the pool of *Top of the Pops* presenters. All the Top of the Tops presenters were Radio One DJs.

Matthew was taken to the Cornflake's dressing room. The Cornflake, who was broad, with oddly flat features under his beard and a nose with unusually long nostrils, did not show any sign of being pleased to meet Matthew. The producer was there, too, and, as often at the BBC, he was surprisingly old: a grey-haired variety show producer who had been given *Top of the Pops* but would have preferred *The Two Ronnies*.

The first thing that was decided on Matthew's arrival in the Cornflake's dressing room was that, uncool as *Top of the Pops* was, it was cooler than him: he could not possibly be seen on camera next to the Cornflake dressed like *that*. It was all too true. He was in a boring pastel-coloured shirt and a pair of cords. He was sent off post-haste to the wardrobe department. A very nice, queeny dresser of sixty, slim, white haired, balding, pulled from a hiding place the sort of trunk a child might keep for his toys, but this was full of clothes. A bright top was picked out, with loud red and orange stripes. It made Matthew look like a Play Away presenter. It was, at least, an improvement on his TV pyjamas.

Matthew chatted for a while to the dresser. The dresser had been in the BBC for thirty years and had worked often on *Doctor Who*. He had dressed both William and Patrick, much preferring William.

Matthew was interested in hearing things which contradicted generally received wisdom. It was in these contradictions that the most interesting approximation to the truth lay. Hartnell had been known as a difficult man. For instance, though he did not fillet scripts as Tom did, he had insisted that all scenes were rewritten so he had the last line. Accommodating this strange demand must have been infuriating for everyone, writers, actors, directors. It was such a legend in the *Doctor Who* production office down the years that, even a decade after Hartnell's death, John Nathan-Turner was aware of it.

"I liked William Hartnell a lot," said the dresser. "You see, he was interested in his costume. Patrick didn't care about his costume very much so he didn't care about his dresser. He wasn't rude but he was indifferent. Hartnell respected his dresser because he respected his costume. Also, he liked to bet on the horses, and he'd send me off down to the betting office with a few shillings to have a wager on his behalf. He was very down to earth."

A conversation about politics started between the dresser and Matthew and a make-up girl.

Matthew had been in a group in the pub with Tom Baker in one of his good moods. Someone had said, "we've got to get rid of this bloody government," meaning Margaret Thatcher, and Tom had said, "yes, but I can't stand those bastards who go on about democracy all the time. I don't trust them at all." Matthew felt this chimed with his own sense of things and decided to remember it for later use. Now he brought it out for the dresser.

"I can't bear all those people who drone on about democracy. I don't trust them an inch."

"You, young man," said the dresser, pointing approvingly at him, "have learnt a very important lesson."

Jane, the *Doctor Who* secretary, met Matthew, ('liaised' was the word, no doubt), accompanied by a small, nervy middle-aged man from BBC Enterprises, the corporation's modest and wonderfully ineffective commercial division. As Mrs Thatcher went to work on the BBC, which she hated, in the 1980s, it became increasingly slick and commercially aware and BBC enterprises eventually blossomed, or at any rate fattened, into the massive BBC Worldwide, described as 'The BBC's commercial arm'. BBC Enterprises in 1980 had no keen young lads with mobile phones and big time media ambitions in it, but was a small and humble thing, it knew its place. Its staff looked like battered husbands. The height of their commercial activity was releasing occasionally a 45 RPM single of a popular TV theme.

This was the point of Matthew's appearance on *Top of the Pops*. He was not only going to introduce himself to the public – if that's what he was doing – he was going to plug the brand new single in its shiny picture sleeve, with Tom Baker grinning on the front in his new red scarf. As Jane introduced him to the little man from BBC Enterprises, Matthew saw that the little man was holding the single.

The Cornflake said he did not want Matthew to plug the record. He should come on without it. Matthew did not know who to listen to. There he was on the studio floor at the edge of the crowd in his stripy orange shirt, with the record in his hands. Should he drop it or take it on camera? Who would he prefer to upset – the Cornflake or the shy man from Enterprises? It was strange, he thought, that he was left to make up his own mind on what was to him a matter of gigantic importance. What would John prefer? What would Jane prefer? He only wanted to be *told what to do.* Anyway, he decided to ignore the Cornflake. The nervous little man looked more easily bruised.

In moments, there he was, swept on the stage, a stupendously stupid grin on his face, the deafening applause, the crowd looking at him adoringly, now he knew what it was like to be David Bowie, the Cornflake's arm around his shoulder, something which passed for banter flashing between them, the grin expanding, oh was he playing a frightening alien ha ha yes he was an alien ho ho but not an odd looking one ha ha at least he hoped not ho ho look here's the fabulous new single ha ha buy it folks ho ho. He held the record up to the camera, the least subliminal advertising ever, the Cornflake still grinning, Matthew still grinning, Tom grinning on the sleeve in his new wine-red scarf and hat, an all-round smiley moment. The applause was shattering, the lights, the cheers, the love.

For the first time Matthew looked out into the crowd.

?

They were not applauding. They were hardly even looking at him. They couldn't care less. They were checking their nail polish.[4]

Matthew was saddened to find out that all the ecstatic cheering every week on *Top of the Pops* as each act mimed to its hit was just as fake as the performances. The audience stood and stared.

Tremendously pleasing to Matthew was that his little talk was followed immediately by Kate Bush: not live, unfortunately, but on video, singing her war song *Army Dreamers*. Matthew and Kate mentioned in the same breath on *Top of the Pops*! Their names would be forever linked. How the crowd shrieked and crowed when the video began, though in the darkness before him they were picking their noses and checking their watches.

Afterwards Matthew went up to the bar with Jane Judge. Nicholas Lyndhurst came up.

"What are you doing? *Doctor Who*?"
"You'd never believe me if I told you!"
"Tell!"

"I've just been on *Top of the Pops*!"
"*I don't believe you!!*"

At a party a few weeks later, Matthew met the man from BBC Enterprises. He came up to Matthew in a state of excitement.

"Thank you for plugging the single," he said. "It sold two hundred copies the very next week."

"Oh," said Matthew, about to say sorry.

"Two Hundred copies! It's incredible. Just incredible!"

Matthew took the praise that was due to him.

3

Matthew got home from school one day. By the way, said his mother, they've announced the new *Doctor Who* actor. Golly, said Matthew, who is it? I've never heard of him, said his mother, he's a man called Tim Barker.

For days Matthew walked around thinking, Tim Barker is the new *Doctor Who*. Tim Barker is the new *Doctor Who*. The new *Doctor Who* is Tim Barker.

Long before Matthew arrived on *Doctor Who*, Tom Baker had become the very standard of bohemian individualism. All of his childish admirers heard the word bohemian for the first time in regard to him, though they had never heard of La Boehme or of Bohemia itself. He was *the* Bohemian, the definitive article you might say. He was 'arty' to people who did not know what 'arty' was. For children of Matthew's age his version of *Doctor Who* was the defining oddity on which they imagined they could model themselves, the embodiment of what it meant to be eccentric in an old-fashioned, slightly poetical way, with his big eyes and unusual dress sense, notably the scarf which in real life you could not wear for more than three minutes without tripping over, and of course his booming voice. That booming voice, almost parodically a 'beautiful' overwrought Shakespearean-style voice, Robert Stephens on uppers, also made him the defining example, to the exhaustively silly boys who worshipped every nuance of his grandstanding, of the stuff of a 'great actor,' though even to them he was a 'great actor' of a somewhat passé kind, as far from the 'kitchen sink' as he could be, the kind who might have strutted Victorian stages declaiming *King Lear* in a glued-on beard, wielding wooden swords, clutching the proscenium with fake exhaustion at the curtain call. Yes, many deluded innocents and holy fools, including Matthew, thought he was a genius.

That Tom could create such widespread delusions among very ridiculous people might be an outré sort of genius in itself. Everyone loved Jon Pertwee's *Doctor Who* but no-one ever called Jon Pertwee a genius. They called Tom Baker a genius all the time. They thought he was 'deep' in some inexplicable way. When he pulled a yoyo from his pocket and ran it up and down along its string suddenly the yoyo, this forgotten wooden toy, which they had never before been interested in, became a desired accessory for unpopular children, who practiced it in the corners of playgrounds in schools the length and breadth of Britain, feeling they were eccentric. Matthew had an official *Doctor Who* yoyo, with a picture of a Dalek glued to the side.

These unhappy boys had read articles about Tom's life and sighed meaningfully that, "of course, he's had a very *difficult* life, you know."

This was a recurring phrase. Later, Matthew got to know a boy who worked in the Soho vegetarian restaurant Cranks, where Tom would show up occasionally for breakfast, looking pale and wan. "Aaaah, Tom Baker," the boy said knowingly, gazing into middle distance, the glisten of a sympathetic tear, "he's had a very *sad* life, he has," as if this would come as interesting news to Matthew, who hardly knew Tom, had met him once or twice perhaps, whereas the Cranks boy and he were really quite pally, though all the boy had done was hand Tom a horribly dry cake made of grains and sawdust and gooseberry skins.

"Really? A *sad* life?" said Matthew. "I didn't know that. When he was around me he was always rather jolly."

The word 'eccentric' did not mean merely odd or alien or weird. No-one called David Bowie eccentric. Eccentric meant Patrick Moore, a clever amateur astronomer with the manner of a barking madman. In the late fifties Moore posted a letter to the BBC suggesting they have a programme about astronomy, and they said they liked the idea and invited him to become its presenter. This programme, which was called *The Sky At Night*, was shown not weekly like other programmes , but once a month, late at night on BBC 2. Hardly anyone watched it, yet Moore became one of the most instantly recognisable people of his time and a favourite of TV impressionists. He was occasionally invited onto entertainment shows to demonstrate his other hobby, which was playing the glockenspiel.

Eccentric meant the poet laureate John Betjeman, with his passion for railways and church architecture and old hymns and his crush on Miss Joan Hunter Dunn, but it did not mean the next laureate, Ted Hughes, though Ted Hughes, who believed in magic, was certainly a more unusual person. It meant Alan Bennett, with his light Yorkshire voice and his

Talking Heads, but not Dennis Potter, though Dennis Potter characters in hospital beds had visions of doctors dancing to forties pop tunes. When she shot to number one with her lovely high-pitched wail Wuthering Heights, it came to mean Kate Bush, whether Kate liked it or not. It was often attached to the adjectives 'much-loved' and 'English'.

The outlines of Tom's life story were known to everyone who had any curiosity about him, because he was the subject of countless newspaper profiles. His story was as unusual and otherworldly as he apparently was. To the readers of hack journalism it was exotic and edgy and appealingly troubled, not enviable precisely but compelling. The earlier *Doctor Who*s had had no great stories to tell or, if they had, they had not been told. William Hartnell, movie character actor, *Brighton Rock*, a sitcom star in the fifties, appeared in the first *Carry On*, known to be a bit grumpy. Patrick Troughton, public school boy, war service, bit part in Olivier's *Hamlet*, jobbing actor, turns up in Hammer Horror film. Jon Pertwee, showbiz family, dad a minor playwright, cousin in *Dad's Army*, radio personality, *The Navy Lark*, *Carry On* films, funny voices. Jon Pertwee had a nice house. This was known because his house was profiled in an article in a magazine, complete with photographs. It was not as nice as Bryan Ferry's house, which was the main article in the first issue of *The World of Interiors*, but not many people could be expected to have a house as nice as Bryan Ferry's. None of these lives were the stuff to grip the attention of the readers of papers, but here, now, the big-eyed maniac with the scarf, here was something else. Tom was the subject of articles all the time, perhaps not only because he was good copy but also because, hanging out in Soho dives like the Groucho Club, he was in the same milieu as countless vile drunken hacks, who, desperate for a few hundred words, found he was easily run to earth.

The scandal rag *Private Eye* threw its free monthly lunches, where anyone with a scurrilous story could pass it on to the Eye editor in exchange for a poorish lunch and some booze, in an upstairs room at the Coach And Horses, while downstairs Tom got plastered.

Tom was a dedicated *Eye* reader, unfolding the inky new issue every fortnight standing at the bar of the Acton pub. Occasionally a satirical jibe about him appeared, and he was a little thin-skinned about these, especially when he was mentioned two issues in a row.

"They don't know when to stop," he sighed.

Strangely, Matthew was also an *Eye* reader, even in extreme youth, because his father got it. So he knew about Tom's most macabre appearance in the magazine. This was an entry in Auberon Waugh's Diary, funny enough to quote in full, in which Waugh writes about the *Sunday Times Colour Magazine*:

September 24th 1978

... On the back page it has a large photograph of Tom Baker, the actor who plays Doctor Who on television. He does not look very healthy, but I gather he once spent six years in a monastery and has been trying to catch up ever since.

He describes a day in the life of a Soho drunk and layabout, but it is the end of his day which catches my eye:

"Then I went back to Gerry's Club for another drink and after I'd cadged some Valium from someone I went home to my padded cell. I thought about Harriet Waugh and fell asleep."

In a free country there is nothing I can do to stop Mr Baker thinking about my Sister when he is alone in bed if that is what he wants to do. No doubt he has spent many years thinking about the Four Last Things, and I can quite understand that he wouldn't want to think about Kate Bush if he has ever heard the terrible noises she makes.

But if any of my female readers would like to think about Tom Baker before they go to sleep, I provide William Rushton's impression of this thoughtful man to assist them in their meditations.

Whatever Waugh said, in 1978 Tom looked a great deal healthier than in 1980. Beneath these words there is Rushton's delightfully amusing drawing of Tom in his scarf, eyes popping, hair wild, teeth bared, one hand holding a novel by Harriet Waugh, the other thrust down his familiar, speckly trousers.

In this little article Tom was inextricably linked with Matthew's heroine Kate Bush, just as Matthew was linked on *Top of the Pops*. Matthew had noticed that when he once commented to Tom on how brilliant and perfect Kate's new album was – it must have been *Never For Ever* – a look of iciness fell on his face. Perhaps he was recalling Auberon Waugh.

Incidentally, when the editor of *Private Eye*, Richard Ingrams, retired from the job, he appointed as his successor a small, brilliant fellow called Ian, who came from Matthew's town. Matthew never met him, but knew his mother, because she worked behind the scenes in amateur theatre with Matthew when he was thirteen. Her son was small but she was big. She was an extremely intelligent, powerful, rather forbidding personality known only as Mrs Hislop.

Not only the *Eye* got Tom's goat. One morning during rehearsals an actor turned up with a copy of the *Daily Mirror*, which he put on the window sill to read later. (If an actor read a tabloid, it was always the *Mirror*). Mysteriously, the paper disappeared soon after.

"What's happened to my *Mirror*?" asked the actor, scratching his head.

The director Peter Grimwade had seen another copy earlier, and he was able to explain why the paper had vanished.

There was a photograph of Tom on the gossip page at some party with his head thrown back, glugging from a bottle of wine. The piece accompanying it was written in 'drunk speech' – "*Yezz another drink tom ooh the room is spinning,*" something like that – implying that Tom had been extremely well oiled. In fact, the bottle had not even been open. A photographer had said, "put that to your lips Tom," and Tom had good-humouredly complied. He felt that he'd been stitched up, and he had.

"But I can just *see* him doing it," said Peter, as if speaking of a wayward child.

Tom Baker!

Born in poverty in Liverpool's Scotland Road area! Goodness, said Matthew's mother, that was the slums. Matthew's mother was a Liverpool girl, she knew all about Scotland Road. And occasionally a character in an early Beryl Bainbridge novel would whisper of it as a place to be avoided.

At eighteen, a monk! Not a religious conversion, but an escape hatch from the hell of Scotland Road. (A sort of TARDIS, really). Three years in a monastery until booted out, told he did not have a vocation. National Service, where he was a lousy soldier, he said, he kept dropping his gun, but, he said, he got by because they thought he was quite harmless, though hopelessly mad.

Matthew identified with Tom's hopelessness as a soldier. On the public school serial, he had had to appear in a scene with the school army corps. This involved a parade, presenting arms, rifle to shoulder, rifle to ground. Matthew could not do it, even when he did not drop his rifle he did not get the timing right, the butt landed on his shoulder a second late and at the wrong angle, on the ground two seconds late. It was as comical as a *Dad's Army* parade. He made every effort. He practiced and practiced in his own time with an imaginary rifle. Eventually the director moved him from the middle of the front row to the back left, and angled the camera so he was out of shot. This was wise. Even his best effort was only roughly right. The military man hired to train the actors for this scene, rotund with a small moustache, unsmiling, hated Matthew, wanted to roar at him and send him off to peel potatoes for weeks and weeks and weeks. He said later, lips peeled back exposing his gums, "I'd *love* to get my hands on you!" Matthew didn't want his horrid authoritarian hands on him and anyway he couldn't touch him because Matthew was an actor and not a soldier. It is just as well Matthew was never called up. He would have been among the worst soldiers ever.

"Wine, women and song!" This was the phrase Tom used about what happened next. Drama School! Matthew overheard an earnest young extra on *Logopolis* – who strummed a guitar in his downtime – introduce himself to Tom.

"I went to the same drama school as you," said the extra.

Tom said,

"Christ, I was the only person ever to come out of that awful place and be successful." Then he strode away. This would have been news to Nerys Hughes, who had also studied there.

In Matthew's town there lived a woman who had been a drama student alongside him. Matthew had long held her in awe. At fifteen, he'd nagged her for information, for further proof of Tom Baker's genius, as if any were needed. You'd have to be a fool not to recognize his genius in every frame of *Doctor Who*. There were subtle suggestions in her umming and aahing that she did not think him all that much of a genius, but she was discreet, became muted when Matthew asked his searching and dreary questions. She knew something of his brief first marriage, which, she quietly said, had come about as a result of an unexpected pregnancy. To Matthew, this was impressively naughty. It was like the decline of the Roman Empire. Sex before marriage! That's what Matthew was into!

Movies. Naked as Rasputin in *Nicholas and Alexandra*, for the premiere of which he turned up slightly the worse for wear. (Matthew was told this by the boyfriend of Victor Pemberton, the man who wrote *Doctor Who and the Pescatons*). Matthew never saw the movie, but he has seen photos of the real Rasputin and the resemblance is uncanny.

At conventions Matthew encountered numerous people whose preferences leant more to *Carry On Don't Lose Your Head* than *Nicholas and Alexandra*, but who had sat through every frame of the latter, simply to catch a glimpse of Tom's penis.

More movies, including *The Golden Voyage of Sinbad*, the only Tom Baker movie Matthew ever saw. When he was a lad, he found it tremendously exciting, with its scary Ray Harryhausen rubber monsters.

Tom was not only in movies, he was on distinguished stages. The National Theatre, under Laurence Olivier! Memorably, as a horse in the first production of *Equus*. More booze, more unemployment. On his uppers, a hod carrier. What's a hod carrier?, Matthew asked his mother. It means you carry around buckets of cement on building sites, she said.

Out of the blue, the best job ever! The builders were readers of *Sporting Life*, and discovered from a front page picture that their hod carrier was the new *Doctor Who*. Matthew wanted to be a hod carrier too so he could become a star and it would be on the cover of *Sporting Life* and his chums on the site would say, *lorks, matey, you're the new Doctor 'Oo, well you could knock be dahn wiv a feaver me old mate.*

It was later revealed to Matthew that the Sinbad film had triggered

Tom's casting as Doctor Who. A senior chap at the BBC – was it the controller of BBC One? – had gone to see it on a whim with his children. Tom was a swashbuckling villain. The Controller of One went to the *Doctor Who* office and said, you should meet this Tom Baker. By then, the role had already been offered to Fulton Mackay, an actor best known as the bullying prison warden in the sitcom *Porridge*. Fulton Mackay's contract was already in the post when the BBC called his agent to cancel it. Afterwards he became the lighthouse keeper in the British version of *Fraggle Rock*.

Also up for the role had been an actor who in the nineteen fifties had played a children's TV character called Mr. Pastry. How on earth did Matthew acquire this knowledge? God knows. Once he saw in an antiques shop some issues of *TV Comic* published long before he was born. He flicked through them and saw a strip about this Mr. Pastry. A problem arose at Mr. Pastry's *Doctor Who* reading, for it became obvious that any part he played, including *Doctor Who*, was going to come out extremely close to Mr. Pastry. Matthew wondered if old episodes of *Mr. Pastry* still existed?

Two other actors had hopes. Jon Pertwee got cold feet about leaving the series and telephoned the office to say perhaps they would like to discuss another season after all. No thanks, they said.

More intriguing was the notion of Patrick Troughton returning. Though a marvellous idea, this was considered by no-one but Patrick. Apparently he was heard to say to actors he was working with when Jon Pertwee announced his departure, if they ask me to come back I'm not sure I'll take the job, but I'll give it some thought.

All these Tom Baker facts were general knowledge to anyone who read the TV pages of newspapers. Matthew found out down the years of his teens more than these, however, because his father subscribed not only to *Private Eye*, but also to a nutty journal called *The Spectator*. This was supposed to be the intellectual journal of the right. It had a small number of readers but claimed to be influential. The tone of the Spectator was clubby, a whisky-and-cheese-and-Cabinet-Pudding-and-cigars atmosphere. There was something endearing about it, as there often is about articulate people with ridiculous opinions.

What he liked in the Spectator were not the political articles but the back pages, where two short weekly columns of great interest appeared. One was *High Life*, by a Greek man who wrote as Taki. Taki described the life of the super-rich in excruciating detail. He spent nearly all his time on enormous yachts. He was in thrall to people with titles. He was always in the company of princesses. All his friends had billions in the bank. Then there was *Low Life* by Jeffrey Bernard. Jeffrey Bernard did nothing all day but sit in the Soho pub called the Coach and Horses from opening until closing time. The landlord, Norman, was the rudest in London. Bernard was drunk all the time. He usually managed to write his column, which could not have taken very long, but otherwise he drank and lay bets on horses.

Matthew would lie on his stomach on his bed and read *Low Life* every week, in between homework and masturbation and *Doctor Who* novels and comics and Hammer Film reviews. It was splendidly sordid. It described Matthew's vision of a perfect life. He liked much more the idea of being a penniless drunk in Soho than being a millionaire with a yacht and a gaggle of princesses. Among Bernard's crowd of drunk friends and a frequent presence in *Low Life* was Tom Baker. Here was a glimpse of Baker when he was not on TV and not talking about himself to journalists. He spent all his free time getting wrecked with Jeffrey Bernard and Francis Bacon and Daniel Farson.

Tom once told Matthew a story about throwing up in a car park. Halfway through, a little boy came up to him and said, *are you Doctor Who*? Hang on a moment, said Tom, and finished vomiting. Then he pulled from the inside pocket of his sick-splashed raincoat a photograph of himself which he signed and inscribed to the child, who walked away blissfully happy.

The *Low Life* column was often described by others as a 'serial suicide note,' though Bernard himself insisted that he had not been depressed for years and was perfectly happy. In the eighties, he became what the British think of as 'an institution,' by which is meant a much-loved scoundrel. The British adored scoundrels, even if, like the Kray Twins, they happened to be murderers. Everyone talked affectionately of the Krays while their victims rotted in the Thames. Jeffrey Bernard was not a murderer, except of his own body. He had been a drunk since his late teens. There was a documentary about him on the BBC in the eighties, complete with scenes in the Coach and Horses, Tom present, in a guise familiar to Matthew, ranting on about how most people were bored out of their minds all the time. This insight, though true, was hardly worth the price of a beer. "Most drunks," said Jeffrey Bernard on the commentary soundtrack over Tom's conversation, "are extremely boring."

Then Bernard was the subject of a solo play by Keith Waterhouse, starring Peter O'Toole. This was called *Jeffrey Bernard is Unwell*, after a footnote which appeared in *The Spectator* on the many occasions when Jeffrey Bernard had not been in a condition to write his column. The play was set in the Coach and Horses. It was the culmination of Bernard's fame, but also the death knell of the Coach and Horses, which swiftly became a tourist attraction.

Matthew dipped into *Low Life* right up until Bernard's death. By this time Tom had disappeared from his circle, or at least his column, so when the effects of all that booze got to Jeffrey Bernard's limbs and first one gangrenous leg had to be cut off, then the other, it was not Tom pushing him around in his wheelchair but the novelist Beryl Bainbridge. Another novelist, the Catholic Alice Thomas Ellis, said she thought there was something angelic about Bernard.

4

Lalla Ward was Matthew's first *Doctor Who* girl. She played the second Romana. Mary Tamm, the first Romana, the most glamorous *Doctor Who* girl ever and the toughest, the first *Doctor Who* girl to represent the 'no crap' vibe of a liberated woman while also being imaginable on the cover of Vogue, had had enough of *Doctor Who* after a single season and hastened off into the night.

So an amusing regeneration scene occurred in a Dalek episode, in which Romana tried on assorted different bodies before selecting the look of Lalla. And why not? Lalla was the kind of actress often called an English Rose, with her petite body and her attractive, dolly face. More inclined to scream in corners than the arctically cool first Romana, the second was less screamy than Zoë or Jo or even Sarah Jane.

On *Doctor Who* Lalla was fortunate to have a new set of clothes in every story. Matthew, stuck with his pyjamas, envied her for this. They were in a wide variety of styles, sometimes a little bit Victorian, sometimes a touch Edwardian, sometimes a bit horsey. Sometimes she had dangly ribbons in her hair. Occasionally there was a hint of a Disney princess, or at least of the maidservant to a Disney princess. (In the seventies, Lalla had cropped up on a BBC serial as a maidservant, complete with a Dick Van Dyke cockney accent).

Like many *Doctor Who* girls before her, Lalla was not a great success as a fashion plate. She was like a Bizarro world *Avengers* girl. When Honor Blackman as Cathy Gale or Diana Rigg as Emma Peel pulled on skin-tight leather trousers on an episode of *The Avengers*, many a sparklingly lusty young English woman could the next morning be spotted going about the King's Road dressed in leather. (Linda Thorson as Tara King had less cachet on the King's Road, but was adored in Paris, where it is *really* cool to be iconic). *Doctor Who* girls did not have this influence. Their costumes served mainly as warnings as to what not to wear this season, or any season. Did Elisabeth Sladen really do a whole story in stripy beachwear, or is this a mis-remembrance?

It seemed that Lalla was being used as a sort of tailor's dummy, on which costume designers could experiment with ideas, rejected before they could find their way into Debenhams. It was not hard to picture the designer of the horsey outfit poor Lalla wore in *The Vampire Lords* standing back and looking her up and down and saying quietly, "naah..." before removing the sketches from her portfolio and dropping them into a bin.

However imperfect in their appeal those outfits were, they must have eaten up a large chunk of the budget. Perhaps this is why *The Keeper of Traken* was a better-looking production than the E-Space trilogy: with Lalla gone, a heap of money was freed up for set dressing.

Lalla was, for many, the living embodiment of the word 'ladylike', the foreigner's idea of an upper class Englishwoman, and in fact she had a title, being the daughter of Lord something or other. She should in formal terms have been called The Honourable Sarah Ward. The childlike name Lalla can be assumed to have come from some cute little brother or sister, who, unable to articulate Sarah, had landed on this babyish alternative, which stuck, as they do. Matthew found the name Lalla slightly silly. Simply *saying* it felt silly. It felt not like a name but an elocutionary exercise. Years afterwards, he worked with a very interesting actress with a very similar name, Lalla Lloyd, which sounded even more like elocution. Lalla Lloyd was also a Sarah transformed by a clumsy childish tongue. Lalla Lloyd, in her eighties when Matthew knew her, had been known as the Queen of Weekly Rep from the nineteen thirties to the sixties. Lalla Ward, though queenly in her own way, might not have survived very long in weekly rep – as who would? -and was unlikely to have ascended to its highest pinnacle.

Long after her liaison with Tom Baker, Lalla married Richard Dawkins, the well-known atheist. Strangely, her very last job as an actor was a role in a play by the Pope, John Paul, written when he was plain old Karel. The Pope was a big draw and free tickets for unemployed equity members never became available, so Matthew did not see it, though many times he walked past the theatre near Victoria where it was running.

Yet Lalla did not come to atheism only when she began going out with Richard Dawkins. Sometimes the subject came up in cigarette breaks on *Doctor Who*. God knows why. She was having nothing of God. Matthew was not sure he believed in God either, but he was already developing his attraction to poetry of an extreme kind, the more imaginative and ungraspable and visionary and barmy the better, so he puzzled over theology in an uninformed but complicated way quite a lot. A large number of his heroes were alchemists or mystics or drug addicts or religious maniacs.

Lalla pooh-poohed it all.

"If somebody could show me the *slightest evidence...* until then, I will not believe a word of it."

This seemed reasonable. Matthew read some of the works of Professor Dawkins, one of them illustrated with terrific line drawings by Lalla. Still, he found he'd rather read the Jesuit priest Gerard Manley Hopkins who was, after all, a better writer. Matthew certainly believed in God for the period of time it took to read a poem or essay by Gerard Manley Hopkins.

Tom Baker in *Doctor Who* still had enough of a religious sensibility to get irritated at a priest he happened to meet. He told the priest that he had hardly committed any sins as a boy.

"My only sin was wanking," he said.

The priest looked smug. That, he said, is no longer considered a sin. *Christ*, thought Baker, *you've just destroyed my entire bloody childhood.*

John Leeson was the voice of K9, the robot dog. On studio days, he was confined to a sort of makeshift booth with headphones and a microphone, from which he would intone his lines in a charming fashion, both robotic and cute. "Yes, mast*uh!*" The voice was not in any way processed mechanically, Dalek-like: what you heard was what came out of John's throat.

During rehearsals, however, he was also the body of K9, crawling around on his hands and knees just as the mechanical hound would scoot across the set on studio days.

It was thought at various times to be sweet if Adric sat astride K9. Adric was not the first character to do this. Doctor Who and Romana had both sat on K9 at one time or another. Not always practical in the episodes themselves, it was good for photo-shoots. But, it seemed to Matthew, Adric was sitting on the dog at almost every opportunity. In the studio, this was fine. K9 was robust enough to withstand Matthew's not very great weight.

But in rehearsals it meant sitting on the back of poor John Leeson himself. This did not appeal to Matthew. He did not want to seem like a spoilsport, but he was worried about breaking John's back. John insisted he was perfectly capable of sustaining Matthew's full weight. Yet Matthew could not stop imagining the sound of John's breaking back, like dried twigs snapping. He pictured John broken in two, his glasses toppling off his nose, one final "yes master..." before he expired because he was ever a trouper.

These gory images in mind, Matthew braced his thighs to make himself as light as possible. This meant that after running a scene three or four times his tendons were sore and his thighs ached. John must have noticed how ghost-light Matthew was, but he never said anything. Perhaps secretly he was scared of breaking his back too.

John had a young son who had recently been in trouble at his school in Ealing for telling lies. This had become such a problem that the teacher had telephoned John about it.

"He keeps claiming his father is the man who does the voice of K9 on *Doctor Who*. Please put a stop to it!"

"But…"

John Leeson was temperamentally the opposite of Tom Baker. He was certainly the calmest personality of the regular cast of the time. Nothing aroused his ire. He got along with everyone and the rows and seizures and rants and dramas which made up a large proportion of rehearsal time passed him by as if they were nothing. When tempers flared he would flip through a paper.

His tin alter-ego was much more difficult than John himself. K9 was radio-controlled, but his radio frequency was *simpatico* with various bits of studio technology, including the cameras, which frequently magnetized him towards them: suddenly possessed, he rushed off towards the nearest camera as if it were a much-missed girlfriend.

When he was supposed to go straight, he veered to the left. When he was supposed to veer left, he went straight. In the middle of an action-free scene which was nothing but dialogue, K9 would dart off at considerable speed towards the white-disced TARDIS wall, into which he would crash excitingly. The Special Effects lads looked as though they were having a whale of a time with him, trying to control him from their portable radio, which was exactly the kind of device used for the toy boats which in those days could often be observed zooming across ponds in parks, to the whoops of their happy if simple-minded operators. Were studio time not so limited, there was potential for oodles of fun like this with K9.

The first day of rehearsal arrived.

Matthew took the train from his parents' house in Sussex to the rehearsal rooms in North Acton. The journey was a long one. It entailed fifty minutes on a railway train, then two tube trains. Matthew was partly glad of the long haul. He wanted it to last forever. It gave him time to gather his thoughts. It gave him time to focus. It gave him time at least to make an effort towards these things. He did not achieve them.

How should he use the time on the train? Should he look over the script for *The Vampire Lords*, which he would soon be rehearsing? Should he try to practice his lines in his head? Should he put the script away and think of other things, while whistling perhaps? Should he read a comic instead or a newspaper? He took the script out of his bag and flipped through it and put it back in his bag and sat there watching the trees and houses and viaducts and sheep and telephone wires go by. Then he took out the script and pretended to read it but the letters came to his brain as blocks and triangles. He kept the script on his knee, the title page up.

Having shown off his script to the nearby passengers, Matthew put it away again and drew out his paperback copy of *2001: A Space Odyssey*. This he read over many train journeys to and from the BBC. He followed it up with *The Worlds of 2001* and then *Childhood's End*.

From British Rail he transferred to the Underground, where the Circle Line, chock-a-block with commuters, took him ploddingly and sweatily to Notting Hill. At Notting Hill, he changed onto the Central Line, for White City on studio days and North Acton on rehearsal days. The enormous platform at Notting Hill Central Line was dark and few passengers waited, because this journey was away from Central London – nearly all commuters were going in the opposite direction.

Emerging from North Acton tube station, a narrow path rose to the street, where a man sold papers. Opposite was the big BBC block. In this building, virtually every piece of BBC material which involved actors was rehearsed. It did not look glamorous in a Hollywood way. It looked as unimpressive as possible, with its low brick wall enclosing its car park, full of the battered second-hand cars owned by actors.

By the time Matthew came to be in *Doctor Who*, casting had taken on a slightly more formal hue, but for years this car park had been a place where unemployed actors hung out in the late afternoons, hoping to catch a director they'd worked with before on his way home.

"Oh, hello, Joe! How are you?"

"Do you have anything coming up that might be right for me?"

"Actually, I need a man to play a bookie on a *Z-Cars* next week. "

Thus were jobs secured.

The lobby was grubbily carpeted. A man in a glass-windowed booth on the right half-looked, moodily, at IDs. Beyond, two lifts led upward. Above the lifts a black display board listed current productions in white plastic removable letters, and their rehearsal room numbers. *All Creatures*, *Juliet Bravo*, *The Two Ronnies*, a new programme called *Hi-De-Hi!*.

Matthew took the lift up to the floor where the *Doctor Who* rehearsal room was. The room –and the floor –was identical to the rooms and floors above and below it. Opposite his rehearsal room was another, the same but reversed, where *Juliet Bravo* or *Hi-De-Hi!* was being rehearsed.

At the end of the corridor was a green room. In one of these green rooms for some weeks in Nineteen Seventy-Four Tom Baker, between addresses, had unofficially lived, all his worldly possessions around him, which amounted to some boxes of books.

Matthew went through the heavy brown swing doors.

5

The read-through was supposed to start at ten-thirty, but by eleven Tom Baker had not yet appeared. In Matthew's stomach the tension was ratcheting up. Everybody sat at the long table, smoking, sipping coffee from Styrofoam cups, waiting for Tom to slope in. Lalla Ward began talking about Claire Bloom. "Lovely Claire," she said.

Matthew sat next to Emrys James, who was playing the leading vampire, Aukon. For some reason, without prompting from Matthew or anyone else, Emrys James began talking to him about *Watch With Mother*, perhaps because, on *Doctor Who*, he decided he had found himself in the world of children's television. *Watch With Mother* was an umbrella title for a number of fifteen minute puppet series shown at weekday lunchtimes for the under-fives, but watched in the school holidays by nearly everyone who happened to be at a loose end. Perhaps Emrys thought Matthew was very, very young and still a regular follower of these table-top productions. Matthew thought: I know I look young, but not *that* young.

He knew the programmes, though, which had been produced in small numbers but (rare for the BBC) repeated ad nauseam for several generations of infants. The mere mention of these programmes can still provoke unpleasantly nostalgic feelings in British people of a certain age: *Andy Pandy*, *The Woodentops*, The Pogles of *Pogles' Wood*, *Bagpuss*, *Trumpton*, *Chigley*, and so on. Emrys had a strong aversion to one called *Mary, Mungo and Midge*, which was made with paper puppets against painted backdrops, about a girl, a dog and a mouse, though he could not get the title right.

"That one, *Mungo and Mudge*, was awful." He went on about how bad he thought it was, calling it by the wrong name. "Bloody *Mungo and Mudge*. *Mungo and* bloody *Mudge*!"

Matthew was not willing to admit to this major Welsh classical actor that he knew the programme well. He made a remembering face.

"O yes, *Mingo and Midge* I think it is."

Emrys James snapped his fingers.

"*Mingo and Midge*! Yes. Bloody awful that one was." Then he began to talk about the train fare from Wales to London, which was high.

*　　*　　*

At 11:05, the doors swung open. Tom Baker came running through.

He looked a bit pale, and thinner than when Matthew had last seen him on TV. He wore a grubby brown raincoat and trousers the colour of milky coffee and a white shirt thinned by too much ironing so that patches of his flesh could be seen through it. He had the remains of a cigarette in his right hand, ash flying behind him as the doors swung closed. He carried a mouldy leather briefcase. He made a small grunt of apology.

Tom came in late probably because he had overslept (or not slept at all), but for Matthew it had the effect of the Hollywood diva, Judy Garland perhaps, who as a custom arrives after everyone else so as to make a grand entrance.

Baker took his seat, in the middle of the row opposite Matthew, where the Queen might sit at a banquet.

The director Peter Moffatt introduced everyone by name, ending with Baker: "Of course, you all know Tom." The Assistant Floor Manager clicked on the stopwatch, and the reading began. At the end of the first episode, the stopwatch was paused, the running time noted, ("nineteen minutes eight seconds,") the watch reset, the reading resumed. Matthew was fascinated to watch Tom Baker, reading lazily, smoking constantly, stubbing out each cigarette with a violent stab at the ashtray so the whole stub flattened, before lighting another. In Matthew's sight he never lit a fresh one from the flame of the last. Lalla Ward puffed away at a fair rate too. So did nearly everyone else, but not Peter Moffatt. Baker and Ward did not for a moment catch one another's eye.

Everyone broke for lunch. Matthew went to the little corner pub called The Castle, a hop and a skip from the rehearsal rooms, where he had spent his lunch-times with Nicholas Lyndhurst and Simon Gipps-Kent on the school serial. He went into the public bar and stood near the Space Invaders machine but Simon was not there and the public bar with its worn wooden floor and its drying cheese rolls under a plastic cover and its pock-marked dart board was dreary and empty.

Over the head of the barwoman, he saw Tom Baker – in the saloon bar! He would go and say hello to him! He would introduce himself! So he went back into the street and around to the saloon bar entrance.

The saloon was lively and smoky. Most of the tables were full and the bar area was jammed with standing drinkers and eaters of pasties.

There, leaning on the bar in his awful brown raincoat looking bad tempered and underweight was Tom Baker! Matthew was overcome with a peculiar sensation of both fear and bravery, but as he neared the bar the bravery vanished and there was only fear. About three feet from Tom he simply stopped for a moment and stood, like a deactivated Auton.

Then he leant on the bar. He bought a beer. He was of legal drinking age though he did not look it, but in those days no-one was ever challenged. There was hardly a boy in Britain who did not drink beers on a Friday night in the pub by the time he was fifteen.

He did not look at Tom but into the air a few inches from Tom's ear. He thought, even as he stood there, I must be completely insane, what am I doing? No doubt he had a slightly stupid grin on his face. What was he expecting? He supposed he was expecting Tom Baker to see him and say, hello, you are the new *Doctor Who* boy, how are you, my name is Tom Baker.

He was fairly sure that Tom Baker did spot him, standing there like a retarded child, but he certainly did not address him.

How long did he stand at the bar, inert except for sips of his beer, his vision a blur of spirits bottles and beer taps and an ear and a curl of hair? Half an hour? Then he had to go back to the rehearsal room. Had Tom already left or was he still in his corner, drinking, ignoring him? This is unknowable now.

The first afternoon was devoted to rehearsal of TARDIS scenes, which Matthew came to understand was the usual pattern. Only the regular cast were there: Tom, Lalla, John Leeson, and now Matthew, with Peter Moffatt and Lynn Richards, the Assistant Floor Manager.

There was an inexplicably heavy mood. Peter did his best to lighten things with his shruggy BBC camp. Baker strutted around the rehearsal room in his grubby white shirt, poring over the script. He moved so fast it was as if he had extra long legs.

Baker would suddenly produce an opinion: "This is whippetshit," he snapped, shaking the script. "Terrance Dicks is a very nice man but he's a bloody awful writer."

And, a little later, "I can't fucking stand adults! I only give a shit about the children. Adults can fuck off."

Lalla Ward was detached and silent, jerking her head sharply to shake hair from her face, more frequently than would seem to be necessary: Matthew wondered if it was an unconscious nervous reaction, like an attic madwoman.

John Leeson did his best to exude forced and unconvincing jollity.

Here was a tension so treacle-thick it was impenetrable. Nothing flowed, nothing seemed natural. Matthew could not read the situation at all.

It was strange. On the public school serial, a 'quality' BBC drama, all had been smiles and lightness, interspersed with concentrated work. Now, here on *Doctor Who*, which anyone would have supposed would be enormous fun to rehearse, more fun than any boring old school drama – if making *Doctor Who* was not *fun,* what was it? – there were no smiles, there was no lightness, there was something troubling and dark. Matthew felt like a swimmer caught in a strong current.

A number of TARDIS scenes were to be to be rehearsed, in which Adric did not appear, but he was incorporated into the rehearsal schedule, in brackets. The list was like this:

```
DOCTOR WHO
ROMANA
K9
(ADRIC)
```

Matthew looked at the list with a little frown on his face. He wasn't sure whether he was supposed to stay around. He would happily have gone for a cup of coffee, but there on the list was his character name. He stood at the side of the markout. What he should have done, would automatically have done later, was to have asked Peter Moffatt if he was needed, but he was too shy to pipe up, so he hovered there while scenes were run and rerun and massacred by Tom's pen. Perhaps he stared, saucer-eyed, like a child who has recognised his telly hero. He lingered near the white line, a little performance of a frown streaking his forehead to give the impression of being thoughtful but unsure.

On perhaps the fourth of these scenes he stood there stupidly. Suddenly Baker turned to him and barked, "Why don't you piss off?"

This sounded fair, so he pissed off and sat on the floor and leant his back against the wall, a few feet away.

Matthew was baffled and upset and determined that tomorrow would be better. He passed the evening silently. Is everything alright, asked his mother. Yes, fine, said Matthew. He thought about the next day. He would smile like crazy, he decided, like Al Green converting to Jesus.

And, indeed, the next day, things were very different. Tom swept in, his grubby raincoat catching the wind of the door as it slammed shut. He grinned like *Doctor Who*. Matthew grinned like Louis Armstrong.

Tom was extremely friendly to everyone, especially Matthew. How are you?, he asked. Fine, thanks, said Matthew, flattered. He was all jokes and Bakerisms. How everyone laughed. How Tom showed off. Things relaxed. A bit.

Tom always set up camp at the same end of the rehearsal room. Each morning he would stalk, usually in a fast-paced silence, to the window directly opposite the swing doors, the most rightward window in the room. When Matthew had found a screwed-up title page from *The Leisure Hive*, it had been dropped directly under this window.

He would place his tatty briefcase and his cigarettes on the ledge. He would bundle up his raincoat. He pulled his scripts from the briefcase and placed them on the ledge next to it. His scripts contained only his own scenes: he had torn out all the others after the read-through. If a newspaper article which had made its way into *Private Eye*'s Pseud's Corner was to be believed, as well as his scripts Tom had in his briefcase at all times a book by Solzhenitsyn and a slice of Parma ham.

When he was not rehearsing, he would lean on the sill, looking out over Acton, hands on his chin perhaps, cigarette between the first and second fingers, or sometimes between finger and thumb. He might flick through a newspaper or make a stab at a crossword, though he was, he said, not much good at crosswords. He once said to Matthew that he was only any good as the second guy, the one who throws in a handful of suggestions.

Almost always he had his back to the room and the cast. When he was in a happy frame of mind, he might turn in from the window, still leaning on his elbow, or sit in a chair facing the rehearsal, though he hardly ever watched a scene he was not in. If he was in an exceptionally bright mood, he might join others at a table, sharing his crossword and his cigarettes.

He would always go round to the pub on the corner for lunch, scarcely ever going up to the BBC canteen on the top floor. He was a pubby, boozy kind of person and anyway the canteen was no better than any other canteen, eminently avoidable. Matthew himself had not taken to it either: he had almost always gone to the pub with Simon and Nicolas while rehearsing the public school serial.

Tom was reputedly the randiest man in Equity, but he did not seem very sexy or adorable at the end of the afternoon. Neither did anyone else. The rehearsal rooms were stuffy and overwarm. By five, there were big oval sweat rings under the arms of Tom's thin white shirt. Oddly, the more temperamental and nightmarish he had been that day the larger the rings of sweat, as if his own dreadfulness had made him perspire, a weirdly appealing failing.

During the bulk of the rehearsal period, nothing was seen of the production staff. Apart from the director, the only non-actor around was the Assistant Floor Manager, usually, in Matthew's experience, a woman. Some had come from stage management in theatre, some were failed actors, some were simply oddities. The job was a mélange of dogsbody activities, marking the set outlines on the floor, following the script and noting down the director's instructions and any rewrites, giving people their call times for the next day, making sure everything was where it should be when it should be. If she was really good, she would also be a mother hen and a comforter of neurotic actors, somebody of whom the cast became fond, without fully appreciating. It was one of those jobs which, the better you did it, the less you were noticed. Lynn Richards, who was the floor manager on *The Vampire Lords* and *The Planet That Slept*, was perfect for the job. Baker took to her and perhaps confided in her, or rather used her as a sympathetic listener, one who could say "umm" and "aahh" and "oooh dear" at all the right times. She knew more about the affair with Lalla Ward than anyone else, including the director.

Still in her mid-twenties, she had come from theatre, to which she yearned to return because she preferred its intimacy and comparative friendliness. Thin-faced with dark hair, she had recently married.

"Everyone thinks my husband is gay, but he's not. However, *all* our friends are gay! We don't have *any* friends who aren't gay!"

Having grown up near Brighton, Matthew as a boy had met overtly gay men on many occasions, working in shops and cafes, but at the BBC he found himself in a world further removed from the middle class assumptions he had grown up around. Almost all dressers were gay. He overheard one dresser discussing with another his hopes of having a sex change in the near future. To the ears of a teenager in 1980, even a gay one, this was startling. Matthew was not shocked by it, but fascinated: the idea that he might meet someone who was considering such an action, rather than merely reading about them as freaks in tatty journalism, was exciting and unexpected.

But it would be a mistake to think that the BBC was an oasis of sexual liberalism. He met at least one gay man in his sixties who was married to a gay woman because they had been afraid that remaining unmarried would stunt their careers. He expressed to Matthew his envy of him:

"To you it's *nothing!*"

After the disaster of the first rehearsal day and the Anabasis of the second, things went downhill again. On the fourth, in the early afternoon, Tom ranting around in an unconstructive fury and Lalla Ward looking bereft, Peter Moffatt made a decision:

"Let's all go to the pub!" he said. "Work's over for the day!"

So everyone ran around the corner and bought each other beers and wines and at five o'clock staggered out to their houses and flats and bedsits. Whether tension was more than briefly relaxed by this boozy afternoon was a moot point, but at least a certain amount of fun had been had.

Matthew found himself standing in a group with Lynn Richards and another BBC staffer and an actor. The other BBC staffer was talking to the actor about the sex life she had with her husband. (This was not unusual. Actors talk to actors they have known for half an hour about their sex lives all the time). Matthew listened prurient, though the conversation was not erotic, but quasi-scientific. Lynn patted Matthew's bottom and said she hoped he was taking notes.

"We're about to try for a baby," said the woman.

"Are you frequent?"

"Yes."

"So are we. We planned the sexes of all three of our children. If you want a girl you must keep on having sex after you're pregnant. If you want a boy, give it up for a while."

The woman found this tremendously interesting and convincing.

"We want a girl first."

"Then you *must* have sex *relentlessly*."

Matthew thought he was making a good show of being happy and smiley, but not everyone was convinced. Emrys James, who had hired a car for his stay in London, gave him a lift to TV Centre, where they were both due for a costume fitting. The drive was silent, until Emrys said,

"You're not happy, are you?"

Matthew wondered whether it would be better to shrug everything off and say he was fine or to tell the truth.

"Well..." he said. "No. Not really."

"I didn't think you were. Why not?"

"Tom Baker was my hero a week ago and now... I mean, he's kind of *mean*. I can't stand it."

"Yes," said Emrys James, "it's all very difficult."

Then the drive was silent again.

The good news was that, much as Tom would have liked *Doctor Who* to be the Tom Baker show with special guest Lalla Ward, neither Tom nor Lalla had it all their own way. Not only was there Emrys James, there were two younger vampires, Vampire Brides so to speak, Zargo, played by William Lindsay, and Camilla, a vampire name if ever there was one, played by Rachel Davies. In a brilliant design decision their costumes were reminiscent of royal playing cards. Rachel Davies had shortly before been in a Hammer Horror TV special called something like *The House That Dripped Blood*. It was rubbish, of course, but Matthew thought it was brilliant. He was a little in awe of Rachel.

"This *Wasting Doctor Who* story is great," he said. "You'll love it," as though she had not read the script.

"I've never seen much of *Doctor Who*," she said. "Something once with a Dalek in it, I think. I thought it was just silly."

"Silly??? Nonononono, it's very clever. It's all very, very intelligent, Rachel. Very inventive. "

She looked reflective.

"Maybe I'll give it another go," she said, in a way that suggested she was not going to give it another go on Matthew's say-so, and probably not on anyone else's.

There was an actor called Clinton Greyn, the unusual spelling of whose last name made it memorable. Perhaps this was the point. He was a Peter Moffatt favourite, employed by Peter at every opportunity. Clinton Greyn was playing one of those *Doctor Who* stock characters, a muscular serf with a knife and a threatening manner, wearing a costume that might have been made from a sack. He lived in a straw house with sad-looking women in equally unflattering clothes. Everyone looked tired and oppressed, like those villagers in Universal horror films who live in fear of the Count in the castle, which is what they were, essentially. Adric was forced to become a sort of waiter to these people.

Clinton had been in LA for many years, where, if he was to be believed, he had come within a spit of being Jones in *Alias Smith and Jones*, the *Butch Cassidy* rip-off, until they decided it would be wiser to cast an American. He was extremely fit and healthy in a pumping-iron work-out way that was rarely seen at the time, at least by Matthew. Matthew preferred the pub to the canteen, but on the few occasions he went upstairs instead of out, he noticed that Clinton finished every lunch with a silver-wrapped wedge of camembert, without bread or crackers. He would unwrap the cheese carefully and eat it in three bites. He seemed to choose his foods carefully for balance, the cheese providing just the necessary amount of calcium.

Matthew loved cheese, the smellier and more exotic the better, but an ordinary camembert was fine with him. Observing the butch Clinton's consumption of it gave him an excuse to eat large chunks on health grounds. He took to buying a camembert, even if it was the only thing he ate for lunch. After the pub, he would swoop to the top floor in the lift. Because the BBC canteen did not store cheese very well, it was likely to be a little too hard, with a chalky streak in the middle.

"I don't eat too much because I'm on a diet," he said, putting the whole creamy piece into his mouth.

"You're on a *diet,*" said Clinton, "and you eat nothing but lumps of camembert??"

"So?"

But he couldn't speak any more, because his mouth was full of cheese.

While Tom added extra layers of amusement to every scene, Peter Moffatt stood by with the look of a man keeping his counsel. When Tom left the room for a moment Peter would say,

"We'll let him do what he likes and cut all of it!"

But he didn't cut much. So lovely Tommish comedy was dotted all over the programme. Matthew's favourite was a scene where Romana came down a ladder. She reached the bottom rung and stepped off. Doctor Who suddenly looked horrified. "What is it?" said Romana, looking for a monster. The Doctor said, "You're standing on my toe."

Kiddies everywhere laughed and laughed.

This moment was sweeter in rehearsal than on tape. On the morning the scene was rehearsed in the studio, Tom and Lalla 'liked' each other, so, a gentleman, he helped her down the ladder. By the time evening had come and taping was in progress, things were sour, so he turned his back on her and she had to clamber down unaided.

Matthew was extremely relieved by one small adjustment Tom made to the script. The last line of The Doctor's to Adric was "Now we'll take you home, young man." With this line was Terrance's instruction: The Doctor pulls Adric into the TARDIS by the ear.

Matthew hated this direction. Fortunately, Tom wasn't having it.

"Why don't I just say the line?" he said. "Pulling him by the ear is whippetshit." And he didn't.

Matthew was by no means a rewrite king, but he threw in the odd thought, one of which, when he saw the episodes again for the DVD commentary, still seemed like a good one. Romana finds Adric in a coffin and wakes him up. Remembering all those Hammer horrors, Matthew said,

"Why don't I, instead of waking up, snap my eyes open, so everyone will think I've become a vampire? It will be a nice moment."

"That's a good idea, Matthew," said Lalla, and Matthew felt extremely flattered to have her approval.

When Matthew arrived at the TV Centre reception desk on the first studio day, a tiny little incident happened which would recur with tiresome frequency. There were lots of child actors milling around in school uniforms. Before he had opened his mouth, the woman behind the desk said,

"*Grange Hill?*"

"No," said Matthew, bursting with pride, "*Doctor Who.*"

By the fifth time, he was fed up with being taken for a *Grange Hill* actor, so he rushed up to the desk and said, as fast as possible, "I'm Matthew

Waterhouse andi'mindoctor*ooooo.*"

It seems unlikely that the receptionist was indulging in deliberate playfulness, but the fact was it became a challenge for Matthew to say *Doctor Who* before the receptionist said *Grange Hill*. He grew to hate the sound of those words. He defeated the receptionist by reversing the order of the information: "*DOCTOR WHO...* and my name is Matthew Waterhouse." Then he would walk towards his dressing room, nose in the air as he passed the herds of *Grange Hill* actors.

Matthew's first ever recorded scene for *Doctor Who* featured only Adric and K9. Doctor Who and Romana, unaware that he had sneaked aboard the TARDIS, had gone out onto the vampire planet. Adric had to squat and pat the dog. The scene was all very sweet and lovable.

Later that evening, an unforgettable few minutes were spent alone in the dark of the TARDIS set. A scene was being shot on another set, at the other end of the studio. There were voices, but far away. The TARDIS set was unlit, the time rotor still. The discs pressed into the flats were deeper than they looked on TV. The backs of the discs were papery, thin as taut drumskins, you could see light through them.

Now, he wondered around the hexagonal console in a deeply private moment, touching the buttons and the big play-pen lever with its round red ball, colourful as the arms of fruit machines at the ends of piers. It was wonderful to touch the console, the lever. He had seen this interior hundreds of times on screen, had imagined operating it. How many boys of his age had not? It was as exciting in reality as it was on screen. More. On TV it looked quite complicated, but in the studio the buttons and screens arrayed on each of the hexagon's panels looked simple, boyish, toylike, hollow. And when he saw old episodes he found that the characters operated the console devices, pushed buttons, pulled levers, in a suitably childish, playful way, with a splendid lack of conviction, this artifice, this intimation that no-one quite believed what they were doing or saying, which ought to have broken the spell, somehow sustaining it. The plastic hand of Scott Tracy seemed to believe more in the levers it tugged than the fleshly hands of *Doctor Who* actors.

There were remarkably few lights on the panels, all the flashing being in the rotor. So the result was not a series of control panels so much as sketches of control panels, the implication of control panels, which the viewers at home filled in for themselves in much the way they filled in the atmosphere and the terror and the conviction.

Tom Baker himself disliked the TARDIS set, for perfectly good reasons. It was hopeless for acting on. There was no easy way to move around it. All you could do was amble in a circle. You couldn't even sit at it. The

TARDIS set was nothing but some walls and a door, and a floor space with this enormous console plonked in the middle, as dumpy as Alice's Queen, built to just the wrong height. All you could do really was to look over the groaning trembling time rotor at your fellow actor or actors. Unless you were tall, your face was lost with each rise of the rotor. You could move a few feet away from it and talk directly to the other actor but this always looked like an attempt to escape the upstaging console, which it was. Sometimes you turned your back to it to look at the scanner screen and then you were wedged between the console and the screen, able to do nothing but stare. The scanner screen was quite large and there was always a sense that the Doctor and the TARDIS girls and boys were standing unnaturally close to it, like children who rush to the front row of a cinema.

But the TARDIS was too ingrained in Matthew's consciousness for him to want to pick holes in it, In *her* it should be, in her, he had known her too long and from too early an age. So he loved her, to him she was glamorous, like Elizabeth Taylor, Ava Gardner, she was like a torch singer, he loved every one of her fake wooden buttons that could not make anything work, every piece of orange plastic, every one of those dials, which so resembled the speed indicators of old cars. Her console was essentially the same object around which actors and, more importantly to Matthew, characters, had stood since 1963.

At the end of the day, Matthew was tired and relieved to get away. He ran to his dressing room and took off his pyjamas and put on his shirt and cords, and pulled off his wig and left it on the table. He ran out to White City tube station.

The next morning he arrived early for the second studio day and he went to make-up where an angrily tight-lipped, pink-faced woman waited with folded arms.

"Where were you??"

"When?"

"Last night??"

"Why?"

"We waited until midnight!!!"

"What for?"

"To take off your wig!!"

"Oooh... I just took it off myself and left it in my dressing room. Sorry... I didn't think it was necessary to... to..."

"It's not a costume! You don't just *take it off!* It's put *on* by make-up!! Make-up has to take it *off*!!"

"Sorry."

She softened.

Blue Box Boy: A Memoir of Doctor Who in Four Episodes

"That's alright."
When the day's work finished, he dashed to the make-up room, barely two seconds after his last scene had been shot, and the woman unpinned his wig with careful fingers. She was talkative and nice to him.

The studio days were a splash of cold water for Matthew. Here he was now, actually making the damn thing! Terror overwhelmed him, which manifested itself in horrendous amounts of giggling, not of course when Tom or Lalla were on the set – they did not induce giggling, but a sort of stiffened tension. But when they were off, unwanted laughter abounded. Clinton Greyn put his arm aggressively around Adric's neck, and Matthew fell about. When Rachel Davies looked at him with her threatening, vampiric gaze, he sniggered. Many more takes of these excellent scenes were required than ought to have been necessary. After the first studio sessions he got over this habit.

Matthew was slightly short-sighted, as has been said, and too vain to wear glasses in public. He persuaded himself that he was not short-sighted enough to really *need* glasses except for reading railway indicator boards. This vanity occasionally led to difficulties. He was sometimes accused of snubbing people, though he had simply failed to recognize them. Worse, he sometimes thought he recognized a person who turned out to be a complete stranger. Once in the BBC Club after a studio day he thought he saw the AFM. He went up to her.
"How do you think it went?" he asked.
"*The Onedin Line?*" This was a historical serial about a ship.
A sensible person would have said, sorry, I mistook you for someone else. Matthew, in an idiosyncratic version of niceness, thought this would be rude, so he pursued the conversation.
"Yes. How did it go? Well, I hope?"
"Yes, very well, thank you."
A conversation of thirty seconds ensued in which she said why it had gone well, Matthew nodding in a pleased fashion.
"Good! I'm glad to hear it, old girl! See you later!"
He peeled away, to bump into John Nathan-Turner. John bought him a white wine and soda.
He remembered from the *Radio Times* Tenth Anniversary Special that his heroine Katy Manning was chronically short-sighted and subject as a result to hilarious misunderstandings, so Matthew's bad eyesight was within a *Doctor Who* tradition. Once, he saw Tom Baker in the office next to the rehearsal room. He was dialling a telephone number, with small frameless oblong glasses on his nose which made him look uncharacteristically

professorial. He never wore glasses in the rehearsal room, though Matthew had noticed that he had a habit of holding the script a long way from his face. Despite the grubby raincoat, Tom had his vanities too.

To compensate for the blur that was the world, Matthew gazed intently at people and things, perhaps sometimes with a slightly mad stare. On *The Vampire Lords*, Lalla Ward spotted him gazing closely at his script.

"I've noticed the way you *peer* at things!" she said. "I'm a peerer too!"

It was a bonding moment.

"I'm a bit short-sighted. Are you?"

"Oh no! I've got twenty-twenty vision. But I like to *peer* at things."

"Yes, I like peering too."

A day or two after the first studio session had ended, John Nathan-Turner called.

"There's a problem with *the union...*" he said. The *dot dot dot* at the end of the sentence was audible.

Matthew was distraught. He had from the beginning been completely frank about his position with the union, partly because it would have been foolish not to have been. At the first meeting with John, he had told him about it. He had been given temporary membership for the public school drama, and, he said, "you know better than I do what this means in terms of *Doctor Who*." John had nodded.

When he was sent the contract for *Doctor Who*, Matthew had written to Equity about it. So no-one could accuse him of being underhanded.

"You are now forbidden from coming to rehearsal until the union committee have had a meeting about you."

Gulp.

"When are they meeting?" he asked, in a very small voice.

"Hopefully tomorrow."

There followed a day of depressed inactivity on Matthew's part, leaning on his arms at the kitchen table drinking endless cups of strong Nescafé.

In the evening, a call came.

"You can come back tomorrow."

"Oh! Thanks."

"They agreed that now material had been taped they could not insist on it being rerecorded with a new actor. And they accepted that I had seen every Equity member who I thought was right for the part, and that you were a member when I cast you."

So Matthew went back to the rehearsals for *The Vampire Lords*.

The climactic scenes for Adric in *The Vampire Lords* were done out of his pyjamas and in a vaguely Elizabethan top with stockings and cloth shoes, and a narrow string belt which held a heavy, rusty dagger which made the belt sag. Early in the morning, after a scene had been run, Matthew walked back to his dressing room. The dagger dropped from the belt and the tip struck his foot. He felt a little sting, put the dagger back in the belt and forgot about it. He was only mildly conscious of an ongoing itch throughout the day. At the end of recording, shortly after ten, he undressed. He pulled off his shoe and saw that his tights were covered in thick red congealing blood at the foot. The tights had in fact adhered to the wound, so pulling them away took a definite tug, with a small tearing sound like elastoplast. The blood on his skin had dried liked thick clots of oil paint, running down the top of his foot and round the toes. Only when he saw the blood did he realised how much his foot hurt.

A BBC nurse came running down to him.

"Are you an artist??" she cried, as though he might be standing there in a dressing room wearing a stylised Elizabethan top for some other reason.

She was not the kind who pats you on the head and pulls up your blanket. She was in a terrible fury, and she had a long bureaucratic form to fill in and her questions were interrogations.

After the six o'clock break before the final taping session of *The Vampire Lords*, Lalla Ward appeared in the studio carrying a card and a small wrapped box. He thought how nice it was of her to give him, perhaps, a box of chocolates as a welcoming gift, even though she had waited until the last day of his first story to do it.

"Have you seen Lynn the floor manager?"

He pointed to her across the studio, and Lalla sidled off and gave her the parcel and they hugged. Matthew wondered if it was a tradition for cast members to give AFMs gifts, so he went to Lynn and apologized for asking such a silly and obvious thing, but was he expected to bring her a present, because he hadn't? No, she said.

"That was nice of Lalla," said Matthew.

"Yes, it was lovely." Matthew wondered why she had done such a thing. "Well," said Lynn, "It's been a difficult time for her. I've tried to be supportive, you see..." She said no more.

In the bar after the last studio day, John Nathan-Turner came up to him.

"Do you know how to *swim?*"

"Yes," said Matthew. "*Why??*"

John smiled and said nothing and walked away.

* * *

Matthew saw the first episode of *The Vampire Lords* in the director's box with John Nathan-Turner and others. It was strange to watch a TV programme in the box overlooking the studio in which it had been taped a few months earlier. Matthew was nervous to see it. There were a couple of nicely played scenes. But then it was a nicely written script. More than this, he liked the whole four-part extravaganza. It was exactly right for *Doctor Who*. Not cerebral exactly, but in a strange way intelligent and certainly inventive. And wonderfully melodramatic. Emrys James as Aukon was one of the most booming and operatic of all *Doctor Who* villains, a Shakespearean actor of genuine excellence glorying in the chance to roar and gesticulate madly without quite – *quite* – mocking the material.

Tom and Matthew later agreed that it was the best serial of the season.

If Equity had had a department for bats, all the Equity bats would have been employed in *The Vampire Lords*, in much the way that, at Christmas, all Equity dwarves find work in various Snow White pantomimes. Matthew was once in a Christmas play for which a non-Equity dwarf had to be hired because all Equity's dwarves were already engaged, there being forty-nine dwarves in the union and seven productions of Snow White around the country. But there were no Equity bats, so the *Doctor Who* office ended up borrowing footage from David Attenborough.

After the story had been shown, an enjoyable controversy began to rumble. Thousands of nature enthusiasts had been campaigning for years for a kinder view of bats. Bats had been misrepresented, they said. They were not remotely mean-spirited, they certainly did not drink your blood. They were shy and friendly and kind and harmless and they ate lots of flies, which was a good thing.

In the opinion of these people, *The Vampire Lords* had single-handedly put back the campaign for the rights of bats by years, which suggests they overestimated the influence of *Doctor Who* on national opinion. They wrote complaining letters to the BBC and to their MPs, and one MP asked an angry parliamentary question about it.

If this was supposed to cow the production office, it had the opposite effect. The day after the matter was raised in the commons, the news circulated around the staff and the cast and everybody was thrilled to bits. Not every TV programme got mentioned in parliament.

6

After the completion of *The Vampire Lords* Matthew had a break of two months. *The Vampire Lords* was the second production of the season but it would be the fourth in broadcast order: now the second story, *Meglos*, was to be produced, then the third, which was Matthew's first in continuity terms.

Matthew heard gossip about the experience of making *Meglos*, in which the Doctor turned into a cactus. Almost all reports were about Tom's tantrums, which were, he was told by Lynn the floor manager, much worse than Matthew had seen on *The Vampire Lords*. Certainly his cactus make-up did not help. Being turned into a cactus entailed hours in the make-up chair and Tom did not take kindly to hours in the make-up chair.

There was a fair quantity of weepiness on Lalla's part.

There was also a problem with the director, a crusty old BBC hack called Terence Dudley, who was also occasionally a script writer. Terence Dudley would not allow Tom to rewrite anything and he had to do exactly as he was told, stand *there* for this scene and after this line move across to *there* before picking up *that* and moving to *there*. (Dudley was so firm about this that, when a *Meglos* computer bank was found on the set to be larger than its markout in the rehearsal room, the computer bank was shifted to accommodate Dudley's directions: he would not allow the actor to change his moves).

On *Doctor Who* Tom had become used to working with very young, inexperienced directors who were easily intimidated. Most of them were terrified of him. Terrence Dudley was too long in the tooth for such nonsense and by all accounts it was a classic case of an irresistible force meeting an immovable object.

It was in this story that the first *Doctor Who* girl Jacqueline Hill made an appearance, as a beautiful alien with complicated headwear. Lalla Ward said only, "she didn't seem very happy…" and left it at that.

A couple of pleasing, small incidents occurred. Bill Fraser – who Matthew would later meet – said he wanted to find a moment in the script where he could kick K9: "I want to be the most unpopular man in Britain!" he said.

Some months after *Meglos* was finished, two BBC location scouts went to a street in Clapham. They knocked on some doors. The first to answer was a man.

"Hello," said one of the scouts. "We're from BBC TV. We're looking for a house to shoot some scenes for *Doctor Who*. Would you let us use yours?"

"Well, of course," said the man. "I've just written a script for *Doctor Who* myself!" It was one of the men who wrote *Meglos*.

And this coincidence is the reason why a *Doctor Who* writer's property became Tegan's flat in *Logopolis*.

Nor had the production of the first serial of the season, *The Leisure Hive*, been unfraught, it was reported to an interested Matthew. Things were not helped by a director at the other extreme from Terence Dudley. This one had experimental ideas. He locked off all the cameras and turned off their lights and edited as he went, so that Baker didn't know which shot was being used at any given time. Tom's whole performance, what might be called his technique, was based on which camera to favour. Wherever the camera was, there was Tom's mug and beady eyes. And now he was scuppered. There was also the difficulty of a smart and able cast member who happened to be a bit of a science fiction fan, a woman called Adrienne Corri. Unfortunately she was the wrong kind of science fiction fan, being a *Star Trek* enthusiast.

The Leisure Hive script had left most of the cast puzzled and uncomprehending. This was common with *Doctor Who* scripts. Actors for whom Shakespeare's most complex sonnets were as luminous as the sun found *Doctor Who* a pit of darkness. But all was clear as daylight to Adrienne Corri.

"Oh, it's all perfectly simple," she would say, explaining some knotty plot problem in a few breezy words. She, Matthew heard, was impressive and in control of herself.

A make-up girl told Matthew that while she was in Tom's dressing room combing his hair and dabbing him with powder, he would rant on loudly and odiously about "that bloody woman", though that bloody woman could hear every furious utterance, because she was in the next dressing room, divided from Tom only by very thin walls.

"Ssshhhh!" said the make-up girl, but Tom wouldn't ssshhhh.

"That bloody woman. Trying to *take over* my programme! Bloody woman!"

Tom could go on as he liked. From what Matthew heard of Adrienne Corri, she wouldn't have given two hoots what Tom Baker thought or said about anything.

*   *   *

Blue Box Boy: A Memoir of Doctor Who in Four Episodes

A day or two after the first episode of *The Leisure Hive* was shown, Matthew saw John Nathan-Turner, and he was, of course, robustly praiseful of this excellent programme, but he had one mild comment.

"I noticed that you called the title character by the name *Doctor Who* in the closing credits. Have you, umm, ever thought of, er, maybe crediting him as just *The Doctor*, the character's actual name being unknown and certainly not *Who*?"

John looked smilingly thoughtful.

When the Fourth Doctor Who gave way to the Fifth, the credits suddenly called him The Doctor. Had Matthew stimulated this alteration?? Should he claim credit for planting the seed? Not impossible, but he would not boast of it, because quietly he preferred the title character being known as Doctor Who. And he was impressed that, when the twentieth anniversary special was produced, though the Fifth was just The Doctor, the aging discards were Doctor Who, Doctor Who, Doctor Who and – frozen somewhere in a time bubble – Doctor Who.

But John was in a fury with the people who put together the preview trailers for BBC One. It was an established policy that trailers should not show the climactic moment of any programme, but the first trailer for *The Leisure Hive* had highlighted the creepy appearance of a monstrous claw, the very shot which was the episode's scary cliffhanger. So the kind of people who had the telly on all day had seen this exciting moment half a dozen times before the programme was broadcast.

For poor Tom, what a long way the miseries of *Meglos* and *The Leisure Hive* must have seemed from polling with his girl on the Cam for a Douglas Adams script, not yet scuppered by strikers! How lovely making the little bits of *Shada* must have been, how lovely that snoggy affair, for a week or two long gone! But of course Matthew knew nothing of any affair, because no-one ever told him and it had not crossed his mind that a man and a woman who seemed to want to throttle each other might in fact be sleeping together. Silly boy. Or that they might later marry...?!?

John Nathan-Turner had toyed for a while, he told Matthew, with salvaging the *Shada* footage, commissioning Douglas Adams to rework the script as four rather than six episodes, and find a part for Adric. Matthew wondered how this could possibly work, because in the existing footage The Doctor wore his old costume, not the slick new wine-red one.

On the first day of filming for *The Planet That Slept*, Matthew sat on the coach, his head in *The Worlds of 2001*. Exterior filming days meant a dawn start from TV Centre, from which a coach ferried bleary-eyed actors and crew to the location. Tom leaned over.

"What are you reading?"

Matthew showed him the cover.

"Oh, that. I always thought that was the most boring film ever made."

* * *

There had been some outdoors filming for *The Vampire Lords*, poor Lalla in an unusual horsey outfit running after a stalking booted Tom, but Matthew had not been a part of it, so on *The Planet That Slept* he made his first filming excursion for *Doctor Who*. (Location material was recorded on film and transferred to tape, the studio scenes were done directly to tape).

So the bus headed out to Black Park, the BBC's favourite location spot for woody scenes. In what always seemed to Matthew a strange policy, *Doctor Who* exterior filming was done before the read-through, and unrehearsed but for a few try-outs at the location.

First of all some young boyish extras had to go into the water and splash at each other playfully. They were dressed in pyjamas very like Matthew's, as all the humanoids in the story were. They were fit lads and were perfectly able to be rough with each other, but this was *Doctor Who* and the playful fighting was quite sedate. They wore nothing underneath and with the wet costumes clinging to them they might as well have been naked. This meant that nearly all the footage filmed for the scene had come out like soft porn, and had to be thrown away. Peter Grimwade, the director of *The Planet That Slept* – broadcast as *Full Circle* – told Matthew a few weeks later that it had been nearly impossible to find the few seconds they had finally used from several minutes of material.

Now Matthew had to prepare for his own scenes in the water. These involved first a shot of him running along the lake at the bank's edge, and then a shot of him swimming towards the bank.

"You'd better sneak off and find a quiet woody spot," said Amy Roberts, the costume designer, who wore moonboots, the footwear of choice for everyone in the costume and make-up departments when on location. So he darted a few dozen yards away into a circle of trees and bushes, to take off his costume and remove his underpants like the extras because they would show through once his costume was wet and clingy.

The film cameraman wore high rubber boots and demonstrated to Matthew what he wanted him to do, though the cameraman did not go very far into the water and did not get his trousers wet. Then he said, now you must do it. Matthew went down the bank and, like the camera man, he clung to low clumps of bushes and ran along the edge of the lake, the water covering only his boots and his legs up to his calves.

"No!" said the camera man. "You must go right into the water."

So he waded in. It was extremely cold as chilly water ran over his legs and thighs and chest. He scrambled energetically through the water at the bank's edge.

Then the swimming sequence had to be done. The cameraman said he must immerse himself over his head. Matthew had visions of his wig coming off and floating to the surface. He dropped down into the lake and waited for the call for 'Action'. It did not come, He waited and felt the water in his nostrils and waited some more until he had to push his head above water and breathe in and say,

"I can't hear 'Action'!"

"We're not going to call it," said the camera man. "Just swim when you're ready."

So he immersed himself again and sprang upward and made his fast but crude swimming strokes towards the bank.

Afterwards the costume lady said Matthew had been immersed so long underwater waiting for 'Action' that everybody thought he had drowned.

Inexplicably, the read-through for *The Planet That Slept* took place not at the Acton rehearsal rooms but in a sort of lounge at TV Centre. The cast sat in comfortable chairs in a circle.

Peter Grimwade had, of course, been on location, but the filming sessions had been run by the film cameraman, a man called Max Samett, Peter standing about exuding neurosis, probably throwing in the odd directorial comment. So it was not until the read-through that Matthew could be said to have met him properly. And this would be the first of many meetings, because Peter would keep cropping up on *Doctor Who* over the next two years.

Peter was perfectly the man it might be assumed would come from his background: he was the neurotic gay son of a Sussex vicar. The impression he gave, in fact, was not so much one of BBC homosexuality as the asexuality of a nervous curate, like those seen in farces. He was short and rail-thin and already balding in his early thirties. His face was narrow and lugubrious. He laughed a lot but it always sounded forced and uncomfortable. He wore grubby jeans. He had no bottom at all, seeming to go from trunk straight into stick legs. He sprang about all over the place like a terrified jumping frog. His intensity was negative in its effects, his movements all elbows and sharp prods of fingers on the air. Rather than directing his cast, he had a habit of *accusing* them, though of what was never clear. He had a high-pitched voice and a clipped accent. The result was like Andrew Lloyd Webber on helium.

He caused those around him to cease up. He meant well. He wanted his productions to be as good as possible. He worked hard on camera angles, for which he had a certain facility, and he did his best to direct his cast, but he didn't understand actors, though he had been around them at the BBC for over a decade. When he tried to 'help' Matthew and others, his input was so unfocussed and confusing that the outcome was simply the loss of their own focus.

The rehearsal room for *Doctor Who* was a tense place at the best of times, Tom likely to go into a temperamental rage at any moment, Lalla with what seemed to Matthew to be teary self-absorption. Matthew himself was tense from sheer nerves. Guest actors looked uncomfortable and embarrassed. A good director needed to let the tension out. Peter Moffatt could do this, even if it entailed sending everyone to the pub for an afternoon. Peter Grimwade achieved the opposite: when he came into a room, the tension doubled.

Matthew did not dislike him exactly, but he found him relentlessly unconstructive. At first he thought this was his own failing, not being adequately responsive to Peter's efforts, (though God knows he tried to be), but he noticed that others agreed with him, including those actors for whom Peter had nothing but slightly unctuous, Uriah Heapish praise – John Fraser, Richard Todd.

When scenes were being rehearsed, he would leap about at the edge of the mark-out, one forefinger touching the tip of the other, one thumb touching the tip of the other, making a square which represented the camera lens. His small eyes would gaze through this 'lens,' his brow creased, occasionally snapping an imprecation – "Matthew! Concentrate!" – but lost in his own directorial visions, his own evocative shots.

He did not like *Doctor Who*. he held not even the mild affection for it of the many who considered it endearing junk. It was junk he was not endeared to. He saw his directing work as a salvage job. He was trying to make what in his mind were inept scripts into something passable. Tom had often said that his own job, too, was alchemical, "turning shit into gold", but no-one could doubt that in his way Tom loved *Doctor Who*. Peter didn't. It did not help that the first script he had to direct was credited to a teenage writer and so could not possibly be any good.

Throughout the read-through for *The Planet That Slept*, Peter Grimwade sat with a dark brow. Afterwards, he announced that everyone could leave except the four Outlers. These were Matthew and three sweet people a little older than him, Richard Willis as Adric's brother Varsh, Bernard Padden, and June Page who, on account of what Peter regarded as her lower-class accent, soon got nicknamed 'Esher Girl', Esher being, Peter must have believed, a depressing Essex suburb. In fact, Esher was one of London's snobbiest outposts. It would have been more appropriate to give the nickname to Lalla, with her accent, partly brittle Chelsea posh, partly elocution lessons. Lalla was the only actor Matthew ever met whose perfect vowels might have come from repeated recitations of 'how now brown cow'.

This was the beginning of a well-meant but badly handled attempt by Peter to turn this foursome into better actors, in the mistaken belief that shouting at them and bullying them would magically bring out everything they were capable of. It had the opposite effect. Matthew lost his bearings entirely. After two years on *Doctor Who* and twenty years in theatre, Matthew never encountered a director so hopelessly incapable of achieving, in acting terms, his aim. It would be an ongoing problem throughout Peter's work on *Doctor Who*. He managed to get up the noses of everybody: from beginners like Matthew to experienced performers like John Fraser and Beryl Reid. The saltiest description of him came from Richard Todd, one of the biggest guest names *Doctor Who* ever had. Richard Todd was a marvel of old English courtesy. But when asked by Nerys Hughes what he thought of Peter Grimwade, he used extremely Anglo-Saxon language.

Perhaps Peter's problem was that he had spent too long in the enclosed world of the BBC. For many of its staffers, the BBC was the centre of the universe. When sometimes Matthew visited the flat of a BBC employee, he found it was almost always sparse and dusty, with a dying plant in one corner and a portable TV in another, and a poster of the kind students put on dorm walls. Their home life was beside the point: to all intents and purposes they lived at TV Centre. On their days off, they could be seen in the BBC Club. It was a joke that TV Centre was circular because its staff were too drunk to walk straight. Once, Matthew saw his Aunt Liz walk directly into a circular wall. Maybe she was too sober for the BBC. Every day, Matthew's Aunt left her house in Mortlake as soon as she had had her bath, and rattled home in her shaky car only when the bar closed. One night, when Matthew was going to stay at her house, they emerged from TV Centre at midnight and found that her car refused to start. A man with a forklift came to help, pushing the car in front of him, Liz and Matthew inside it, up the hill to the gates, where fortunately the engine caught.

Peter Grimwade had toppled into the BBC while still very young, and had been working as a floor manager on *Doctor Who* ten years before *The Planet That Slept*, his first directing job. Surprisingly, he was not much interested in directing. He wanted to write. In the end he wrote nothing except a couple of *Doctor Who* scripts and a slim children's story called *Robot*, which was put out by the publishers of *Doctor Who* novels. *Robot* was one of the most remaindered books in publishing history. For years, copies could be found in the red wire bargain bins at Woolworth's everywhere, often for as little as 25 pence. Perhaps it was a gripping read. Matthew read the first page. It felt even then old-fashioned, something like the space adventures of Captain W. E. Johns of *Biggles* fame. Perhaps the writing of it had given him pleasure. There was no evidence the *Doctor Who* material gave him any pleasure at all. These were written, it must be supposed, purely for the money, such as it was. His dislike of the series was often expressed, and with his high-pitched, bitten-off consonants he sounded inexplicably angry about it. Yet the series gave Peter his only chance to direct and later to write. He was involved mainly because he was a friend of John Nathan-Turner's, though at some point after Matthew left the friendship evaporated.

Peter had a strong dislike for Jon Pertwee, on whose *Doctor Who* episodes he had occasionally worked. He always called him 'Old Mother Pertwee'. He had tales to tell about those productions. He claimed to like Tom, though, while being unable to handle him, like most directors.

Though he gave many actors a hard time, there was one kind of person he would bully more intensely than others: young males who were obviously homosexual. This meant especially Matthew but also others, including a couple of young men who appeared in *Kinda*. Between Peter and Matthew there was a layer of sexual tension. Peter would bully and criticize him and then hug him very close. This was not relaxing.

Richard Willis was a very serious young man and his physical qualities underlined this. When his face, which was attractively sculptural, was not expressing any specific thought it fell into a light frown, just a little moody in a way which appealed to women. He was cool, laid back. His skin was slightly dark as if there were Spanish blood in him. His hair was raven black. He had been an actor on TV for many years, most famously as the editor of a school magazine in a series called *A Bunch of Fives*, but now he had plans to go off to RADA. He was interested in classical theatre, as was Matthew. He was particularly in thrall to Laurence Olivier and was seen to read Olivier's memoir *Confessions of an Actor* in every spare moment of rehearsals. In one corner of the rehearsal room, Lalla Ward crocheted. In another, Matthew read *The Glass Teat*. In a third, Richard studied Olivier with a frown of attentiveness.

When Matthew saw Richard as Varsh thirty years later for a DVD commentary, he recognized instantly an astounding and impressive feat which had been missed at the time, certainly by the kiddies who watched the programme and, more surprisingly, by the cast and production staff: Richard had turned his appearance in *Doctor Who* into an opportunity to experiment with assorted Olivierisms, not least in his vocal inflections, but also in a certain way of leaning in his chair, as Olivier had leaned on the arm of his throne in the Granada TV version of *King Lear*. The result was unusually intelligent, truly delightful and just a little silly in the best possible way.

By this time, Olivier's career was nearly over. He was infirm and could not stand up for very long. Matthew was too young ever to have seen him act live, though even in cinema his technique was apparent and fascinating and brilliant. He was still the hero of several generations of working actors. Actors as young as their early thirties talked wistfully about 'Larry' and every Shakespearean lead in rep was an Olivier impersonator to a greater or lesser degree, often to a greater degree.

Richard, though very young, was an old hand in the acting world and had a strong sense of ethic. Matthew had a liking for Catherine Schell, the actress from *Space: 1999* who had turned up in the *Doctor Who* Paris episodes, smoking fags flamboyantly through a long holder and camping it up to luscious effect. Once Matthew mentioned this to Lalla Ward.

"I like that Catherine Schell," he said. "I loved, loved, loved her in The City of Death."

"Yes? Her? Did you indeed?" said Lalla, looking superior. "Yes, she's nice, though of course she can't act."

In conversation with the outlers, Matthew said, "I really like that Catherina Von Schell." He spoke her name in a German accent. He went on in his innocent, big-mouthed way, "Yes, I adore her. Lalla says she can't act, but still I like her, I like her lots."

"Well," said Richard, like a fifty-year old trouper who had seen too much bullshit to put up with any more, "Lalla Ward *should not say things like that!*"

For any actor tired of bullshit, *Doctor Who* in 1980 must have been a very trying engagement.

Bernard Padden was less interested, perhaps, in Laurence Olivier than Richard was. He was a Manchester lad who had found success as a working actor in London, and for many years after *The Planet That Slept* he worked regularly, until returning to Manchester to be, as he put it, a 'theatrical landlady'. He was happy to embrace any form of showbiz that would have him. Just as comfortable in pantomime as in drama, he briefly became a TV presenter and caused a mild furore in the tabloids by coming out as gay on breakfast TV. Matthew did not see this exciting broadcast.

Matthew had something else in common with Bernard Padden. Richard told Matthew about an evening spent with Bernard while working on *Doctor Who*. After a few drinks Bernard went skipping down the street and ran right into a lamp post. He's a very strange boy, said Richard with narrowed eyes. Perhaps. But Matthew had once or twice, in a state of intense conversation with a friend after a night in a pub, walked into a lamp post himself. He had assumed he was the only living person to whom this happened, otherwise it being the stuff of slapstick comedy. What a thrill it was to hear that Bernard had a similar quirk.

For the first time in his life, Matthew was working with a movie star. Unfortunately, he did not know he was working with a movie star, having never heard of him, and he was not as impressed as he ought to have been. As far as Matthew could make out, George Baker was a tall bloke who could hold a ray gun.

George Baker – extremely unrelated to Tom – had made lots of movies in the fifties and sixties. Matthew had never seen any of them, not even the James Bond movie, *On Her Majesty's Secret Service*, though eventually he would see this. The best thing about the movie was Louis Armstrong's performance of a John Barry song, a miniscule footnote in the career of a gigantic American genius, comparable in twentieth century art only to Picasso in the view of the poet Philip Larkin, but even here Armstrong managed to make a light, camp movie song sound profound. But George Lazenby and Diana Rigg and Telly Savalas were very good too, and so was George Baker. Everyone was good, and there was lots of skiing.

At the start of the eighties, George's career was in a bit of a trough, hence his acceptance of the role in *Doctor Who*, unimaginable a few years earlier, or a few years later, after he got the part of Inspector Wexford in the endless series of programmes made from the Ruth Rendell novels, which put him back on top again.

Tom Baker and Peter Grimwade would not stop going on about how awful the script was. This got a bit dreary after a while. "How they can produce this garbage by this *child*,'" spat Peter," is beyond *me!* There are countless good writers who can't get their work produced and they commission this bilge!" Matthew suspected that the particular writer Peter Grimwade was thinking of in this respect was Peter Grimwade. Matthew felt embarrassed. This was partly because he was virtually the same age as Andrew Smith but also because, though Andrew had sent in his idea, he could hardly be accused of forcing the script on anyone. Tom and Peter droned on and on about the author's age.

Matthew had picked up a remark, perhaps from Andrew or John, that had led him to believe the script had been heavily reworked by Christopher, so it was not exactly Andrew's material in its final form. Andrew was not an exception in this: Christopher had the habit of rewriting everything he got his hands on, which left writers more experienced than Andrew feeling ill-used. Later, at the recording for the DVD commentary, the first comment Christopher made in Matthew's hearing in thirty years was to Andrew. It was, "Of course, I wrote that script, didn't I?" Andrew was non-committal. This seemed to confirm what Matthew had long suspected, that the script as produced was not written by a teenager but by a script editor in his early forties. Tom and Peter simply did not know what they were on about.

One of the lowest moments in Tom Baker's company occurred on the set of *The Planet That Slept*. He was in a grotty mood. He began stalking about the set, ranting on loudly about "that bloody spotty-faced writer." What he didn't know was that that bloody spotty-faced writer was up in the bloody box.

This unedifying moment entered Peter Grimwade's lexicon of funny stories. During a *Logopolis* rehearsal he narrated the story to Tom himself, who looked a little sheepish as it unfolded. Peter didn't look sheepish at all. "Ha ha ho ho that fucking spotty-faced writer, ho ho! Oh, he began crying, people were scrambling around for tissues! Ho ho ha ha." Matthew and Anthony Ainley walked away.

"I think that's horrible," said Anthony. So did Matthew. He glanced across to Tom, who looked sad and ashamed. Peter guffawed.

Though all the humanoids except The Doctor and Romana wore pyjamas, the monsters did not. They wore nothing, not even loin cloths. Like the Silurians and other reptilian monsters, though not *The Sea Devils* who wore blue fishing nets, they walked around starkers. This was sensible. If you lived in a swamp clothes would get ruined quickly.

Amy Roberts, the costume designer, had not asked Matthew which way he dressed, but she had no illusions about the body, human or otherwise, and as the monsters were naked she supplied both the males and the females, in her original designs, with genitals. These marsh creatures were certainly the first, and perhaps the only, *Doctor Who* monsters to be designed with genitals. She told Matthew this in the bar one evening. Not knowing much about *Doctor Who*, she was taken aback when she showed John and Peter her designs and they reacted with horror.

"This is tea-time entertainment!" they gasped. "Get rid of them!"

"But they're naked…"

"Beside the point! Get rid of them!"

So she had to rub the genitals out. The monsters were still naked, but they were now quite sexless.

Sexuality or sexlessness! Everybody was curious about sex, or the lack of it, in the universe of *Doctor Who*. It became something of a joke that the only companion with whom the Doctor was allowed physical contact was Adric, and indeed the Fourth Doctor had a habit of putting his arm around him, which was sweet. John Nathan-Turner, who loved all dealings with the press – photo sessions, press releases, press conferences – was extremely proud of his much-quoted answer to the sexual question: *No hanky-panky in the TARDIS!*

The rubber monster costumes, now without genitals, posed a problem for one of the actors, Norman Bacon. He was playing the marsh child, though he was twenty-seven years old. He was short. He was also claustrophobic. So the minute he put on his rubber costume, skin-tight as a diving suit, he began to feel hot and bothered, and became increasingly uncomfortable as the day went by.

This reached a climax during a scene in a laboratory which the marsh child had to smash up. Rarely has a set been smashed up with such passion. The poor man was having a kind of seizure. Matthew stood a few feet off the set, watching. Wires were torn out, glass flew from the set to the studio floor beyond. Pieces smashed near cameramen, and a couple right near Matthew's boots. Matthew didn't know whether to run for cover or applaud. It was one of the most intense scenes ever to appear on *Doctor Who*.

It must be admitted that Matthew was slightly more impressed to be in the company of Norman Bacon than George Baker, because the Marsh Child had appeared in a Hammer Dracula film, where he rode a bicycle down the street of a fake Appalachian village in a pre-credits sequence, until he was killed by Dracula and tied to the clapper of a huge Church bell. As far as Matthew was concerned, he was a star.

One little piece of excitement on *The Planet That Slept* was the arrival of the man from Viewmaster. He was to come to the location filming and then spend two days on the studio set. He carried with him an enormously complicated 3-D camera, which looked like the kind of device Jack Kirby villains used to drill trans-galactic gateways in the air.

A Viewmaster was a sort of 3-D binoculars. Discs containing fourteen images, (seven different photographs twice) were inserted into the top, the pictures becoming three-dimensional when looked at. When a lever on the side was pressed, the disc revolved to the next picture. Very lo-fi by the standards of DVD, it was a marvel of a toy in its day, though the 3-D effect was not one of natural depth: it was as if cardboard cut-outs of actors had been placed a few feet in front of a backdrop.

Matthew had got a Viewmaster one Christmas countless years earlier and a number of 3-disc sets of photographs from his favourite TV series. There were also educational discs available on subjects like outer space and undersea corral and the life cycle of dolphins, but such boring subject matter could not deflect Matthew from Gerry Anderson's *UFO*, with its fabulous 3-D images: of Sky One shooting down a UFO, of a green-skinned alien in his red spacesuit pointing his gun towards a SHADOmobile, of the Moonbase staff at their silver consoles. The Moonbase staff were pretty women in green cat-suits and, inexplicably, purple wigs, which they removed in their off hours. One of these purple-wigged women was Gabrielle Drake, who became an accomplished comic actress and was the sister of Nick Drake, the brilliant, unhappy musician. Gabrielle Drake now writes sleeve notes for reissues of her brother's albums.

It had always puzzled Matthew that Viewmaster had never done a *Doctor Who* set. Now this was to be rectified, and he was going to be on it himself, in glorious 3-D!

The man arrived at Black Park and went to work snapping his pictures. He snapped lots of pictures of Matthew sitting on K9. Matthew was extremely co-operative, because he liked the idea of being on a Viewmaster reel, but Tom and Lalla, neither of whom had any previous knowledge of Viewmaster, were less welcoming.

The next day Matthew had a chat with the man from Viewmaster. It turned out he had photographed the cover of the very issue of Sussex Life which had a picture of Matthew inside, albeit one the size of a passport photograph. This was, to Matthew, a tremendously curious coincidence.

The Viewmaster man came back for two days in the studio with his large camera. If he had not endeared himself to Tom and Lalla on location, he set about making things worse for himself, though he was only doing his job. During the run-through he sneaked in and out of the set, clicking away. Once, he came fairly near to Lalla Ward and pushed his camera towards her and she jerked her head away from him in a manner identical to Miss Piggy in pre-karate mode. A few minutes later, the Viewmaster man tried again, this time pretty much shoving the camera up her nose. Lalla shrieked.

"I can't possibly work with this frightful little man constantly sticking his camera in my face!"

The studio fell silent. The photographer apologized and said he would try to be less intrusive. In the bar afterwards, Matthew had a drink with John and others. John was cross.

"I can't have my leading lady being distracted like this," he said decisively. "I'll have to have a word with that man!"

Matthew sipped his white wine and soda and said nothing. He thought Lalla was being mean and stroppy and self-important. The man had to do his job and it wasn't as if Lalla was playing Hedda Gabler. She could churn out her lines as Romana perfectly well whether or not someone shoved a 3D camera up her nose. But the next day the photographer crept about the set unhappily, doing his best to remain unnoticed. Perhaps John had had his 'word' with him. Matthew made a point of grinning his head off whenever the photographer came near him.

At the end, the Viewmaster man said to Matthew that *Doctor Who* had been the worst experience of his working life. This was a pity.

Matthew could not stop being photographed. Not only was the man from Viewmaster capturing him in wonderful 3-D, there was also the photo session which would yield the image for the postcard he would have to send out in answer to whatever dribble of fan mail came to him. The photographer found a nice barky tree for him to lean against next to the lake at Black Park and pictures were taken, showing all his expressions from A to D: some frowning and intense, some thoughtful, some grinny, a couple smiling his head off in a great wide split.

A few weeks later, John came to him with the photograph, now printed onto hundreds of postcards.

"I love this picture," said John. "It's so characterful! So you!"

Matthew looked at it. He did not love it. His wig hung at the back in a rather fake way and his ears seemed to stick out as they did not in life, and he had a little triangular grin on his face. The grin reminded him of the black triangle on the front of the electric stopping trains which ran along the coastal lines of Sussex. This triangle, with two oblong driver's windows above, gave the impression of a face, happy but babyish.

What could he say? Later some other images from the same session, much better, cropped up in articles. Why hadn't one of them been picked?

"Thanks! It's great!"

There was in this the difficulty of Matthew's innocence and youth. Most actors would have been consulted before their picture was selected. Secretly, he thought not to be asked was a bit rude. He was merely presented with heaps and heaps of the dreadful thing. When, a few months later, Janet Fielding saw it, she gasped with horror and went straight to John about her own card, the photo session for which had already taken place. She insisted, in a splendid show of forcefulness, that she was going to choose her *own* picture. But then Janet was a worldly twenty-five, Matthew was a young eighteen. He was in that strange place of being neither a child exactly, nor an adult.

The postcard went into more than one reprinting and he signed hundreds, perhaps thousands, of them, always with a small rush of annoyance.

*   *   *

An actor called Tony Calvin reminded Matthew of Eeyore the donkey. In a location scene Tony had to slice in half a watermelon which was painted to pass as an alien fruit, which he did with concentrated solemnity, and when the film stopped rolling the solemnity remained on his face. He had a permanently down-turned mouth and his bushy eyebrows curved downward too, so he looked unhappy and angry all at once. Matthew was unsure whether this look was physiological or a barometer of his mood. Then Tony told him, over taramasalata in the bar.

He had, he told Matthew, been seriously ill, confined to hospital for a year, and, he said, "not a single actor or director or anyone in the business visited me." So, though he was now working again he no longer liked his professional world. Matthew did not say what he thought, that perhaps those actors and directors hadn't known he was ill. Tony suffered over what he regarded as his abandonment.

Tony was an active member of the Labour Party. He would talk about his political activities with intense earnestness. He was not a witty man. Matthew said that maybe it would be a mistake for the Labour party to continue to move leftwards if it was ever going to be elected again.

"Well," said Tony, "the Tories have moved rightward so why shouldn't we move to the left?" Matthew nodded as if he accepted it as a fait accompli.

Many actors read political books of the left. One man, appearing in *Doctor Who* for a small part, was up in the bar at TV Centre and Matthew saw him reading a volume, his large hands concealing the cover as if it was *Delta of Venus*. When Matthew approached him, he turned the cover towards him and said, in the muted way he might have asked if Matthew was into being tied to the bed, "do you like *him?*" It was the diary of Tony Benn. Matthew said yes, he did, and the man looked pleased.

After supper on the second day of taping Matthew came back to the studio a little early. He decided to sit down on the studio floor, between two cameras, while something was being done to the laboratory set. The stone floor was hard and cold on his bottom. It was interesting to look into the set from outside, at a low angle. It seemed surprisingly high and well-built and permanent from there, running through thick double doors to a workbench at the other end with a microscope on it. It was a view of the set no-one normally got.

Then he lay on his back, stretched out, as he sometimes did in parks and fields to look at the sky. Though this was a studio floor with feet moving about on it, he was quite relaxed: not at all afraid that he would be run over by a camera. He looked all the way up to the ceiling, to all the lights above, and the booms, which had not yet been swung over the set, and to the very top of the set where it simply stopped and looked paper-flimsy.

He rolled onto his stomach.

Tony appeared, all bushy eyebrows and arched mouth. Tom was standing about looking mournful.

"What's that boy up to?" whispered Tony, but not so quietly that Matthew could not hear it. "That *lovely* costume which Amy has designed for him and look how he's treating it."

It was a fair point. Matthew found himself wondering why on earth he was lying on the studio floor like that. He stood up and made a show for Tony of dusting himself down. But he did not regret lying there. He had seen something no-one else in the studio had seen.

The last studio day on *The Planet That Slept* was one of great tension. At nine o'clock at night, with the last cycle of scenes to be shot and everyone tired, Tom came on to the set in a spitting mood, Lalla behind him, teary and furious. Tom was swearing like a trooper between scenes, ranting at no-one in particular, or at everyone.

"Just shut up," mumbled Lalla. "Awful man. Awful man." Tom didn't shut up. He said something particularly infuriating.

Matthew said, quietly,

"Oh, *fuck off.*"

He could scarcely believe what he had said. Tom Baker had been his hero a few months earlier and he had now become the first and probably only person Matthew had ever told to fuck off. Coming from him, it was absurd, comical, and might under other circumstances have broken the tension. It did have a goodish result. The whole studio fell silent. For the half hour of shooting time that remained, Tom, though seething, said absolutely nothing between takes. Lalla looked thrown. Perhaps her thoughts had switched from Tom to Matthew, from "awful man, awful man," to "awful child, awful child."

Matthew was reading a lot of short stories by Harlan Ellison, who wrote science fiction stories and peculiar fantasies and teenage gang stories and drug addict stories and dark city-set mystery stories. He also wrote journalism, most famously a column of TV criticism, collected as *The Glass Teat* and *The Other Glass Teat*.

Matthew read *The Glass Teat* during breaks on *The Planet That Slept*. It was exhilarating to read a book so vehemently hostile to television while sitting in the heart of an institution which made TV programmes – something like, perhaps, reading erotica in church. While Lalla was crocheting and Richard was seeking advice from Olivier's memoir, Matthew was in his corner engrossed by *The Glass Teat*.

The original columns which made up the book had been written in the sixties for an alternative paper and were, of course, published only in America. Matthew had heard of almost none of the programmes that Harlan Ellison slagged off, which made the criticisms abstract. What remained were the salty flakes of his rage. What exactly *was Gilligan's Island*, the most moronic programme ever according to *The Glass Teat*? What *was Dark Shadows*, dumb beyond words? Who *was* Julia Child, whom Ellison actually admired? It would be years before Matthew found out…

Actually, when he saw some segments of *Dark Shadows*, repeated infinitely at ungodly hours, he was taken, not with admiration quite, but with a gripped astonishment. It was a weekday afternoon soap opera made in the late sixties, starring a vampire, featuring a witch, a werewolf, a Frankenstein monster and assorted ghosts and gypsies. Oh, and the Devil. (Old Scratch!) Zombies pushed up foamy earth and rose from the dead in front of cardboard headstones. One headstone had the name of a dead character mis-spelt. There was a mystical professor who was a little like Doctor Who. There was a mystical villain with a pointy beard who was a little like the Master. There was a diner waitress who screamed and screamed and was a little like a *Doctor Who* girl. It thundered all the time though it never rained.

New York theatre actors performed a script they had received the night before, which had been rehearsed once, then taped as if live. There were no retakes. The brooding leading man, who was a good actor but ill-suited to quick study, struggled to remember even the gist of his lines, there were strange pauses, there was repeated squinting at the teleprompter. The struggle of the very decent cast was fascinating for an actor to watch. It was *Doctor Who* as remembered by many people, though *Doctor Who* was Powell and Pressburger compared to *Dark Shadows*. Because of its frequency, five half-hour programmes a week all year round, more episodes of *Dark Shadows* were produced in its five year run than in the nearly three decades of the original *Doctor Who*. The sets wobbled not occasionally but frequently, the fans which made the curtains gustily blow could be seen, cameras crashed into each other, cameramen got fits of coughing. It was all charming.

Harlan Ellison outspokenly loathed television, despite – or because of – having written for it on a regular basis. Yet he liked *Doctor Who*, and once wrote a flattering but realistic essay which formed the introduction to American reprints of some of Terrance Dicks' adaptations, in loud new covers. Christopher Bidmead admired this essay and asked all potential writers for *Doctor Who* to read it. Chris was impressed to see Matthew shyly but furiously reading *The Glass Teat* during a coffee break on *The Planet That Slept*.

* * *

Matthew, over a drink, suggested to John Nathan-Turner that he telephone Harlan Ellison and commission him to write a script for *Doctor Who*.

"He will probably write the best *Doctor Who* story ever," said Matthew. John smiled ironically.

"I would consider it," he said, "if Harlan Ellison will accept a *special low*." He arched an eyebrow and widened his eyes.

All freelance contributors to the BBC had a set fee, based partly on age and partly on how many BBC contracts they had worked before. If they were to be paid less than their official fee, their contract was called a special low, if more it was a special high. Most actors, most of the time, were on special highs or special lows, almost no-one was paid their actual designated fee. Even Matthew's pathetic wage on *Doctor Who* was a special high. It was a macabre and nonsensical system. A very distinguished actor who had starred in twenty series for ITV might be offered the Equity minimum amount because he happened not to have worked for the BBC before, and occasionally the contracts office would go back to a director and say they'd rather he cast someone else, this person not being a BBC person, not "one of us." In fact, Matthew once met a director who told him he had been left with no choice but to recast, because, said the contracts office, "we *cannot* pay this man what he is demanding." His replacement, having done a great deal of BBC work, was paid more than the earlier choice had wanted. No-one in the contracts office seemed to consider this crazy.

John Nathan-Turner told Matthew that Harlan Ellison or his agent had approached the *Doctor Who* office, saying he would like to write a story for the series and stating his fee, which, being a Hollywood-style fee, was enormous.

"But," said Matthew crossly, "Harlan Ellison is very ethical." Harlan Ellison, though famously temperamental, (he had once kicked over a model of the submarine from *Voyage to the Bottom of the Sea* in a fit of pique during a troubled script conference), was always talking about ethics in his writing. "If you *explained* to him that the BBC has no money and everybody works for next to nothing, but you say you will produce his script as written, which never happens in LA, I bet he will accept." John looked sceptical. "All he wants is r, e, s, p, e, c, t!"

Harlan Ellison was never to write for *Doctor Who*. Matthew remained curious: would he have written a *Doctor Who* script for peanuts if he had known his work was to be respectfully treated? Ah, but *would* it have been? How would Harlan Ellison have coped with Tom's 'improvements'? A shiver runs down the spine. Perhaps he would have kicked Tom in the knee, or at least gone to Madam Tussauds and kicked his wax effigy in the knee?

7

After a fortnight's break, what might laughably be called 'the team' gathered to start work on *Warriors' Gate* by Stephen Gallagher. This was the most ambitiously impenetrable script the series had ever commissioned and the first from a published writer of 'serious' Science Fiction. Not a single participant in the production really understood *Warriors' Gate*, though Matthew thought it was brilliant.

Stephen Gallagher was the first 'legitimate' science fiction writer to bring a *Doctor Who* script to full term, but he was not the first to be considered. A man called Christopher Priest had also had a story in the pipeline for the same season. How much of Christopher Priest's script was ever written, if any, would never be known to Matthew, but it was certainly at one point listed on production schedules.

When he met some lads from the *Doctor Who* Appreciation Society they mentioned Christopher Priest. They knew he was a published science fiction writer and perhaps they thought he would lend *Doctor Who* some needed credibility. They talked of him in hushed, weighted tones, almost in whispers. "Christopher Priest," "Oh, the brilliant Christopher Priest…" ""There are rumours that Christopher *Priest…* how exciting…a *major* writer…" "The great Christopher *Priest…*"

As Matthew listened further, an amazing fact came to light: none of them had ever read a word of Christopher Priest. Neither had Matthew. For these boys, Christopher Priest was an unknown entity, they knew only that in some way he was 'serious'. Their excitement could not have been more sweetly devoid of knowledge.

Stephen Gallagher was the least present of all *Doctor Who* script writers of Matthew's time. He came to the read-through, thin with longish hair, denimed, young but slightly stooped, like the kind of shy rock musician who hides at the back of the stage, playing second guitar – this, at least, is how Matthew remembered him countless years later. He puffed on roll-ups all through the reading. His face expressed nothing. Then he disappeared, never to be seen again.

The director of *Warriors' Gate* was a man called Paul Joyce. He was remarkably nice. He was far too nice to direct *Doctor Who*. If Peter Grimwade was the very type of the queer son of a Sussex vicar, Paul was everybody's idea of a junior school teacher who cannot quite control his class, the kind who the naughtier boys might lock in a cupboard. Tall, narrow, bony, nervous and slightly camp, in the way of a Yorkshire school teacher, a bit Russell Harty, a bit Alan Bennett, he would try to be stern, but to little effect.

Once, while Matthew and Tom were talking through a scene featuring just the two of them, Matthew was noisily scraping a spoon around the bottom of a plastic yoghurt carton, trying to get the last bits of creamy strawberry yoghurt from the edge.

"Have you nearly finished that?" asked Tom, a little shirtily.

"Yes," said Matthew, diving for one last scrape.

"Would you," said Paul like a *Coronation Street* character, "kindly *finish it off and dispose of the container in the bin!*" It would be impossible for anyone to give this order in a manner more perfectly like a mild-mannered but infuriated primary school teacher. Perhaps it was the word 'kindly' that was so suggestive of school: "Clarence, will you *kindly* stop daubing Violet with that paint brush!" What was even more adorable was that Paul had not himself been remotely bothered by the sound of the spoon in the carton.

On the first day of full rehearsal after the read-through, before work started, Lalla Ward went up to Paul Joyce.

"I will need to take Thursday morning off," she said. "I have an engagement."

"I can't promise that," said Paul, mustering his pallid version of firmness. "You may well be scheduled to rehearse. I can't give everyone time off just because they want it."

Lalla smiled her most radiant smile.

"If you *could,* I would be extremely grateful."

Paul ignored this and looked down at his script. The smile vanished from Lalla Ward's face. She said to Matthew in a perfect stage whisper,

"I'm bloody well not coming in that morning, whatever that bloody man says." She didn't. Thus was the director *instructed* by his cast. If Lalla Ward was going to do whatever she bloody well wanted to do, it can be imagined that Tom was going to do whatever he bloody well wanted to do, to the nth degree. Paul allowed Tom to walk all over him. He was terribly frightened of him and Tom picked up the fear like a stalking cat.

It was a baptism of fire. Paul had never directed anything before: he was a photographer. He had been the set photographer for some of the BBC Shakespeares, and one (at least) of the cast of *Warriors' Gate*, David Kincaid, had been plucked by Paul from a BBC Shakespeare set. David had been jobbing around as an actor for years and would do so for a long time afterwards. Matthew worked with him a couple of years after *Warriors' Gate* in a production of *Treasure Island*. He told Matthew that, though he had had dozens of jobs, his children only believed he was really an actor when they saw him in *Doctor Who*.

David Kincaid knew Tom of old. They had been National Theatre players under Olivier. When Tom was an *Equus* horse, David was the horse next to him. They had been drinking partners. David could keep up with anyone when it came to booze. It was from David that Matthew learnt of the concept of the 'hair of the dog,' which Matthew took to enthusiastically. David was disappointed and a little hurt that Tom virtually ignored him on *Doctor Who*. They had, after all, thrown up together.

David Kincaid had come up from his house in Wales to do the job and had to pay for a room in London. He was a little low on funds. He was used to working in theatre, where, by Equity rules, a subsistence fee had to be paid on top of the wage so rent and food would be covered. The BBC did not pay a subsistence fee. David was extremely put out. He went to accounts and said,

"Could I have a few pounds now, in advance?"

The clerk looked at him as though he had just escaped from an asylum.

"You get paid when you get paid," he said and that was the end of the matter.

David was insulted and upset by this.

"The smug bastards," he said. "The bastards. They don't give a shit about anyone…"

David lived in Wales but was Scottish. He mentioned an audition he had once had with an American director, who was looking for a Scottish actor. David read his lines and the director said,

"Now would you do it in a Scottish accent, please?"

"I did do it in a Scottish accent. I'm Scottish."

"No, in a proper Scottish accent."

"It was a proper Scottish accent. I'm Scottish, I speak with a perfect Scots accent."

"But I mean *really* Scottish."

"I am *really* Scottish, and I speak with a *really* Scottish accent."

David did not get cast. He supposed the director must have meant an accent like Scotty from *Star Trek*, an accent which had never once been heard in Scotland, anywhere from the Borders to John O'Groats.

Rehearsals started sunnily. This was a good example of the calm before the terrible storm. The first day was spent running TARDIS scenes. The

TARDIS mark-out was right by the wall, near the doors, so the full day in the massive rehearsal room was spent squashed into one little corner. A hexagonal wooden cut-out placed on a table represented the console. Only Tom and Lalla and John and Matthew were present. Tom was in a disconcertingly jolly mood. He skipped around the console. He made funny remarks every moment of the day. How everybody laughed. He was merry with Lalla, he was fond of Matthew.

Paul lingered with fiddly fingers on the side of the scene, pretending he was having a lovely time too, though the terror was plain to see behind his eyes.

Lalla Ward had been polite enough to Matthew, but never particularly friendly to him. She had no reason to be. On the second day of rehearsals for *Warriors' Gate*, this suddenly changed. Usually the read-through table was folded up and put away after the first morning but Paul had left it out, under the huge window just to the right of the piano. Matthew sat on a chair at the edge of it, Lalla right next to him. She fiddled with her crocheting. She chatted to him often. It was always about Tom.

"That awful man," she said, in quiet rage. "Dreadful man." Remarks like this occurred throughout the day, in between dives of her crochet needle. Baker was, as always, based a few yards away at the extreme rightward window, his tatty briefcase and written-over script on the ledge. Though Lalla was seemingly talking to Matthew, it was possible that she hoped Tom would overhear her. Tiny whispers travel a long way in a rehearsal room.

Matthew was emotionally illiterate and did not know what to say to Lalla, or what he was *expected* to say. Should he make grunting noises of agreement? Was he supposed to defend Tom in some way? Probably he was expected to say nothing, just be the wailing wall off which Lalla's misery could bounce. He had begun to develop a suspicion that Lalla and Tom had had a fling at some time, but it was not clear to him how serious it had been and there was no evidence that it was still going on. By 'evidence' Matthew meant affection, humour, kindness, the things one expects of lovers to each other – at least, what one expects if hopelessly naive.

So he sat there listening to this stuff for first one day, then another, then a third. He felt uncomfortable, but he liked the fact that Lalla was showing interest in him. Actually, she wasn't, but because she was talking to him it felt like she was. When he tried to make what he thought were supportive remarks he made the wrong ones.

"Dreadful man," Lalla whined.

"Was he *always* so horrid?" asked Matthew.

"What do you mean?" she asked, eyes wide, offended, even rather shocked. "He wasn't *horrid*, not *last* season, he was *wonderful!*"

"Oh."

"I don't know what's gone *wrong...*" She looked teary. Matthew wanted to cry too, from embarrassment.

But Matthew's value as a listener, as quickly as it had begun, was as quickly spent, and she was back in her corner crocheting in silence. What had happened to make this change? She never said.

Perhaps Lalla clumsily turned to Matthew – if that is what she was doing – because the saintly floor manager Lynn was not on *Warriors' Gate* to mop up her misery. Instead there was Val McCrimmon, efficient, unsmiling, not as sympathetic a person as Lynn Richards. When not being an AFM, Val earned extra money as an actress; she had a small part in *Earthshock*. She was not taken by Matthew, thinking him a bit spoiled. Once at a party Matthew, having twisted the corkscrew into a bottle of wine at a funny angle, found he was having difficulty pulling the cork out. Val came up to him.

"Here, I'll do it!" she snapped. "You're so spoilt!" Matthew could not for the life of him work out what struggling with a tight cork had to do with him being spoilt.

A scene required Doctor Who to stalk out of the TARDIS saying he would be back in a few minutes.

"Minutes!" blurted Tom. "*Back in five minutes?* How boring! How dull! What about something more inventive! Ninods! Yes, ninods! *I will be back in seven and a half ninods!*"

"Oh how *delightful!*" said Paul, with an enthusiastic clap. "Marvellous. Yes, ninods, ho ho!" So ninods were officially incorporated into the script.

Matthew had very little to do in *Warriors' Gate* except flip a coin, but this he had to do a lot. He was rubbish at flipping the coin. He could flip it into the air well enough, but it refused to spin downward onto his hand. Instead, it flew over his shoulder or off across the room. It hit Paul's chest or Tom's nose. Matthew spent hours in corners during rehearsals and at home, tossing coins.

Stephen Gallagher wrote a delightful scene in which Adric puts on the Doctor's hat and scarf. He then spends half an episode wearing this outfit. Matthew loved these scenes and was looking forward to rehearsing them.

The costume designer, June Hudson, was at the rehearsal room getting measurements, and she came to Matthew carrying the scarf and hat. She told him to put them on so she could see how he looked. Paul Joyce stood nearby. It was agreed that Matthew looked marvellous. These scenes are going to be lovely, said Paul Joyce. At that moment Tom returned from lunch. He swayed to the window ledge. He looked across at Matthew. Matthew had never before seen the expression on a human face so like that of a cat, jealous to see the attention another cat is receiving.

Shortly after, the first of these scenes was to be rehearsed. In it, the Doctor had to leave the TARDIS for a while. Baker looked up from the script.

"I think," he said, "it would be much better of I *took my hat and scarf with me.*"

"Oh *yes!*" said Paul, waving his lower arm with a dismissive gesture. "Yes! Much better!"

Matthew didn't know whether to be annoyed, impressed or amazed. Annoyed at the loss of some nice moments, impressed at the shamelessness of Tom's gall, amazed at how easily Paul let him get away with it.

Romana and Adric had to hide behind a large machine and look over it. Tom said,

"Wouldn't it be sweet if the children stuck their heads over it at exactly the same moment?"

Lalla was not pleased to bracketed with Matthew as one of the children.

But the idea was nice. So Lalla and Matthew lifted their heads slowly and simultaneously over the top of the machine and looked from side to side, like cute little cartoon mice.

A very nice man called David Weston played Biroc, the leading Tharl. He regarded himself as essentially a Shakespearean actor and perhaps Paul Joyce had plucked him from a BBC Shakespeare set, like David Kincaid. Naturally, Shakespeare cropped up in his conversation. Lalla Ward nicknamed him 'Banquo's ghost'.

Before each block of studio days, there were two run-throughs at the rehearsal room, one for the technical crew to discuss matters of camera work and effects and so on, the other for the producer and various office staff, essentially a dress rehearsal without costumes. After the producer's run, there was a private meeting where John Nathan-Turner gave the director notes and talked things over.

After lunch Paul Joyce padded back into the rehearsal room. He was clearly uncomfortable. He approached Matthew, holding a small white envelope. He passed it to him silently. An envelope, quietly slipped to him in a corner? A dismissal notice! At the very least, a slew of notes so damning they could not be spoken in front of others!

Seeing a similar white envelope passed to Lalla Ward did not placate him, Lalla had already been 'axed'. Then one was passed to John Leeson. But he was on his way out too!

Finally, Paul slipped an envelope to Tom Baker, with an embarrassed smile. Good grief, thought Matthew, Tom too. A red letter day in *Doctor Who* history: everyone was being fired. Perhaps the series had been cancelled.

Matthew pulled the paper from its envelope. There wasn't much writing on it. It doesn't take many words to fire someone. He unfolded it.

There were three short numbered paragraphs, neatly typed. The most damning one was this: "The producer does not approve of the word 'ninods'." The note went on tremulously, "We must use minutes. I suggest three and a quarter minutes."

Yes, those frightening envelopes contained acting notes, remarkably tame ones. As regarded the giving of acting notes, Paul's timidity was unique in all Matthew's experience. Paul was too petrified of Tom Baker to say, *John hates ninods and so do I.* He had to hand him the news on paper.

A *Doctor Who* fan called Ian Levine had wormed his way into John Nathan-Turner's good books. Ian was the DJ at the gay club Heaven in Charing Cross. He was also a producer of Hi-Energy dance records. These were okay for sweating to, but actually listening to one had the effect of a Mind Extractor's cigarette. When Quentin Crisp said the worst thing about being gay was having to listen to all that dreadful dance music, he was probably referring to Ian's records.

Matthew never knew Ian Levine well but met him occasionally, at the BBC and once or twice in Heaven. He liked him well enough.

Ian was allowed to hang around the set occasionally, piping up his opinions. He must have been in the box for at least one of the first round of *Warriors' Gate* studio days, witnessing some scenes featuring the Tharls.

"Thals? Thals?? Those monsters sound like they're called Thals!" he said. "Thals are the handsome blond enemies of the Daleks. The moment Terry Nation hears of this, he will sue the pants off everyone."

Back at Acton, the message was relayed to everyone that Terry Nation was considering bringing a case against the BBC. Only if he's a moron, thought Matthew. He was narked when he next saw John Nathan-Turner, because John, not rudely but firmly, implied that *he* should have pointed out the coincidence. Matthew had certainly noticed it when the script came through his letter box and perhaps so had Tom. But who could possibly care? Every third alien in pulp science fiction was called a Thal, or something like it. A further problem was, there were already loads of scenes in the can where the Tharls were called Tharls. Three studio days had passed, half the material was on tape. A decision was made: they would now be called Tharils. But they could not be *pronounced* Tharils, because everybody had already called them Tharls. So they were *called* Tharils but pronounced Tharrrls, with a rolling Somerset 'R'. Not every cast member could keep up with these new strictures, so in the resulting episodes they went from Tharls to Tharrrls to Tharils willy-nilly.

The tensions in the rehearsal room deepened. After a particularly miserable morning, Kenneth Cope, the star of many *Carry On* films and of *Randall and Hopkirk (Deceased)*, was talking in the restaurant upstairs, sighing about the dreadfulness of it all.

"I have come to the conclusion," he said, "that I don't like temperamental actors." This was an elegant bit of understatement.

Matthew had seen *Randall and Hopkirk (Deceased)* as a child but he had never registered the names of the cast and had not made the connection between the actor in front of him and that programme: to Matthew he was simply an Equity member who seemed like a nice bloke, a very good thing to be, especially on *Warriors' Gate*. In fact, he never talked about his acting career. He was more preoccupied now with running a restaurant. Foodiness had not yet overtaken Britain, which was still reputed overseas to be a bit rotten when it came to dining out, but Kenneth Cope's restaurant was generally thought to be very good.

"I'm really a restaurateur more than an actor now," he said.

He made an offer.

"I always say this to actors." He opened his palms to take in everyone at the table. "If you come to my restaurant, make yourself known and I'll bring you into the kitchen and show you around and give you a free dessert and a glass of wine. This offer is open indefinitely. The weird thing is that in the years I've been running my restaurant and telling actors about it, only one has ever taken up my invitation." Matthew was to be another of the many hundreds of actors who did not take up the invitation and even if he had gone to the restaurant he would have been too shy to make himself known. In this he was like a surprising number of actors. Shyness is often a characteristic of show-offs.

On the day of the final run-through, before the second batch of studio days, Tom was in an unusually gruesome mood. Everyone was tense. The room was fogged with his rage. An old, damaged pushchair had been serving during rehearsals as a machine which at various points the Doctor had to carry about. Matthew was standing near Val McCrimmon. Val picked up the pushchair.

"Give this to Tom," she said, not as a request but as an instruction. Matthew looked across to an ugly, seething Baker.

"No, I don't think that's a good idea," he said.

"*Give it to Tom!!*" she hissed, the bossy woman who has had quite enough of a stroppy boy. Matthew gave in, and rather self-consciously carried the pushchair to Baker, standing on the edge of the mark-out.

"Here," he said, embarrassed.

"I don't need that fucking thing!" said Tom, who snatched it from him so sharply that the canvas across the back burnt Matthew's fingers. Tom threw it all the way across the room. It shot over the heads of actors and collided with a pole which wobbled but did not fall over, reminding Matthew of bar billiards.

A man called Freddie Earlle was among the crew of the *Warriors' Gate* spaceship. Freddie was humorous and loud, short and chubby and very London, a sort of Bob Hoskins type. He probably spent much of his career playing market traders and small-time crooks and small-time crooks who were market traders. During recording, Freddie decided impulsively to try a bit of method acting and, when his scene began, he pulled from his pocket a big fat red apple and bit into it, speaking his dialogue between juicy crunches. This failed to impress the people up in the box, perhaps because it was impossible to understand a word Freddie said with his mouth full of apple, so the scene was stopped and the apple spat out and the scene recorded in more orthodox fashion, the words easy to follow but a nice touch of life eliminated.

After a studio day Matthew had to make the train journey back to his parents' house in Sussex or cross London to one or another acquaintance who had a spare bed or a sofa. On *Warriors' Gate*, he decided to try an experiment. He would spend the night in his dressing room. This meant he could stay longer in the bar and would not have to get up early to make the journey back to TV Centre.

He was not sure if this was allowable, but he had overheard Lalla Ward say that Derek Jacobi had occasionally slept in his dressing room during the making of his TV Hamlet. It was possible to interpret this as meaning that Jacobi had stayed the night. Matthew supposed that, as long as he did not ask anyone and risk a firm no, he could get away with it.

So, after the story's first studio day, he sneaked down from the bar and into his dressing room. He undressed and stretched out on his lounger. There were sounds of movement outside. After an hour or so he heard the rattle of keys some way down the corridor and the click of first one lock turning, then another, then another. My God!, thought Matthew, they lock the bloody dressing rooms! He made himself as still and silent as possible, then he heard the insertion of a key into his own lock, a turn and a click. Well, he thought, let's hope there isn't a fire.

He tried to sleep, but was repeatedly drawn back into half-consciousness. TV Centre was patrolled throughout the night: the frequent pad of footsteps in the corridor, mingling with quiet chat which sometimes rose as guards passed by his door. And it was extremely cold: the heating had been switched off. Yet the pipes, though cold, were noisy as a zoo. A great variety of moans and gripes and huffs came down them. The small window overhead was curtainless, so the orange of outdoor lighting spilt on him. For much of the night he was more awake than asleep, until, at about four, he finally drifted off. But not for long, because shortly after five there was the rattle of keys again and the distant sound of unlocking, until, a few feet from him, his own lock was turned. The door was pushed slightly open. Matthew tried to make himself invisible, but he need not have worried because no-one looked inside. And half an hour later he heard more voices, different voices, these were women. The last thing he wanted to do was give a cleaner a heart attack, so he dressed and sat up and prepared to act as though his being there was the most ordinary thing in the world. When a middle aged woman with a mop opened his door, he threw his sweetest grin at her and said, *Good morning!* She stepped back for a moment and then joined him in pretending that all was as it should be. *Morning, dear!*, she said. She was quite chatty as she set to work. *I'll leave you to get on with it*, said Matthew, all friendly. He ambled out into the corridor and went to the coffee machine. It was not yet six.

Matthew could not say his night in the dressing room had been particularly restful, and he did not intend to make a habit of it, but he thought that, now he had experienced its rhythm, he could sleep at TV Centre on the odd occasion, and next time it would be easier.

Matthew was sad at the thought of Lalla and John Leeson no longer being around. John had always been fun and lively. He had not always found Lalla so easy a personality and had not understood the dynamics of her relationship with Tom, but obscurely, perhaps sentimentally, he suspected that he would miss her. He had a strong dislike of sentimentality, in part because he was prone to it. He bought 'Good Luck For The Future' cards. In John's card he drew a crude but recognizable cartoon of a winking K9 drinking wine. He took the card to John in his booth, just before the evening came to an end. In Lalla's he drew a crude but recognizable sketch of Tom, all big eyes and dangling scarf. He shoved a corner of Lalla's card into the metal square of her dressing room name plate. The card curved above it precariously.

John thanked him and seemed touched. Lalla came to him after she had changed into her street clothes. She seemed very buzzy, excited to be free of *Doctor Who* at last. She smiled and gave him a gentle little peck on his cheek. He felt himself turn pink. She ran off down the curve of the corridor towards the exit. He felt a welling in his eyes.

Neither Tom nor Lalla went to the last night party for *Warriors' Gate*. Matthew went, of course.

Matthew's inability to shut up sometimes got him into hot water. At this party, he found himself talking about theatre to David Weston, the leading Tharl. He mentioned that, a year or two before, while studying Macbeth at school, he had gone to see a production at the Gardner Centre on the University of Sussex campus. Oh yes? said David. Yes, said Matthew, it had starred an actor from *Survivors*.

Survivors was a Terry Nation series. It was a post-nuclear drama, or post-plague, post-something, anyway, but it quickly became cosy. The survivors formed a farming collective and after that their biggest worry was mucking out the sheep pen. It was like a cross between *Emmerdale Farm* and *The Good Life*, science fiction elements far in the background. (*Survivors* would cause a rift between Brian Clemens of *The Avengers* and Terry Nation, because Clemens had once mentioned to Nation that he was developing a series along these lines, and was more than miffed to see his idea suddenly crop up on BBC1, with the name Terry Nation all over it).

"It was very good," said Matthew chattily about Macbeth. "The man from *Survivors* was terribly good. There were only a couple of low points. They had this bloke do King Duncan very camp. It was terrible, that. It didn't work at all."

"Oh," said David Weston. "That was me."

Matthew thought fast.

"It was a great performance. Only the concept was wrong. The acting was great."

"Thank you."

"The other bit that didn't work was, they had this *really boring actor* as Malcolm. The Malcolm scene dragged on forever. It was *so boring* I wanted to cry."

"Ah," said David. "That was me too."

When the party ended and everybody was going home, David shook him warmly by the hand.

Paul Joyce was in a very bouncy mood at the party, drinking white wine and smiling a lot. Much of this must have been sheer relief that the whole horrific experience was over. He came up to Matthew and thanked him for his hard work.

"And you learnt to toss a coin beautifully!" he said, in his brightest school teacher's cadence. Matthew felt as if he had won a school prize.

The costume designer for *Warriors' Gate* was a wonderful, slightly melancholy woman called June Hudson. She drank a lot and was always emotional. She was thinking of leaving the BBC.

"I've had this offer to design clothes for dolls. I don't know if I want to take it or not. It's very well paid but I like the fact that TV is so full of people. I might find designing for dolls rather lonely and dull."

In the way of many insecure people, she was open to advice on this matter from anyone, including Matthew.

"I asked Tom his opinion. He said, oh you should leave the BBC immediately, June. But I don't know…"

Matthew did not say that taking advice from Tom was the worst move possible. Whatever Tom said, it would be wise to do the opposite.

"It would be great to design costumes for dolls," Matthew said, "but you're so good at this, why give it up?"

"Oh, I know," she said, "I know."

Browsing in Foyle's one afternoon several years later, Matthew came across a book of moody photographs of the Yorkshire Moors. The photographer was none other than Paul Joyce.

In the late '90s, Paul directed a two-hour TV interview with Dirk Bogarde, Matthew's favourite actor. Bogarde was and remains an iconic figure in British and European cinema and a major gay icon. In fact, in the early sixties he was the first movie star to play a 'serious' gay character in a film, though not the first actor: that was Murray Melvin, who was later to become a friend of Matthew's, in *A Taste of Honey*. Bogarde's six volumes of autobiography were the finest books any actor ever wrote. He invented his life as he wrote them. "I never believed more than a single sentence," Glynis Johns said, but it had seemed to Matthew that Bogarde was not asking for belief exactly. He was one of a miniscule number of actors thought to be interesting enough to deserve a movie-length documentary, though it was really a grandiose plug for the books. It would be Bogarde's last TV appearance. Paul told Bogarde's biographer that he was not in the end satisfied with the production because Bogarde, at first cooperative, became difficult as filming went on. Surprise. Paul, it seemed, drew difficult people.

Warriors' Gate was a thrillingly baffling piece of fiction, a heroic attempt to transfer 'proper' science fiction to the lowlands of TV. That lazy, over-used word dreamlike seemed to apply to it, with its leonine Tharrills and its all-white scape. The viewers did not understand a word of it, but were swept up by the time winds. It opened with lingering interior shots of the spaceship, gantries and ladders and unpeopled corridors, shots familiar to fans of *Alien*. These *Warriors' Gate* shots were so successful that they were replicated in *Doctor Who* less than a year later, in *Earthshock*.

It had a fabulously wicked spaceship captain in it, who went crazy in the last episode and had the cackliest laugh of any *Doctor Who* villain. He was played by Clifford Rose, a delightful and gentle man who had made a career out of playing evil Nazis. Clifford was sometimes punched in pubs by morons who did not know what a 'character' was. TV people have often been accused of cynicism about their audiences, but there are large quantities of breathtakingly idiotic people in the world and most of them watch a lot of telly.

Stephen Gallagher did not hand his script over to Terrance Dicks to turn into a little book. He wrote it himself, and it wasn't so little. Matthew was told that the office boys at Target Books, used to slim volumes with short sentences, had a breakdown when they saw Gallagher's huge manuscript. They set about editing, by which is meant butchering, it. Gallagher took his name off it. Lads who turned to the book to clarify the complexities of the episodes found they were none the wiser.

Gallagher became an extraordinary writer. There had been, by 2009, around two hundred *Doctor Who* stories, written by a hundred or so writers. It seems odd that only one of them, Gallagher, ever became a really terrific writer of prose fiction, both novels and short stories, in the way Harlan Ellison or Theodore Sturgeon or Norman Spinrad, contributors to *Star Trek*, were. (It has to be said that all those writers hated the watered-down *Star Trek* episodes which had their names on them). Of course, Douglas Adams had enormous commercial success with his wonderfully arch English humour – the long dark tea-time of the soul! – but Gallagher's novels, two of which Matthew read, were much more interesting and wide-ranging. There were a number of other good British science fiction novelists – Brian Aldiss, Michael Moorcock – who expressed a mild liking for *Doctor Who*, but none ever showed the slightest interest in writing for it.

8

Very different from *Warriors' Gate* was Johnny Byrne's *The Keeper of Traken*. Matthew loved this script. It had something of that mystical streak to be found in many episodes of *Space: 1999*, which Johnny had script-edited and written for. A wise, bearded old man, like a hermit, magically appeared in the TARDIS on a throne and said things, pregnant with warning, to Doctor Who and Adric.

The day of the read-through for *The Keeper of Traken* was also the day the first episode of *The Planet That Slept* was to be aired. Before the read-through, Matthew had to do an interview for a local BBC radio station in Wales, plugging his first episode. This was to go out live at nine a.m. The only way Matthew could fit it in was by getting to the rehearsal room extremely early and using the office telephone and this was agreed among all concerned. But this good idea hit an unexpected difficulty. There were horrendous delays on the London-Brighton line and the train arrived at Victoria an hour and a half late. That is, a fifty minute journey took one hundred and forty minutes. Matthew was in a terrible stew. It was nearly nine o'clock. There was no way he could get to Acton in time. He decided to call Wales right from Victoria station. This meant stocking up with a large number of ten pee coins to pump into the telephone, so he rushed into the station branch of W H Smith and bought a comic. Then he went to the little court where the public telephones were.

Victoria was a noisy place at the best of times but this morning, with all the delays and cancellations, the high, cavernous building echoed relentlessly with blurred announcements and apologies and people ran about looking furious, and those cars which carry goods to guards vans hooted and screeched with unusual frequency, a few inches from where Matthew had flattened the balled-up piece of paper with the number on it on top of the coin box and was now shakily dialing BBC Wales.

He got through to the radio station and pushed in some money and a clear-voiced woman with a lovely Cardiff lilt answered and he gaspingly explained his predicament and the woman said she would call him back, "so you won't have to bother about putting in all those coins." Not all public telephones accepted return calls so there was a moment of worry before the ring. The clear-voiced woman said how nice it was for him to do the interview and she was putting him on air now. A van hooted behind him. There was a click on the phone.

An interviewer asked him a question. He could not hear a word of it, there was no more than a crackle and the distant chunner of a male voice.

"Er, I didn't quite catch that, what did you say?"

The chunnering voice repeated the question, but it was incomprehensible.

"Yes," Matthew said, "well, you see…," and he made some general and dull remarks related to being in *Doctor Who*. The voice chunnered another question.

"Ccrrrzzzzz@#@?"

"Well, this is an *especially* exciting episode, with terrifying marsh monsters in it. I'm certain all your listeners in dear Wales will enjoy every moment, when they are not hidden behind their sofas, teehee."

"Gobbleooooodyerfillagleik!?"

"Absolutely, Tom is a charmer and Lalla a joy. Very fanciable, hahaha. It is unbelievably exciting being the new *Doctor Who* boy. Incredibly."

They kept up this exchange for two or three minutes: the interviewer saying something in what might have been Croatian, Matthew sounding interested and then whirling away on some new rush of invention.

"NincompeeeeelllyoxbreathBBCwho?"

"Quite right. And it is on this very afternoon at 5:15. It's quite hard work making it, long studio days, scarcely a moment's rest."

Finally the crystal clear woman's voice came on.

"Thank you," she said.

"Was it alright?" asked Matthew

"It was fine," said the woman warmly, though she had probably not paid much attention to it.

Matthew slapped down the receiver and rushed to Acton, his pocket rattling with ten pee coins.

Matthew tried to put the fact that today was the day of the first episode with him in it out of his mind as the reading for *The Keeper of Traken* started. Tom swept in to the read-through as if he had wings on his feet. All was jollity. Everybody was in a remarkably good mood. Afterwards, everyone went to the pub. Johnny Byrne and John Nathan-Turner took a seat in an alcove in a bay window with Matthew, and John Woodnutt joined them. Gary Downie, JNT's partner, was also there for some reason. Perhaps he had been floor-managing another rehearsal. Tom and Anthony Ainley stood at the bar, apart from the rest, Tony smiling broadly as Tom regaled him with tales of Anthony's wilder brother, whom Tom had known. Matthew overheard one story while lingering at the bar buying a round of drinks. This brother was something of a womanizer and Tom described seeing him disappear into a car with a girl. A second later the car started creaking and rocking, energetically and rhythmically.

Tom eventually rolled out, perhaps to Soho and booze and dope, and Tony joined the others at the round table. A happy lunchtime extended into the mid-afternoon, everyone drinking to Matthew's first episode. Everyone was buzzy, the pub was lively with that distinctive Saturday afternoon all-the-time-in-the-world friendliness which felt different from a weekday lunchtime. Johnny spoke with a priestly gentleness. He discussed character.

"I always try to write real characters, even for small parts," he said.

Matthew said he had certainly written a character for him. He was delighted with the script, he said.

But all the time in the world too quickly came up against closing time, which was three. John and Gary gave Matthew a lift to Victoria station. Matthew was nervous about *The Planet That Slept* and had hoped to stay in the pub all afternoon and so miss it. John was congratulatory. Matthew occupied a strange mental place, a sort of emotional high but with butterflies in his stomach. They waved goodbye.

Matthew went to the platform for his train and then realized with a spinning feeling that he had left his bag in the Acton pub. This was a substantial disaster, for in it was not only his *Traken* script but his wallet. He had nothing at all with him but the clothes he wore. He did not have the train fare to Sussex, nor even back to the North Acton tube station.

Fortunately, travelling free on the London Underground in 1980 was not difficult, rarely necessitating even the mildly mischievous act of jumping a turnstile. There was usually an open gate by the ticket inspector's box, and most ticket inspectors were not profoundly taken up with the matter of inspecting tickets. So Matthew slipped onto a train and the tube rattled him back to North Acton. The pub was as silent as a Church. He bashed on the door and only after some minutes of knocking and loud calling did the woman who ran the bar rustle towards the door and open it blearily, as if she had been woken from a nap.

"My bag!" cried Matthew. She produced it instantly. "Oh thank you!" said Matthew and he kissed her. Then he darted away, bag under arm. He jetted back to central London – as nearly as the London Underground allowed it – and hopped on a British Rail train. He made a show of studying the script for *The Keeper of Traken*. He arrived in Sussex as the *Doctor Who* theme began to roil around his town and he ran the three minutes to his house and darted upstairs and turned on the TV, which was old and took a minute to warm up. Then he watched, or rather half watched, the first exciting episode of this classic adventure, mildly drunk and, mainly, relieved that he had not lost his wallet.

The scenes of everybody splashing about were appealing, and the final scene, where the monsters approached the shore from a foggy lake, was dramatic, if overly suggestive of the Gila Monster. By uncanny coincidence, Matthew had seen *The Creature from the Black Lagoon* shortly before, because it was on virtually permanent show at a 3-D cinema on the Piccadilly edge of Soho, the only such cinema remaining in London then, and perhaps in the world. (There was also, attached to Victoria Station, a Cartoon Cinema, which showed *Daffy Duck* and *Tom & Jerry* and *Mighty Mouse* all day).

This wonderful, smelly little movie palace, a few doors away from Soho's many porn cinemas, somehow drew big enough crowds to stay open by showing *The Creature from the Black Lagoon* and *The House of Wax* over and over and over again. Perhaps the rent boys who waited outside Boots in Piccadilly – Dilly Boys, they were called – went in to see a 3-D movie as a respite from thick-walletted clients. Apparently, they, and punters in raincoats, (perhaps some of them the same thick-walleted gentlemen who would later pick them up outside Boots),in between stronger, stickier fare, were delighted to don 3-D glasses, issued at the ticket counter, and sit through *The Creature from the Black Lagoon*. This was a dated, plodding film, but it was terrific to see it in 3-D on a largish screen, with four other customers, all propped on the kind of lumpy seats which encouraged fidgeting. This was the sort of cinema where the punters kept having to shift their bottoms because of tiny, itchy, needly flea bites, which caused a definite stinging sensation, though the fleas were just as likely to be imaginary as real. Matthew thought, watching *The Planet That Slept*, that it would have been even better in 3-D, the children of Britain on their haunches, cardboard glasses itching the ends of their noses, scared out of their pants by the approaching bog creatures.

Countless years later, while doing the DVD commentary, Andrew told Matthew that he had not had *The Creature from the Black Lagoon* in mind at all. He had meant the monsters to be cavemen. Upright humanoids evolving from cavemen: a very different thing than from Gila Monsters. Had the production therefore made nonsense of the script? If so, none of its millions of viewers noticed.

This thrilling *Doctor Who* story also included some brilliantly creepy spiders, which broke out of eggs. The effects man was extremely proud of them, and a year later another guy from the same department said to Matthew, "he *still* goes on about those bleeding spiders!" But he had reason to be pleased with himself.

While watching *The Planet That Slept*, Matthew kept feeling his wallet in his trousers pocket, enormously relieved that it was there.

Matthew had watched the first episode of *The Planet That Slept* in black and white, because his parents had never got around to buying a colour set. Here he was, a TV actor, and yet he had to watch his own work in black and white. Probably he was the only BBC worker who watched black and white TV. This could not go on. He decided to buy a colour set.

His father worked for an electric company so he could get a TV at below the shop price, but it had to come by post and it took a long while to arrive. John Nathan-Turner had had the excellent idea of showing on BBC 2 a sampling of old *Doctor Who* episodes, one story from each of the four Doctors' oeuvres, starting with the very first episode, *An Unearthly Child*, then the deliciously creaky and entertaining *The Krotons* with Patrick, then

Robert Holmes's gem *Carnival of Monsters*, ("Roll up! Roll up!" said Jon Pertwee in his *Navy Lark* comedy voice, Katy looking enchanted), finally *Logopolis*. This was the first time in *Doctor Who*'s eighteen years that early episodes had been repeated. Matthew's TV arrived just in time for the first broadcast in this special season, and it is absolutely true that the first thing he ever saw on his new colour TV was *An Unearthly Child*, broadcast in its glorious original black and white.

Matthew was by now spending less time at home. The breaks between stories were spent in Cambridge: he was having his first serious relationship, with a post-grad student he'd met at a party in Brighton, and he had some friends in London. By the time he left home in a formal way he was hardly ever there. So the TV got very little use, and sat in his room acquiring an ever thicker coating of dust. It was the only TV he would ever buy in his life. It got so clotted with dust that, when he turned it on for the first time in two or three years in the late nineties, there was a smell of burning and flames leapt out of the back.

The second Saturday of rehearsals for *The Keeper of Traken* was also the day the second episode of *The Planet That Slept* was due to air, and it was the day he was to appear on the live children's programme *Swap Shop*. This ran on Saturday mornings, for hours and hours. It was a very peculiar entertainment indeed. In the studio, pop singers sang hits and amusing games were played and 'celebrities' answered telephone questions. Meanwhile, an ex-child actor called Keith Chegwin, known as Cheggers, went out to various parts of the country with a sort of road show, and children in that week's locality could gather and get their little faces on the telly and, presumably, swap things.

The studio portions of *Swap Shop* were presented by a tiny but slick and bearded gent called Noel Edmonds who was also a Radio One DJ. Matthew had seen the show only occasionally, when somebody he especially liked was scheduled to appear on it, the most memorable being, of course, Kate Bush. Whereas the naffness of *Top of the Pops* somehow eluded people, absolutely everyone knew that *Swap Shop* was naff, but they watched it anyway.

One of the programme's elements was a competition in which a 'celebrity' posed a question. Children sent in their answers on postcards and a winner was drawn from a hat the next week. This meant that, if there was a good guest one week and Matthew entered the competition, it was annoyingly necessary to watch the programme the next week too, to see if he had won. Matthew entered Kate's competition three times and got the answer dead right on all three postcards, but he did not win the fabulous prize, which was assorted promotional goodies tied in with her second album, *Lionheart*. Matthew would be disgruntled for many years about never owning a *Lionheart* umbrella.

So, on this particular Saturday morning, Matthew was going to appear and answer some phone questions and give away a large heap of goodies. He had to come up with a question for the competition. He thought and thought and thought, and then he came up with a terrific, fiendishly difficult question for the *Swap Shop* viewers. It was sure to cause humiliated silences in the houses of *Doctor Who* know-alls.

Lying on the grass one lunchtime with Andrew Smith, the writer of *The Planet That Slept*, during location filming, Matthew had tried to catch Andrew out with *Doctor Who* minutia. This was nearly impossible to do. Matthew asked questions to which he himself did not know the answer, hoping to bluff his way through, but Andrew knew everything. "Oh aye," he said, "Avon from *Blake's 7* did *indeed* appear in *Doctor Who*, in a small role." He then named the character and the episode. Matthew wanted to strangle him.

But Matthew had his trump card. He asked, very slowly, for Andrew to "name...the...actor...who ...played Doctor...Who... in the... *stage version*... called *Seven Keys... to ... Doomsday*. Ha!"

Andrew went white. He began to pull up blades of grass. A long pause followed.

"Well... *I don't know!*"

"Heavens! I *am* surprised. Why, it was Trevor Martin!"

Even at the time of *Swap Shop*, Matthew did not have the faintest idea where he had acquired

this priceless piece of info. He had certainly not seen the play. He once asked someone about it and was informed that it was very light and amusing and was written by that hurricane of *Doctor Who* script-writing, Terrance Dicks.

He once saw Trevor Martin in an RSC production. He was a very fine actor. His stage Doctor Who had apparently been a variation on the First Doctor. Matthew became acquainted with a friend of Trevor Martin's and was at least once in a crowded room with him. Matthew's friend admired Trevor Martin and thought he had not done as well in his career as he deserved.

"You see," she said, "Trevor is lazy."

Just as he had zoned in on Andrew's tiny fragment of ignorance, Matthew wanted those inactive *Doctor Who* viewers at home who watched *Swap Shop* (rather than kicking balls around in town parks and on village greens as they should have been) to rip threads from their parents' carpets in a fury over this obscure but beautiful diamond of fact.

John Nathan-Turner was having none of it. He had come up with a much better question, he said. It was about a professor in the previous season. It was so boring, Matthew wanted to yawn in John's face. It would make *Doctor Who* know-alls smug with their despicable knowledge, as if they were not smug enough already. Yet John was in charge and Matthew had to ask the professor question.

Before he was interviewed Matthew sat on a set which was a sort of faux café decorated in playpen colours at the edge of the studio. It was full of children and balloons. Occasionally the programme cut to the café where bubbly fun was being faked. Matthew sat at a round table. Next to him was a man from British Marvel comics. He had a high pile of the first issue of a Marvel space comic which he was going to plug on the programme. He had an unintelligent grin on his face and a sneery manner and he began to talk to Matthew condescendingly, even while he offered Matthew a copy of the comic, which Matthew politely declined.

Then Matthew was taken to a sofa and introduced to Noel Edmonds.

If the question Matthew had to ask was disappointingly easy, he was undoubtedly a king of prizes. Perhaps he outshone even Kate Bush, with his cornucopia of merchandise, enough toys to cover a coffee table, and tickets to a *Doctor Who* event. As he pointed out all his stunning prizes, he felt like one of those game show girls who open refrigerators and cars while dressed in skimpy swimwear. A gentleman from BBC Enterprises, which was promoting the *Doctor Who* event, gave him the prize tickets. He was not the same man as the *Top of the Pops* fellow, but from a similar mould. He hovered off camera near Matthew, and looked extremely chuffed when Matthew said what a great event it was, though Matthew knew nothing about it except that he was giving away tickets.

Also hovering nearby was John Nathan-Turner, in his sheep-skin jacket, fists pressed into the pockets, looking very pleased at how well everything was going. People telephoned Matthew and he answered their questions fully. For some reason, someone asked about the age of Doctor Who – the character, not the programme. This might have been an instance where a person had telephoned without the slightest expectation of getting on air and had to invent a question at the last moment. Fortunately, Matthew was able to pluck from his memory the stimulating information, revealed in *The Making of Doctor Who*, that *Doctor Who* was six hundred and fifty years old. Golly, said the boy on the line, that's old. Yes it is, agreed Matthew.

Matthew asked John if he had appeared too nervous.

"It's really scary," he said, "but that Noel Edmonds is quite good at putting you at your ease."

John said, on the contrary, he was extremely pleased with Matthew. He took him out to the front of TV Centre and put him in a cab to the Acton rehearsal rooms. Matthew looked through the back window as the cab spun away. John was waving at him, a broad happy smile all over his face.

At Acton, John Black and Tom Baker were waiting for him. Matthew felt lively and happy.

"How did it go?" asked John Black warmly.

"It's really scary," said Matthew, "but that Noel Edmonds is quite good at putting you at your ease."

Tom Baker piped up.

"Did you say what a complete bastard I am?"

"No."

"Really?? Why not??"

"Well, I didn't want to…"

"Really??"

Over the two or three weeks following *Swap Shop*, many impressively pompous pieces of correspondence drifted to him, in various colourful inks, all starting with a phrase like, 'you obviously know a great deal about the subject' or 'you are very well informed, but…,' until the nitty-gritty was reached. *Doctor Who* was, said these many letters, not six hundred and fifty years old but seven hundred and fifty…!!!

Matthew hoped that none of these dreadful letter writers had won the myriad goodies he had given away.

Was the *Doctor Who* event for which Matthew gave away tickets on *Swap Shop* the one at Madame Tussauds, the London waxworks emporium? Probably not. The Madame Tussauds event included wax simulacra of The Fourth Doctor Who and the Second Romana. Matthew was a bit narked not to be asked to pose for a waxwork of the first Adric, though this was later made up for when Adric became a chess piece.

The Second Romana stood around in Madam Tussauds attracting dust for a few weeks before being melted down, turned perhaps into Mrs Thatcher or Jack the Ripper. The Fourth Doctor remained unmelted a little longer, and, as everyone knows, was found useful when in 1983 Tom Baker refused to have anything to do with *The Five Doctors*, that enchanting twentieth anniversary special. For the publicity photographs the waxwork took the place of the real Tom.

This had the effect of drawing all eyes to the sculpted figure. The other Doctors hovered about in poses reminiscent of life and action, while the Fourth Doctor Who stood as stiff as a propped-up corpse, blank-eyed, unwell, with shiny skin and a sickly grin and possibly a little tipsy. The William Hartnell substitute, Richard Hurndall, clearly had a few good years left in him yet, but the waxwork Tom looked likely to topple over at any moment, landing face-first in the mud, broad but anaemic smile intact. Doesn't the Fourth Doctor look *odd,* said those innocents who saw one of the pictures in their parents' newspaper. Tom's ego was so huge that he sucked all attention to himself even when he wasn't there, which must have pleased him a lot.

Among the fabulous cast of *The Keeper of Traken* was Sheila Ruskin, a smart, talented woman who was with Matthew's agent. She was also quite hard-boiled. She had lived for a few years in the heart of Soho. When Tom Baker heard this, he was impressed.

"Christ," he said to Matthew, "you have to be bloody tough to live in Soho."

There was also a terrific middle-aged actor called John Woodnutt. He had one of those faces which seem to have disappeared from the modern world, distinguished and yet clerkly, perfect for historical dramas of any era, imaginable in *pince-nez* or little round Berlioz glasses, poring over music scores or illuminated manuscripts in candlelit rooms. He was a talkative man, and was just as happy to moan about the awfulness of the acting profession to Matthew as to anyone else. He was by any standards a reasonably successful working actor but seemed to regard himself as a terrible failure, or at least feared that others regarded him as a terrible failure.

"People say, why do you act? *After all, you didn't, ummm, make it, did you?* That's what they say. They haven't the faintest idea what it's like!" But not long after *Traken* he would appear in the BBC drama serial of Kipling's novel *Stalky and Co.*, and would later regard this as the best job he had ever had.

He had appeared in several earlier *Doctor Who* stories, going all the way back to 1970.

"Oh yes," he said, "I was in the first one with Jon Pertwee."

Matthew was interested by this. *Spearhead From Space* had been a particularly exciting and scary episode.

"That's amazing. What was it like, working with the Autons?"

"The what? I can't remember a thing about it. They're all completely forgettable."

"That story, *Spearhead From Space*, is an absolute classic," said Matthew, believing this would please him. He didn't care.

"And I was in one with Roger Delgado, but I can't remember anything about that either."

"What was it like, working on Jon Pertwee's first story?"

"Lovely man. Absolutely lovely man."

"Jon Pertwee?"

"Roger Delgado. Lovely man, Roger."

John was, in the way of many actors, both warmly sociable and socially uncomfortable. He would take the tube from North Acton station back to his house in Ruislip. Sometimes after work he would arrive at the station just as Matthew was buying his own ticket, or would be in the ticket line when Matthew arrived. Friendly at the rehearsal building, he was suddenly distant and distracted away from it, even if only by a few minutes and a few hundred yards. Matthew said a clumsy hi and he looked surprised and said a hasty hello before darting down the steps to the platform. Sometimes they stood in the same ticket line, one behind the other, neither acknowledging the other, as if they were complete strangers. It was a matter of the strange shyness of actors.

He battered Anthony Ainley into becoming his friend. Anthony went with him to a wine tasting. After that, John was always calling with plans for evenings of activity. Anthony got worn out by it.

"I went to this rather dull wine tasting with him and now he wants me to go to something every night. I'm getting fed up with it."

Robin Soans, an extremely able working actor, did not seem to Matthew outstandingly magnetic in sexual terms but he had a colourful past. For some reason an old copy of one of the women's volumes of *Spotlight*, the photo directory of actors and their agents, was found in a corner of the rehearsal room and Robin flipped through it. "I've had her," he said, pointing to a picture of a radiant blonde. He turned a few pages. "And her." He turned a few more pages. "And her." A few more, pointing to a well-known face. "And her…" Matthew was impressed.

The Keeper of Traken introduced two new ongoing cast members to *Doctor Who*, Sarah Sutton as the life-affirming Nyssa and Anthony Ainley as the revived, magisterially evil master. Later on, Matthew got the impression from Sarah that this would always be her favourite *Doctor Who* story. She found Tom difficult to be around, and behind her smile she was not thrilled to be known by him as Miss Basingstoke, after the town she lived in. But the fact is, Tom rather liked her.

She had been an actor for several years and had starred in a serial on BBC1 called *The Moon Stallion*, though she had trained as a dancer. She occupied her space beautifully. Matthew worked over the years with several woman actors who had trained as dancers and they had a particular physical self-containment in common. Dancers were taught to occupy an invisible bubble.

Matthew loved everything about the script for *The Keeper of Traken*, but most exciting of all was the revival after many years of The Master, played in his fire-baked melted form by Geoffrey Beevers, who was, impressively, the husband of Caroline John, transforming right at the end into the sinister and glamorous Anthony Ainley, who for most of the story had played the kindly father of Nyssa, called Tremas. (This was an example of John Nathan-Turner's unhealthy attraction to anagrams). The burnt Master opened the door of his TARDIS, which was in the guise of a grandfather clock, and grabbed Tremas by the throat, and all was darkness for the poor gentle fellow. It was one of Matthew's favourite *Doctor Who* moments ever.

Tony was the son of Henry Ainley, who had been a heart-throb leading man in the early decades of the twentieth century. Matthew's mother told him that the young Henry Ainley had been something of a pin-up for her own mother. Matthew once heard an early audio recording, made during the first decade of the twentieth century, of Henry Ainley in Shakespeare, and it was in the tooth-rattling style of a Victorian ham. Henry had been a womanizer and Tony was the outcome of one of his liaisons. Henry had no objection to guys either. He was a lover of Laurence Olivier, if Olivier's authorized biographer is to be believed.

Anthony had done a fair amount of work as a young man, cropping up in *The Avengers* and similar programmes, and occasionally he got a movie role. Before the BBC supplied him with a postcard of The Master for signing purposes, he fobbed off autograph seekers with a photograph of him in *The Guns of Navarone*, one of countless old action movies Matthew has never seen, this one from an Alistair McLean novel, the kind of stuff Matthew found unreadable even as a boy. He'd liked the James Bond novels, but compared to Alistair McLean, Ian Fleming was a literary genius.

Anthony had been in the running for the part of James Bond, to the extent at least of meeting Cubby Broccoli. But Broccoli had taken one look at him and said, "not tall enough," and that had been the end of that. Anthony's smile was wiped away when he mentioned Cubby Broccoli.

Yes, Matthew loved *The Keeper of Traken* more and more with each passing day. He was in awe of Johnny Byrne anyway, because Johnny had worked as script editor on the Gerry Anderson series *Space: 1999*. Matthew had a slightly skewed memory of this programme, because in his area it had been scheduled on ITV directly opposite *Doctor Who*. This meant that Matthew saw only the first half of each episode before switching over to BBC1. So *Space: 1999* was a melange of strange, often slightly dreamy situations which were never resolved. He only saw the complete episodes when they were repeated on Saturday mornings. It was a tremendously peculiar series because its atmosphere, with white metal walls and *Eagle* spacecraft and military-style uniforms, was, on the surface, that of 'hard,' technological science fiction. But underneath, there was absolutely no science in it. In this, it was like *Doctor Who*. The individual stories, like the premise – the moon, blown out of Earth's orbit, flies from planet to planet through the cosmos – were fantastical and mystical, not science fictional at all.

Matthew loved the scene where the Master took over the body of Tremas. He was full of praise for both Johnny Byrne and John Black. Up in the bar, sitting in a cosy corner with JNT and John Woodnutt and Geoffrey Beevers and Robin Soans, he was going on about ways the scene could be done.

"Of course, you don't *have* to witness the transformation," he said authoritatively, enacting the scene as he described it, his voice dropping to a dramatic Halloween whisper, "it would also be tremendously effective... if you seeeee Tremas and/ then!/the *burnt-up Master* reaches OUT to him!!... and Tremas t-u-r-n-s away and then turns b-a-c-k, his face *hooded*, and he slowly pulls down the hood and – *it's the face of the Master!!* Eeek! And he *laughs MAAADLY!!*" It felt tremendously effective as he worked it out. John Nathan-Turner said it was a good idea.

"I think I see a director in you... but," he added, "I still think it's better to see the face change, actually..."

The conversation turned to ambitions. Everyone was asked to name their biggest ambition. Matthew couldn't think of one, so he said, "To be as great an actor as Olivier by the time I am twenty!" This was greeted with approval all round, as a reasonable ambition for a lad to have.

John said,

"I want to be Controller of One by the time I am forty!"

Controller of BBC1!! Everyone gasped at the scale of this, yet knowing that it was not impossible: it just might come true...

On the last day, at the party, John Woodnutt said goodbye to him.

"You are going to make a brilliant director," he said. Apparently, from Matthew's brief conversation, he had concluded that this was where his heart lay. Perhaps he was hoping that when it came to pass, Matthew would hire him, which in fact he might have done, except that he had never had the slightest ambition to be a director...

Matthew made his first 'public appearance' at John Woodnutt's behest. Every year John arranged a visit from a minor celebrity to open the school fete near his house in Ruislip. Matthew turned up at the school with a heap of his BBC postcards for signing.

He gave a little speech. "What a lovely, sunny, perfect day..." All the children were excited to meet him, but they were equally excited by the sweatshirt he wore, which boasted a lovely image of K9... Assorted parents asked Matthew how they could get hold of one of those shirts.

During rehearsals for *The Keeper of Traken*, the astounding news came out that Tom was to marry Lalla Ward. Marry Lalla Ward??? But he didn't even like her! In the canteen of the rehearsal studios, actors in great numbers gasped and spilt their teas. The circles of Equity could hardly have been more incredulous if it had been announced that Jesus had risen and was joining the cast of *Are You Being Served?*

Peter Moffatt said he'd telephoned to tell them they were out of their minds. "Call it off, now!"

Soon, cartoons began to appear in all of Britain's newspapers. These cartoons tended always to be the same joke: Tom and Lalla at the altar, a vicar asking if anyone knew just cause why these two should not be joined together in matrimony, a gaggle of familiar monsters in pews with their arms and claws and suckers up.

Perhaps it was this news which made *Doctor Who* fans feel frisky. John Nathan-Turner was delighted to show Matthew the Lonely Hearts pages of Time Out, where one entry said: *Doctor seeks his Romana.*

And, further down, another entry: *Gay Doctor seeks his Adric.*

Perhaps also on account of the happy news, Tom Baker, who would never claim to be a generous actor, was often quite sweet to Matthew on *The Keeper of Traken* and *Logopolis*. The quality of a day still depended on his mood, but misery of the scale of *Warriors' Gate* was gone for good. Perhaps it was that he and Lalla were very happy at the time. Perhaps also Tom saw that Matthew was so fragile he needed all the kindness he could find. There were a number of terrific two-hander scenes between the Doctor and Adric, and they came out with a nice warmth. Tom gave him quite a lot of attention, played scenes *with* him rather than *at* him, made useful suggestions and could be friendly, on and off camera.

9

Work on *Logopolis* began with some filming days on a grass verge alongside the M1. Compared to this, a day at a quarry would have been a luxury. It was an old and tired joke about *Doctor Who* that it was all filmed in quarries, but in his two years Matthew never went near a quarry.

It was mid-December. The sky was steel grey when it wasn't raining, which for much of the time it was. A big chunk of those days was spent waiting for breaks in the rain, to snatch the time to shoot a short scene. Matthew's pyjamas quickly became damp and muddy.

Drivers spotted the TARDIS and slowed, like they do at the sight of an accident. Occasionally a car stopped and a parent got out, dragging a wide-eyed boy. The child stared at Tom, with a look as much of bemusement as awe. Tom would wave, and throw his Bakerish smile, sometimes scrawling an autograph on a motorway café serviette hastily pulled from the parent's pocket. It was interesting for Matthew to observe how often these children showed *him* not the slightest glimmer of recognition, though he had been on air for a couple of months by then. It illuminated the strange world of TV stardom: millions of little kiddies who could recognise Tom instantly and would stare at him in wonder, briefly treasuring his signature, on a serviette or on graph paper torn from an exercise book, did not watch his programme.

One of these filming days was Matthew's birthday, most of which was spent standing under big umbrellas. John Nathan-Turner presented him with a birthday cake. Everyone stood under their umbrellas, slices of the cake circulated on tiny white cardboard plates which bent with the weight of rain. The sponge got damp. Lorries roared past. Tom ate some of Matthew's cake.

Rehearsals for studio days began. Val McCrimmon from *Warriors' Gate*, who was also the floor manager for *Logopolis*, was setting things up when Matthew and then Tom arrived.

"Did you see *Doctor Who* on Saturday?" she asked. The first episode of *Warriors' Gate* had been shown. "My God, wasn't it *boring?*"

Tom grunted. Matthew laughed.

A new *Doctor Who* girl called Tegan Jovanka appeared in some M1 location scenes, but Matthew was not around on the day they were filmed, so he did not meet Janet Fielding, the Australian who played her, until the read-through. How the character's surname got past the script-editing stage was a mystery to Matthew.

Janet Fielding was in many ways an impressive character, even intimidating. She was a strong personality. She had a way about her which said 'no bullshit'; tough as old boots. She certainly was pretty tough, having absconded from Australia to make a new life in London. Her given reason for this was men: Australian men were all Neanderthal, she said, she much preferred British. Matthew was willing to believe, having no opposing knowledge, that Australian men had the minds of cave dwellers, but was uncertain as to the liberal fabulousness of the generality of British men.

   She was only twenty-five, though even twenty-five was thought to be over the hill for a modern *Doctor Who* girl, so in newspapers she was twenty-two. She may have been the first *Doctor Who* girl to have had a degree, but this was a degree in journalism, which to Matthew did not quite count. He had no degree in anything, of course.

Most actors smoked, including Matthew very occasionally, and Janet probably smoked no more than the majority of the cast, but afterwards she became so strongly associated in Matthew's mind with a burning cigarette that he could not picture her without one. Many times he was afraid that if he made a silly or naive remark she would stub her cigarette out in his eye. Eventually she gave up smoking and by the time Matthew met her again to do DVD commentaries, she had been fagless for years. He commented on this to her: "What, no cigarette?" Characteristically, she took a veiled, spiky offense, as if he was making a criticism. It is true that Janet without a cigarette was weirdly jarring, like Lord Charles without a monocle.

She found Matthew uninteresting and unintelligent, so it was impossible for him to engage her in conversation. He once made some mild remark about politics and she snapped at him.

"You didn't come up with that on your own! You're regurgitating something you read!"

Matthew, though no whizz kid, had achieved an A in Politics at A level, so he was as competent on the subject as pretty much any boy of his age. But rather than arguing with her, her let it go and said nothing. Oddly, it had crossed Matthew's mind that Janet's own views were plucked from exactly the kind of newspaper column she had been trained to write.

Early on, during *Logopolis*, she made an astonishing claim to an actor during a coffee break.

"I planned my career," she said, puffing away.

The actor was impressed, but Matthew thought that if this was so she had made a terrible error. Matthew knew enough about *Doctor Who* girls and boys to be aware that the series was the worst stepping stone to success imaginable: the kind of stone you leap on to cross a river, only to find it sinks under you and you are having to scrabble back to the shore. One of the *Doctor Who* girls to have had what might be thought a distinguished career, Maureen O'Brien, had had to flee to Canada to achieve it.

   No-one on the series except perhaps Peter Grimwade had more strongly expressed reservations about *Doctor Who*. After they were finished with the series, Janet and Peter became friends and it is easy to imagine their livid discussions on the subject.

Janet's criticisms were acute and often valid. Many of them had to do with her offense at the traditional patriarchal narrative stereotype. The audience, male, adolescent, watched every week a strange but heroic chap rescue incompetent screaming females who turned too easily to jelly. This was completely outmoded in Janet's view. "New formulas for the nineties!" This was a refrain she used on convention panels. "New formulas for the nineties!"

Matthew would not have argued with Janet's views – they were obviously right -but he thought that nominally feminist entertainment like *Star Trek* was more dishonest, putting women into important positions on starships, but only if they had nice legs and huge knockers. If they were fat and dumpy they were allowed on board the Enterprise for comic purposes only. Even in the twenty-first century, long after the end of the sexism-riddled original *Doctor Who*, woman-friendly *Star Trek* saved a tanking spin-off by introducing a female android so tightly dressed that every wobble of her breasts and ripple of her bottom could be observed by the salivating viewers at home. *Doctor Who* was indefensible but it was not fraudulent. And for people bothered by *Doctor Who*, the BBC did at least provide *Blake's 7*, where the women were tougher than the men.

"The trouble with you, Matthew," she said more than once, "is that when it comes to *Doctor Who* you suspend all your critical judgment." This was a well-made point, but then she had no emotional involvement with it and Matthew did. He was intelligent enough to know that if too tough a critical approach was taken to *Doctor Who*, every last moment of it would collapse to dust. It was no good to say *Paradise Towers* was crap but *The Talons of Weng-Chiang* was a classic, without, if you were smart, going to the end of the argument, which was that *The Talons of Weng-Chiang* wasn't all that good either.

This he did not want to happen. Matthew recognised the fragility of the object of his mad affection.

She made a shrewd deduction about Tom Baker. On her first day, she found herself in the pub with him at lunchtime and he was, of course, breathtakingly rude to her.

"I think it's marvellous that they can cast someone like you as a *Doctor Who* girl. You're plain and you've got fat legs. It's very refreshing." It goes without saying that Janet wasn't plain and didn't have fat legs but there was nothing she could say except, *yes, isn't it great?*

The next day, he was sweet as apple pie. Janet decided that he treated people shoddily so that when he was nice to them they would be eternally grateful. Oh, Tom was *nice* to me today, yippee. Janet was, wonderfully, not having it for a moment.

But in a perverse way Tom may have meant what he said. The *Miss World* beauty contest had not yet been banned from British TV and had been shown a few weeks earlier. The next morning Baker had mentioned it.

"I can't stand that bloody *Miss World*! The idea that a woman can't be sexy because she happens to have a big arse..."

Janet noticed that Tom always wore long coats.

"He's tall, but with rather short legs," she said, "short legs on this incredibly long torso. That's why he always wears long coats: so people won't notice how short his legs are."

Peter Grimwade made a suggestion: "Matthew, how about wearing a pair of plimsolls to rehearsals? It will loosen you up."

This sounded to Matthew like a good idea, and he had a pair from school which he had hardly ever worn, being so non-sporty. They were still a nearly pristine white, marked only with one scuff of green, from when he had walked across a wet cricket pitch. He took off his black shoes and put on his plimsolls and felt freed and ready for anything.

Tom spotted him in his plimsolls.

The next day he arrived not only with his dusty old briefcase but also with a brown paper bag. Inside the bag was a pair of plimsolls, not as unworn as Matthew's. He put them on. This was amazingly sweet. So the first batch of rehearsals for *Logopolis* was spent with the two 'stars' skipping around the rehearsal room in light and airy footwear.

Logopolis was not a script which delighted Tom Baker. It did not help that it was written by Christopher Bidmead. These two had not hit it off. It was Christopher, of course, who had – meaning well – warned Matthew about Tom's difficult temperament.

Lynn Richards the floor manager mentioned that they had had a clash on *Meglos*, the cactus episodes. Assorted actors were gossiping before the producer's run. The chattering went on after the run ought to have started and Tom called out, "Come on, let's get to work, this is serious."

Bidmead had snapped back at him, "That's a bit much coming from *you*."

This remark was certainly unhelpful. Tom Baker looked as though he had been kicked in the balls. He never forgave Christopher. An indelible image from the rehearsals for *Logopolis* was of Tom on his knees, drawing with a piece of chalk the arc of a grave, and inscribing within it 'Christopher Bidmead RIP'.

But there was a *Doctor Who* world unknown to the actors, which was the production office. Christopher Bidmead and John Nathan-Turner were not, it was much later revealed to Matthew, finding each other especially comfortable company. Matthew knew nothing of this. Cast members had next to no contact with the production office and were blissfully unaware of its dramas. One staffer, the Production Unit Manager Angela Smith, who worked on the series throughout Matthew's time, was hardly known to him at all. The secretary Jane Judge was a much more prominent figure than Angela in Matthew's world. As far as Matthew understood the job, the Production Unit Manager was the person who oversaw the budget, making sure it was not exceeded.

Bidmead could be a genuinely considerate man. Matthew's contract expired at the end of *Logopolis*. There had been an option to get rid of him after eight episodes, (hence the ambiguous last line of *State of Decay*) but the contract actually expired at the end of the season, with an option to renew on the part of the BBC. Strangely, though Matthew was outrageously happy to be in *Doctor Who*, his new, important agent, Kerry, wanted him out.

"You're a talented young man," he said. "You're too short ever to be a leading man, but you could potentially be a very good working actor. But not if you get stuck with *Doctor Who*, you'll never escape it. I would like you out of it as soon as possible. I know John quite well and I'm going to ask him to let you go."

Whether this conversation ever took place was not to be known to Matthew, and yet he was never formally told by John that he would be coming back. It was only Bidmead who had the courtesy to tell him.

"By the way," he said, almost confidingly, "You *are* being renewed."

That was it. No phone call, ever, from John, just, after a few weeks, a new contract in the post. Thrillingly, it came with a raise of five pounds an episode.

Matthew was once again playing scenes with a movie star. Like George Baker, he was past his peak, or else – Matthew imagined – he would not have consented to play an old fool in a fake beard on *Doctor Who*. This was the charming and extremely friendly John Fraser. John had the rare quality among actors (or anyone else) of finding other people interesting. When he talked to people, he asked about them with more than mere courtesy, as if he was really curious.

Shortly after they met Matthew was up in the canteen with him during a coffee break.

"What do you want to do after *Doctor Who*?"

"I've always wanted to act, but the weird thing is if you'd asked me what I wanted to act in, I would have said first of all *Doctor Who*."

"Really? So all your ambitions have been fulfilled. How wonderful." He looked enormously pleased on Matthew's behalf.

"Not *all,* but it's true that this is the only job I *specifically* wanted."

"Look," he said, when Anthony Ainley joined them, "all this boy's dreams have come true! What is he going to do *now??*"

"Find some more, I suppose," said Matthew.

The subject of sex came around. Anthony mentioned casually that he didn't really have sex much.

"I live without it," he said, apologetically.

John leapt in with his live-and-let-live liberalism.

"That's absolutely fine! You don't have to apologise! Whatever suits a person! If you don't want it, fine! Me, I'm an old scrubber!"

Matthew kept quiet at the time, but he loved the phrase 'old scrubber,' though he was not entirely sure what it meant. He assumed John was saying he slept around a lot, though it was not clear from this whether with men or women. Matthew toyed with adding the term to his lexicon of phrases but it never felt appropriate to use it and did not seem the right description for him. Perhaps if he lives to be eighty and still has sex, he will use it then, proudly, even boastfully. "Me, I'm an old scrubber!" He decided, anyway, he would like anyone who described themselves as an old scrubber.

A particular scene with John Fraser required Matthew to enter in the middle. During rehearsals, Matthew's entrance never occurred at quite the right moment. This was because John did not have his lines memorized yet, and was approximating them. So Matthew made a guess each time and stepped in, always at the wrong moment. With each try, Peter grew more apoplectic.

"Matthew! Get it right!"

John tried to calm him.

"No, Peter, it's not Matthew's fault, it's mine. I keep giving him the wrong cue."

"Oh *no,* John, you're doing everything absolutely right, Matthew's messing it up."

"No Peter, he's doing it right. *I'm* messing it up! I keep giving him the wrong cue!"

"No! No, no, no, it's Matthew's fault. You're doing it perfectly in every way."

"*But I'm not*! I'm *fucking* it up!"

John was a stubborn man and he was not going to allow Grimwade to apportion blame in the wrong quarters. This was an enchanting, unforgettable instance of generosity, and also quite surreal, Peter red-faced, no doubt baffled as to why John was rejecting the praise and claiming the blame. The argument went on like this – "it's *not* your fault, John, it's *not*!"

"But it *is!*" "It's *not!*" "It is!" "It's bloody well *not!*" – for a good few minutes. For this, Matthew felt a little glow of love for John, which never vanished.

Tom began to miss rehearsals more and more often, with less and less advance notice of each absence. Sometimes Peter Grimwade would arrive, to be informed by the assistant floor manager that Tom would not be in 'til two. Tom made most of his money from voiceovers – "Good food costs less at Sainsbury's". A morning doing an ad could net him thousands of pounds.

"Tom… *not here again?*" There wasn't much to rehearse when Tom was away. Instead, there was a lot of coffee and gossip. "I'm not putting up with this." Peter said he was going to ring Tom's agent Jean Diamond and insist he show up for rehearsals every day as required. The next day, Tom turned up.

"I'm afraid that tomorrow morning I won't – "

Peter went white.

" – be doing anything except *Doctor Who.*"

Peter let out a brittle laugh.

It has to be said that the subject of *Doctor Who* cultism cropped up fairly often when Peter Grimwade was around. He was appalled by fandom, and also fascinated by it in a car crash way.

The meaning of the terms 'fan' and 'fandom' were flexible and might even change during a particular conversation. For Peter, who could not abide *Doctor Who*, it seemed to mean anyone dumb enough to switch on the programme at all, for Tom anyone over about ten. (He claimed to adore the little kiddies, but certainly not their parents, who squatted beside them and said, "say hello to him, Gerald, it's Doctor Who!") But sometimes perhaps it meant only those who wrote to the office with sternly expressed but bleakly sub-literate 'opinions'. (Often these came from America where – it seemed – it was possible to enter High School incapable of writing a sentence). It might sometimes have meant only the producers of fanzines, or the one or two individuals who interviewed actors for the Marvel comic. These were men for whom Tom's favoured word for them, 'sententious,' might have been invented. Unlike the rump of *Star Trek* and *Blake's 7* fandom, the *Doctor Who* cult was almost entirely male.

John Nathan-Turner at this time took a purely practical view. "Until they turn on me, I'll be polite to them." Did he suspect that one day they would, in spades? But he was not dazzled. "Think of the most vicious, bitchy queen you've ever met. The worst of the fans are much, much worse."

Shortly before work started on *Logopolis*, there had been a *Doctor Who* convention, at which both Matthew and Peter Grimwade had appeared, along with a busload of other *Doctor Who* people. Peter would not stop bringing it up.

"Those sad gits! What do they want *my* autograph for?" This was a fair question, which Matthew had asked himself. "It's pathetic."

Peter was unwilling even to accept a compliment from a fan.

"A woman wrote to me saying how much she liked my direction of *Full Circle*. She said it had made her weekend. Silly cow!"

Peter shared with Tom an antipathy to the story called *The Robots of Death*. He had worked on these episodes, though not as a director. (Was he the Production Assistant?) This story would be brought up as proof of the chronic ignorance of 'fans'.

"You remember that piece of *crap*, *The Robots of Death*, Tom?" he would ask, in his offended curate's voice. Tom Baker said he did and looked pained at the thought. "Christ, wasn't that a complete mess? That was the worst piece of writing I've ever seen! And those *fans* think it's an absolute classic!" He would emit a small snorty laugh. "They keep voting it the *best story ever!* They haven't a *clue!*"

The script for *Logopolis* that dropped through the letter box was weird and inventive, with its Russian Doll effect and its shrinking ray and its computer language. Perhaps because Chris was script-editing himself, an occasional story contradiction had slipped through. For instance, there was a scene where the Doctor said to Adric that he thought the Master was on *Logopolis*. Two scenes later Adric asked, in cross-eyed amazement, whether the Master could *possibly* be on *Logopolis*, as though it had never been suggested.

The bulk of filming days had been spent doing little scenes going to and from the TARDIS and the first scenes to be done in the studio were the reverses of those scenes, going out and coming back in. The continuity woman was aware that, because it had been so wet on the filming days, Matthew's pyjamas had been damp and muddy, so someone from make-up stood just off the TARDIS set, spraying him with the kind of narrow nozzle used for weed-killers in greenhouses. He never looked quite as dripping wet for the interior scenes as he had out of doors, but no-one could deny that the effort was being made.

There were enough TARDIS scenes to fill up the whole of the first studio day. Perhaps because there were so many the time rotor gave up the ghost. Before it could be mended a question had to be addressed: was the TARDIS console a set or a special effect? Some minutes were spent ruminating over this matter. It was important. The BBC was a strongly

Blue Box Boy: A Memoir of Doctor Who in Four Episodes

unionized institution – which was fine with Matthew – and if the wrong department set about repairing it a strike could quite easily ensue.

A tense, whispery few minutes ticked by. It was eventually decided that Mat Irvine of the special effects department should take charge but he repeated the question a couple of times for reassurance to a person from the sets department, his arms open, hands out, as if to underline his appeal: are you sure? Are you okay with that? Are you quite sure? Yes, grunted the set person. It was not in any official way agreed as a precedent that the time rotor was a special effect. All that was agreed was that for now Mat Irvine and his colleagues could repair it.

Or try to.

Tom and Matthew stepped off the set. A bearded man from Special Effects squatted under the console and removed a panel and set to work. For ages all anybody saw of him was his bottom. He tugged wires and hammered but the rotor remained stubbornly as dead as a doornail. Half an hour of valuable studio time went by before the man emerged and said, sorry, it's completely broken. It'll take hours and hours to mend.

But there were not hours and hours available. By ten o'clock the TARDIS scenes had to be on tape, or else.

Mat Irvine had an idea. He and his colleague would manually operate the time rotor. This meant squatting under the console again, from where the rotor would be pushed up and down by hand.

After a while this must have been extremely tiring. And thus the scenes were recorded.

When Matthew saw the episode, he was impressed to see that Mat Irvine and his pal had operated the rotor with a fair approximation of the familiar up-and-down rhythm, though Matthew thought that occasionally there was a wobble and occasionally a loss of rhythm which the average viewer was unlikely to notice. As the *Acorn Antiques* producer said in a faux documentary, "we professionals notice but Joe Public never clocks a thing!"

A couple of weeks later, back in the studio, Peter Grimwade said that a problem with the microphones which had only become apparent later when he looked at the tape meant that a couple of lines from these TARDIS scenes had to be rerecorded. Matthew assumed this meant sitting in a booth watching the tape, but this was not so.

"Just say the lines, we'll put them on."

"But how will we know we've said them at the same speed?"

"Oh, just do it."

So, standing on the studio floor, they said the lines again. The result was that for a few seconds on the episode neither Matthew's nor Tom's lips were in sync with their voices, which was rather sweet.

Tony Ainley said how he hated leaving TV Centre after a long day in the studio and having to drive all the way to Hampstead. Matthew said, in a casually throwaway manner,

"Oh, I just sleep over!"

"Really?" Tony was stunned. "Maybe I'll try that."

"The only thing is, they lock the dressing rooms, so if there's a fire..."

"Well, there won't be, will there!"

"And you must take care not to give the cleaner a nervous breakdown."

And on one *Logopolis* studio day, Matthew arrived to see Tony looking extremely tired and distracted.

"I slept in my dressing room! It was awful! Noisy and cold! I didn't sleep a wink!"

"Sorry! I did warn you!"

Tom arrived and began talking in the corridor off the dressing rooms about the BBC Shakespeare production of *The Merchant of Venice*, with Warren Mitchell as Shylock, which had been shown the night before.

"After five minutes of Alf Garnett doing Shakespeare -" he quoted a line in Warren Mitchell's style – "*Has a Jew eyes??* – I switched the bloody thing off."

Tony tried to look interested, an artificial smile fell on his face, but he was too tired to care about *The Merchant of Venice*.

Matthew's own occasional staying over came to an abrupt end. Up in the bar with John Nathan-Turner, he lost track of time, so when he came down he found his dressing room had been locked.

This was worrying, because the last tube had long gone from White City. He decided sleeping in his dressing room was a perfectly respectable thing to do so he went and found a security guard.

"Open my dressing room this minute!"

"Why?"

"So I can sleep in it!"

The guard looked put out.

"You can't sleep in your dressing room, young man!"

"Why ever not? Open up!"

"This is a most unusual request. I can't just let you in. I know! We'll ask the boss!"

Rats, thought Matthew. They took a lift up to the floor above, where a uniformed man with the face of a nark sat at a desk.

"What???" said the man. "You can't possibly sleep in TV Centre. It's not safe! We lock all the doors! What if there was a fire?"

"There won't be, will there!"

"I can't possibly allow you to sleep here, young man. It's out of the question! More than my job's worth!"

"But the trains have gone, and I have to be back here tomorrow morning." Plus, he wanted to add, I know Tom Baker lived in an Acton green room for weeks, so what's the difference?

"There are a number of Bee and Bees on Wood Lane, young man. I suggest you go and ask at them!"

Matthew left TV Centre and turned right and, at half past twelve at night, thumped first one bell then another. The houses were very still and dark, the curtains very drawn. At the fourth house, he decided he was not going to stop ringing until someone answered or the police arrived so he could sleep in a nice, cosy cell. He rang and rang and rang until a small Pakistani man wearing only his pyjama bottoms answered the door. He looked hardly awake.

"Yeeezzz?"

"I need a place for the night!" Matthew made an effort to sound both desperate and completely unthreatening. He made his accent as posh as he could so that he would not be taken for a criminal.

The man looked at him and weighed him up. In a room off the hall, a woman lying on a mattress on the floor pulled a sheet over her breasts.

"Twelve pounds!" he said. "Including breakfast!"

"Fine!"

He handed over the cash and signed the guest book. He noted that all the other guests had paid seven pounds. The man took him up to a plain single room with a sink which had only a cold tap.

Matthew fell into the bed, and slept deeply, but woke early and scarpered from the guest house long before breakfast. He had an orange juice at TV Centre. Sarah Sutton showed up, perky.

"Slept in your dressing room again, Matthew?"

"Yes, he said. "And a very restful night it was too."

Matthew had mentioned to John and the Production Unit Manager, Angela Smith, that he occasionally dossed in his dressing room, so, though it did not have official approval, it was by then known to the *Doctor Who* office.

A stern note was sent to them from the security office, to the effect that *Doctor Who* cast members were not permitted to use TV Centre as a hotel.

"You've been found out," said Angela Smith. "Sorry, but you can't do it anymore."

"Bum," said Matthew.

He mentioned it to Lynn Richards.

"It's incredible that you were able to stay even for a single night. Those security guards are supposed to check inside every dressing room before it's locked. That's their job. "

"I've listened over several nights. They never look inside. They just lock them."

"They're supposed to look into every single dressing room every time!"

In the Castle on the last day of rehearsal for *Logopolis*, Tom was in a good mood. He bought Matthew a drink and talked to him. Matthew asked him if he thought he would ever watch *Doctor Who* again.

"That's a good question," Tom said, putting on his thinking face, "*I don't know.*"

And what, Matthew asked, trying not to sound overly probing, did he want to do now?

Tom's eyes widened in the way of the Fourth Doctor.

"I want," he said in his biggest voice, "*to be a huge star.*"

The set for the planet *Logopolis* was one of the most delightfully artificial of all *Doctor Who* 'exterior' planet sets. When characters ran across its rocky terrain, the hollow indoors thud could plainly be heard of boots on papier-maché over a wooden frame. This leant it the intimate quality of village hall theatre.

Peter sprang about on the set in his usual way, vaguely furious with everyone. Tom said on his breath,

"What does that man think he's doing, running around as if he's got a snake up his arse?"

Coming to the end of shooting on Tom Baker's last day as Doctor Who, Tom and Matthew were standing together in the dark, waiting to enter a scene. Tom suddenly said, out of the blue, "The thing I always hated about this programme was that they never let us have a live audience. Every other bloody sitcom is recorded before a live audience, why not *Doctor* bloody *Who?*"

Matthew agreed that it would have been nice, though *Logopolis*, whatever its merits, was not very funny.

"Now, Tom," said Peter Grimwade, "we're going to record your dying shriek." The final scene before the regeneration of Doctor Who was his fall from a gantry hundreds of feet above ground. Smashing to earth, his body was internally broken into a million pieces, though on the outside he looked only slightly pale, as if getting over the flu.

*   *   *

It was intended that, during the fall, a terrible cry be heard, shattering the tea times of millions of viewing kiddies, like this:
Aaaaaaaaaaaaaaaaaaaaaaahhhhhhhhhhhhhhhhh!!!
Tom Baker thought it was ludicrous. Peter didn't. Here was a rock-and-hard-place collision. But no-one could get Tom to do something he was determined not to do, so no cry was ever taped. This is why the awful drop was eerily silent. Peter had been wrong, of course, and Tom had been right: the silence was more effective than all the shrieks of hell.

Christopher was fascinated by computers and he talked romantically of floppy discs and bytes. He and John had presided over what would remain the single most cerebral season of *Doctor Who*, making many brave, adventurous commissions. The script editing job had first been offered to Johnny Byrne, who had turned it down because he wanted to stay in Norfolk.

There were viewers who thought *Logopolis* was a *Doctor Who* masterpiece.
"Christopher Bidmead is the best *Doctor Who* writer ever," said one humourless elf, "even better than Robert Holmes." "His dialogue is like *poetry,*" said an earnest boy who had never read a poem. Not all lads were smitten. Gary Russell said to Matthew, "the *only* good thing about that *load of bollocks* is John *Fraser!*"
"It's an intellectual wank," Tom said of *Logopolis*. Matthew liked the episodes as they finally came out, particularly the first, with the ever-darkening TARDIS set, the laughing master, the Russian doll effect, the shadowy atmosphere. The first episode cliffhanger, Tegan's aunt shrunk to the size of a Barbie doll, was weird and impressive.

It was one of those stories which took place on a *massive* scale. Occasionally, between the little invasions of England which the Doctor dealt with snappily, there were aliens and monsters with much grander ambitions, whose planned conquests were not of Earth or the galaxy, but of the entire universe. Something *vast* might happen: Douglas Adams caused the Big Bang, Adric wiped out the dinosaurs and created the conditions for the human race. Talk about Big History! In *Logopolis*, the Master managed to destroy large swathes of the universe, including Nyssa's home planet Traken, witnessed by Nyssa in a moment wonderfully done by Sarah Sutton. Barry Letts bumped into Christopher in the corridor.

"What are you going to do next, Chris, now you've blown up half the universe?"

The episodes went from a rainy motorway to the exterior of the universe. The TARDIS went outside the universe and looked back into it. The universe looked very like a galaxy.

A few years later Matthew lived in a flat with some actors who had acquired satellite TV for a month as a free trial offer. They were not really interested in TV and this subscription had been taken out in a spirit of giggling exploration – queeny Equity members dying to see what American daytime soaps were like – with the intention of cancelling when payment was demanded. The free month coincided with a repeat of *Logopolis* at the unusual hour of weekday midnights, no longer aimed at families with teenage kiddies, but at actors and waiters and bar staff and other booze-soaked insomniacs. It was watched by Matthew and his friends while circulating a two litre bottle of plonk. After agreeing that Matthew was a genius, they all said they thought the programme was good fun, and at the last shot of the first episode – the shot of the miniature aunt – Matthew's friend Helen gave a little squeaky gasp. "My God!" she said.

Matthew was pleased with the midnight serial, and he found himself thinking with pleasure and amazement and relief, "Gor Blimey! *Doctor Who*! I still bloody like it! I still effing enjoy *Doctor* bloody *Who*, even when I have to watch myself."

After the final studio day of *Logopolis*, a small farewell party was thrown for Tom, but he did not turn up to it, so various cameramen and floor managers stood about, drinking bad wine, talking about nothing but the fact that Tom had not shown up. Tom had in fact flown off to Soho, where two separate parties were being thrown for him by assorted alcoholic bohemians, no doubt with his fragrant fiancée in attendance. Matthew did not doubt that the parties in Soho were much to be preferred to the miserable little do in a TV Centre dressing room, windowless and with harsh strip lighting and the nasal complaints of floor managers and the drinking of paint-stripper wine and the talking of shop.

Matthew had given John Leeson and Lalla Ward 'Good Luck' cards when they'd left, but he did not give one to Tom. A few weeks earlier Tom had mentioned that his birthday was coming up soon. "We'll have a bit of a knees-up at lunchtime!" he said.

Matthew bought him quite a funny birthday card and brought it in to work but he realized sinkingly when Tom arrived, in a perfectly good mood, that he could not bring himself to wish him a happy birthday and hand him a card. It would have been vastly embarrassing. In the evening, he dropped the signed, enveloped card into the bin by North Acton tube station, near the newspaper seller. No lunch-time knees-up had occurred.

A grander party was to be thrown a month or so later. Matthew received a gold-embossed invitation, RSVP. He wasn't certain he wanted to accept, not being one for parties at the best of times, but in the end he went, out of curiosity mainly. Tom Baker's farewell party: a red letter day in *Doctor Who* history. It was weird to think that he was going to such a party, both because it was unimaginable for him that he was in a position to be invited and also because it was incredible that Tom, who it might be imagined would have clung on to the series until death's door, had given it up. (It was never flatly stated to Matthew that it had been a decision other than Tom Baker's, and it was none of his business).

At least this party was not taking place in a dressing room, but in a spacious room with a burgundy carpet. A long table covered in a cloth was lined with an array of snacks and cheap wine. Surprise: Tom did not come – and of course neither did Lalla Ward – so the conversation, infuriatingly, turned again to the fact that Tom was not there. Matthew didn't care. He wished he wasn't there too. He stood in a group with Janet and Sarah. A thin, small, serious-looking man in a jacket, clutching a glass of wine, came up to Sarah and said hello.

"Hello," said Sarah.

"Sorry," said the man with a smile, apologizing for interrupting the little group, "but Sarah and I know other."

They chatted for thirty seconds and then the man went away.

"That was Philip Hinchcliffe," said Sarah. Matthew felt a stab of excitement. He had heard of Philip Hinchcliffe, of course, because Hinchcliffe had produced Tom's earliest programmes. He did not look as Matthew had imagined him, as far as Matthew could be said to have imagined him at all. He had produced more than his share of *Doctor Who* 'classics'. Recently, he had had a mild success with a TV series about a soldier, which had elicited less than admiring remarks from John Nathan-Turner, and later he produced a dreadful but well-meant film version of a novel by one of Matthew's favourite writers, Beryl Bainbridge.

Who knows what other 'geniuses' of Tom Baker's run as Doctor Who were present in that room? Was Graham Williams there? Or was he already dead, shot – Matthew was told – in a terrible hunting accident, taken for a deer, a fox, by one of his friends, in much the way the protagonist of an old folk song shot his woman whom he mistook for a swan? But would Graham Williams have wanted to come to the party, his relationship with Tom being so fraught that the Controller of BBC 1 had gathered them in a room and knocked their heads together and told them they had to make the effort to tolerate each other, or he would fire them both? Perhaps Robert Holmes was there somewhere, and it would be surprising if Terrance Dicks, never one to be absent when bottles of wine were uncorked, even bad bottles, had not made an appearance.

Anthony Read and David Fisher? Were they there? Matthew had met David Fisher at an earlier party and David Fisher – very white-haired, plump, with tired eyes – had looked, not unreasonably, extremely uninterested when introduced to Matthew. He had shortly before written a script for the TV series *The Hammer House of Horror* and Matthew said how much he liked it. David Fisher gave him a blank look.

A few years later, Matthew bought a remarkably fat book about Hitler and Stalin. After twenty pages he decided that it was not his kind of book. When he had put it down he began to wonder about the names of the authors: David Fisher? Anthony Read? *Why on earth do I know those names?* Then it clicked. Good grief. For the *Doctor Who* actor, *Doctor Who* comes up all the time in the most unexpected ways.

Was Douglas Adams there? But Douglas Adams had brilliantly made his escape from any association with *Doctor Who*, having already become a household name for *The Hitchhikers' Guide to the Galaxy*. Douglas Adams had even refused to allow Terry Dicks – or anyone else – to get their hands on his *Doctor Who* scripts, and they remained probably the only *Doctor Who* stories from the old run never to be sculpted into little novels.

Whoever it was among the milling crowd, there was a fairish turnout all told, but of course all anybody could say was, Tom's not here, isn't he *strange?* That, and the usual TV chatter. Matthew could not wait to leave, and to go to Ronnie Scott's where dedicated artists made intelligent music and it was all right – *de rigueur*, in fact – not to care about what was coming up on BBC1. Telly talk drove him to distraction.

Once an actor is a *Doctor Who* actor he is a *Doctor Who* actor forever. Not everyone was delighted by this association, but Matthew of course was perfectly happy with it. When actors he worked with in theatre found out he had been in *Doctor Who* for a long time, those that had stories about it would tell them to him, whether he wanted to hear them or not. Those that had had no direct experience would come up with some tiny childhood reminiscence: "That William Hartnell was so great…" … "Wasn't that Roger Delgado scary?" … "Were you a Sea Devil?"

Sometimes they would ask, which Doctor Who? Tom and Peter, said Matthew, feeling smug to have straddled, so speak, two of them. (Arguably three, if you counted his ghost-like floating head as Peter turned into Colin). It sounded as if he had been in the programme for years and years and years. "Peter Davison, nice man, I was in *All Creatures* once." "I really liked Peter Davison. I had a scene in *Campion* with him, in an old car. What a *nice* man." But: "Tom Baker???" "You worked with *him*? Isn't he supposed to be a nightmare?"

Tom Baker stories occasionally flew to Matthew, like interesting but doubtful news of a far-off relative brought by carrier-pigeon. An instance came from a woman Matthew knew who had worked with him on a

191

z-grade medical soap. She encountered at a party a man who described himself as Tom Baker's best friend!

"I've been Tom's best friend for years and years," he said. "It's always seemed strange to me that in all these years I have never once met anyone who worked with him. It's odd. What's it like, working with him?"

The woman was direct. It was her way.

"@@#!^&&&!!?@!"

"Yes, yes," said Tom's friend, laughing. "I've always suspected that."

He heard another story, bizarrely, in the flat of a guy with whom he was having a brief fling. The girl in the upstairs flat came down one morning for some sugar. Matthew was tidying up the kitchenette.

"Bloody hell," said the girl at the door to Matthew's friend. "We had that Tom Baker in our shop the other day."

Matthew's ears pricked up.

"He's a one!" said the girl. She worked in Freeman, Hardy and Willis, a shoe shop in Oxford Street, a spit from Soho. "Last Friday afternoon he comes in to the shop and he says really loud, 'I want some shoes!' So I say, well, Mister Baker, we've got *lots* of shoes, what size are you? So I get out box after box of shoes and he tries them all on and he doesn't like any of them. There are shoes all over the floor and he puts on his old bashed-up shoes and he walks right out, saying, 'You haven't got the shoes for me. Christ, no wonder people take the piss out of Freeman, Hardy and Willis'."

In the strange way in which memory stimulates memory, this reminded Matthew of a hitherto entirely forgotten childhood moment. In the first episode of *Spearhead From Space*, the new Third Doctor is in hospital obsessing about his shoes. "I want my shoes!" he says repeatedly.

Not long after this episode was broadcast, Matthew had to go to hospital, and he spent the first hour in the bed asking the nurse where his shoes were. "I want my shoes!" he said, just like Doctor Who. "I want my shoes!"

He dearly wished he had two hearts, because he would love to have baffled the doctors with the unique arrangement of his insides in the way those *Spearhead From Space* doctors had been baffled.

EPISODE THREE
FORTH TO DOOMSDAY

Life that begins absurdly will go on absurdly to the end. The lines don't change on the palm.

Graham Greene, **Ways of Escape**

One recalls Irving's wife, "Tell me, Henry, do you intend to spend the rest of our married life making a fool of yourself in public?"

Peter Vansittart, **Quartet**

1

As if Tom Baker had not already been getting enough press attention from his engagement to Lalla Ward, it was announced, just before rehearsals began for *The Keeper of Traken*, that he was to leave *Doctor Who* at the end of the season. After seven years! Two more than Jon, more than twice as many as William Hartnell or Patrick Troughton!

Tom and John Nathan-Turner had kept the news close to their chests, so Matthew found out at the same time as everybody else. Tom went on the BBC1 evening news magazine *Nationwide* – the programme for which Matthew had cut up newspapers a few months earlier. He wore his tatty blue pinstripe and blue shirt, open-collared, the outfit he pulled from his wardrobe whenever a nod to formality was required. He looked like somebody you wouldn't buy a used car off. It was a look which Matthew found charming. He leant against the TARDIS, which appeared to be propping him up. His arms were folded. It was possible to suspect that he was a bit the worse for wear, though John Nathan-Turner, who was hovering off camera in his customary way, later told Matthew that Tom had not had very much to drink. "Only a couple..."

He was interviewed by a presenter called Sue – the wife, at the time, of the guitarist John Williams. Matthew had met her at Pebble Mill on the day of his first TV appearance. Interviewing Tom Baker, Sue looked distinctly uncomfortable. She asked him about his future plans.

"Do you want to move on to more serious work?"

Tom looked insulted and barked at her something to the effect that *Doctor Who* was perfectly serious. He half-mitigated his cantankerousness with the familiar toothy grin, and Sue looked apologetic, her mouth formed a peculiar gritted half-smile which she held for the rest of the interview, which was stilted, long pauses between questions and answers, Tom's wide stare boring down on Sue as though she had profoundly affronted him.

It took only seconds for an ITV children's producer to come up with an idea: Tom and Lalla, radiant newlyweds and now both about to be unemployed, should have their own show! An educational series about astronomy was in preparation, and Tom and Lalla would be the perfect presenting duo!

But Tom, and perhaps Lalla too, thought the idea was a bit, well, exploitative, so they said no. When the programme appeared it was presented not by Tom or Lalla or actors at all, but two professional astronomy experts, a girl and a guy, young and with a hint of glamour. For a while Heather Cooper, the woman, became the go-to girl for opinions about astronomy on BBC news programmes.

Matthew had *The Hound of the Baskervilles* in his bag one morning alongside his script and had read the first chapter on the train. His head was full of it when Tom arrived and said he had just been offered the part of Sherlock Holmes in a theatre version of the novel. This sort of coincidence, without particular meaning but strange, happened often to Matthew. He said how great the book was, though he did not say he had been reading it twenty minutes earlier.

"I love that scene with the reflection in the silver tea-pot."

"Oh yes!" said Tom, who had perhaps flicked though the book that morning as well.

"And of course," said Matthew, remembering the character as pictured by him, "Sherlock is very arrogant, isn't he?"

"Very!"

"And he never *smiles,* does he?"

"Never smiles, not at all!" Tom made an expression which said, to smile would be fatal.

As far as Matthew knew, the play was never produced with Tom in it, but some time later he played Holmes in a TV serial version, produced by Barry Letts and script-edited by Terrance Dicks. Tom's Sherlock was closely modelled on his Doctor Who, with the familiar wave and, many times at moments of high drama, the very familiar smile. The production, though thrilling, was reduced in its impact by a rather sweet and pettable hound which, even covered in glowing paint, could not scare anyone.

If Tom was going, the question came up, who will take his place?

The BBC was crawling with *Doctor Who* fans, including the man who ran the *Doctor Who* Appreciation Society, who had some position somewhere in TV Centre, perhaps as a labourer in the *Blue Peter* garden. He was pleasant enough, but he had the brashness of a cocky teenager, even though he was creeping into his thirties. He came up to Matthew after a studio day and slapped the bar and said, "So, who's the new Doctor then?"

Matthew didn't know and if he had he wouldn't have been allowed to say, but he was irritated at the way the question had been asked. He

Blue Box Boy: A Memoir of Doctor Who in Four Episodes

leant in to the man and, perhaps thinking of Richard Willis, he said in a melodramatic whisper, "*Don't tell anyone this,* but they've offered it to Laurence Olivier."

"Really??"

"He hasn't accepted it yet, but he's considering the offer at this moment. *Keep it to yourself.*"

Even if this had not been totally absurd on the face of it, it was general knowledge that Olivier was aging badly and could now scarcely walk. Matthew was taken aback to see from the bright light in the man's wide eyes that the joke had been swallowed whole. A month or two later, a short piece appeared on one of the gossip pages of *Private Eye* reporting the latest rumour running rampage in the BBC: the role of *Doctor Who* had been offered to Laurence Olivier. Which says something profoundly unnerving about the way in which gossip flies from one big mouth to another.

More concretely, in 1966, one actor of very high calibre *had* been approached. The part of the Second Doctor had first been offered to Michael Hordern, long before he became Sir Michael. He turned it down flat.

"If I'd done that, I'd never have bloody worked again!"

When journalists asked Tom Baker about who the next Doctor should be, he said, "It should be a woman!"

This superb, constructive suggestion was reported in every newspaper, and caused an influx of furious letters to the *Doctor Who* office, all of them beginning, "I am not sexist, but..." and going on to say that if the Doctor was a woman "I will never watch the programme again!" JNT did not think the world was ready for a female Doctor, but he loved the publicity.

A friend telephoned Matthew. "Have you heard the news?"

"What news?"

"About the new Doctor Who?"

"No."

"It was announced on the nine o'clock news. It's Peter Davison."

"Peter Davidson? From *All Creatures Great and Small*?"

"Yup. It's not Davidson. It's Davison."

"It's an interesting choice."

"Yes. Very."

With Olivier out of the running, John Nathan Turner could hardly have chosen any more unexpected actor.

*   *   *

Peter Davison was, in his way, as unusual a figure as Tom Baker. He was the most visible actor on TV. He was a kind of sex symbol among Britain's housewives. When the news came out, no-one said, "Peter who?" as they'd said, "who's this Troughton person?" or "Who on earth is Tim Barker?"

All Creatures Great and Small was his most famous series. The blend of cute animals and country nostalgia and old cars and bucolic shots of the moors was not Matthew's thing, and he was hardly alone in this among teenage lads. But *All Creatures* was not the whole story: Peter was also in two sitcoms simultaneously, one on ITV and one on the BBC. Once he started to appear in *Doctor Who* he was on TV, or so it seemed, more nights than he was not. Nothing like it had ever happened before on British TV.

As an actor, he was able to suggest competence in all things. He needed only the right togs. If you supplied him with greasy overalls he would instantly look like an able car mechanic, if you put a horsehair wig on him he would look like a brilliant lawyer, if you put goggles on him like a race car driver, if you put him in a silk dressing gown, like a twenties wit. Give him a machine gun and a homburg hat, he looked like a gangster. If you put him next to a cradle he looked like a loving if overwhelmed father. If you stood him beside some stumps, he looked like he could go into bat for England.

So persuasive was Peter's aura of competence that – he told his *Doctor Who* girls and boy – he had been hired for his first job in a commercial as one of several young men who were to ride huge Harley motorbikes across a muddy field. Having convinced the director of his skill, he found himself in a bit of a tizzy when he was offered the job, because he had never touched a motorbike in his life. When he got to the location, he found that none of the other cast members could ride either: every single one of them had conned their way into the job. Bloody hell!, said the director, just sit on the bloody things and make them go.

Peter found himself in a quandary – it seemed to Matthew – when he was offered the part of Doctor Who. His career was going fabulously well as it was. The last thing he wanted was to become associated only with *Doctor Who*, finding after he left that the flow of work dried up. And he was much younger than the other Doctors: it must have been possible, on a sleepless night, to imagine the future a terrifying fifty-year tunnel of *Doctor Who* conventions. It took some energetic persuasion on the part of John Nathan-Turner, including no doubt many free lunches at the French restaurant on Wood Lane, the munching of countless snails in garlic butter and bottle after bottle of freely flowing wine, to get him to sign.

For Peter, the doubts about *Doctor Who* – Matthew deduced – never quite vanished. He would much rather have been larking about in Yorkshire with Christopher Timothy and Robert Hardy than stuck in the Tunbridge Wells rain with Matthew, and he could hardly have been blamed for this.

He was the first Doctor young enough to have grown up watching the early episodes, though, being around eleven or twelve when the first programmes appeared in nineteen sixty-three, perhaps just a sliver too old. The series had made only the vaguest impression on his boyhood and he rarely expressed a clear memory of a particular moment, though when talking about *Earthshock* he mentioned the early Cybermen with their cloth faces. "Oh yes, them," said Matthew knowledgably, remembering *The Doctor Who Monster Book*. "This boy," Peter said, turning to Sandra, his wife, "knows *everything*."

Did Peter ever own a ball-bearing Dalek? It seems unlikely.

He was a tiny bit nervous about promotional interviews for *Doctor Who*. He had never been in a series which had such a history, and it was inevitable that he would be asked what he thought of the old Doctors. He probably didn't have particularly strong views on any of them, though he made a polite comment about each. But when one interview appeared in print, he was afraid that it might offend Jon Pertwee, though the remark which worried him was a masterpiece of blandness: "Jon is a comic actor, so it's surprising that his *Doctor Who* is the least jokey."

Peter's arrival coincided with a major change in the scheduling of *Doctor Who*. Having been established since November 23rd 1963 as a part of Saturday tea-times during the darker months, it was now to go out on Monday and Tuesday evenings at 7:00, or thereabouts, for thirteen weeks of the year. Matthew himself felt sad about this change, if only for sentimental reasons, but perhaps, along with the Fifth Doctor, it had a refreshing, new-minting effect.

When Matthew later met *Doctor Who* fans who told him they would watch *Doctor Who* videos *only* at half past five on a Saturday, he thought they were ridiculous, but to be fair, there was something strongly associative about the time slot, as there was about the twenty-five minute running time. In the mid-eighties he saw a repeat of *Warriors' Gate* on PBS in a hotel room in Boston. It had been edited into a TV movie and ran from ten until midnight and it felt very strange indeed.

John Nathan-Turner liked Peter Davison very much as an actor and as a person. They had worked together on *All Creatures*. John and his boyfriend Gary had a dog called Pepsi, who had made regular appearances on the programme.

In the bar John narrated an example of Peter's exceptional niceness.

Peter was doing a publicity photo shoot when a boy on a bicycle, passing in the background, began showing off, indulging in little stunts.

This resulted in the boy and his bike toppling into a pond. Peter ran across and pulled the boy from the water.

The photographers begged Peter and the boy to re-enact this moment for their cameras. Peter refused.

"Isn't that incredible? He's *such* a nice man," said John.

Peter was certainly good-humoured. He had a favourite film from which he could quote large chunks. This was *National Lampoon's Animal House*. Matthew never saw the film, but after a few months in Peter's company, it was as if he had.

Peter's first story in production order, though not the first to be broadcast, was *Four to Doomsday*, long-term BBC hack Terence Dudley's sole stab at writing space opera. Peter knew Terence Dudley of old, and had not warmed to him. It would have been interesting to overhear Tom and Peter sharing their views of Mr. Dudley.

Matthew met Terence Dudley once or twice and thought he was nice enough as crusty old BBC fellows went. He was reputed to be an enormous snob. He always went First Class on the train, and said that this was because he couldn't possibly concentrate on his writing in the noise of Second Class.

He did slightly bother Matthew by saying to him at a party:

"I've been commissioned to kill you off!"

John Nathan-Turner got wind of this and the next day rushed to Matthew.

"I hear one of my writers has given you the wrong information. He has not been commissioned to do anything of the sort."

Weirdly, *Four to Doomsday* had a one-off script editor. This was a young guy called Antony Root. Intensely polite, he occasionally faxed to Acton, where rehearsals were well underway, new, substitute pages, the only time this happened while Matthew was in *Doctor Who*. He was never formally introduced to Matthew or, as far as Matthew knew, to other cast members. Having finished *Four to Doomsday*, he disappeared as swiftly and silently as he had arrived, eventually to become one of the most important people in British TV.

The BBC bureaucrats loved having committee meetings and changing things around. Perhaps it was their idea of fun. Angela Smith, who had been the Production Unit Manager on Matthew's first season, was now called the Production Associate. Her job was exactly the same, nothing but the name had been changed. The reason for it had been, apparently, to make the job sound more important. In the view of every Production Unit Manager Matthew ever talked to, including his Aunt Liz, this was not the effect. They all thought Production Associate sounded like a demotion.

Peter was so overwhelmed with work that *Doctor Who* was essentially a part-time job. He spent the mornings rehearsing a sitcom set up North, and the afternoons on *Four to Doomsday*. The Doctor is such a prominent presence in the programme that, though there were other scenes to rehearse, there were moments when, without Peter, everything ground to a halt and people twiddled their thumbs, as when Tom had disappeared to do a voiceover.

Terence Dudley may have claimed to know little of science fiction, but *Four to Doomsday* was a very decent space entertainment, with an appealing blend of the futuristic spaceship and ancient rituals, including a stunningly beautiful Chinese dragon. It had a cast unusually exotic for *Doctor Who*, with Chinese and Indian actors all over the place. The TARDIS children bickered with each other in scenes of unusual life and fizz. It was rare for *Doctor Who* companions to behave like real people, and in these scenes they pretty much did.

The whole thing was helped by another terrific cast, including Matthew's third encounter with a movie star he had not heard of. This was Burt Kwouk.

Burt Kwouk was one of the most relaxed actors Matthew ever met, a wonderful man extremely happy with the success he had enjoyed, and completely unpretentious. Everything was lively when Burt was around. He was best known, of course, for *The Pink Panther* films. These comedy classics were yet another example of Matthew's boundless ignorance. He'd only ever seen one, and had found it cruel. He could not figure out what was so funny about watching the Herbert Lom character having a gradual nervous breakdown over two laboured hours. Chuck Jones had pursued a similar theme in *One Froggy Evening*, but that had only lasted seven minutes. Matthew did not make the connection between Burt and the Chinese man in *The Pink Panther* until the AFM Val McCrimmon told him. Val had worked with Burt of old and greeted him like a friend. She struck Matthew as slightly flirtatious in Burt's company.

Burt liked all his jobs.

"Doing the *Pink Panther* films is fun," he said in the make-up room, "but doing *Doctor Who* is fun too."

Just as a tiny number of black actors had cornered the market in virtually the only employment opportunities available at the time, African dictators bedecked with medals walking down aeroplane steps on TV thrillers – and one Noble Savage in a Patrick Troughton Cyberman story – so Burt had cornered the market in Chinese characters. There weren't many Chinese characters, but when there was one it was Burt.

Stratford Johns was not a movie star, but he was, though South African by birth, one of the most recognisable faces in Britain as a result of playing a fat detective called Barlow, first on *Z-Cars*, then on a spin-off called *Softly, Softly*, then on another spin-off, *Barlow At Large*. The character was even roped in for a BBC2 documentary series about Jack the Ripper. Barlow filled up twenty years of Stratford Johns' life. Barlow must have been the first TV character to have multiple different series. Yet a woman who knew Stratford Johns told Matthew that in his early career work had been sparse and he had been forced for several years to run a hotel.

Stratford Johns was cited by Tom Baker as an example of an actor who could, if he chose, go into a pub and punch someone, to the delight of everyone else because it was in keeping with his TV character. Tom contrasted this with the frustration of being *Doctor Who*: he could not afford to punch people in pubs however much he wanted to, because it would be shocking to see the Doctor behave like that...

In real life there was not much evidence that Stratford Johns – whose real name was Alan Stratford-Johns, and who was known as Alan in rehearsal – wanted to punch anyone. But there were many scenes between Adric and the green frog which was Alan's character, and John Black was afraid that by Alan's sheer hugeness, of body and of personality, Matthew would be out-acted into total invisibility. This did not occur and rather generously John Black credited Matthew's hard work and excellent acting for being able to remain a living presence in these scenes, though in reality Alan could have smothered Matthew if he had chosen to do so, or any other cast member for that matter. His frog, though hardly muted, was subtler than it might have been.

The rubbery frog costume worn by Stratford Johns was very effective on camera, and it would have been impossible for viewers at home to guess that it had been made of hundreds and hundreds of condoms.

Though Val McCrimmon was the AFM on *Four to Doomsday*, she must have been ill or unavailable for a period of rehearsal because for several days her place was taken by an unforgettable woman of an intensity which, in the impression it left, bordered on madness.

She seemed at all times on the edge of a nervous breakdown. She chain-smoked all day, each intake accompanied by a distinct sucking noise, and the skin over the lower joints of the first and second fingers of her right hand were permanently stained an unpleasant tobacco brown/yellow. In his memory, Matthew saw this yellow hand as always shaking and as slightly dried and withered, but this must be a misremembrance. She was not Davros.

After rehearsal one afternoon, Matthew bumped into Philip Locke, who was playing a wise, bearded android in *Four to Doomsday*, on a central London underground escalator. Philip was carrying a bunch of flowers.

"Hello," said Matthew. "What are you up to in these parts?"

"I'm going to see a friend in hospital."

"Oh! I'm sorry. I hope he gets better soon."

He answered with an intense gentleness.

"He won't. He's dying."

The studio days started with a small difficulty. On *The Vampire Lords*, Matthew had developed the habit of giggling at inopportune moments. This he had soon learnt to stifle, but now, perhaps because there was a new Doctor on the set, his giggling returned. The meal scene with the android was a particular problem: every time Matthew asked for the sodium chloride, he was struck by how incredibly funny it was. Laughter rocked around the table, except from Philip Locke. At first Philip allowed himself a small smile at Matthew's giggles, but his expression soon became frosty until, after the Nth take, he suddenly barked out:

"Stop it!!"

He achieved his aim, because seriousness dropped over everyone and the next take was perfect. Up in the bar, John was cross with Matthew, who said he would never do it again and pretty much kept to his promise. Peter Davison was amused by the whole thing.

"It's funny," he said, "but you haven't learnt when to stop."

"It's not about not knowing when to stop," said Matthew, "it's about being *unable* to stop." The next day in the make-up room Matthew apologised to Philip and he accepted graciously and was nice ever after.

Tom Baker rewrote scripts so heavily they took on a tone unintended by their authors. Peter made fewer changes, but the dining scene was subject to an adjustment, memorable perhaps because it was so tiny. As originally written, Adric asked for someone to pass the salt. Philip Locke's android, Bigon, looked puzzled. "Sodium Chloride," advised the Doctor. Oooh, said Bigon, comprehending.

Peter thought the scene made no sense as written. Why would the android not know salt? So it was decided that the android knew perfectly well what salt was, and Adric didn't. Adric said, "pass the sodium chloride" and Bigon looked at him as if he was mad and the Doctor said "salt." In Matthew's view, it didn't make much sense either way: why should Adric, a speaker of perfect English, know the scientific term but not the quotidian?

You didn't want to think too deeply about it. But it was a sweet enough scene, which was the intention.

Adric the character contradicted himself from story to story, and in *Four to Doomsday* he became the easily gulled innocent. Won't it be heaven, he says to the Doctor, when technology, chips in our brains and plastic in our bodies, will make us perfect? This represented not so much a character's organic reaction as a writer's schematic need for an opposing view to the Doctor's. But the corruptible innocent is one of fiction's great subjects.

One of *Four to Doomsday*'s studio days was a Saturday. A worker, a cameraman perhaps or a boom operator – once when a boom operator had made a cock-up causing a retake, Tom Baker had murmured, "those sound people never bloody apologize!" – had arrived that morning for the live broadcast of *Swap Shop*, the kiddies' time killer, which took up most of Saturday mornings on BBC 1. This person was displeased to find out that the car park at TV Centre was full. He was under the impression that he was guaranteed a space. Sorry, said the man at the gate, it's full, you'll have to park down the road. The man decided he was not *going* to park down the road, he was bloody well going to park at TV Centre or not park anywhere. Sorry, said the man at the gate, full up.

Every union worker at the BBC walked out in sympathy. The live broadcast of *Swap Shop* was scrapped. No taping for *Doctor Who* would take place. Everyone might as well go home.

"Why couldn't the fat git walk the few minutes from the car park down the road?" said Matthew, hitting the table. "Or better yet, get off his arse and take the tube and leave his effing car at home??"

John Black handled it all with great calm. *Ah well*, he said.

Matthew was always pleased to get out of his pyjamas and into another costume, so he was delighted to see in the script that he had to do a fight scene in an astronaut suit. This suit looked superb and Matthew loved it when he tried it on at the costume fitting, but the designer, swept up in the joy and challenge of making a spacesuit, overlooked the fact that it was to be used in a fight scene. The fight had been choreographed in rehearsal but until the studio day it had never been run with Matthew wearing the costume.

Matthew climbed up to the grilled gantry, high above the studio floor, where the fight scene was set. It was hot up there, near the studio lights. He and his opponent began to run the fight, and the design's weakness became apparent: the heavy helmet, not being attached to the collar but only propped on it, toppled off with every energetic movement. Far from being able to roll across the floor, Matthew could hardly walk across it. So even to approximate the fight as rehearsed, he had to put his hand on the helmet's plastic visor to hold it in place, looking completely absurd.

It must be said that, between takes, a photographer snapped some very nice pictures of Matthew in his spacesuit.

2

Work began on *The Visitation*, the fourth story in the season cycle, the second to be made. This script by Eric Saward was a delight. Everybody loved it. Eric had managed to write a *Doctor Who* story very much in the spirit of the better episodes of the past, but with the faster pace which eighties TV apparently required. The script itself was a terrific read. Matthew had loved *The Vampire Lords* and *The Keeper of Traken*, but in many ways *The Visitation* was the most magical of all his scripts in pure *Doctor Who* terms. When Matthew read it, it struck him, particularly in the first episode, as foggy and candle-lit, with something of Daphne Du Maurier, a maid carrying a sputtering candle through a large dark house, rolling thunder, fog on the hills. Peter Davison had read it a couple of months earlier and had enthused about it. The climax, with its burning London, was entirely unexpected but when it came it seemed inevitable. It hardly mattered that, like the unveiling of the killer in a detective story, the twist could work only once: it was only supposed to work once. *The Visitation* was rare among *Doctor Who* scripts – rarer than might be imagined – in another regard: without too much alteration it could have been produced with equal effect at any time in the programme's run. It would have worked perfectly well in 1965 with William Hartnell and his school teachers and would have fitted snugly into the twenty-first century version of the series.

Peter Moffatt was to direct. This was happy news. Matthew had found in the Soho science fiction bookshop *Dark They Were And Golden-Eyed* – named after a Ray Bradbury story – a t-shirt of Steed and Mrs Peel from *The Avengers*, and was pleased to wear this on the first day of rehearsal. Peter Moffatt recognised them instantly.

"Mrs Peel – how *lovely!*"

When he had first read the script, Matthew had supposed that some semi-glamorous chap with a penchant for light comedy like Nigel Havers would be cast as Richard Mace the highwayman, so it was a shock to him when he read the cast list to see that it had gone to a little bald sitcom actor called Michael Robbins. When Matthew met him, he was delighted by Michael Robbins, who was a unique and characterful person.

Michael Robbins had done countless seasons of the inexplicably popular sitcom *On the Buses*. This programme was a truly mysterious phenomenon, because it was a gigantic hit, while never coming within range of a remotely funny moment, despite having a good cast which included Theatre Workshop actor Stephen Lewis. It was so successful, in fact, that Hammer Films, having given up on horror, produced two *On the Buses* movies, which broke the rule that people will not buy cinema tickets for what they can see on television. They were extremely profitable, and ushered in perhaps the lowest point in British cinema history, when the only movies that could find finance apart from *Carry On* films – themselves past their best – were spin-offs from TV sitcoms.

In *On the Buses* Michael Robbins played a hen-pecked husband with a permanent look which was at once beaten down misery and sour complaint. He was married to Olive, who wore horn-rimmed spectacles. In one of the movies Olive became pregnant, or perhaps only thought she was pregnant, and ate nothing but pickled onions throughout. This was as memorably horrible as anything in Hammer's Dracula films, but not necessarily in a good way.

Michael said that he cared very little whether he worked or not. He had probably made a fair sum from *On the Buses*, because it ran for many years and ITV paid much more than the BBC, so perhaps he could afford to be picky. It seemed that he accepted or rejected a job purely because of his mood that day.

"I was up a ladder, doing some decorating," he said, "and my agent calls and says they want you for such-and-such, this is the fee. And I said, I don't care if I do it or not, tell 'em to double the offer, and I slammed down the phone and five minutes later my agent said they'd doubled it, so I said okay. But I don't care about the money, I do mostly for nuthin's."

Michael was heavily involved in charitable activities. These activities took up much of his time and much of his conversation. There is no doubt that he genuinely cared – he was, essentially, a good man – but he didn't half go on about them.

"I do mostly for nuthin's," he said, over and over again. For nuthin'. This lovable phrase became Michael's refrain, just as indelibly as "whippetshit!" was Tom's. Looking across the rehearsal room at Peter Davison, Michael said to Matthew, "do you think he'd do a for nuthin'?" Matthew said he didn't know but expected he would if asked nicely. It seemed that, in all his paid engagements, Michael was scouting for celebrities, minor or major, who could be brow-beaten into doing a for nuthin' with him.

"People say, you're so caring, Michael, so generous, all this charity work, it's beeyootiful, but I say, no, I'm not generous, I'm not giving, I'm taking, because the joy I see in their little eyes is all the reward I need. That's why I do so many for nuthin's."

Michael felt strongly that even when a fee had been agreed for a charity appearance, the 'celebrity' had the moral duty to spurn it. An appearance which had been negotiated with an agent as a for somethin' should be understood to be a cleverly disguised version of a for nuthin'. This was not a custom Matthew had heard of, but of course he knew little about such things. One well-known figure, having spent a day hugging special needs children, asked Michael in a rather embarrassed way about the agreed payment.

"I was furious," said Michael Robbins. Matthew imagined Michael's lip curled as he addressed his victim, like his character from *On the Buses*, or like his Highwayman, but he did not need to imagine it for long because as the terrible memory came back to Michael his lip lifted in the familiar way, like a shrivelled, balding, contemptuous Elvis. If Davros had been a rock 'n' roller, he might have looked like Michael in this frame of mind.

"'Alright,' I said, 'just one moment'. I went to the cash box and very slowly took out the fee – in one pound notes – and I counted each note right in front of him, onto a table. 'One-ah, two-ah, threeya, four-ah, five-ah,' all the way up to five hundred pounds. Then I turned my back on him!"

He liked to present himself as being unusually sensitive, as perhaps he was. He hated rock music. Once at supper over a plate of taramasalata in the BBC club he complained about the rubbish that people listened to. "Once, I saw this violinist, and he was playing absolutely beeyootifully. *Beeyoootifully.*" He savoured this word. For a moment all that could be seen of his eyes were the whites as if he had been momentarily transported by remembrance of the lovely music. "Hardly anybody in the audience, of course, though he played so beeyootifully. But some long-haired oik with a guitar," his lip twisted in disgust, "and they'll lap it up. Pathetic. Talentless rubbish."

Matthew made noises which were neither agreement nor disagreement. He liked violins but he also liked The Kinks.

Peter Davison struck few people as an especially dangerous or edgy person, and yet he had as a lad been a rock drummer and had perhaps had youthful fantasies of pop stardom. He took polite offence at Michael's remark, pointing out in his nice but firm way that rock musicians work extremely hard, which was true. Michael said nothing. Perhaps he was busily remembering the violinist. He put a hunk of bread topped with a big pink dollop of taramasalata in his mouth.

In the studio, he was a chatterer while other people did their scenes.

Often his whispered grumble-mumble passed over the flats. But when he was on the set himself, a pin-drop was enough to distract him. "Can we have *silence,* please. Some of us are trying to *work.*"

On the last day of *The Visitation,* hovering a few feet from a set, he said to Matthew out of the blue, lips drawn down and eyelids lowered,

"This is the worst job I've ever done."

Matthew was fascinated but flabbergasted to hear this and it took all his willpower to keep from asking how someone who had spent a decade in *On the Buses* could possibly think *Doctor Who* was the worst thing he'd ever done. But perhaps he said it about all his jobs, except of course the for nuthin's.

One of *Doctor Who*'s legendary figures was the stuntman Stuart Fell. Stuart had put himself in danger for *Doctor Who* on many occasions, plummeting from on high or catching fire. Now he was to throw himself through a glass window in Matthew's costume. He was in fact almost exactly Matthew's height, though in other ways not of a similar build. He was talky and friendly and interesting. He was a trained fire eater.

"I could teach you how to do it if you like. It's easy. You just put petrol in your mouth, then insert a burning stick."

Matthew had no intention of learning fire eating.

"All you have to remember," said Stuart, "is not to swallow. Keep breathing out."

Matthew said he would remember that.

The Visitation was a fire-filled epic, so the climactic scenes could not be shot at TV Centre. They had to be done on film at the Ealing studios. This was a studio for which the word legendary was hardly an overstatement. All the Ealing comedies, the heart of Alec Guinness's film career, had been made there. *The Lavender Hill Mob, The Man in the White Suit.* Now it was the place where a bakery was to spring alight, Adric and Nyssa trying to stamp on the flames.

Some months after *The Visitation* was completed, Michael Robbins got in touch with Matthew's agent, and asked if Matthew would make a charity appearance. There was no danger of Matthew making the mistake of the man who had asked for his fee, because no fee was offered. This was, from the get-go, a for nuthin'.

Matthew said okay, so on a bright summer day he took a train out to a field somewhere on the outskirts of London, where he found himself in the company of Anthony Ainley and Sarah Sutton, who had also been brow-beaten into doing a for nuthin'. Matthew and Sarah and Anthony smiled down at the Downs Syndrome children with their big, friendly, uncomprehending eyes, and other children scarcely aware of the world, rolling about in wheelchairs. There was a large tent. There was a clown. There were balloons.

Anthony said, after a particularly long and dribbly hug,

"Of course, none of them have a clue who we are."

This was true. But everyone, actors and children, smiled as if they were in heaven.

Once the *Doctor Who* pay cheques began to flow, Peter Davison rushed out and bought himself a splendid, sporty car. He was earning so much money now that someone – his agent? His accountant? – said he should without hesitation buy the most expensive car he could find, to reduce his tax bill. He looked into buying a Saab. The Saab was the trendiest car to be had. It was so trendy that it had just become the new James Bond car, in the first Bond novel in years. This novel, one of what turned out to be many by John Gardner, was called *Licence Renewed* and was an honourable attempt to revive Ian Fleming's Bond of the books, with the scar across his cheek. The dust jacket was designed in the manner of Richard Chopping, who'd done most of Fleming's originals. Matthew read the first few of these Gardner books, including one where the villain was revealed to be Blofeld's daughter, but when they dropped the Chopping-style jackets he lost what mild interest he had had.

Peter Davison's dealer told him about the Bond car, and said that for promotional purposes Saab had built a one-off version with all the extra equipment Gardner had described. It was all found to be perfectly feasible, but made the car so heavy that it would not break fifteen miles an hour.

This was not a problem for Peter's car, which in the end was not a Saab but – if Matthew remembered right – a Porsche. Anyway, it was a very nice car. He showed it off in Tunbridge Wells. Janet and Sarah and Matthew went for a spin with him around the countryside, if spin is the word for an exhilarating drive which reached a hundred miles an hour, rising and falling on the hilly little lanes, the hedges and the cows gazing stupidly over them mere impressionist streaks of green and black and white.

Perhaps the man who had advised Peter to buy a car was his personal manager, a gentleman called John Mahoney, the shape of a chess pawn with a round red face. He had the single worst hair piece in history. It looked as though every morning he plonked this on his bald scalp in the dark. He was blissfully unaware of how amusing he looked.

He was a frequent presence on *Doctor Who*, on studio days, at American events, at BBC parties. This was very unusual for an agent. Matthew's

Aunt Liz, who had encountered John Mahoney, remarked on it.

"Doesn't that man know he's not *supposed* to come to our parties? He's not *invited*?"

Most agents sat in offices sending ten by eights of their clients to casting directors. Not John. John had a small number of household names on his books who took up all his time. His less well-known clients sat around in outer London flats, waiting for him to call with an audition. This he never did, because these unfortunates did not cross his mind. He was wholly occupied with his little bundle of celebrities.

He ran his agency out of his attractive Baker Street flat. In legal terms, running a business from home was more complicated than buying a desk and sitting at it. Peter, having worked in a tax office, once smilingly said he was sure that John would eventually be found out.

But if you happened to be Peter Davison, he was a good manager. After the success of *All Creatures Great and Small*, Peter was indubitably his number one client. Another celebrity was Robin Nedwell, who had been a big sitcom star in the seventies, appearing in the long series based on Richard Gordon's *Doctor* books – *Doctor in Charge, Doctor at Sea*, etc. Robin Nedwell's star was now fading. When Peter had to cancel a personal appearance because of work, it was always Robin Nedwell who took his place. Once there was an ad in the *Evening Standard*: Robin Nedwell was appearing at an event, landing in a helicopter. "That was supposed to be me," said Peter.

John had a penchant for youngish boys so it was perhaps inevitable that he would corner Matthew at parties. Thus Matthew was forced to talk to him for half an hour at a time. Eventually, in the mid-eighties, Matthew became a client. This was mainly because he liked the idea of having an agent with a Baker Street address, being a fan of the Sherlock Holmes stories. (Yes, Matthew thought like this. He lived too much in his own head. He could not walk through Soho, which he did thousands of times, without thinking of lines from William Blake, who lived most of his life there. Matthew's favourite living poet, Jeremy Reed – the last bohemian poet? – stands at the turn of each season with a musician friend on the ground where Blake was born, and recites Blake's work, rain or shine, snow or hail. Matthew thinks this is a wonderful thing to do.) By this time John's face had turned from red to beetroot. A huge, beautiful print of the famous painting of a naked boy looking contemplative, elbows on knees, hung over the fireplace in his lounge. Regents Park could be seen through his window, and the Sherlock Holmes museum. Having taken Matthew on as a client, he clumsily slipped a naughty video into his machine. Boys moaned lustfully on the TV and Matthew talked about the weather.

The law caught up with John and he was turfed out of his Baker Street flat, moving to an office nearby and buying a flat in Brighton. Having not had a job for months and having heard nothing from him, Matthew made an appointment to meet him. John looked awful. His face had now gone from beetroot to the glossy dark red of a ripening blackberry. He was very distracted, puffy, slightly drunk, breathing heavily, the hair piece more askew than ever. He was full of slurred praise for Matthew's talent. He pulled a file drawer too far out from the cabinet and it dropped onto the floor, papers fell out.

Matthew thought, *this man is about to have a heart attack. He is knocking on death's door.* On the train back to his flat, he wondered whether he should call the office and get them to send him to a doctor. Two days later, he made the call. The secretary sounded depressed. John died last night, she said. This was the least surprising thing Matthew ever heard.

3

Castrovalva arrived in the post. This outstanding surrealist epic by Christopher Hamilton Bidmead was inspired by the prints of M. C. Escher. Escher's work was an excellent choice of inspiration, because he was every teenager's favourite artist. His bizarre woodcuts and lithographs were wide ranging in subject, everything from Saint Francis to ghosts in a crypt to globes and crystals and flat, papery swans, to, famously, a hand drawing a hand which was drawing the first hand. But best of all to the adolescent mind were his fantastical, slightly medieval townscapes, with flights of steps which appeared to lead downward but in fact lead upward, some coming out onto walls rather than floors, some double-sided, a hooded figure walking down the top side while, beneath him, another hooded figure walked up the underside. In one, a waterfall recycled itself, seemingly continuing at the bottom to roll downward but actually going back up to the top. So appealing to the childish mind were these wondrous puzzlements that boys with no other interest in art would lie on their beds poring over them and would bring books of his work to school to amaze their friends. Matthew knew about Escher because he was himself one of those poring boys, having an Escher album, as did at least a couple of his class mates. Magical in his way, Escher wasn't remotely as great or resonant as his contemporary Giorgio de Chirico, compared to whom his art was not much more than clever, but schoolboys, all ignorant of de Chirico, beheld an Escher image and thought it was amazingly profound.

Fiona Cumming, the director of *Castrovalva*, was the definitive picture of a bohemian woman with artistic leanings. She had a pleasant round face, with boyishly short brown hair, and she always wore loose-fitting and colourful clothes. She was always associated in Matthew's memory with knitted ponchos, but this may be an invention. Certainly she was the kind of woman who it might be imagined knew how to wear a poncho elegantly, which not everyone can pull off. She had, unexpectedly, a passion for the cartoon cat Garfield, and her flat was – Matthew was led to believe, or at any rate liked to imagine – full of collectable Garfield figurines. This flat was in Saltdean, a suburb of Brighton, in the same building where John and his boyfriend Gary spent their weekends. The main attraction of the building was that it had fabulous picture windows onto the ocean. John and Gary's flat was bookless and sparsely furnished, the main point being the view, but they had an attractive sculpture of a naked woman with her back arched.

Fiona had an older husband who, it seemed, had nothing to do with *Doctor Who*, but who was often seen hovering around the set and at parties and in pubs. Matthew met him many times and said hello and he said hello back, but they were never formally introduced and Matthew never knew his name or exactly what his job at the BBC was. He assumed he worked in the BBC, but even this was never said. As far as Matthew could make out, he was just Mr. Fiona Cumming, who hung around a lot.

Castrovalva was Matthew's first experience on *Doctor Who* of location filming away from the environs of London. Off to the wilds of Kent!

"Location hotels are always pretty bad," said John. The hotel in Tunbridge Wells, not horrendous, was of a fairly basic sort but with pretensions, the kind which twenty years earlier might have earned a part of its living from resident guests, like the old ladies in *Fawlty Towers*. It was used regularly by film crews in the area. The hotel was putting up not only the *Castrovalva* crew but also the crew of a movie. Janet talked briefly to the movie director. About five minutes of *Castrovalva* had been filmed on the first day. "Wow!" said the movie director. "*We* got about fifteen seconds."

Tunbridge Wells was one of those very conservative English towns packed with prosperous old people, ancient generals and colonial widows, including the last residue of those born in the Victorian age.

The hotel was located above the town, with nice views over rooftops and fields. With its solid Edwardian exterior, once a bright white and now in need of touching up, and its threadbare carpets on the stairs and a strong scent of beeswax on the banisters and its creaky floorboards and its pre-war baths, it reeked of faded gentility. Its reception area, of heavy wood and poorly lit, felt like evening whatever the time of day. The bar was airier, perhaps to entice customers who liked some light, the furniture bright-wooded, a large window onto the car park.

Everyone went to their rooms and dumped their bags and then went down to the bar and an evening of drinking began. This was a rare occasion when cast and crew drank together. At TV Centre, the directors and producers might drink with the cast, but the cameramen and the effects lads hung out with each other in a different corner.

Matthew had a great time. He bought lots of rounds and John bought lots of rounds too and so did everybody else. Matthew's favoured drink was a spritzer. A spritzer was white wine with a splash of soda, all the rage in the BBC. Even Peter Davison bought him a spritzer, before leaving. Peter never, while in Matthew's sight, drank more than one glass of wine. He was not a man who hung around in bars.

Matthew would pour the new drink into the old glass, which John remarked on.

"Only Matthew would pour the full glass into the empty glass!" he said. Matthew liked this observation and decided to make it a permanent eccentricity, and he kept the habit up for some years.

Matthew had another eccentricity which was remarked on, though this one was perfectly logical and easily explained. He put his jacket on when he went to the bar, a habit which he still occasionally maintains. Sometimes people thought he had taken offence at something and was leaving in a rage, though he was perfectly calm and happy.

"Why do you do that?" asked John. "Put on your coat just to go to the bar? It's not that cold!" He seemed to think it was some old world genteel courtesy, forgotten everywhere but in Matthew's family. In fact, it was practical: Matthew hated having loose coins in his trouser pocket so he dropped them into his coat pocket and he found, when he bought drinks, that it was easier to get the loose change out if he was wearing his coat than if he were holding it up and feeling for coins, while it hung loosely and swung and twisted. So you see, it is all logical.

The evening wore on. Greasy food was ordered to soak up the drinks: chicken fingers and deep-fried clams and chips. More drinks came. Matthew lost count. New rounds were being bought with such pleasing frequency that at one point Matthew had three full glasses in front of him. It was lovely. Eventually midnight came, the crowd thinned until only John and Matthew and the assistant floor manager Val remained. The conversation turned to *Doctor Who*. Matthew said he liked the fact that though it seemed to change it never really did. He understood perfectly well what he meant by this but could not put it clearly. Rubbish, said Val, it changes all the time. Yes, yes, said Matthew, but not really. Well it does,

He dashed out of shot, past the camera and the boom, and threw up at the foot of a tree.

For lunch, he ate nothing but he drank gallons of orange juice, on the grounds that this was indubitably good for his health. After downing it, however, he felt a little bit worse.

He went and lay in a field nearby where the grass was tall and there were lots of dandelion clocks. He plucked a clock and blew it. He felt the imprint of his body under him on the grass. He looked up at the sky, which was very blue; the sun was warm.

People with hangovers often think cosmic thoughts. He thought of how he would not very long from now be dead, and so would everybody else involved in the making of *Castrovalva*. But the sun would still shine and there would be other people and other dandelions and the grass would still sometimes be dewy, until eventually there were no people left but there would still be stars. He thought about how the human race had ruined the Earth, and the Earth would be better off when there were only cats and butterflies and roses.

He felt exquisite, delicious melancholy at the thought of his mortality.

Then these reflections were cut short by a face looking over him. It was the face of Peter Davison.

"Hello," said Peter. "Are you alright?"

"I'm fine, thank you," said Matthew.

"I saw you lying here and thought you'd died."

"In fact I'm feeling a little better."

"Good."

But Matthew was annoyed with Peter for disturbing his melancholy.

The cast were being treated to tea with the lord of the manor, or whatever he was, but Matthew could not face tea with anyone, Lord or not. So he was driven back to the hotel.

In the lobby, he saw the hotel manager with his Fawltyish moustache. The manager rushed to him, looking slightly put out.

"We had a strike of the cleaners this morning," he said. "They stopped work for an hour."

"Ah."

"They said that they're not paid to clean up sick."

"Oh dear."

"The strike only lasted an hour, then I managed to persuade them to go back to work. But it might be nice of you gave them a tip."

"Is ten pounds okay?"

"Ten pounds will do nicely."

said John, they had the earth season and the space seasons. Sometimes it was jokey, now it isn't. Yes, but in a way it doesn't change, insisted Matthew.

This conversation, as far as Matthew was concerned, had become inarticulate and he said it was time for bed. They all went up in the lift together. Matthew waved goodbye. He went into his room. The curtains were drawn and it was dark. He could not find the light switch. He took off his clothes and climbed into bed and, the moment he lay down, he felt ill. He lay wide awake and his stomach was busy and he felt sick. There was a sink on his left, he remembered. *I think I should go across to it.* He rose to get out of bed and at that moment a jet of vomit splashed onto the edge of the bed and the carpet. He didn't care. It was a double bed and he rolled to the other side and fell asleep.

The next morning, early, the phone rang. It was an unwelcome, knife-edged sound. It was his wake-up call. He was not sure how much sleep he had had but it wasn't much. He knew he had to clean up the mess, but when he looked at it in daylight it was worse than he had thought, a large, now drying river the shape of Bermuda running to the sink, and drips running down the side of the bed.

He showered and dressed and brushed his teeth. He did not feel well but there wasn't time to think about this. Well or ill, he had to go down and get on the bus and turn out scenes for *Castrovalva*. He went down to the heavy wooded foyer and a few people were already milling about. He was not in any mood for breakfast. He went up to the desk where a woman was looking at a ledger and he said, as quietly as possible.

"I was a bit ill last night, so I'm afraid that I was a bit kind of sick…" he made an apologetic smile. The woman beamed brightly. "Don't worry," she said. Matthew wondered if she had grasped his full meaning.

Then he was on board the BBC coach to the lands of a grand country house where assorted outdoor scenes would be filmed. This was the country house used soon after in *Black Orchid*, but of course the house itself did not appear in *Castrovalva*. Everybody talked as the coach bumped along, except Matthew, who felt every rise and fall on the narrow country lanes wobble through him as if there was a go-go dancer in his belly. His head throbbed.

The scenes to be shot involving Adric were late in the story, after he had been saved from the Master's web. So it was fortunate that he looked a bit the worse for wear. How's that for method acting? One scene had the boy and Tegan and Nyssa and the Doctor all trotting back to the TARDIS. Before filming began, Peter asked Matthew if he was okay. Yes, said Matthew, in a way that meant no. The cameras rolled. The four heroes trotted along. Matthew began to feel wobbly in his stomach.

Matthew handed the money over.

"That'll keep them happy," said the manager, folding the note.

Fiona Cumming appeared, well stuffed with the lord's tea. They sat on a bench in the lobby.

"Now," she said, "about last night."

"Well," said Matthew. "I don't think it was the drink. I think it was the chicken."

"The chicken?" Fiona looked doubtful.

"Yes, those chicken fingers. They didn't taste right. They were a bit off."

He went upstairs, but he found he didn't want to sit all evening in this grey cold tatty room. So he decided he would go down to the bar, but only for a short period, and that he would drink a glass of water for every spritzer.

Fiona Cumming and John came in to the bar. Fiona had a serious look on her face – or at least a faux-serious look – but John was unusually jolly.

"I have asked around," said Fiona, "and no-one who ate any of those chicken fingers got ill. Except you. I don't think it was the chicken." She wagged a finger and paused weightily. "If you are not used to alcohol, you must be more careful. You mustn't drink so much."

"Not used to it???" barked John. "He invented it!"

Matthew laughed at this. He was narked by Fiona's teacherly pompousness. She was one of those people who had no youthfulness left in her, it seemed to him. Had she never done anything silly when she was a teenager? He was still a boy, he was *entitled* to be silly, he would be like a dead person if he wasn't. He was pleased that John implicitly supported him. After all, John had plied him with half those drinks.

It was mentioned by John with amused pleasure that, when Matthew had thrown up at the tree, some of his vomit had splashed onto the sound recorder. The poor sound man had had to clean it up.

Christopher Bidmead visited the location.

Matthew had noticed that he'd put on a little weight around the time of *Logopolis*, but now he looked thinner and very pale and he seemed bit detached from the goings-on around him.

"You've lost weight," said Matthew.

"I'm on a diet."

"Oh? What sort of diet?"

"I've given up eating."

"?"

"It's the best way to lose weight. Don't eat for a week."

For Christopher, it worked.

Matthew asked Christopher if he had handed the script of *Logopolis* over to Terrance Dicks yet, to be transformed into a Target book. Christopher was not too weakened to produce a forceful answer.

"No! I'm doing the adaptation myself! It's already nearly finished." Not a man prey to self-doubt, it appeared, he added, "It's a ripping good read!" Matthew said he was sure it was.

Matthew had discovered the wonder of credit cards. It was exciting to feel rich while having no money. His credit card statement said he could spend hundreds and hundreds of pounds. All he had to do was hand over his lovely card. He carried less and less cash. Credit cards would cover everything.

One evening, John said it would be nice to go to a restaurant. This appealed to Matthew, he liked restaurants. A sweet little restaurant was found and nearly everyone went, cast and crew, though not Peter Davison. Perhaps Sandra Dickinson was visiting. Twenty BBC people sat at one long table and a slim, aging, polite waitress brought them steaks and beers and bottles of wine. When the bill arrived Matthew said he didn't have enough money to pay his share so he would put it on his card if everyone would give him cash. His wallet was suddenly obese with fivers and tenners.

When his credit card statement arrived the food bill was nowhere to be seen. He had visions of the restaurant having to close because of the massive losses incurred by the BBC meal. He imagined the polite, good-humoured waitress without a job, signing on the dole. He wondered if he should telephone and offer to send a cheque. But this guilty feeling lasted only for a few moments. Anyway, he could not remember the name of the restaurant.

During rehearsals, Fiona Cumming conned Matthew unforgettably. As so often on *Doctor Who*, everybody was going on about how incomprehensible the script was and how the viewers would never understand it. Fiona Cumming was trying to explain a particularly problematic scene, though she was completely in the dark. Eventually, after tying herself in knots, she gave up pretending she knew what she was talking about. She sighed.

"We'll have to call Christopher and ask, "she said.

"Does it matter?" said Matthew cynically. "No-one'll understand it anyhow."

Fiona looked put out. She wagged her finger and spoke heavily.

"If we understand it, they'll understand it."

"Of course," said Matthew, feeling a fool for not knowing this. It was obvious. If we understand it, they'll understand it. If we understand it, they'll understand it. Plain as a pikestaff. Fiona might have had less of a science fiction mind than Matthew by far, or anybody else, but she knew how to direct TV.

Matthew thought it over. After about two minutes, he realized he'd been conned. Fiona's answer had been glitteringly free of concrete sense. By the time this clicked, the conversation had moved on and he could not challenge her, which of course he would not have done anyway, being shy and insecure. But it remained in his memory ever after as his favourite example of director's flannel.

By wonderful coincidence, Fiona had a very similar opinion of Chris Bidmead.

"I always feel when I ask him a question that he explains it very clearly, and it's only a while later I realize I'm none the wiser."

An unexpected excitement was the return of the man from Viewmaster! This poor fellow, who had had the misfortune to be on the set of *Full Circle*, was now to make a series of discs featuring the brand-spanking new Doctor Who, the old Doctor forgotten, consigned to the memories of aging nostalgists, his outdated Viewmaster reels for sale at very reduced prices. "Tom who?" said all those forgetful kiddies.

After the misery of his first experience, the Viewmaster man was in heaven on *Castrovalva*. How different everything was! Matthew was the only actor he knew, and he greeted him warmly. He clicked away at Matthew between takes, up there suffering in the web. And how relieved he must have been to meet Peter and Anthony and Sarah and Janet, all willing to grin and pose and look frightened at his gentlest request. No Lalla, no tantrums, here!

The special guest star was Derek Waring. He was one of those male actors, like Michael Williams – Mr. Judi Dench – with a more widely known wife, Derek being married to Dorothy Tutin. She, of course, had been wowing classical audiences for decades, while he was best known as a *Z-Cars* policeman. When interviewed, he was always asked by vile journalists what it was like having a 'more successful' – their phrase – wife. This must have been tiring, but Derek Waring could be imagined to have handled it with great aplomb. He handled everything with aplomb. He talked to everyone as if they were equals. He seemed interested in everyone, in the way of John Fraser. Once, in the bar, he *asked* if he might join Matthew and Janet, an astounding courtesy. One middle-aged actor, friendly but deeply boring, droned on one lunchtime about wine, on which he believed himself an expert. (Very slowly and mumbly, "certain...Burgundies... er... even quite... *ordinary*... bottles... I suppose... one ... might call.. them... these *Burgundies*... do you not... *find?*...have... a stronger...bouquet than...*many* ...a more...ummm... *high-priced* ...red of... ummm...say... the Marseilles...region... or... thereabouts...Those burgundies... really... ummm... *tickle*...my nose... *hairs*...") Everyone else mentally absented themselves, glancing across perhaps to the line at the food counter, trying to spot minor telly faces, but Derek looked consumed by the conversation. At the read-through, this boring actor misread the name of the planet as K'*stroev*'lva, until corrected by Christopher Bidmead. Later, he began to get invitations to conventions, where he could talk slowly and tediously to the crowds too. He was actually a nice man.

Matthew, on the stairs, said to Tony, who had also been present at the wine talk,

"I think that is the most boring person I have ever met."

Anthony laughed more loudly and longer than this deserved.

"You," he said, "will be a great wit." Matthew was vastly flattered, though he could not see how observing that someone was boring was especially witty.

Nearly all of Matthew's part in Christopher's wonderful story was spent in the Master's TARDIS, tied up in what must be nearest to a bondage scene ever to appear in *Doctor Who*, at least until the Master tied David Tennant to a chair while taking over everyone on Earth. Matthew's hair style changed from story to story, though the cut looked cool only rarely. He was under instructions not to get haircuts between stories, allowing the make-up designer to decide what she wanted to do. On *Castrovalva*, the make-up designer, Marion Richards, though excellent, did not apparently notice the voluminous quantity of his hair and left it untouched. So in the web Adric had possibly his least cool hair style of all, looking like a wild jungle boy who had never heard of scissors. Matthew was becoming to hair styling what Lalla had been to clothing fashions.

Matthew was high up above the black TARDIS floor in the Web. Far, far below, Anthony Ainley made ranting speeches. The Web was simply a disc cut in wood, against which Matthew leant, angled slightly forward. It echoed, probably not by accident, that old image of the figure of man in a circle, though the figure of man had not worn little green boots and a blue star badge, or in fact anything at all.

A thick rope had been tied around Matthew's waist and fixed at the other end to a railing, several feet behind him. Matthew was not particularly nervous – in fact he thought the whole thing was very cool -but was later told that the set had been at the very edge of permissible safety measures for actors.

After *Castrovalva* had been shown, Peter Moffatt came up to Matthew at a party.

"*Well!* There you were, this little innocent off the street in *State of Decay*, and now, in *Castrovalva*, you're the *best thing in it!*" Matthew went pink. He doubted Peter felt quite as strongly as he said, but he did not argue with him.

4

The actor who played Boba Fett in the *Star Wars* films was working at the BBC on a drama serial about football. He was sometimes magnetized to the *Doctor Who* table in the canteen, perhaps because of some science fictional empathy. He mentioned that when he had signed on for *Star Wars*, he had been asked to fill out an information sheet with questions on it, which could be sent out in reply to fan letters. These questions were of the 'What is your favourite food?' variety.

"One of the questions," he said, "was, 'What is your favourite pop group?' I don't have a favourite pop group, so I thought about it for a moment, and put down The Bee Gees. So now, somewhere in the world, there is a *Star Wars* fan who thinks I like the Bee Gees, though I have never listened to them in my life."

A frequently cited example of the most banal possible fan question was the one about favourite foods. Matthew quietly thought this easily mocked question was in fact less dreary than many others.

There *was*, in fact, something interesting about food preferences, it was an illuminating detail. It would be interesting to be reminded what kind of sandwich the Doctor ate in *The Sea Devils*. Was it ham? Cheese and pickle? And it was interesting to know that Kate Bush at nineteen was a vegetarian. This information was added to thirty years later by a remark made by a musician that "she makes a mean ham sandwich!" It would be revealing to know that Greta Garbo loved Chinese takeaways, just as it would be interesting to know what particular drink or drug had intoxicated the junkie William Burroughs on the day he shot his wife.

They were playing William Tell, a glass on her head in place of an apple. He fired too low. The glass was fine.

*   *   *

Work was to begin on *Kinda*, one of the most unusual *Doctor Who* stories and one of the most interesting, quite by itself in the arc of the original *Doctor Who* series, genuinely cerebral without falling into the trap of mere cleverness. The writer, Christopher Bailey, was a Buddhist. He looked exactly as he was supposed to look: tall and thin, he had the beard of a hippy prophet, hair hanging loose to his shoulders while thinning on top, and he always wore sandals.

If the script was unusually original and stimulating, it must be said that Peter Grimwade had brought together a quartet of superb actors to bring this rich material to life. Many guest stars took on a part in *Doctor Who* while waiting for something better to turn up. The *Kinda* cast, expecting perhaps to play Robomen or thickly made-up hissing aliens, must have been surprised by the quality of the material. (It seems unlikely that even Richard Todd saw the script before signing on, but who knows?) When Simon Rouse played madness, it was not the melodramatic madness so wonderfully done by Geoffrey Beevers as the burnt-up Master; this was the kind of mad person you might spot from a distance and cross the street to avoid. These characters had actual psychology. Here was the most terrifying of all *Doctor Who* monsters: real life.

Kinda was the only *Doctor Who* story where it was possible to discuss the meaning of a scene and the implications for its characters without being hopelessly pretentious. There was some debate over whether, when he escapes from the box towards the end, Adric was worrying only about his own skin or the skins of the people he might have injured. In the end, the scene was shot both ways.

Nerys Hughes was a big TV star as a result of a long-running sitcom set in Liverpool called *The Liver Birds*. She turned up to the read-through with her contract in her handbag.

"I *never* sign until the first day of rehearsal," she said.

Of all the movie stars to crop up in *Doctor Who* while Matthew was in the series, Richard Todd was the one whose career had, at its peak, most glittered. In the fifties, he had been a genuine, major star. Matthew had not seen any of his movies, but was assured they were all classics. Uniquely on *Doctor Who*, when Richard, who had an anecdotal nature, told amusing stories, they were not about rep theatre or the dear little BBC but about Hollywood. He had a tale about 'Ronnie' Reagan, the details of which are forgotten, except that it ended with Reagan's flies down.

His knowledge of the technicalities of a studio was second to none: like Judy Garland, he knew exactly how the light affected his face in any given shot. Nerys, despite twenty years in telly, had never given such movie star considerations a moment's thought. Matthew overheard her discussing between shots the mysteries of light with the *Kinda* lighting man, who told her to observe Richard. "He's the only one who knows what he's doing."

Simon Rouse was a very intense young man who played a very intense young man in the story. His intensity spilt over into a nervy temperament. He was snappy and irritable, and slightly erratic, so that in the studio his scenes took more takes than was usually permitted for *Doctor Who*. He was all tightly wound energy. He spun neurotically in his spaceship chair between takes. Once, in the studio, Matthew entered a beat late and when a retake was called Matthew admitted to the box, "that was my fault," and Simon agreed: "You hear that? That was Matthew's fault! That was *Matthew's* bloody fault! Yes, it was! Matthew's fault! Not mine, you hear that?" And he spun in his chair. "*Matthew's* fault!"

For Matthew not even Simon Rouse was the highlight of this extraordinary serial. The highlight of *Kinda* was Mary Morris, who came onto *Doctor Who* only for the second batch of rehearsal and recording days, making the trip over from Switzerland, where she lived. She had been a brilliant Number Two in *The Prisoner*. She played a familiar *Doctor Who* type, a witch with a staff, but from her expressive and characterful map-lined face and her exquisite voice she made it new. She had been acting so long that she was fully relaxed into herself in an ideal and rare way.

She was funny and chatty off stage. Someone sneezed in the make-up room and she informed everyone with a huge smile that a big sneeze was the sign of a person who has intense orgasms. Matthew was pleased to hear this, because he always sneezed fit to burst.

With this cast Peter Grimwade could do very little except shut up. The smaller roles were excitingly cast too, especially Anna Wing, a year or so before starting on *EastEnders* as one of those characterfully eccentric women who are the life blood of British soap opera, as a plump dream Tegan, playing chess with an aging dream Adric.

Fortunately there were two lads on whom Peter could focus his criticism: one was a handsome, buff young shirtless jungle man, who soon gave up acting to become a TV presenter, the other a sort of dream-world trickster figure. Peter's familiar curate's squeal could be heard issuing directorial instructions to the trickster, as always in so bullying and disorienting a way that no discernible improvement could ever be detected or even hoped for. When Peter turned to Matthew, Matthew ignored him, and instead worked out his performance by responding to the intensity of Simon Rouse.

In the bar after the first group of studio days, Matthew asked Christopher Bailey how he thought it was going. He shrugged.

"It's alright," he said, non-committally.

"Only alright?"

"Not everything is the way it should be."

"Like what?"

"The box. I had envisioned something entirely different. Bigger. More robotic."

Matthew felt a little thrill of pleasure.

On the space ship set, things fell silent while Peter Grimwade in the box fussed over something. Matthew suddenly looked right at Richard Todd and blurted out in comic self-deprecation,

"Of course, the secret to TV acting is *not to look at the camera!*"

Thirty years later, he was told that a version of this incident had become one of Peter Davison's favourite convention anecdotes, Matthew's humour removed to imply that he had said it in the spirit of *giving advice* to Richard Todd. Matthew liked Peter's version of the story very much because it was funny but it was, of course, fictional. It could only have been true if Matthew had been retarded, and he wasn't.

In the bar after the last day, Matthew hugged Nerys and said how nice she was. Nerys looked a bit uncomfortable, but could hardly object to the compliment. Then Matthew hugged Mary Morris.

"You are brilliant, the best thing ever on this programme!" said Matthew, and she looked pleased and laughed and said how sweet he was.

Matthew bought everyone drinks.

"What do you want?" Matthew asked Simon Rouse.

"I'll have a double whisky," said Simon greedily. For some reason Matthew never forgot this.

After Matthew had seen the first episode of *Kinda*, he said to Val McCrimmon,

"Simon Rouse is brilliant, isn't he?"

"Well," she said dryly, "he's only playing himself. He's exactly like that. So it's not really acting, is it?"

After the usual break, everyone was off to Tunbridge Wells again, to shoot location scenes for *Black Orchid*, a stab by Terence Dudley at a twenties mystery thriller, Doctor Who filling the detective role, a sort of Sexton Blake in cricket togs. The script glistered with shards dug up from Agatha Christie and Charlotte Brontë, complete with a thick policeman and a lunatic in the attic, though on this occasion the lunatic was not the first Mrs Rochester but a man, a troubled brother or cousin of the owner of the stately home which was the story's setting.

Strangely, though it ran to only two episodes *Black Orchid* unfolded in a leisurely fashion, with long, lingering shots of Peter Davison pretending to be good at cricket. This was another example of Peter's talent for exuding competence where there was none: Only at the DVD commentary did it come out that he was hopeless at the game.

It was a happy production. The director, Ron Jones, was pleasant and calm. He was a tall, slim gay man with a neat moustache and dark, thinning hair, the very type of the 'clone,' the fashionable look among gay men at the time.

Ron dealt well with John Nathan-Turner. While working on the cricket scenes, things ground to a halt. Ron spent ages squatting at the camera trying to get the angle he wanted. John stood at his shoulder, nagging him.

"Stop faffing around, Ron!"

Ron ignored him, with all the grace of an indifferent cat. He continued to gaze through the lens.

For the location filming they stayed at the same hotel they'd used for *Castrovalva* and the scenes were shot on the same estate. Matthew hoped the hotelier would not remember him but the man's expression said he remembered him perfectly well.

The TARDIS materialises on a railway station platform. The BBC had hired a lovely old car to ferry the Doctor and his girls and boy to the manor where the story was set, but the budget would not stretch to a railway engine, so everyone stood on a sweet old country platform with dry ice up to their knees, the engine itself being stock footage. This was an example of how, in real terms, the budget for the series had dropped. Ten years earlier, the Jon Pertwee episodes had often made use of helicopters, which would have been unimaginable in the early eighties.

But Matthew found talk of the budget wearing. It was brought up all the time by members of the general public. They would say, as if it was the first thing that came in to their heads, and they always looked commiserating as they said it, *of course, it's got a very low budget, hasn't it? It's made very cheaply,* isn't it? To Matthew, the look of *Doctor Who* was not a limitation, it was a style. The scripts were as inventive as they were precisely because of the way the programme was made.

Matthew, as Adric, spent much time lingering outdoors by a table of food, including a delicious-looking roast chicken. It was sometimes tempting to tear a tiny piece off between shots, but, reaching out, Matthew found the set designer, Tony Burrough, standing beside him, asking him not to eat the props. This was a fair request but it passed Val McCrimmon by. Val was standing near Matthew, talking. She had warmed to him since Tom's departure. ("She says you're *much* nicer since Tom Baker left," Janet informed him.) She could not keep her mitts off the chicken until Tony Burrough came and bawled at her. "Don't eat my set!!" Val looked apologetic and when he had gone away made a twisty smile as if to say, *he's bonkers, isn't he?*

The party scenes required a fair amount of dancing from a tiny number of extras and from Sarah and, more surprisingly, Janet, who made a noble effort to do the Charleston. The choreographer was none other than John Nathan-Turner's long-time boyfriend, Gary Downie. Gary had lived in London for years but was South African by birth and South African vowels remained in his speech. Gary, with his unusually long jaw and little neat beard, looked like a musketeer reflected in a funhouse mirror. He came one morning to the rehearsal room and took everyone through a few simple steps, including Matthew, though Matthew did not have to dance in the programme. When asked in the story if he would like to dance, Adric says simply, "I don't dance," and spends most of the party standing by the food table.

The BBC frequently used a small number of extras to suggest a crowd, and this was much mocked. In the BBC Shakespeare production of *Julius Caesar*, for instance, the 'Friends, Romans, Countrymen' speech was orated to a handful of middle-aged blokes, who stared indifferently at Mark Antony, like a scattering of seaside holidaymakers half-watching a Punch and Judy show, wishing they were paddling instead.

These extras did their best to people the BBC's Rome and Arden, and school quadrangles and alien planets and Home Guard units.

This reminded Matthew of a remark made by a traveller in the early nineteenth century, who, seeing some distant slaves on an orange plantation, wrote that "their lives must be hard, but perhaps it would give them pleasure to know that they are helping to people the landscape for travellers such as I."

It has to be said that the tiny number of dancers peopling the background of *Black Orchid* failed to imbue the party around which the drama turned with much of a sense of life. Even before all the killings and kidnappings occurred, Lord and Lady Cranleigh must have looked at each other once or twice, their eyes saying, *it's not going very well, is it?#*

* * *

Real-life drama occurred during the fakery. At the climactic moment of *Black Orchid*, the lunatic in the attic kidnapped Nyssa, mistaking her for her identical twin, and took her up to the roof of the manor house. Once up there, he decided life was no longer worth living, and threw himself off the roof. Everyone wanted to watch the filming of this spectacular moment, because dangerous stunts were scarce on *Doctor Who*. The whole cast and crew were dotted about on the grass, craning upward.

The stuntman, Gareth Milne, had piled a heap of cardboard boxes fifteen feet high against the wall underneath him, to break his fall. He leapt from the parapet into air, but he had disastrously overshot the boxes, and plummeted downward, nothing between him and the ground but air. He managed to reach out a hand to the uppermost box, and hit it with his palm. This slowed his descent enough to make a difference. The box spun in the air and dropped after him.

He landed on wet grass with a terrible thump. Everyone stood absolutely still. The whole world fell silent. Then he stirred and people rushed to him and an ambulance took him away. Later, it transpired that he had suffered only a few bruises. Matthew said to John that he had been sure for a long, terrible moment that Gareth had been killed. John said, so had he.

Among the cast was a gentleman called Ivor Salter, playing a police sergeant. Ivor was a jobbing actor who had worked for years and years, including a long stint as a mad farmer in *Crossroads*. Matthew asked Ivor what Noele Gordon was like. This fascination with Noele Gordon on Matthew's part is inexplicable because Matthew had not seen much of the programme, and though one of his grannies had been a fan, she had died in 1970. And yet he loved to hear about the horrors of making *Crossroads*.

"I hear she's difficult," said Matthew, fishing for scandal.

"She can be," said Ivor, with lips pushed forward and a look of self-regard, "but she was always lovely to me, because she instantly recognized a *fellow professional* when she saw one."

Ivor was certainly a professional if ever there was one, and remarkably dedicated. He lived a long way from London, in the pretty but poverty-stricken city of Lincoln, with its hilltop Cathedral and its sharply inclined cobbled streets and its dirty, shouting urchins. Lincoln was a place where attractive ivy-covered cottages could be snapped up for next to nothing, as long as you didn't mind the urchins.

Lincoln was a long schlep from London. This did not bother Ivor. Whenever he was called to rehearsal, he made the two-and-a half hour Inter-City train journey out from and back to Lincoln. He might have paid a refreshingly moderate sum for his ivy-covered cottage, if such it was, but after coughing up the enormous train fare it is unlikely that Ivor saw much profit from *Black Orchid*, even though, his part being smallish, he did not have to show up every day.

It was a splendid idea to follow two completely contrasting *Doctor Who* gems – *Kinda* and *The Visitation* – with this light conceit, almost a throwaway, before springing into the big-news return of an old monster. In this way, Peter's first season was beautifully structured.

Black Orchid was not the slickest of scripts. One of the challenges for a writer of *Doctor Who* is putting plot explication into the mouths of characters while disguising it as something more. It would not be unjust to say that few writers really solved this problem, but Terry Dudley seemed not even to have acknowledged that there was a problem, but rather to have shrugged his shoulders and said sod it and stuffed the dialogue with unvarnished plot points. Even a superb cast – including Moray Watson as Sir Robert, and Barbara Murray and Michael Cochrane as the Cranleighs – sometimes had a challenge with Terence's lines. In one scene, Moray and Barbara had to give out the kind of information which might take up thirty pages of a novel in a few information-crammed exchanges, and speaking this dialogue they looked like they were eating stones.

It says something about the acting profession that Moray Watson, a superb and distinguished actor, then and later, mentioned to Matthew that shortly before *Black Orchid* he had toyed with giving up acting entirely.

Matthew mentioned to Michael Cochrane that he wondered whether he would go on acting after *Doctor Who*.

"I think I might be too giggly," he said. "I laugh too much."

"Well, I think," said Michael, "that that is a *very* good sign."

Around this time, a fourth season of the BBC's other space adventure serial, *Blake's 7*, went into production. This was supposed to be the BBC's answer to *Star Trek*, and was thought – by the BBC at least – to be more serious than the knockabout melodrama of *Doctor Who*, seriousness in these terms meaning only an absence of jokes. Like *Star Trek*, it was loved by women. *Doctor Who* cultdom, of course, was wholly dominated by queer men of a bitchy nature. All the *Blake's 7* fanzines, on the other hand, were produced by women and they all had the hots for Avon, though many of them were lesbians. Like the Australian soap opera *Prisoner: Cell Block H*, *Blake's 7* became a true lesbian classic. What is it about lesbians and prisoners? *Blake's 7* was about a bunch of intergalactic criminals, among them a couple of exceedingly tough women in jumpsuits who looked like they would kick the balls of any man who got in their way. They were all on the run in a stolen prison ship. Their foe was an enormously evil woman called Servalan who was in charge of the dictatorial Federation.

She seemed to have nothing better to do than chase the Seven from corner to corner of the universe.

For gay women, Paul Darrow, whose character Avon became the central figure of *Blake's 7*, has a status akin to Dusty Springfield's among gay men, with the added advantage of still being alive.

Dudley Simpson, fired from *Doctor Who*, continued to turn out his suspenseful fragments of melody and rhythm for *Blake's 7*.

The cast were of a more straightforwardly heroic stripe than the oddities of *Doctor Who*, the tall white man with tight curly hair who moved well and knew how to draw a ray gun fast, the tall black woman with beautiful eyes who also knew how to pull a ray gun fast. And, in the midst of them, Paul Darrow. Blake himself left the programme as soon as he could wriggle his way out of the contract, so for much of the series there was no Blake in *Blake's 7*.

Matthew had not seen much of *Blake's 7* – for some reason, he had always had to stay late at school on the weekday evening on which the early episodes had been shown – was it a Monday? – otherwise he would have been glued to it, for sure. He was told by fans that *Blake's 7* had started in a dark and sinister and unsmiling tone, but soon the temptation to archness could not be resisted and it became over its run ever more camp. Somehow it got darker and more of a romp all at once. That lovely close-cropped villainess Servalan, played by a former Hammer film ingénue called Jacqueline Pearce, and Paul Darrow turned *Blake's 7* increasingly into a comic two-hander, Paul's remarkable performance becoming bigger and bigger by the moment, dwarfing Blake and all the others.

What Matthew saw of *Blake's 7* was all marvellously entertaining. He was impressed to hear that it had been created by Terry Nation off the top of his head, Nation having no idea what he was going to say when he went in to the BBC conference, coming out ten minutes later having conceived the title, the characters, the situation, all on the spur of the moment.

Paul Darrow ended up having lunch every so often with Matthew and Sarah and Janet, though he hardly knew them. He had lunch with them, he said, because the cast of *Blake's 7* were so incredibly boring. Matthew and Sarah and Janet were all flattered to be thought more interesting than the *Blake's 7* cast by that spectacle's towering icon. Paul was very actory, which appealed to Matthew.

He mentioned that he had once had lunch with Tom Baker, "which was very peculiar, because he began throwing his food at me…"

He said that he had suggested Peter Davison for a guest appearance in *Blake's 7* and the producer had pooh-poohed the idea. "Peter Davison in science fiction? Don't be ridiculous!"

Paul was extremely happy to report to this coterie of admiring *Doctor*

Who girls and boys that *Blake's 7* was about to have its own monthly comic. There could be no further doubt that *Blake's 7* was every bit as fabulous a cult as *Doctor Who*, and any feelings of superiority *Doctor Who* actors entertained on account of having a comic were as dust. The first issue was to come, he said, with a lovely free gift: a *Blake's 7* sticker, which would soon be attached to satchels all around the British Isles.

Shortly after this conversation, Matthew found a *Blake's 7* sticker on the floor of his dressing room, which he supposed must have been the gift that came with the first issue of the *Blake's 7* monthly. (How many *Blake's 7* stickers could there be?) It was certainly a nice sticker. He assumed that his dressing room had last been used by a *Blake's 7* actor, who had dropped the sticker while looking through a complimentary copy of the comic, no doubt thinking, *this'll* silence those *Doctor Who* companions with all their swagger and crowing… Matthew, not having a satchel on which to attach it, nonchalantly put the sticker in the bin…

Back at rehearsal, somebody asked if a nice lunch had been enjoyed by all.

"Well," said Janet, "ours was a Darrowing experience."

Never has a person looked more delighted by her own word play.

John Nathan-Turner was underwhelmed by *Blake's 7*, and his always cool view of it chilled when a *Doctor Who* monster showed up in a *Blake's 7* episode. Matthew mentioned it to John.

"Did you spot that Sea Devil walking through dry ice on *Blake's 7* the other day?"

"I was furious! I went to the producer and had a stern word with him. How dare you! I said. Oh, he said, we found this dusty old monster mask in the back of a storeroom and thought it looked quite nice. Didn't know it was from *Who*. Sorry."

John was mystified, with reason, as to how anyone could come across a monster mask in a storeroom at TV Centre and not immediately suspect that it was from *Doctor Who* – if not *Who*, what ?

Of course, John might have been miffed for another good reason. He was becoming infatuated with the idea of a full season of stories making reference to old episodes, and to this end was contemplating a revival of *The Sea Devils*. It must have been galling for him to think of all those kiddies saying to their mothers, "Coo! What's a *Blake's 7* monster doing on *Doctor Who*?"

Some years after *Blake's 7*, Paul Darrow played Macbeth. A friend told Matthew that he went to the first night, and the audience was the most unusual he had ever seen at a Shakespeare play, consisting of large numbers of butch women in *Blake's 7* costumes, complete with ray guns. They loved every minute of Paul's performance.

5

Peter's first season, already nearly perfect, was about to take a further leap upward with the return – top secret! – of the Cybermen. This was a tremendously exciting idea, because the Cybermen, though known to all *Doctor Who* viewers as the best monster after the Daleks, had appeared only infrequently.

During the ten years the series had been made in colour, there had only been one Cyberman story, and that had been quickly overshadowed by the arrival of Davros. They were essentially a monster of the Second Doctor's time. Their first story, *The Tenth Planet*, ended with William Hartnell regenerating in to Patrick, and then, for three years, they cropped up all over the place: on the moon, in a weird tomb, in the London sewers. Once they were accompanied by little rodent-like metallic Cybermats, tiny slithery things which gave children nightmares. In the time of the Third Doctor, they made no more than a cameo appearance, in the *Carnival of Monsters*.

For the average *Doctor Who* enthusiast in 1981, the Cybermen where mysterious, known only through the novels and through many vivid photographs. From story to story, their look changed, in a way the Daleks did not: first, there had been the cloth-faced Cyberman with the circular mouth, caught in a famous close-up shot, head half-turned, and in a mid-shot, a bunch of them walking through a blizzard with Davy Lamps around their midriffs. Later, there had been the sewer story, Invasion, with handlebars on the sides of their heads, the faces now metallic, the mouth a letter-box slit. Each eye was a disc with, on the lower outside edge, another, smaller disc, like a teardrop, which made them look rather sad.

Years earlier, a photograph had been taken of a Dalek on London Bridge, which many innocents had believed to be a scene from *The Dalek Invasion of Earth*. Not so!, said smug 'experts,' no such scene existed! That was only a publicity shot! The second opportunity for dreaded 'authorities' to show off their superior knowledge was a much-reprinted shot of several Cybermen on the steps of St. Paul's, taken during the making of the sewer episodes. Cor!, that must have been a great scene, thought thousands of kiddies. *Actually,* said the nasal, purse-lipped experts, the Cybermen *never* walked down the steps of St. Paul's on the telly...

Adding to the mysteriousness of the Cybermen stories was that so many episodes had been destroyed. In 1981, this was academic, because it was no more possible to see the extant episodes than the lost ones. But the thought that they were not to be found in a dusty vault at TV Centre, that they did not exist anywhere on earth, added to their piquancy. Of the quartet of early Cyberman adventures, none existed whole. One, *The Tomb of the Cybermen*, had been entirely lost.

Here is an interesting example of the workings of memory. It was said by every *Doctor Who* viewer old enough to remember it that *The Tomb of the Cybermen* was a classic. It was, in fact, *the* classic, the ultimate *Doctor Who* story. This was so widely said that it solidified into a concrete fact, as much-repeated falsehoods often do.

Around 1990, someone found the lost 'classic', every last moment of it! Once remembered only from a couple of photographs, the complete story was now there for all to see, released on video with a great deal of fanfare. Matthew found a second-hand copy in Soho, and impulsively bought it for two quid.

It was a delightful entertainment. Patrick was as adorable as ever, the girls and boys splendid, the atmosphere strong, but it was not as utterly terrific as had been said, though the tomb set was very cool. But then, nothing could have been as utterly terrific as *The Tomb of the Cybermen* had been reputed to be...

After their huge first success in the serial *The Dead Planet*, the return of the Daleks was promoted aggressively on every occasion, their names, (the main draw, a bigger draw than the Doctor himself), were blazed across the titles. *The Power of the Daleks*! *The Evil of the Daleks*! *Day of the Daleks*! Viewers were never allowed to be surprised by their appearance. Many of the Cybermen stories, conversely, did not mention Cybermen in the titles. What was on *The Moonbase*? You had to tune in to find out. *The Invasion*! But of what? They appeared as a gasp-making surprise. *Earthshock* followed this tradition. John Nathan-Turner was determined to keep their comeback a secret. He came to Matthew in the Castle and told him not to mention them to anyone:

"It's stipulated in your contract. Don't talk about them!"

The poor man was, of course, defeated. There were a number of viewing galleries from which anyone in TV Centre could watch the proceedings of a studio, and a producer who wanted these galleries to be kept off-limits had to request a 'closed studio' – a studio would be 'closed' for the shooting of a nude scene, for example. John 'closed' the studio for *Earthshock*. One evening the man who had circulated the news of Olivier's casting approached him in the bar.

"I had to try every single gallery, and the last one I came to was open. The new Cybermen look great!"

But secrets were impossible to keep anyway, despite closed studios and Matthew's zipped mouth. A number of 'fans' managed somehow to get their hands on scripts. Perhaps someone in the office secretly passed them on, (there was a rumour to this effect), or perhaps they were being stolen. Once in their hands, these 'fans' flaunted their advance knowledge.

"I've just read *Earthshock*," said one bald little fellow, before a moment had been rehearsed. "So have I," said Matthew.

For Matthew, who loved *Doctor Who*, this desire for inside information was weird. If you really liked the programme, surely you wanted to come to each episode with as little knowledge as possible? That was the only way to see them fresh, as intended. Why spoil the effect?

The other big secret was that Adric was to die heroically attempting to save Earth, the first time a companion with any public profile was to be killed. A couple of girls had died in an interminable Dalek story, *The Dalek Masterplan*, which ran for twelve episodes and was the longest *Doctor Who* serial to date. These women came on board the TARDIS in an early episode and died in a later episode of the same story so they were not ongoing cast-members. Later, Matthew worked with one of them, Adrienne Hill, when they were both hired to read at a poetry event in, of all places, the Natural History Museum in Kensington. They intoned poems together among dinosaur bones. Adrienne was interested to hear that Matthew had been in *Doctor Who*.

"I hold the record," she said, "as the shortest-running *Doctor Who* girl. But..." she added in a whisper, "*they* tracked me down. It's all very odd, isn't it?"

"You mean the fans?"

"A Scottish man called Gordon found me."

"Oh, Gordon, yes. He's a nice man, actually."

Another cast member at the museum got a crush on Adrienne and, not receptive to small hints, had to be told where to go in no uncertain terms.

Adric was the second *Doctor Who* regular to be killed by the Cybermen, the first being, of course, the First Doctor. Matthew worked with the woman who had vision-mixed the transformation of William Hartnell into Patrick Troughton. Crikey, said Matthew, that's a big *Doctor Who* moment. She didn't seem to regard it as a highlight of her career, though half a century later writers and effects people were still fascinated by it. She could not have imagined that, forty years later, the Doctor's regeneration scenes would be built up to ever greater grandeur, Chris Bidmead and

Blue Box Boy: A Memoir of Doctor Who in Four Episodes

Russell T. Davies making huge-scale epics out of the Doctor's death.

Long before rehearsals started for *Earthshock*, long before the scripts landed on his mat even, Matthew knew about Adric's death. This was because, for some inexplicable reason, Peter had been walking around with an advance copy, which Matthew happened to flick through, while it was at Peter's elbow in the canteen.

Probably he looked visibly upset when he saw the last page. He was, but not for the straight-forward reason Peter and others assumed. Of course, romantic as Matthew was, he liked the idea of his character snogging another character and moving to another planet. The universe of *Doctor Who* was not ready for a boy who fell in love with boys, so it would have been a girl, but that was fine, he liked girls.

And yet, he knew that the death of an ongoing character was a brilliant, unique way to go. He should, knowing the programme as he did, have been thrilled. In some sense he actually was. But there was such a thing as reality. His own brother had ended his own life a couple of years earlier and Matthew felt he would in some way be re-enacting something that had already happened. Any actor will tell you that they draw on their own experiences for the people they play, and here he was – he felt – being asked to touch on something very dark in a programme which was essentially light and throwaway.

No-one on *Doctor Who* knew about this, he had never brought it up, and even if they had it would not and should not have made a difference, but the fact was that, as far as Matthew was concerned, the character of Adric was touching on something very dark – darker in fact than the sensational, manipulative moment itself. Talk about taking it all too seriously! Janet had once said to him,

"The trouble is you are always trying to find things in these scripts that aren't there."

But Janet did not have a clue what it was he'd found. And, in the end, she was wrong: it was there.

Peter Grimwade had the outré idea of adding further spice to the already flavourful concoction which was *Earthshock* by casting a comic actress in the leading roll of the spaceship captain. Beryl Reid was known mainly as a comedienne from the radio, though known to Matthew only as one of those 'celebrities' who seem to make a full-time occupation of appearing on game shows, on the strength of which they are invited to open supermarkets and fetes, for which they perhaps charge hefty fees. Beryl cropped up most weeks on Blankety-Blank. She had an ongoing joke about a little man who lived under her desk. There was more to her than this: she had won a Tony award on Broadway for her work in *The Killing of Sister George* and she had appeared in the BBC adaptations of John Le Carré's Smiley novels.

Matthew was warned to watch out for her.

"She'll eat you alive," said James Warwick, who was having a nice time toting a laser gun with vast, camp energy.

Beryl was completing another job and did not come onto *Earthshock* until rehearsals were well underway. When she arrived she did have the forbidding manner of a furious granny, but in fact she took to Matthew and flattered him and patted him on the head a lot. She might have felt a certain bond with him, because Grimwade was giving him a hard time and, with his usual incompetence, giving her a hard time too. She told Matthew that after one rehearsal Peter took her aside and said, with his bitten consonants,

"Beryl, you are not up to standard."

This seriously upset her. She had been an actor for forty years and had won awards and acclaim. It was unclear to her how this criticism was meant to help. If he wanted her to get *better,* this was the least effective way of achieving it.

It turned out that the job she had just completed was an episode of *Worzel Gummidge*, a successful ITV series based on the children's novels by Barbara Euphan Todd, developed by and starring Jon Pertwee as a scarecrow who walked and talked, and, on a single which was a minor hit, sung after a fashion. Matthew asked her how she had liked making the programme. It was horrible, she said, though she liked the two child stars. It rained all the time, she said. One afternoon, she was standing in the rain after shooting had finished and Jon Pertwee sped past her in an enormous, empty Land Rover with enough room for seven Beryls. His thick tires ran though a puddle and soaked her. It was unfortunate that when Matthew encountered Jon Pertwee at events, he could never get this image out of his mind: a spray of water drowning an old woman. The Land Rover zooming away.

She talked a lot about her cats. She had a dozen of them. Matthew liked cats himself, but found hour-long lunchtimes with Beryl a little draining. After a glass of wine she could talk about her cats at considerable length, leaving Matthew with a small, dull headache. Perhaps because of this, she struck him as a lonely, though essentially a kind old woman.

Beryl lived in a little ivy-covered house which she had tweely named Honeypot Cottage. Or perhaps it had always been called that? She was badly dyslexic and had to learn her lines from tape recordings. She claimed always to develop her characters starting with their shoes. She knew nothing of *Doctor Who*, not even what a TARDIS was.

When the programme finally aired, she turned out to be the most colourful thing in it. She was not slick but nor was she bland; she had her own strong presence. Matthew loved Eric Saward's *Doctor Who* scripts, and he didn't think Eric would be offended if it was said that the spaceship captain as written was a formula character, with hardly a line which could not be found in a guidebook to science fiction clichés. Beryl's sheer confusion gave her captain a kind of bewildered life, which a more robust version would have missed. To add to the spectacle, she wore a butch leather coat and her hair was dyed a curious marmalade.

The Cyber-Captain was played by a tall man called David Banks. David was open and chatty and exuded extraordinary self-possession. For David, *Earthshock* was only a beginning. Throughout the next six years, with each new Cyberman story – and there were many of them, each a little less effective than the last – David was back, booming his way from planet to planet as the Cyber-Captain. He had that skill for squeezing every last penny out of his association. He turned out a paperback novel about the Cybermen, and a coffee-table book. He was pleased to inform Matthew a few years later that he had also played the Doctor, in the theatre. This was not in *Doctor Who and the Seven Keys to Doomsday*, but a brand new piece put together in the mid-eighties, though apparently incorporating plot elements from the earlier play. It toured the provinces for many months. The Doctor was played for the first half of the tour by Jon Pertwee and then by Colin Baker, and David Banks was to be seen nightly as the – it can be imagined – delectably evil villain. But David was also the Doctor's understudy, and when Jon Pertwee was unable on a couple of occasions to appear, David stepped into his shoes – which must have been fun – and somebody else, presumably, played the villain. Initially, the hope had been that the *Doctor Who* boy and girl would be played by Jason Donovan and Kylie Minogue, at that time stars of the Australian soap opera *Neighbours*. They said no.

Matthew would have been interested in seeing this play, which was apparently a merry romp suitable for those attractive Victorian theatres in seaside towns where what actors call Tatty Tours circulate, promoted with posters featuring half-forgotten TV heads, TV policemen appearing in old thrillers, sitcom actors in Ray Cooney farces. The West End might have been whispered of by producers of the *Doctor Who* play, as it is for many of these tours, but the bus broke down countless miles from Shaftesbury Avenue, as it usually does.

Alongside David was a Cyber-lieutenant, played by an equally tall, slightly gawky Sussex lad scarcely twenty-one years old. He did not have the presence or the distinctive voice of David Banks but he worked hard and he could not believe his luck in finding himself on *Doctor Who*.

The story included a scene featuring the Doctor and Adric, where a wall blew up. For this, explosives were laid behind the wall. Matthew had never been in the vicinity of an explosion before. He asked the effects man who was laying the explosives if it was safe.

"Oh, completely!" said the man. Then he left the studio. The make-up girls left the studio. Lighting technicians left the studio. The cameramen made reassuring grunts, then they locked off their cameras and left the studio. The boy on the boom left the studio. The Production Assistant left the studio. The cat left the studio. The mice left the studio. Peter and Matthew looked at each other. There was no-one in the studio but them. This was not reassuring. But when the wall blew up and the Doctor and Adric threw themselves on the floor it was a very exhilarating sensation.

A couple of days before the last batch of *Earthshock* scenes were to be recorded, a phone call came from a journalist.

"I hear you're leaving *Doctor Who*," said the journalist.

John hadn't given Matthew any instructions on what to say if asked but he supposed he should deny it.

On his last day, as he entered the studio after supper, a man he had never seen before came out from the shadows and approached him. He was friendly.

"Is it right you're about to leave the series?"

Something clicked in Matthew's head. The BBC was crawling with people who got extra money from passing tips to journalists.

"Oh no!" he said. "I've got ages and ages!"

The man disappeared back into the shadows.

A couple of hours later, Matthew shot his last scene.

The usual little dressing room party took place, everyone saying goodbye to Matthew under unflattering strip lighting. The party dragged on. Eventually, in the small hours, John got Matthew a cab, and the driver drove him all the way to his parents' house in Sussex, two bottles of champagne and a huge bouquet of flowers at his side. It was a long, depressing drive.

Ten minutes before the final episode of *Earthshock* was to be broadcast, the phone rang. It was Peter Grimwade, full of praise.

"It's very moving," he said. "The explosion is spectacular. Good luck for the future."

Poor Peter. He meant well, but he could never make the right judgement,

Blue Box Boy: A Memoir of Doctor Who in Four Episodes

not even at the final moment. The last thing Matthew had wanted was a phone call from him. Dear Peter. But Matthew realised that he actually liked him and was touched by the call, even while he put the phone down in a fury.

A fortnight before *Earthshock* was aired, Matthew got a less predictable call: from *This is Your Life*. Peter Davison, though not thirty, was to be a victim, and, said Matthew's agent, would Matthew come along and appear on it? Well, he supposed he would. He had only seen little bits of *This is Your Life*. Every week an Irishman called Eamonn, who had been a boxer, sprang out at an unsuspecting but famous personality and presented him with a vast book about his life, a sort of grand photo album which Matthew assumed to be empty. Then the victim was taken to an old music hall theatre which had been dedicated exclusively to *This is Your Life* for years. For the next half hour people ran onto the stage into his arms saying how marvellous he was. They spoke for a few seconds or, if very important, for half a minute, and were then ushered to a bank of chairs, which filled up throughout the programme. The lives were presented free of any darkness except the sentimental kind – the early death of a parent, a tough job in a blacking factory. Real suffering was expunged as firmly as same-sex lovers. First wives were forgotten. Instead, aging schoolteachers talked of the victim as a young and talented scallywag, Mums and Dads said they'd always known he was a bit special, and perfect wives and kiddies said what a great dad he was and how he loved gardening. The result was that even interesting people were reduced to *Radio Times* smugness. Yet it was the most widely watched programme on TV – more popular even than the soaps – and, because none of the victims or guests were paid, it cost very little to make, though Eamonn the boxer was probably a bit pricey. After the recording, a party went on into the small hours. The programme was recorded eight days before it was shown, but a gentleman's understanding existed and the TV pages kept the victim's name a secret.

Only one victim, as far as Matthew knew, had ever refused to appear. This was Richard Gordon, who wrote large numbers of reputedly amusing books about a doctor's life. They were the forerunners of the James Herriot vet series. They were filmed successfully, launching the career of Matthew's favourite movie actor, Dirk Bogarde, and in the seventies they became that long series of sitcoms starring Robin Nedwell. When he spotted Eamonn, Richard Gordon sprinted away and ITV had to show a repeat instead.

The trap for Peter was set in Leicester Square, where he had been led to think he was making a promotional ad for *Doctor Who*. He approached the TARDIS and was surprised to see Janet Fielding emerge from it, then Sarah Sutton, then – gasp! – Matthew. Then Eamonn! Matthew hoped that

Peter might run away like Richard Gordon so they could all go home early, but he made a brave stab at looking pleasantly surprised. Matthew never did ask whether the huge album presented to Peter contained anything but blank pages.

At the theatre where the bulk of the programme was to be taped, Matthew was stunned to see Beryl Reid in the make-up chair, because apart from their brief encounter on *Doctor Who* she didn't know Peter Davison at all. Matthew had thought the guests on *This is Your Life* were supposed to be close friends and relatives of the victim, and, of course, pals from drama school who had less luminous careers. He could not understand why Beryl was there. He hardly knew why he himself was there, though John Nathan-Turner told him that it was good timing, because Peter's *This is Your Life* was to go out only a day or two after the last episode of *Earthshock*. All those weeping kiddies could see that he was not dead after all. Matthew had his doubts, because he thought most *Doctor Who* kiddies did not watch *This is Your Life*. Anyway, he always resented the assumption, common in TV, that outside its own glamorous circles, Britain consisted solely of viewers in suburbs with dreary lives who spent all their spare time in front of the telly, watching absolutely everything. Matthew's Aunt Liz once referred to those who did not have the special qualities it took to work for the BBC as 'ordinary citizens', implying that those within its walls were not.

Beryl entered grandly, the final guest. She hugged Peter and said how great he was. Eamonn asked her about her career. This was the highlight of Peter's *This is Your Life*: Beryl talking about herself. She said that she had always loved *all* the jobs she'd had throughout her career.

Except, she added in an undertone, one.

Matthew sat there next to Sarah and Anthony, wondering which job she was thinking of. *Doctor Who* or *Worzel Gummidge*? It had to be one of the two. But Beryl was taken away in a limo before the after-show party got underway and he never had the chance to ask her. He pictured the whole gathering at Peter's *This is Your Life* being splashed by muddy water, spurting from under the wheels of Jon's enormous Land Rover.

Peter Grimwade was bursting to be a writer, and now he found his dream a reality. The final story of the season, *Time-Flight*, was his first TV script. Unfortunately, it was for that series about which Peter had such enormous reservations.

In Peter's action-packed story, Concorde goes through some kind of dimension doorway and ends up a long way from London, or even Sydney. Matthew had heard detailed descriptions from Peter of his day of research, spent in the Concorde cockpit. In the episode as it finally appeared, you could be certain that the lingo the pilots used in preparing for take-off was exactly the lingo of Concorde pilots in reality. It took up half the first episode. Every fact Peter had gathered was included. Most of the rest of *Time-Flight* was written not by Peter but by Eric Saward, in his capacity as script editor. Eric told Matthew this in crystal clear terms:

"It was a mess. I had to rewrite the whole thing."

Matthew appeared for a second or two as a ghost. He had to let out exactly the kind of loud, eggy shriek which Tom Baker had refused to do at the end of *Logopolis*. Tony Ainley appeared as the Master in a very peculiar disguise. Memorably, the guest star, Nigel Stock, who had had his own series in the seventies, called *Owen MD*, and was among the very best Doctor Watsons, taught Matthew how to play golf in the make-up room, folding Matthew's fingers around a club which happened to be to hand and demonstrating how to swing, to the amusement of the make-up women.

Matthew later asked Peter if he would have preferred to have directed *Time-Flight* himself rather than entrusting it to the hands of Ron Jones.

"That," he said, "would have been a disaster. No writer should direct his own script." This was wise.

Matthew was miffed to hear that now he was gone, the *Doctor Who* crew were boarding planes for glamorous locations like Amsterdam and Lanzarote. These were a big improvement on Tunbridge Wells.

But it would be disingenuous to pretend that Matthew was not quietly pleased, when he saw a number of episodes from the following seasons, to observe that though they were absolutely excellent, they were a teensy bit less good than his own episodes. (This might have been wishful thinking on his part). Johnny Byrne brought back the Time Lords in an excellent story which was not quite as magical as *The Keeper of Traken*, despite some lovely shots of Janet in Amsterdam. And then the Sea Devils and the Silurians teamed up, now inexplicably wearing heavy helmets. Eric Saward developed a terrific line in fast-moving thrillers featuring Daleks and Cybermen, though these were *events* more than they were stories, chock full of references to older episodes. Eric was one of those brilliant *Doctor Who* writers who, far from pushing boundaries, burrowed to the very heart of the format, making his scripts both familiar and at the same time fresh and new. Terence Dudley wrote that splendid period piece *The King's Demons*, which had the edge on *Black Orchid*, but only just. One of the best *Doctor Who* cliffhangers ever came in a vastly camp story starring a plump comic actress as a space pirate, complete with eye-patch, when the final shot of the first episode revealed that what had appeared in its control room to be an ordinary spaceship, though with maritime influences, was a gigantic clipper ship sailing through the stars.

Kinda, a story which did not need a sequel, had in fact yielded one, but Matthew was able to see only a single episode of this when it was shown, because he was in a play. Another actor watched it with him, and he said what a strange actress Janet Fielding was, failing to understand that Tegan had been 'taken over' in the story. He was more impressed by Martin Clunes, not yet famous. "He's got a very nice bottom," said the actor. Matthew only saw this story in its entirety in 1992, when a friend leant him the tape. It was brilliant, but less brilliant than *Kinda*. Martin Clunes clearly had more going for him than just a bottom.

The gifted Mark Strickson arrived as a public schoolboy, wearing a school uniform for ages and ages. John mentioned to Matthew that the public school idea was found in a submission that was not otherwise of the slightest interest, so the *Doctor Who* office bought not the offered story but simply the idea. Mark was followed by the humanoid robot called Kamelion, visually impressive but inert, though voiced by a considerable actor called Gerald Flood.

Matthew was summoned back to the studio for the final moments of *The Caves of Androzani*, in which Peter turned into Colin Baker. This marvel of a serial was directed by the ebullient, neatly bearded Graeme Harper, who had been an extremely bubbly Production Assistant on *Warriors' Gate*. Graham was a man of enormous energy, who could sometimes be spotted recharging his batteries by snatching thirty-second naps at the edges of sets. He was short and stocky, and as a PA he had seemed slightly swamped by the headphones and radios and other equipment he had carried on his person. Shouts and complaints and curses from the box had to be transformed by the PA into gentle requests. "Get that fucking actor out of shot!" had to be relayed as "Sir, would you move just a little to the left?" Few people did this job with Graeme Harper's diplomacy.

He was a superb director, with inventive use of cameras and a gift for keeping his actors happy. *The Caves of Androzani* may have been his first directing job. A thousand years later, he was still to be found working on *Doctor Who*, this time with David Tennant.

Matthew was delighted to do this little cameo, because it meant he finally got to be in a script by the doyen of *Doctor Who* writers, Robert Holmes. It was pleasing to the ego to find that the Fifth Doctor's final pronouncement before he expired was "*Adric...*"

*   *   *

One way or another, for Peter Davison, *Doctor Who* worked out brilliantly. He made a firm commitment to doing three seasons only, and when John implored him to do a fourth, he declined. He was the only one of the original Doctors not to find himself associated with the part to the exclusion of everything else. For Peter, thirty years later, *Doctor Who* was a job on his CV among many others: vets and hen-pecked husbands and detectives and professors and murderers and pools winners and galactic cowboys and edible aliens.

Has any Equity member had more leads in more series than Peter? Whether this was because of his flexibility as an actor, his temperament, which was always spoken of as exceptionally equable, or skilled management, or a combination of all of these, he escaped the shadow of *Doctor Who* – that creepy shadow which turns all its other actors into walking skeletons.

And Colin arrived in his Technicolor coat in a marvellously enjoyable oddity called *The Twin Dilemma*, and Nicola with her American accent. The Doctor was tried by the Time Lords in the longest-running *Doctor Who* story. Unfortunately the writer entrusted with the resolution to this epic, Robert Holmes, died before he could write it and he had kept his intentions close to his chest. Other writers were hired, and had to scrabble about trying to come up with an ending.

Then Bonnie Langford, floating in a bubble created by Kate O'Mara, and Sylvester with his puckish sweetness and Ace with her explosives and her battle cry.

Occasionally a friend or acquaintance would crop up in an episode. A young actor called Adam Blackwood had been a star of the Barn Theatre in Ansty, Sussex, where amateur actors were directed by the professional playwright James Forsyth.

Adam, six or seven years older than Matthew, was at RADA, returning to the Barn between terms. There was an implication in the air that, instead of sitting about reading comics, ignorant boys like Matthew should be watching and learning from Adam's every move. There, the ladies who hung about backstage seemed to suggest, was a real actor. Adam Blackwood was the only professional actor Matthew would ever know to have a huge wooden Victorian make-up box, stuffed with lipsticks and greases and powders and puffs and eyebrow pencils and a mirror, smeared, as if from decades of use. He loved to coat his features in slick creams to play Dickens lawyers. He found work easily after RADA, as doomed soldiers in trenches and assistants to policemen. In *Doctor Who*, he had to wear one of the strangest costumes ever seen, reminiscent of a baby's pyjamas, floppy at the toes, like Winken, Blinken, and Nod. He maintained a remarkable dignity even in these astounding clothes.

Georgina Hale, a rare, extraordinarily creative actor, for whom *Doctor Who* was no more than a job for the money, nevertheless threw all her talent into it, coming up against the wall of its limitations. "I'm trying to make something interesting out of a load of clichés and I'm getting no support from the director at all. And Sheila Hancock isn't much help either!"

Clive Swift said to Matthew that he had been flattered to be offered *Doctor Who*.

"Then I knew I'd made it!"

Murray Melvin was summoned to meet Russell T. Davies, who puzzled aloud about the fact that Murray had never appeared in the programme.

"I wonder why not?" mused Russell T. Davies.

"That," said Murray, "is not for *you* to ask. That's for *me* to ask." Murray ended up not in *Doctor Who* itself, but in *Torchwood*, which he enjoyed, "though a lot of the cast spend all their time between takes on their mobiles."

EPISODE FOUR
SURVIVAL

Boyishly pleased, he contemplated a silver candlestick as if testing its authenticity. "One meets people, Della. Yet must move on. O my Fairbanks and my Barrymore long ago."

Peter Vansittart, **Aspects of Feeling**

Gregory resisted the temptation to open his eyes, and immediately found himself inside a television set. The cathode tube, he saw, was womb-shaped, with the fundus (on which coloured pictures were projected) pointing out into the room and the vestibule packed with electrodes like so many penises projecting visions into a womanly organ. He looked about him at the small shelves of transistors like a neat library, or a coloured garden of electrical scaffolding, and perceived that the basic pattern of the whole thing was also yoni-lingam since straight currents everywhere were modulating circular ones that travelled in coils. At this he realised that the set was turned on and that he was caught up in a great hot orgy of electricity. Turning about to find some escape, he put his hand on a wire and with a green flash along all his nerves was pulled in among the jockeying currents.

Peter Redgrove and Penelope Shuttle, **The Terrors of Dr. Treviles**

1

One of the nicest things about being on TV was that it made it easy for Matthew to have lots of sex. He was, after all, eighteen, the age when nearly everyone has just lost their virginity or is just about to lose it.

He supposed others must have experienced a similar link between their work on *Doctor Who* and an improvement in their sex lives. Tom Baker was at the time reputedly the randiest actor in equity and it is unlikely he would have had women by the dozen without the *Doctor Who* character lending him an unearthly glow. His second, brief, marriage, of course, came directly from *Doctor Who*.

Homosexual activity was still illegal in Britain for people under twenty-one, so for three years Matthew was a lawbreaker, and this appealed to him. There were debates on the radio about whether gay sex should be banned entirely, with crazy people saying how disgusting and sinful it was. This gave him a thrill. He liked the idea that people thought he was decadent, though he was not especially.

The London gay scene was centred around Earl's Court at the time, with a couple of bars on the Kings' Road and a ginormous dance club called Heaven underneath the arches at Charing Cross. Heaven was the main meat market of the London scene if you were determined to get laid on a Saturday night. It was not really Matthew's cup of tea but it was interesting. There were countless tall, narrow men with dark hair and neat moustaches all over the place.

It turned out that the DJ at Heaven was a *Doctor Who* fan called Ian Levine, the man who had made a fuss about the Tharls on *Warriors' Gate*. Of course, Heaven was not a very unlikely place for a *Doctor Who* fan. Matthew did not assume that absolutely every *Doctor Who* fan was gay, but that heterosexuals were a peculiar minority, as in certain corners of New York after dark. In a reversal of the usual assumption, it could be taken that any particular fan was gay until it was revealed that he wasn't.

Sometimes Matthew would see Ian Levine at Heaven. He played dance music but did not look as if he danced much himself. He was plump in a Bunterish way. He had small, currant eyes in one of those round, expressionless faces which give nothing away.

Ian occasionally hung around at TV Centre in the director's box on studio days and may have had some semi-formal post on the series as an adviser for while, though Matthew was never sure about this. John would sometimes ask Matthew for some information on a long-forgotten episode under the mistaken impression that he knew the history of *Doctor Who* in detail. When Christopher Bidmead was writing about the Master's shrink-ray, if that's what it was called, John asked Matthew how the shrinking effect had been done on the Jon Pertwee programmes. Matthew had no clue. He had not seen them since he was ten. He scarcely remembered the shrink-ray. He didn't want to disappoint John so he invented an answer, vaguely remembering an Action Man in *The Deadly Assassin*. Ian, on the other hand, with his priceless stash of episodes, could be relied on to have accurate knowledge.

Ian co-wrote the theme tune for the first *Doctor Who* spin-off (with a good musician called Fiachra Trench, who soon abandoned Ian and did some terrific arrangements for Van Morrison). This thriller was produced while Matthew was in *Doctor Who*. It was called *K9 and Company*, and starred Elisabeth Sladen as Sarah Jane Smith and John Leeson as the voice of K9. Hopes of it becoming a series were dashed, but the one-off episode, shown as a special on a Bank Holiday Monday, was jolly enough in its way. It was written by Terence Dudley and was about witchcraft. It had more of the spirit of those old adventure programmes of the 1960s, *The Avengers* or *The Saint*, than *Doctor Who*. The BBC production style was not at its best in fast-cut action *a la The Avengers*, and the K9 opening credits weren't swift enough for the effect of excitement they aimed for. Elisabeth Sladen looked slightly embarrassed to be jumping over walls and leaping about in the mode of Tara King. Ian's theme had John Leeson saying "K9!" over and over to a merry synth-driven riff which moved along nicely. John Leeson had been surprised to go into the studio to record this theme and, having said "K9!" once into the microphone, been immediately sent away.

Strangely, Eric Saward, the script editor for *Doctor Who* and *K9 and Company*, asked Matthew for his opinion of the special over a drink, which was very thoughtful of him. Matthew said he had enjoyed it greatly, but after years of watching the Doctor saving planets and galaxies once every four weeks, despatching a couple of witches from a local graveyard seemed a bit *small*.

Ian was partly responsible – Matthew was led to believe – for the idea which John took up shortly after Matthew had left the series: all the stories across a whole season should have references to past episodes.

Ian had two overarching obsessions in his life. One was *Doctor Who*, though his emotional loyalty was mainly to the early episodes, which he had seen as a child. In some shadowy way he had acquired a number of reels from the BBC. As well as being a DJ, Ian was a record producer, which sprang from his other passion, Motown records. He was sometimes credited with inventing Hi-Energy dance music, which was all the rage in the gay clubs at the time. The words he wrote were modest adjustments of Motown lyrics. He used black soul singers, sometimes aging Motown stars.

In the mid-nineteen-eighties criticism began to swirl around *Doctor Who*, triggered in part by Michael Grade, who was the controller of BBC1 and hated the programme as it then was. Obviously, controllers of BBC1 scheduled programmes they didn't care for all the time. By making his hostility public, Grade was indulging in political game-playing. It was suggested by Grade that the programme might be suspended for a while. The word 'suspended' was ambiguous. Ian threw himself into the fray. A short while before, the Band Aid single had been a big success, raising money for the starving of Africa. Ian thought a similar record could be made to save *Doctor Who*. John told Matthew about this over breakfast at a Science Fiction convention.

It was none of Matthew's business, but he thought the idea was simply horrid. Saving a rocky TV show seemed a very modest ambition for a charity single, quite different from saving people wracked with famine. The word 'pathetic' might have crossed his lips while he chewed his croissant.

Ian must have struggled to find what are now called A-List names, because the contributors, among them a singer from Bucks Fizz and a lady who did comedy impressions on TV, were hardly likely to send your average rocker running to the record shop. It shifted few copies.

Matthew will never know what happened to bring the friendship of John Nathan-Turner and Ian to an end. But when it ended, it ended bitterly.

There was a critical programme on BBC2 called *Did You See...?* in which three talking heads discussed a couple of chosen programmes from the previous week's television. Then there would be a short film on some TV-related matter. With *Doctor Who* under intense criticism, the *Did You See...?* producers decided to do a mini-documentary. Matthew did not watch *Did You See...?* (or anything else) on a regular basis and only happened on it by accident.

John Nathan-Turner had turned down the invitation to appear. He had, in fact, always disliked *Did You See...?* "I don't think the BBC should be slagging off its own output," he said. So the time was taken up by the gabbling heads of a couple of ex-enthusiasts. Ian was among these chattering nitwits. Ian said how terrible the programme was now. It had been worthless since 1980, he said. This, of course, was the year John had taken over. Watching Ian's jaw go up and down with his opinions struck Matthew as one of the most macabre things he had ever witnessed. Ian did not mention that he had been involved in some of those programmes. He did not mention that he had produced a charity record which was a great deal worse than any episode of *Doctor Who*. As a trivial matter of opinion, it was impossible to care what Ian thought, but as far as Matthew was concerned, if he had had the slightest sliver of grace he would have refused to do the programme. In the interview, Ian looked unnervingly like one of the race of *Doctor Who* space warriors called the Sontarans.

2

The *Doctor Who* cult could be said to have begun formally with the founding of the *Doctor Who* Appreciation Society around 1977. As the title implies, this was not a fan club of a jovial, celebratory sort. When you sent off your membership fee of three pounds you did not receive the fan club goodies you hoped for, like Tom Baker stickers and TARDIS key rings and Leela fridge magnets and UNIT badges. Instead, you got newsletters, written in the prose style of a slightly sprightly WI bulletin. There was never any news to report because the *Doctor Who* office did not care for the *Doctor Who* Appreciation Society and did not tell them anything. Instead there were 'departments' with slightly silly, important-sounding titles. There was a president, an archivist, a historian, a reviews editor, even a co-ordinator, whatever that was supposed to mean. To the observer, there was something playful about its grandiosity, as when boys sleep in tents in the back garden pretending they are in the African veldt.

The moment there was a *Doctor Who* Appreciation Society there was a rump of members who did not 'appreciate' the programme. They complained that it wasn't as good as it used to be. (This had always been a cause for complaint. One actor Matthew worked with said that when William Hartnell had turned into Patrick Troughton, for him the series had been ruined. "I thought, why are they doing it all *funny?*")

Committee meetings took place, Matthew was told, where minutes were taken and arguments were hot. Fists thumped on tables, bitterness was rife, unpleasant sects were formed, plotting the destruction of other unpleasant sects. It was a caricature of village life, lots of bloated feuds over matters for which 'insignificant' was too grand a word. Committee members lay sweating in the night over their hatred of other committee members and, in a weird twist, of the programme itself.

An extreme example of this darkness was a young man, the kind of muscular gay man who goes to clubs in army fatigues. He had developed a cordial loathing for John Nathan-Turner and his work. He launched a fanzine exclusively devoted to whinging about John, pages and pages of vicious bile. John could do nothing right. Everything was crap. When a comic sketch about *Doctor Who* for the *Children In Need* appeal was allotted a production number in line with the episodes, this boy concluded that the sketch therefore had 'official' status, lodged forever in *Doctor Who* continuity, a wicked ploy by John to make the programme a laughing stock. Things ended unhappily for the boy. He had a huge mental collapse and his psychiatrist instructed him to apologise to everyone he had ever treated badly. So he went to John and begged his forgiveness, which of course was granted.

Among the members Matthew liked was a boy called Gary Russell. Gary was only a year or so older than Matthew. Like many *Doctor Who* fans, Gary Russell was shy in the outer world but confident in the circles of fandom. He had been a child actor, starring for some years in a TV version of *The Famous Five*, Enid Blyton's long series of children's mystery stories. Enid Blyton was one of the most prolific writers ever. She wrote over five hundred books, only twenty-one of them about *The Famous Five*, though there was also a series, identical but for character count, called *The Secret Seven* and a third, with '*Mystery of...*' in the titles, featuring a boy called Fatty. Many dozens of a different stripe were about a boy called Noddy, who lived in Toyland and drove a taxi and shared his bed with a fat elf called Big Ears who was much older than him. Noddy was, literally, a toy boy. Enid Blyton was the favourite author of several generations of British children and is still read today in rewritten versions from which 'outmoded social assumptions' have been eliminated. Gary was excellently cast in the TV rendition of *The Famous Five*, having the good fortune to fit exactly Enid Blyton's description of his character. He was a hero to countless little ones. Have these episodes been released on DVD, in sumptuous boxed sets?

He was once photographed for a *TV Times* article sitting on a pile of *Doctor Who* annuals. He published his own little fanzine. Matthew thought he was quite sweet. He might have been in *K9 and Company* as the boy character, because John Nathan-Turner didn't know about his *Who* interest, until halfway through the reading Eric Saward wandered in and said, "Hello, Gary," and that was the end of that. Instead he rocketed through the skies of fandom, editing the Marvel comic for a while, insisting it wasn't a comic but a magazine. After having done a dreadful interview for the comic many years earlier, Matthew swore he would never talk to it again. Gary was the only person on Earth who could persuade him to relent.

Gary Russell left Marvel to write large numbers of pastiche novels and what were called 'audio dramas,' of which there were many hundreds, released on CD. Then he found himself at the BBC, script editing *The Sarah Jane Adventures* – the modern version of *K9 and Company*, its title inspired presumably by *Batman Adventures* and *Superman Adventures*, the comic book versions of those fabulous TV cartoons made in the nineties. It starred Elisabeth Sladen, whom Matthew had met more than once and liked a lot. Lis's character had for thirty-five years been – "you can't doubt it!" – a blinding sun in the *Doctor Who* firmament. In *Doctor Who* terms, Gary was that rare person of whom it could fairly be said that all his dreams came true. This was pleasing.

A moon-faced gentleman called David Saunders was an interesting character. He was the co-ordinator of the *Doctor Who* Appreciation Society. Perhaps he had a talent for co-ordination. John Nathan-Turner said of him, "He's exactly like a bank manager." Matthew had never met a bank manager but he could not imagine NatWest having much of a future if people like David Saunders ran its branches.

Matthew already fancied himself as a bit bookish and had developed the vile habit of making literary references at unexpected times. When he referred to some obscure writer, David, startlingly, always knew of him. "Well, of course Graham Greene, who I love, is only the *second best* living writer! The best writer of our time is Norman Lewis!" said Matthew, an accurate enough observation but snobbishly inflected. Oh! Norman Lewis! said David Saunders. Matthew was impressed. He went further. Of course, he said, Vernon Watkins is a much better poet than Dylan Thomas. Oh, Vernon Watkins, yes, mumbled David Saunders. Edmund White is all very well, added Matthew affectedly, but Denton Welch was a *genius*. Denton Welch? said David Saunders, oh indeed, Denton Welch.

It turned out that David Saunders was a librarian. He had never read any books in his life but he had shelved them all.

What he had read were comic books. He had a collection of sixties Jack Kirby comics likely to arouse envy even among more down-to-earth personalities than Matthew's. Matthew loved Jack Kirby and owned a couple of his original pages. These pages were in frames on his bedroom wall at his parents' house so they were seen by few. This meant that, for them to earn him social kudos, Matthew had to boast about them. Unfortunately, as he knew no comic book fans, even in this way kudos were scarce. David Saunders was unimpressed, not being a huge Kirby fan. Why, then, don't you *give me all your bloody Jack Kirby comics,* I who will *appreciate them?* This strategy failed.

David Saunders was in his early thirties when Matthew knew him, but he looked older. He gave the impression of having suffered, in an unexplained way. He had perhaps had a stutter as a child because a comment to him, however scintillating or dull, would be followed by the same infuriating pause of two or three seconds before a reply came, rarely one worth the wait. Maybe he had had a fair sized breakdown at some point. He was one of those people who appeared to live with a vague, just tolerable depression all the time, but Matthew found him hard to dislike: He was honest about his need for the simple escape of TV fantasy. "I had to choose whether to get into *Star Trek* or *Doctor Who* and I tossed a coin."

David Saunders had unpretentious tastes. He was an addict of the TV soap *Crossroads*: he was upset when Noele Gordon was 'axed' from the series – photographs of her in a headscarf and sunglasses looking extremely put out were plastered over the tabloids – and again when she died. He always called her Nolly, under the impression that this was her nickname on the set, which may have been so. Saunders also liked the *Carry On* films and the James Bond films. He had a complete run of the Bond novels in hardcover, which were rejects from the library where he worked. Ian Fleming was no Norman Lewis, but he was better than nothing.

"Do you like the novels as much as the movies?"

"I've never read them," he said in his lugubrious voice. "I just have them. All I do is watch the films."

Matthew also liked a stocky Scottish reverend called Ian, who worked in schools for years until getting his own church. Matthew had been in a choir in his mid-teens, touring the churches and cathedrals of Lincolnshire every summer, and he liked the buildings, the swing of the censer, the smell of the incense. He liked talking about theology with Ian, because he knew hardly anything about it and had only the vaguest religious feeling: it was all incredibly abstract and elusive. It was nice to meet at a *Doctor Who* event a person who wanted to talk about something else. In one corner Matthew would discuss with Ian the nuances of transubstantiation while in another Gary Russell answered *Doctor Who* trivia questions.

One *Doctor Who* fan alone received the approval, indeed the admiration, of Peter Grimwade. This was John McElroy. John was darkly handsome. His sex life was rumoured to be full and rich. John had a modest tint of glamour. Grimwade said, "He's lovely, he's the only one of those people I can stand, though because he's a *Doctor Who* fan he must be just as mad as the others." He was one of those whose emotional loyalty was primarily to the black and white episodes, the earlier the better.

When not being a *Doctor Who* fan John was loopy about Dusty Springfield. He ran her fan club and contributed to an admiring book about her. He called her just Dusty as if they were lovers. Matthew had a good feeling about Dusty, but he did not love her enough to join her fan club, though the tone was probably more celebratory than that of the *Doctor Who* Appreciation Society.

3

One of the strange phenomena of science fiction cultdom is the convention. Presumably, in the early days these gatherings spun off from what was horribly called the 'fanzine'. Those now defunct amateur journals seem to have appeared for the first time in the nineteen thirties or early forties, some of them written by people who would later become science fiction writers. Ray Bradbury ran a fanzine as a teenager, copies of which can now be purchased from rare book dealers for thousands of pounds.

Conventions – as far as Matthew could make out – began around the same time as a means of meeting the people known only through correspondence and fanzine subscriptions. These early conventions, about books and comic books, involved no more than a few dozen people. The scene grew fatter with the start of the *Star Trek* cult. *Star Trek* events drew many hundreds, even thousands. Also, they were, in large part, women. This was a change. Women had never been readers of science fiction in great numbers, but the *Star Trek* cult was triggered by them.

People who know nothing about science fiction cultdom tend to assume that it is one huge monolithic block of like-minded creatures. In fact, it divides into countless different categories, the twain meeting only occasionally, like those set circles in maths. There are science fiction fans who watch *Doctor Who* and *Star Trek* and also read J. G. Ballard and Philip K. Dick and Michael Moorcock and Philip José Farmer and keep up with developments in Marvel and D.C. and underground comic books. But these people exist in small numbers. Most *Star Trek* fans have never opened, and will never open, a book by J. G. Ballard, and most comic book enthusiasts do not follow *Doctor Who*. In his stunning naïveté, Matthew, at his first American events, would sometimes drop a reference to someone he liked, Farmer or Ballard or Jack Kirby, expecting admiring cheers and applause for his good taste, receiving instead complete silence.

The first *Doctor Who* conventions occurred, apparently, in the late seventies. What is striking to think now is that the 'celebrities' attended these early events free of charge. Matthew went to his first convention in, probably, 1980. Why on earth did he go? He didn't really want to, and he was not being paid so he had no financial motive, and he had no desire to be any kind of 'celebrity'. He went, he supposed later, to be nice...!

The 'celebrities' were ushered on to a stage where they were interviewed on uncomfortable plastic chairs. Being interviewed, Matthew had no objection to the shy, rather clumsy lads who tried to make a go of it. What appealed to him less were those, stars perhaps of their local amateur dramatics societies, who modelled themselves on the interviewing techniques of Parkinson. These interviewers believed, Matthew suspected, that they were themselves 'celebrities,' and possibly they thought themselves the biggest celebrities of all. Thus fake versions of TV chat shows would take place in hotel ballrooms and campus lecture halls, the interviewer being, he appeared to think, by turns 'witty' or 'controversial' or 'shrewd'.

At the first convention he went to, nobody was too insignificant to be interviewed, nobody had a job too lowly to be without interest to the gaping crowds. Thus, the secretary Jane Judge, a very nice woman, was dragged onto the stage to be grilled by a Parkinson *manqué*. What do *you* do, Jane? Well, I type John's memos... Fascinating!

Then there was the autograph session, a long line, nearly all males: the large bearded men, effete boys, lads in anoraks. And there were the young men with chiselled semi-model features, determined to be what they called an actor, though it was not character but fame that interested them. They did not doubt their potential. "If Matthew *Waterhouse* can do it, I *certainly* can."

Everyone from Chris Bidmead ("I thought you played rather to the gallery, Matthew.") to the unhappy Peter Grimwade to JNT to Janet Fielding to Jane Judge, scrawled in autograph books.

Then, America Called...

By the early eighties, *Doctor Who* was being shown regularly on PBS channels in America. It was not the first time. The Jon Pertwee episodes had been shown on PBS years earlier, then the early Baker programmes, syndicated to commercial stations for showing in the children's after school slot, complete with a newly filmed introduction by an American actor explaining who *Doctor Who* and the Time Lords were and what had happened in the previous episode. But only when these Tom Baker episodes were moved to PBS, *sans* the introduction, did *Doctor Who* catch fire. This was why *Doctor Who* in America was seen very much as The Tom Baker Show, in a way it wasn't quite in Britain, despite Tom's best efforts. Every *Doctor Who* enthusiast in Britain knew before he was ten years old that Tom was one of, so far, four Doctors. One day there would be a fifth. In America, the *Doctor Who* cult and the Tom Baker cult were indistinguishable.

Matthew received a letter from a man whose name ended in '-stein'. He remembered this because he had never met anyone whose name ended in Stein and could think only of Frankenstein and Einstein. Of course, in America, loads of people have names ending in '-stein', and there are some for whom Stein is the whole last name, including the brainy 'celebrity' Ben Stein, a right-wing intellectual who had been an adviser to Nixon and who became a hero to drunken students as a presenter of 'alternative' game shows, a weird career trajectory if ever there was one.

The Stein who wrote to Matthew was a lawyer and, perhaps, a *Doctor Who* fan. It was never quite clear how much of a fan he actually was, and how much his event was merely a business venture, that familiar American act of leaping on a speeding bandwagon that promises $$$$.

Mr. Stein was organizing, said the letter, the biggest *Doctor Who* event ever, to coincide with the twentieth anniversary. Thousands upon thousands of 'fans' would be descending on a hotel specially booked for the event, and Matthew was invited to attend. There had already been a big anniversary event in the UK, which Matthew had taken great pleasure in turning down on the grounds that he was in a play. But now he was available and, further, a fee was offered of considerable enormity. It was, in fact, the smallest fee being offered to anyone. Tom himself was paid, Matthew was later informed, twenty-five thousand dollars to attend this event and even Anthony Ainley got eight, which was more than twice what Mr. Stein had offered Matthew. But his fee would cover his rent and wine bills and book purchases for several months, and his travels. (He liked to travel alone and in this way he wandered through Ireland and France and Italy and Spain). Plus, he had never been to America, and this was his chance to go. Disappointingly, the city was to be Chicago, not New York. For Matthew the idea of America was inseparable from the idea of New York – Matthew's version garnered from Fantastic Four comics and Woody Allen films. Apart from New York there was only, to him, New Orleans with its jazz and the great big river, and the places along its banks that Mark Twain wrote about. Chicago meant nothing but wind and gangsters. Still, it was America.

So he decided, yes, he would go to glittering America, where everyone was beautiful and wealthy and had subscriptions to Marvel Comics and liked jazz! He signed the contract. Mr. Stein was staying for a few days in a plushish hotel in central London and Matthew was living nearby, so he went to the hotel to drop the contract off. He went to the desk with his envelope. At the checkout desk across the lobby, he overheard a hotel employee say, "Yes, sir. We'll take your key for you and look after it. For security purposes, you understand."

An American voice said, very loudly so that it crossed the foyer like a shout though it was really only a remark,

"Really, it's that bad around here, huh?"

Could that be Mr. Stein? wondered Matthew. He did not stay around to find out, but left the envelope and darted away, hearing behind him the footsteps of the American man crossing to the desk to enquire about the envelope.

The organisers had arranged special work permits and Matthew had to go to the American embassy at Grosvenor Square to get his passport stamped. 'Temporary work permit,' said the lovely blue and red stamp. It looked good in his passport. But the taut efficiency of the organisers slackened. The day before he was theoretically to fly out, he had heard nothing from Mr. Stein, so he hadn't a clue what time the plane was, or even which airport it was flying from. He phoned John Nathan-Turner in his Threshold House office and John gave him the necessary information.

When he got back to England, his mother told Matthew that at two in the morning on the day he was due to leave, a man in a postman's uniform had appeared on the front doorstep carrying a large clean card-backed white envelope containing all the information he needed. Matthew opened the envelope – weeks after the event -and there, in slick neat fashion was the flight information and the name of the hotel and a fictional name, under which his room had been booked. Here was drama, albeit contrived: a secret name, documents delivered in the small hours. It was the kind of correspondence it might be imagined spies receive before an important secret mission. Later he found that many Americans loved playacting, the more melodramatic the better. Often they lived hermetic lives and left their houses only to climb into their cars and go to their offices from which they returned in their cars, and their nights were spent watching TV, so their sense of life's excitement had nothing to do with the outer world, of which they were ignorant. What they 'knew' came to them from Hollywood, undiluted by the danger of real lived experience.

But, not living at his parents' house, Matthew did not see this envelope, so it was on account of John that he caught the plane. He had never taken a long flight. Once he had flown to Brussels, and that was it. On other occasions, he had gone to Ireland and Europe on water. He could not wait for the channel tunnel.

It was a Pan-Am plane. Nowadays Pan-Am is so strongly associated with the mistaken prediction in *2001: A Space Odyssey* that it would still be around to build moon shuttles that it is odd to think the company ever really existed.

The Pan-Am plane was jammed with *Doctor Who* actors, not to mention the odd 'fan,' including one who was travelling with a full-sized K9, and another, a distinctive little chap calling himself J. Jeremy Bentham, who had set up his market stall as the world authority on *Doctor Who* and was now off to Chicago to rattle his wares. J. Jeremy Bentham was convinced that Christopher Bidmead was a genius and he "predicted" that Sarah Sutton would be one of the great actors of our time. He had made a weaker impression on the cast than he supposed. On board the flight, he came up to Ian Marter, who was sitting with his son next to Matthew, and engaged him in five minutes of conversation. When he left, Ian said, "Who on earth was he?"

"I'm not sure," said Matthew. "I think he's called Jan."

Notably absent was Tom Baker, who had gone on a different plane. Also absent were Lalla Ward, the only *Doctor Who* actor not invited, to avoid embarrassment re: the now defunct marriage, and Mark Strickson, who was flying in later because he had a rather grand movie audition.

"How did it go?" asked Janet.

"I never get those really big jobs," said Mark with a shrug, though he did get this one, playing a young Scrooge who grew into George C. Scott.

The Second, Third and Fifth Doctors were up in first class with John Nathan-Turner, the lowly boys and girls in the cheap seats at the back.

The pilot could not contain his excitement. He announced over the Tannoy how pleased he was that dozens of *Doctor Who* actors were on board, to the embarrassment of all of them.

"I want to be a huge star!" Tom had said to Matthew. He had now decided, it seemed, that he was well on the way to this goal. He was far too big to stay in the same hotel as the rest of the *Doctor Who* gang. So, with his agent Jean Diamond in tow, he was put up in a special hotel. It must have been a bit lonely. Perhaps Jean Diamond was marvellously witty and entertaining company. After the convention, Tom was to fly on to LA, to launch himself into superstardom.

A special bus met the gang to ferry them to the hotel. Matthew found himself sitting next to one of his favourite *Doctor Who* girls from the past. He made light conversation with her.

"It's bizarre, isn't it? In England we're all on the dole, and here they're acting like we're enormous stars."

"I know," she said. "Good heavens, that reminds me, I quite forgot to sign on last Monday!"

*   *   *

In the lobby of the Marriott airport hotel where the convention was to take place, everyone waited at reception while they were issued with their room numbers and their secret names. Credit cards were demanded. Tony Ainley looked extremely put out.

"Our rooms are being paid for!" he said.

Yes, said the suited man at the desk, with the efficiency of courteous indifference, but just in case there's a problem...

Matthew was quite nervous. He knew Tom and Peter and Janet and Sarah of course, and JNT, but also attending this event were people he had never met but had adored from time immemorial. My God, Lis and Louise and Mary and Katy! And Doctor Who!! Jon Pertwee! Matthew was never to be relaxed around Jon Pertwee, though Jon was polite and charming on the occasions they met. He introduced himself to Matthew in the Marriott hotel lift, and though this was the wrong way round it must be admitted that Matthew would not have spoken to him unprompted, being very shy. He would have counted the numbers as the lift rose, perhaps humming a tune. Then there was Patrick Troughton, who also, incredibly, introduced himself to Matthew. Troughton, a legend in Matthew's mind – he had known the name almost from the moment he knew the name of any actor, perhaps he was the *first* actor whose name Matthew knew – was completely unpretentious, simply a good working actor who behaved like one.

Key in hand, Matthew went to his room and fell asleep.

In an upstairs lobby, outside the ballroom where some of the panels were to take place, sat Tom Baker, on a plastic chair. He was leaning forward. In a semi-circle at his feet sat and knelt a gaggle of young people, mostly girls, shapeless with ample bottoms, chins already starting to double though they could scarcely have been twenty-one. Tom was in full *Doctor Who* mode, all toothy grin and rolling eyes.

It was a perfect Baker moment: he was Jesus, they were the sheep and goats, staring up at him in a kind of mindless worship. Oh, Tom, Tom!, thought Matthew, this is your dream come true...

If Tom was enjoying the worship of the sheep, he wasn't getting such unmitigated adoration from the other actors. Mark Strickson put it plainly: "Tom Baker can disappear up his own arse." Patrick Troughton looked baffled. "I don't understand it, it's so strange..."

Thousands of people descended on the Marriott, many wearing scarves. How many thousand? This was open to debate: Matthew was under the impression it was around six thousand but Sarah told him she thought it was nearer fifteen. It was more than enough.

Some of these people, eyes bulged out, could be heard quoting Tom

Baker's TV lines. "What's the use of being grown-up," they said, "if you can't be childish some of the time?" To listen to them, you'd think this was the wittiest thing since Oscar Wilde and the most poetic thing since Yeats.

A miscalculation had been made, for each of the ballrooms in which the panels occurred held only a few hundred. Even the ballroom dedicated to Tom Baker's appearances held only a thousand or so. At any one time, the great majority of the crowds who had paid several hundred dollars to attend were unable to get into any panel. They stood in line for hours, becoming increasingly disgruntled, before being turned away. So they went to the dealers' rooms and bought jelly babies.

Tom had decided that he was Mick Jagger. During his appearances, which were solo affairs, he would speak for a few minutes when he was not being drowned out by cheers, then he would jump into the audience like Jack Flash, to the orgasmic bleats of his flock. It was all very funny and a little sad.

Matthew was not a sporty person but he had always been a walker of streets and paths. He had never been trapped for days in the air conditioned misery of a hotel and it began to drive him crazy. He wanted to see real people, real life. But beyond the Marriott's walls were only highways and runways. There were no streets to walk down. So he took to ambling about the car park. At least the air had not been cycled through a machine.

This habit caused untold alarm among the fat gentlemen who had appointed themselves security guards. "Matthew Waterhouse has left the building!" said one into his walkie-talkie. "Bring him back!" said another. "He's walking towards the parking lot!" said a third. Soon one of them would chase after him. He protested that he was only getting some air, but he would be ushered back to the lobby.

Matthew was reminded of a story by Ray Bradbury called *The Pedestrian*. It was about a time when walking would be against the law. These men, who called themselves Science Fiction fans, were on the wrong side: Like the policemen of the story they thought the pedestrian must be mad. What a terrible irony.

There was a lounge where the guests could sit around. A table with snacks ran along one wall, and at the end was a large television. This television burbled on and on and on until Peter Moffatt cried out: "for God's sake, turn it off!" Matthew was grateful to him, though sometimes in the evening it would be switched on again so Mr. Stein and his friends could watch the newest episode of *Taxi*.

One good use of the television was the viewing of the twentieth anniversary special called *The Five Doctors*, by Terrance Dicks. This was shown on PBS and everyone (except for Tom, ensconced grumpily in his special hotel) gathered in the lounge to watch it. Matthew was not in it, but he was surrounded by people who were, including Jon Pertwee and Peter Davison and Elisabeth Sladen. It was strange for Matthew, who found he still loved the programme, to be watching it surrounded by its cast. It was ninety minutes of glorious rubbish, enormously pleasurable. At the end, Matthew spontaneously applauded, and John said how nice that was of him.

Matthew said to Peter Moffatt, who had directed the piece,

"It's a pity Tom was too busy to do *The Five Doctors*!"

"Busy? He wasn't doing a *thing!* He turned it down only to be difficult!"

When JNT returned to Britain, he found himself in hot water with the BBC, because *The Five Doctors* had been broadcast in the US in advance of the UK, if only by a few hours. This was not only a first for *Doctor Who*, it contravened BBC policy, which was that programmes must never be shown abroad until they have aired in Britain.

One of the weirdest traditions of science fiction conventions was started at this Chicago event: the cabaret! It was essentially Jon Pertwee's idea. Jon was, as everyone knows, an accomplished comedian and he suggested he might present his night club act. Someone else said, maybe the other actors should do something as well, as an opener. So the first half consisted of *Doctor Who* actors demonstrating that, however competent they were as actors, they were not cabaret performers, which was fine because they had never claimed to be: Nick Courtney demonstrated that he was not a comedian, Sarah Sutton did what seemed to be an audition piece. Mark Strickson wrote and played a song about *Doctor Who* on an out-of-tune piano. John Leeson scratched his head over an old lyric: "I don't understand it! 'I say patayto and you say potayto, I say tomarto and you say tomarto..'." Tom, of course, was nowhere to be seen. Then Jon swooped on and did the act he had perfected over forty years. It was amateur hour followed by a true professional. Matthew, who had said he wouldn't do anything, thought the whole thing made able working actors look less gifted than they were by putting them in completely the wrong context.

But the cabaret idea, which it might be supposed would be a failed one-off, in fact expanded. Matthew decided at a British event he might as well give the thing a go. This was a mistake. He made some very peculiar last-minute choices. He started with a folk song, accompanied on piano by the brother of a *Doctor Who* fan, who had been roped in for the evening, but Matthew had brought along the Benjamin Britten arrangement, which is brilliant but demands virtuoso singing and playing, and there was no danger of virtuosity on that evening. Then, thought Matthew, he would stun everyone with – very entertaining! – a depressing poem by T. S. Eliot called *The Hollow Men*. He ended with a Bryan Ferry song, sung not in the style of Bryan Ferry but aiming for a bizarre cross between two other performers he admired: early Tom Waits and a great trombonist called Jack Teagarden, who had worked with Louis Armstrong and had a vocal style which slipped and slid like his trombone, making a relaxed, mellow, lazy, drunken quality which Matthew loved.

Painful as this must have been to sit through, it was equally painful to do, though it was praiseworthy perhaps for its sheer lunatic courage. Afterwards, Matthew avoided cabarets wherever possible, but they continued, if not to thrive, at least to stagger on, now incorporating *Star Trek* actors and *Babylon 5* actors. A Klingon did Pinter, a woman from *Babylon 5* sang terrible complaining pseudo-folk songs, each three-minute song introduced by five minutes of explanation, usually about how awful men were. Then she plugged her CD. Colin Baker squeezed comic juice out of a recitation of the US customs forms.

Matthew managed to turn his favourite *Doctor Who* record, *Who Is The Doctor*, into a sort of music hall turn which always went down well. And, though slightly out of context at a cabaret, readings of short pieces by Matthew's favourite satirist, Mark Twain, genuinely made people laugh, Mark Twain being, as he said of himself, that rarest of creatures, a humorist who is actually funny.

A bus was arranged to take those who wanted to escape the Marriott into downtown Chicago for a couple of hours. As the bus arrived back at the hotel, Matthew, laden with books by Harlan Ellison, felt a bit of grit in his eye and he rubbed it. This was unfortunate. His contact lens flipped out. It glittered at his feet. He did not want to crawl about on his hands and knees in front of everyone. He was right by the exit door, but he stayed sitting while everyone else got off, ushering them along with a little grin. Off climbed Peter Moffatt and Peter Davison and Ian Marter, and Mark Strickson with Mrs Strickson, and Patrick Troughton with Mrs Troughton. But Jon Pertwee, the last person on the bus apart from Matthew, courteously insisted he go first. "No, you go first!" said Matthew with a big smile. "You first, I insist!" Jon was determined to be more gentlemanly than Matthew. Matthew was determined to be more gentlemanly than Jon. "You first." "No, you first." Matthew had no choice but to tell the truth. "My contact lens is on the floor and I have to get it back!" "Ooooh." Jon gave that enormous familiar smile he'd thrown on the programme, when, asked his real name, he had said, "John Smith!"

* * *

A spectacular faux pas ended the grandiose event. A line-up of the cast was to take place on an enormous stage. First of all, the Doctors were to be introduced, then the boys and girls. These announcements were entrusted to a woman of prize-worthy stupidity.

So, first: "The Second Doctor, Mr. Patrick Troughton!" Patrick went on the stage, whistles and cheers. "The Third Doctor, Jon Pertwee!" Pertwee entered, whistles and cheers. "The Fifth Doctor, Peter Davison!"

Backstage, a stunned silence fell. Peter looked about. Everyone gazed at him. Nothing happened. Baker looked at his shoes and at his agent. Davison turned to a fat suited man with a radio, the 'fan' nearest to hand. He said,

"I'm not going on."

Time passed, what felt like bails of minutes and might have been only thirty very long seconds. Then the silly cow with the microphone made a coughing noise and said,

"I'm *so* sorry! I forgot the *Fourth* Doctor, Tom Baker!"

Tom threw Jean Diamond his widest smile, and disappeared onto the stage, to squeals from his flock.

4

After the Chicago spectacle, which had felt bloated and under-organised, Matthew, like other *Doctor Who* actors, was put off the idea of conventions. But then a smaller organisation, called Creation Conventions, got in touch and asked if he would he do some appearances around the US, Chicago, San Francisco, Philadelphia, New York. New York!! Plus, these events would be more modest in scale and not dedicated only to *Doctor Who* – instead, a mixed bag, a *Doctor Who* actor, (in these cases, him), a *Star Trek* actor, a comic book illustrator. Matthew was out of work and could use the money, and anyway he wanted, finally, to see romantic New York City!

So, for a long weekend once every two or three months, he would leave his little flat and jet off, star-like, across the pond. Other *Doctor Who* actors made appearances for Creation, too. At any given time, one plane or another was carrying a *Doctor Who* actor to the United States or back to London. Just as Matthew landed at JFK, Mark Strickson or Sarah Sutton or Mary Tamm would be arriving home to Gatwick. Sometimes perhaps they passed each other in the sky.

Among the people who came to these conventions was a memorable, very thin woman in her early thirties called Suzanne Muldowney. Suzanne must have had access to money because she was to be found at conventions all over the country, coast to coast, LA to Chicago, like Sade's smooth operator, though otherwise she bore no resemblance to the western male of the song. She had long brown hair and a long glum face and looked more like Lalla Ward than Mary Tamm, though not much like either. She was very intense. It was hard to imagine her being relaxed.

She had a deep interest in *Underdog*, a comedy TV cartoon about a dog who was secretly a superhero. *Underdog* was Suzanne's *Star Trek*, she knew its history and its characters down to the minutest detail and its imagined universe was more vivid and colourful for her than the real one. This passion must have been a lonely one. There was not a large *Underdog* cult to share it with. She was working, when Matthew knew her, on a movie screenplay. With the LA Olympics on the horizon, she thought it would be the perfect opportunity for a revival of *Underdog*, and she worked through many drafts of *Underdog* at the Olympics, hopeful of selling it to Hollywood. *Underdog* at the Olympics was not to be a cheap five-minute slapstick cartoon like the TV episodes, but an earnest widescreen spectacle with few jokes. She sincerely admired the genius who had created *Underdog* but it was not wise to refer to her passion too often, and certainly not with a smile. She suspected that other people brought it up in scarcely disguised mockery. This was an acute insight.

Matthew was not always able to remember her name and would say to her,

"Hello, *Underdog*."

She would frown and say, with a constriction in the throat, her eyes moving away from him, a crease on her brow,

"Suzanne *Muldowney*!"

When Matthew knew her, she had not achieved the pinnacle of fame which she would later enjoy, but there was always a sense that she occupied a strange place somewhere between ordinary convention attendees and the 'celebrities'. She did not talk to Matthew as if she were in any way impressed by him. They were equals as far as Suzanne was concerned. He once asked her what she thought of *Doctor Who* and she shrugged and said, not much.

"Of course, other people have their interests just like I do. You have your interest, I have mine."

To Suzanne he was '*Doctor Who* boy' in exactly the same way as she was '*Underdog* lady'. Maybe she thought Matthew went to conventions as a hobby.

She was not a one-issue obsessive. She regarded herself as a dancer, and was then in the process of developing a ballet version of *Dracula*. Many of these conventions had costume competitions and Suzanne would enter, dressed in a diaphanous blue gown. She had a cheap little cassette recorder which she placed on the floor, and she danced to music of a new age kind which she had composed herself. Coming from her little player, the simple music, though striving for a dark and misty dreaminess, had a cheap, synthy sound, as if it had been recorded in a bathroom. She would float long veils on the air as she danced.

Matthew was one of the judges of these costume competitions, often with the fragrant and humorous George Takei, Sulu of *Star Trek*, who attended science fiction events as a full-time career, or so it appeared. The eyes of the competitors suggested that to them the results were very important. Matthew giggled and George's eyes twinkled while they deliberated. It was rarely if ever possible to place Suzanne in the top three. The winners were announced in ascending order. The third place, then the second, and Suzanne's eyes turned shiny as if they were reflecting the gold medal which she already clutched tightly in her palm, before, a moment later, the first place winner was revealed to be someone else, her hopes were dashed, the gold medal a chimera.

There were tears in her eyes. She was both upset and puzzled by her loss and Matthew would say to her when he bumped into her later that she had placed fourth, only a point behind the third. Perhaps this was true. She would dry her eyes and lift her head. Next time, she would say, she'll make it. *Just one extra point!* She would walk away with a new burst of that optimism which Americans admire so much.

Suzanne had a good reason to be miffed: her efforts at the costume competitions were at least original. The other entrants slavishly copied the TV and movie costumes of their favourite characters. Matthew and George had to judge countless plump Uhuras and fat Darth Vaders and sawn-off Tom Bakers. Matthew loathed the *Star Wars* saga, as it was already called, so Skywalkers and Stormtroopers and Leias, however excellent, stood no chance of winning on his watch. Thus were prizes won or lost on a matter of mere prejudice. These costumes were often marvels of accuracy and must have taken weeks of concentrated work. One woman who had come as Tom Baker – gender was no barrier – gave Matthew her scarf. It was a completely accurate reproduction of the long wine-red scarf of Tom Baker's final season, in terms both of colour and of length. Matthew had no choice but to accept the gift gratefully, though he wondered why she thought he would want it. When he was packing in his hotel room he found he could not fit this endless woollen monstrosity into his bag, squash and squeeze and press as he might, so he left it behind, thrown over a chair. Thirty years later, perhaps it is still in the lost property department of the Marriott hotel in Manhattan.

The convention organizers showed Matthew round their office in Long Island. "Do you see that metal filing cabinet?" they said. Matthew noticed that the bottom drawer was bulging. "All our business documents are packed into the top two drawers. Do you know what is in the bottom drawer?"

"What?"

"Hundreds and hundreds of letters from Suzanne Muldowney."

Suzanne was the unlikeliest person to find herself on a yellow brick road to stardom, but this was the case, to an extent. She was taken up by the shock jock Howard Stern as one his menagerie of interesting people, along with an alcoholic midget, a manic-depressive transsexual, a female porn star still making movies in her eighties, and a man who received messages from aliens. When she went to science fiction conventions or to parades she was acclaimed by the crowds. Howard Stern even gave Suzanne her own radio show for a while, which Matthew regretted never having heard. He would like to have called her up for old time's sake and said hi.

The trip to Long Island to see Suzanne's file drawer occurred while Matthew was sleeping on the streets of New York. This adventure took place after he had spoken at a convention in the city. It was his second Manhattan appearance: on his first, he had booked a hotel on the upper west side and had spent ten days exploring every nook and cranny of the island, which he had loved.

Now, he decided it was about time to try something crazy and the dangerous streets of New York were it. He was in thrall to the American picaresque hero: to Huck Finn, the boy on the raft, and to Jack Kerouac, bumming from one end of America to another. On this occasion Matthew would not travel but he would have a new experience fraught with risk, at least potentially. He decided to *sleep on the streets.* He was going to take in heaps of jazz and hang out on Christopher Street. He would save all his convention fee except for a food allowance of a few bucks a day and enough for the Village Vanguard or Eddie Condon's jazz club.

He changed his clothes at the convention hotel on the Monday morning, thinking he was insane. He went to Pennsylvania station. Here there were lockers which could be rented for a very small daily amount. He stuffed his bag into a locker and went out into the city. The convention people said if he got tired of the streets he could stay with one of them, a man called Gary, on Long Island for a couple of nights in the middle of the week. Gary had a spare room.

It was a hot day and he wore only a t-shirt and shorts and trainers. He went to museums and at night to Eddie Condon's Jazz Club on 45th Street.

Blue Box Boy: A Memoir of Doctor Who in Four Episodes

Eddie Condon's Jazz Club had been around for decades, though this was not the original club building.

He sat at the bar and ordered a drink. An old man came in and took the only remaining stool, which was the one next to Matthew. The old man was clearly a regular because several people came up and chatted to him and patted him on the back. The barman gave him a free drink. When he was left alone, Matthew began to talk to him. He was under the impression that in American bars people made casual conversation with strangers by second nature. Perhaps he had gathered this from movies. The old man asked about his life. Matthew said he was English. The old man said, "Funny, I've never heard an English accent like yours." This was bizarre to Matthew, who had what everyone thought was a very English accent indeed. But it was interesting that the old man had met other English people. The talk turned to British jazz, about which the old man knew something. Then he talked about Eddie Condon's Club in its heyday.

The band came on to play a set. They were players in the early New Orleans style, what journalists called Trad Jazz and musicians preferred to call Classic Jazz. At the end, the band leader said how sorry he was that this was the club's last night and what a terrible loss it was for New York City. Everyone applauded and cheered. Then they played some more.

A film crew arrived and set up cameras and began to interview the members of the band. Finally, the interviewer came up to the old man next to Matthew. He was taken shakily, supported on both sides, to a banquette. What do you think about the club closing, Mister Goodman?

So Matthew had spent half an hour in a bar talking to Benny Goodman.

As the interview went on, Matthew began to feel a bit uncomfortable. It was becoming clear that he was the only person in Eddie Condon's Jazz Club on its last night who was not a musician, and the only one who was not a pal of Benny Goodman's. So he quietly went outside.

An evening chill was coming on and Matthew in his t-shirt and shorts began to feel cold, so he went to Penn Station and took out his bag and pulled out a long shirt and a jacket and a pair of cords. He went into the toilet at the station, which was smelly and disgusting, and changed into his 'evening wear'.

Then he wondered across town and came to Union Square. Though shortly before it had been a den of drug dealers, the trees around it had recently been cut down and the square opened up and the drug dealers had gone elsewhere. There were benches along the path which ran down the centre of the square. They were long enough for a sleeping person but a third armrest divided them up in the middle. Matthew decided he was small enough to fit into one of the halves if he pulled up his legs and propped his head on the cold wrought-iron outer arm.

Quickly it became clear that his hope of getting a short but decent night's sleep, maybe five or six hours, was a fantasy. Cars sped past, sirens called, there was never any silence. It was noisier than the pipes at TV Centre. He felt squashed on his little half-bench. Even in this hot midsummer the City was chilled at three a.m. He remembered a comment Tom Baker had made one morning. "I slept on a bench in Green Park all night on Saturday," he'd said, "the coldest night of the year." This was very Tom – sleeping rough was not enough, it *had* to be on the coldest night of the year.

Matthew drifted in and out of a semi-doze. A sound of scrabbling near his ear woke him. A fat rat was climbing up the trash can by his bench, swooping over the lip and clawing about inside. Another followed it. Soon they emerged and scooted down the path to the next one.

By four a.m. he had given up. His back ached and the night was cold. He went up to Times Square where there was a twenty-four hour McDonald's. For the first time he ate a McDonald's breakfast, with its yellow glob of reconstituted eggs and its English Muffin which was neither English nor a muffin. There were other customers, all looking tired and unkempt.

Sitting on the steps of the public library the next afternoon in his t-shirt and shorts, he ate a sandwich. A girl stopped her bike and stared at him and climbed the steps to him, pulling her bike with her. She sat right down next to him and propped the bike against the step below her. She was a boy-thin lesbian with small breasts and close-cropped hair, the kind of gay woman Matthew found sexy. As with many gay women, her conversation was impassioned. She began talking about troubles with her girlfriend, asking if Matthew minded that she was gay. No, he said. She talked all about her life. After an hour, she left. I have to go back to work, she said, wheeling away on her bicycle.

Had she seen him on *Doctor Who*? Had she been at the convention? She never said she had. Did she just like talking to a little English guy in shorts on the steps of the New York library? Perhaps.

In Central Park an old man with white hair and a collar shirt and jeans came to him and began talking as dusk fell. He said he liked Matthew's face. "You have a nice, open face," he said. A lot of people were not very friendly in New York, he said. He seemed a bit nervous. Perhaps he was one of those people who had wound up in the city a long while before and had found it too much for them but had somehow never got around to leaving. There were a lot of people like this in New York. He talked to Matthew for over an hour and when Matthew said, as an excuse, that he had to get a train at Grand Central, the man said, "do you mind if I walk with you?" Matthew felt hard-hearted when he said he had to walk very fast because his train was leaving in twelve minutes. The man looked sad and abandoned.

The next morning an attractive black boy in his early twenties came up to him on his bench and asked if he had heard the good news about Jesus. I used to do drugs, he said, and had women all the time and now I have Jesus in my life and I'm free of sin and saved. You look like you've been up all the night, you look like you need saving. You can be saved too, like me. I want to share the good news.

A real New York experience happened near Times Square in the early hours. Matthew was ambling down forty-second street when two young men sprang out at him.

"We've been following you," said one. "Give us your money. We've got guns," he added, though he did not pull one out.

Matthew was carrying his bag with a few hundred dollars in it. Bloody hell, he thought. He did not hand over the bag, but dipped into his pocket and pulled out a few coins, which he sprinkled over the hand of the man who'd spoken. While the man looked at the coins, perhaps not quite believing how little they added up to, Matthew darted across the street. The man called out to him.

"Hey!"

"Look, old chap," said Matthew, astounded at his own calm, "I don't have any money, and anyway you can't kill me, I'm in *Doctor Who*."

"You what?"

By then Matthew was in a crowd. This must have been the tamest mugging in history and, though relieved, Matthew was slightly disappointed not to have had a more exciting adventure, but it was pleasant to be able to boast that he had been mugged in the most notoriously dangerous city on earth.

After three days and three nights of this, with hardly any sleep at all, Matthew's mind began to blur. He decided to take up the invitation to stay for a night on Long Island. He took the train out, and Gary took him to a restaurant and showed him the comic book shop which the organisation was due to open the next week. Matthew was interested, though very, very tired.

In Gary's house, Matthew was in one room watching a Fleisher *Superman* cartoon on video while in another Gary watched the news. He called to Matthew. "You must see this!"

The 'light' story at the end of the news was about the closing of Eddie Condon's Jazz Club, and there was Benny Goodman, in the club, reminiscing about the good old days.

The next morning there was a noise of activity in the kitchen. Voices were raised. Matthew pulled a towel around his waist and went to have a look.

Gary was arguing with his mother, who was a Jewish mother of perfection. She lived elsewhere but she had gone grocery shopping and let herself into his house and now she was filling his fridge. He said pleadingly that she didn't have to do all this shopping for him, but she said, how a mother worries about her son when he leaves home, she has to make sure he eats right. Years later, Matthew would have a Jewish partner for a while and they were always grateful when, on every visit, his mother drove down to their flat from Manchester, loaded with groceries, including matzo crackers and jars of gefilte fish.

Matthew left Long Island and returned for three more days to the streets of New York and the bench at Union Square. His adventure ended unexpectedly with a romantic encounter with a Mexican boy whose hair was dyed in orange and black stripes like a tiger, but that is outside the scope of this book.

Matthew had loved *Star Trek* as a boy but for some reason this affection did not last. When as an adult he came across old episodes, he did not get even the mild nostalgic tingle he felt seeing a repeat of *Thunderbirds*. Yet when he attended these American science fiction events he found he liked the *Star Trek* cast members very much. Regrettably, he did not meet Leonard Nimoy or DeForest Kelley, nor the astonishing William Shatner, but he briefly met Scotty, who loved bars, and Chekhov and, more frequently, the tremendous and lovable George Takei, Mr. Sulu, who came out as gay in the early twenty-first century, which must have had all the shock impact of learning that Louis Armstrong was black. Friends of Matthew had seen George occasionally walking along London streets looking glistening and available.

Matthew did not yet understand the workings of America, as far as he ever would. When he overheard *Star Trek* actors talking at conventions, he noticed that they could make utterly banal comments which brought whoops and hollers and enough applause to rock the building. In fact, it was a mistake to say anything interesting or unexpected, because this would be greeted with confused silence. All Trekkies asked for was simplicity, so they could whoop and holler and crow.

Matthew had agreed to do an interview in a hotel room after George Takei had done one. He sat outside the room, listening to George go on about the magnificence of *Star Trek* and the wondrousness of its fans. Everything George said was going down well with the interviewers. But, thought Matthew, does he really believe it? Perhaps he does. Matthew liked *Doctor Who*, that was for real, but he could not sit in front of an interviewer and say how profound it was and how it was like touching the face of the stars. He could not have kept a straight face. In fact, at an event with John Nathan-Turner, John and Matthew were to be interviewed together in front of a camera, but every time John tried to embark on his promotional speechifying Matthew could not stop falling about. He politely dropped out of the interview, so John could talk rubbish with a straight face.

Just as delightful as George was Grace Lee Whitney, who played Yeoman Rand. Yeoman Rand was supposed to be in *Star Trek* on a long-term basis but lasted for only a few episodes, perhaps on account of too much booze. In her later life Grace Lee Whitney had a splendidly cigaretty laugh. Matthew listened in to some of her convention talk, where she said crowd-pleasing things like, "I didn't have the best career but all these years later all the successful people I knew are forgotten and I'm *remembered.*" This remark was greeted with enough cheers to drown out the Beatles.

When they were sitting together signing autographs, she laughed with more than polite appreciation at Matthew's every amusing remark. At the end, she hugged him close. She told him he was wonderful. He said so was she.

Equally jolly was a character player called Roger Carmel, who had been in two *Star Trek* episodes as Mr. Harry Mudd, a disreputable cad with a waxed moustache who built android wives with perfect bodies, his real wife being a nagging old bat. As satire, this was not sophisticated, but his two episodes of *Star Trek* – 'classics', apparently – were sufficient for Roger Carmel to become a 'convention personality,' much cheered at his every utterance.

Matthew assumed Roger Carmel was gay, but in the bar at the airport where they spent an hour before getting their separate flights, Roger showed great interest in the Baseball game on the screen. One of these facts did not automatically eliminate the other, but for some reason Matthew was surprised by Roger's detailed knowledge of the sport. When they parted, Roger gave him his address and number.

"All actors end up in LA, so when you come out here give me a call. Don't worry, I often give out a false number but this is the real one."

Matthew was curious as to who asked relentlessly for Roger's number and had to be fended off with a dud.

Also much loved by the whooping crowds was Mark Lenard. Mark had played Mr. Spock's father and had been a regular on the *Planet of the Apes* TV series. Matthew had dinner with him and asked him about Roddy McDowall, whom he loved as an actor. Roddy McDowall was, and is, an adored figure by many gay men, an under-the-radar icon. He was without the dark complexity of Dirk Bogarde, but the definitive glistering Hollywood queer, going to lots of parties at the house of Elizabeth Taylor.

Matthew has heard countless people say out of the blue how much they love Roddy. In the twenty-first century, Matthew had a friend called Jason of only twenty-one who said, in between offering his views on amazingly obscure musical theatre failures like Pretty Belle, how he absolutely loved everything about Roddy McDowall. Jason was interested to hear authoritatively from Matthew that Roddy was famously well-endowed. When Matthew said that though he knew this for a fact he was not claiming to have slept with hIm – or even to have met him – Jason did not quite believe it. He continued to suspect that he had and was a bit envious.

Mark was reserved on the subject of Roddy. Matthew said he loved Roddy's accent, which was totally Hollywood, with just a distant remaining hint of Englishness in between the broad LA vowels. Mark was taken aback to hear that Roddy did not sound as utterly and unquestionably English in every vowel and consonant as the Queen. No, indeed not, said Matthew. Many years later, Jason was also surprised by this accentual fact.

"And your Scotty does not sound even a tiny bit Scottish. He makes our Jamie sound like Rabbie Burns."

"Goodness."

"And," added Matthew, "cockneys don't sound like Dick Van Dyke."

"They don't??"

Mark was less upbeat than other *Star Trek* actors, the abysmal frustrations and cruelties of Hollywood having, it seemed, got under his skin. When Matthew made a praising remark about F. Murray Abraham in *Amadeus*, Mark flared his nostrils and said,

"Of course, there are many actors who could have done the part just as well." He sipped on his wine. "Including me."

This was probably true.

Yet Mark Lenard was very tolerant of Matthew's smoking throughout dinner. Matthew did not smoke much in Britain and then usually little cheap cigars bought in flat tins rather than cigarettes, but in America he puffed through packet after packet of deadly Pall Malls, partly because he knew Kurt Vonnegut smoked them. Later he would spend a day in Kurt Vonnegut's company, but that was far in the future. Pall Malls had a toasty flavour unknown to horrid Rothman's and Silk Cut and Marlborough in England. This was partly because they were unfiltered and so even more lethal, though Vonnegut lived to his late eighties. Incidentally, when Matthew was a small boy, his mother, who hardly smoked at all, would once or twice a year after a special dinner – children long since banished to bed – indulge in what she called an 'American cigarette', which was understood to be exotic and sophisticated, set apart from the junk available in newsagents.

Mark Lenard drank cautiously, Matthew getting through three glasses to each of his one. Going back to their rooms afterwards, on the same floor, Mark stopped outside a door. Matthew continued to chat for a while, then walked on. "No," said Mark. "This is your room – mine is further along." Matthew did feel a bit woozy when he got to bed.

One element of *Star Trek* Matthew continued to admire was its mixed race cast, which extended to a mixed race following. Autograph lines for *Star Trek* actors included Asian and Hispanic and black people, while the line for *Doctor Who* was almost invariably white. Matthew had been quite surprised that, by the mid-eighties, John had not cast a black companion. It had seemed by then an obvious step. *Doctor Who* only began to represent the racial make-up of Britain when Russell T. Davies took over.

John Nathan-Turner loved flying to America and talking at conventions. He loved the roars and applause. He admitted to Matthew that this was because he had always wanted to be an actor and these appearances got his performing ambitions out of his system. His acting career had not got very far, though he had once toured psychiatric hospitals throughout Britain in a play. He had performed to people who moaned and groaned at random moments and to people who were too depressed to make any noise at all and to people who were apparently happy and stable and laughed a lot, the only clue to their true state the scars on their wrists.

John was good at conventions. He liked being the king of all *Doctor Who* media, a sort of Gene Roddenberry figure. He fed the people what they wanted. He was in thrall to showbiz America and would often, after a convention, spend a few days in New York catching up on all the new Broadway shows. He felt strongly that American actors were better than British ones, which contradicted the received wisdom of the time. "Watch them do musicals," he said, "and then see a British production of the same piece. We haven't a clue."

John's absence from the *Doctor Who* office was noticed by others in BBC drama. Matthew's aunt Liz, still working on serious plays, said that everyone at Threshold House had cottoned on to the fact that he was never around, and they complained about it in a small-minded way. He should have been looking over budgets and consulting with his script editor, they said. But John was enjoying the limelight. And as relations with his script editor, Eric Saward, had by this time become icy, it might have been for the best that he was often out of town.

A certain ambiguity in his professional relationship to American convention organisers apparently developed, whereby he became not so much a guest as an organiser himself. This led to a rift with Anthony Ainley which never healed. Ainley believed that John was being 'encouraged' to persuade actors to attend conventions for very low fees, and that John was being paid for this service. Matthew had no idea whether there was any truth in this. Tony said he accepted fees which he would not otherwise have tolerated because John said there was hardly any money available but it would be a nice thing to go along anyway. Tony did not want to argue with his producer and employer.

Tony's irritation over this was exacerbated when Barry Letts told him that Tony was cast as the Master at his, Barry's, suggestion. "There I was," said Anthony to Matthew, "sucking up to John all those years because I thought he'd chosen me! Then I found out it was all down to Barry Letts!" In fact, it turned out that Anthony had been on the short list the first time round, when the part had gone to Roger Delgado.

Tony was very conscious of matters of money. He lived with his aging mother somewhere in Hampstead. *Doctor Who* gave him a long-running job, but it seemed to close off other avenues for him, as it so often did for its cast. Tony always said he did not like to work too much anyway, particularly during the summers, which he spent playing charity cricket matches. He was utterly in love with the game of cricket. There was supposedly some private money floating around, but it could not have been a huge amount: when he sent out Christmas cards, they were previously used, with the back half neatly torn off. The envelopes were often reused too, a label covering an old address, and stamps which the post office machinery had failed to frank – a frequent occurrence in those days – had been steamed off and glued on. This economy, in its way admirable, was not uncommon for a generation that had experienced war austerity.

After his difficulties with Americans, Tony became incensed at any convention invitation which did not come with an offer of thousands of pounds. He would dismiss anything lower as a profound insult.

Many convention organizers gave up on asking Tom Baker to attend. He was a good draw, they said, but such a difficult man that they'd rather rake in less money and have a happier time.

One tough no-shit lesbian dealt with him rather well. When she picked him up at Toronto airport he was in a foul mood and complained all the way to the hotel, barking instructions about what he would and would not do. This pissed the lesbian off so much that, when they arrived, she said, unplanned,

"Right, Tom, you stand *here* at the convention entrance and as each fan comes in you *smile,* you give them a *free signed photograph* and you *shake their hands."* She planted him at the door, passed him a huge heap of pictures and a marker pen and marched away. So poor Tom in a furious mood had to stand stock still and grin his head off for two hours, while the lesbian drank coffee in her hotel room.

Doctor Who enthusiasts could often be found in theatres. The boy behind the ticket counter or the assistant stage manager or the set carpenter: somebody, somewhere in the building, was liable to be a fan. Or, if there was not a fan on the staff, somebody who passed evenings in the bar: there was a memorable woman, one of the 'friends' of a theatre where Matthew worked. The 'friends' of rep theatres were an important source of extra money, but they were often a rum lot. Among the bonuses this theatre offered their 'friends' was an afternoon sitting in on rehearsals. Only the most extreme of the 'friends' took up this invitation: a couple of very old women, and this youngish woman, who looked down on the actors from high-banked seats with staring intensity. Inevitably, rehearsals ground to a halt, so that, far from getting an insight into the working processes of actors, they got an insight only into how actors and directors behaved when deeply self-conscious and embarrassed.

She was in the bar nearly every night, even when there was not a play on, though she never drank alcohol. She drank only orange juice. At the time Matthew knew her, she was in the process of having new teeth put in, and had temporary cardboard teeth as a stop-gap. This gave her mouth something of the graveyard. She said to Matthew:

"I was brought up on three things – Jesus, Tarzan and *Doctor Who*! I love them all!"

"I hope your number one is *Doctor Who*?"

"No – my number one is Jesus!" and she walked away. But Matthew had not offended her enough to keep her away from the theatre, where she could be found night after night, because, presumably, she could not think of anywhere else to go when there was not a Church function. He never saw the day her cardboard teeth became splendid new clackers.

5

Over the years ITV tried to produce its own variations on *Doctor Who* and some of these were successful. As a boy Matthew watched *Ace of Wands* with a hero called Tarot, and *The Tomorrow People*, about a group of teenage children called 'Homo Superior'. These children had special powers, including the ability to 'jaunt' – to disappear and seconds later reappear in another location. These powers lay dormant until they 'broke out,' with much sweat and anguish. Matthew completely missed the obvious allusion to puberty.

Their headquarters was an abandoned underground station, where there was a computer with a posh voice. The programme was very much rooted in London, and had a wonderfully mixed-race cast. *The Tomorrow People* had a long run and Matthew discovered it late, so, like *Doctor Who*, there was a mysterious past of now departed characters and unknown adventures.

These programmes were exciting in their day, including one with oil paintings which moved. One story, though, was extremely silly. It was also the first episode Matthew ever saw. It starred none other than Peter Davison with his wife of the time, Sandra Dickinson. They were alien cowboys speaking in Wild West accents, or at least having a go at them. Peter, Matthew suspected, would have much to be embarrassed about if this marvel were dug out. Peter said that the regular cast of *The Tomorrow People* had loved this comedy western story. Normally, they told him, the programme was incredibly po-faced, so it was wonderful to take the piss out of it for once.

Peter Davison was so famously nice that many people failed to pick up on his surprisingly well-developed waspish streak, though Matthew, always sceptical of mere niceness, found the waspishness a delightful extra dimension. Peter once took great, even mean-spirited, pleasure in saying that an ex-*Tomorrow People* boy was now working as an extra in the Midlands.

Much the best of these ITV series, to Matthew's mind, was still in production while Matthew was in *Doctor Who*. Matthew simply loved it. It was called *Sapphire and Steel*, a slightly naff title which sounded like it had Robert Wagner in it. Surprisingly often, when *Sapphire and Steel* was mentioned, people thought it was *Hart To Hart*. But it was a very clever, genuinely original series which starred Joanna Lumley, post-*Avengers* and pre-*AbFab*, and David McCallum of *The Man from UNCLE*, as alien agents about whom nothing was known. The fabric of time would sometimes rip and things from the past or the future would break through to the present and the agents had to repair time. It was on the whole better written, scene by scene, than *Doctor Who*, though it moved less snappily. It used the *Doctor Who* format of four, six and eight twenty-five minute episodes. Like *Doctor Who* it had been conceived for children but had a wider appeal. Like *Doctor Who* it was dismissed by mothers as rubbish, but they kept watching while their children explained what was happening.

It was all very dreamy and engrossing. The settings were enclosed, airless, claustrophobic: an abandoned railway station, an isolated cottage, a greasy spoon attached to a garage. The stories had very small casts. Sometimes six or eight episodes were sustained by, essentially, four or five actors, including the stars.

A nice link was made between *Doctor Who* and *Sapphire and Steel*. Matthew was in a play with an actress called Jenny Stoller. Jenny said to him about one of the other actors, Peter Laird,

"We've worked together before, but he doesn't remember me."

"What in?"

"Some absolute rubbish. I can't even be bothered to talk about it." She shrugged and the conversation returned to the vagaries of the Royal Shakespeare Company. Jenny and Peter were among the finest actors Matthew ever worked with. Jenny was an actor of great technical skill. Her closest friend was Diana Rigg. Peter was one of a dying breed of authentic, protean character actors who, in theatre, got to play an astoundingly wide range of characters and styles.

A year or two later, in the early nineties, Matthew came across on VHS a rather splendid wooden box containing all the six serials which made up *Sapphire and Steel*. I wouldn't mind seeing those programmes again, thought Matthew, I wonder how they've worn? So he took the box back to his flat. And there, in the fifth story, were Jenny and Peter.

Jenny was wrong to think *Sapphire and Steel* was rubbish, Matthew reflected. Her particular serial, the fifth, was slightly less idiosyncratic than the others, the only one not written by *Sapphire and Steel*'s creator, who was one of those writers who went by his – or her – forename initials, like W. S. Graham and J.K. Rowling and R.S. Thomas and E. F. Benson, though he – or she – was none of these people. But Jennie and Peter's story was still a terrifically inventive pop fiction. It made a science fiction twist on the Agatha Christie formula, and was written by a couple of *Doctor Who* hacks.

So the actors playing both his mother and his father in the play had appeared together in a *Sapphire and Steel* story, their son a *Doctor Who* lad. Lovely. This is one of the obscurest facts in the history of TV trivia. Over the ten or twelve weeks they worked together, Peter Laird never did remember that he and Jenny had known each other of old.

Matthew found himself at TV Centre at a BBC party around 1990. He was delighted to see June Hudson, the costume designer for *Warriors' Gate*. He went across and said hi.

"I don't know if you remember me. I was in a *Doctor Who* story you designed."

"Of course I remember you," she said, buoyantly. June was already well oiled, but together they drank a couple of glasses of wine each.

"So, how are things?" he asked.

She looked a bit depressed.

"I left the BBC long ago," she said. "I design miniature clothes for collector's dolls."

Matthew remembered she'd been thinking about taking this job years earlier.

"That's wonderful! How do you like it?"

"It pays well, but I wish I'd stayed in the BBC. It's lonely, I never see anyone. And I only took the job because Tom Baker said I should."

"Really?"

"He said, do it, June! And I did." She glugged her wine. "But it was a mistake."

At first, Matthew, being very young, had been bothered by rumours which circulated back to him. Assorted fictional versions of him were being created, often vindictively. Why? For what gain? It was very weird. Early on, he heard a rumour, apparently widespread, that he had been spotted insulting people in a night club, though he had never been in a night club. Later, as he began to understand more about the human race and to feel less contempt than pity for the whole benighted species, he found these rumours not so much offensive as comical. One of his favourites was when someone, years after he had left *Doctor Who*, mentioned in passing the affair he, Matthew, had had with Anthony Ainley.

Matthew was flabbergasted that this affair should be general knowledge among gossipy cultists, though it had never existed or remotely been on the cards. Matthew wondered for days how such a tale could have started. Then he had a thought: Every so often, when there had been a couple of hours when neither he nor Anthony had been required, he had sat in Tony's dressing room. Perhaps someone had seen him emerge from the dressing room and drawn a conclusion? No sex had taken place, but rather a conversation about Noël Coward – scarcely even a conversation really, but a monologue, Tony talking, Matthew listening. Tony was a big fan of Coward.

Tony had a catchphrase. It came from a remark Coward was supposed to have made to his actors. "I'm very, very pleased with you," said Coward, "and I'm especially pleased with *you!*" Tony used this phrase frequently, for no particular reason: to Matthew: "I'm very, very pleased with you!" Then to Sarah: "and I'm especially pleased with you!"

By the early twenty-first century, the strange cult of celebrity had reached newly incredible heights, and in addition to *Doctor Who* conventions there were other signing events, in which 'celebrities' sat at tables with enormous pictures of themselves in their familiar roles above their heads, and spent all day signing pictures, or twirling their pens in their hands waiting for someone to ask them to sign a picture. Matthew attended a couple of these events in a spirit of exploration, as an extremely minor celebrity among much flashier presences in, once, a gigantic sports stadium in Birmingham and, another time, a massive shopping mall in Milton Keynes.

At Milton Keynes, Matthew sat near Sarah Sutton, and they waved to each other while waiting for customers, sighing, thrumming their tables. Opposite, Lalla Ward gossiped to John Leeson, their autograph lines equally sparse. This little group of minor *Doctor Who* actors was placed in a dusty corner at the edge of the mall, opposite a cut-price clothes shop, right by a row of massive plate-glass windows, and it was a sunny day, so by lunch-time they were all parched and had throbbing headaches. At right angles to this quartet from the old programme was Barnaby Edwards from the new one, at a rather larger table. He was the star Dalek in recent episodes. Barnaby Edwards was an old friend of Matthew's, but it was irritating to see that Barnaby's autograph line was seven times as long as his, or Lalla's or Sarah's or John's. Barnaby could barely draw breath before a fresh gaggle of obese kiddies shoved pictures and ten pound notes under his nose, while Matthew had plenty of time to work through a large chunk of the second volume of Norman Sherry's ginormous life of Graham Greene in unbroken silence. Lalla had all the time in the world to chat about Darwin. It underlined how passé the old lot now were, if this needed underlining. Barnaby was a part of the new lot, and by no means passé. Nor was the outstandingly likable and gifted new *Doctor Who* boy, who came up to Matthew and said he was his hero, a compliment which Matthew accepted graciously. Matthew had not seen him in *Doctor Who*, but did see him in a movie made by the producer of *Queer as Folk*, in which he was sweet and excellent.

Away from Matthew's little group of minor TV hacks were the big name draws, even bigger than Barnaby Edwards. These 'stars' were in the centre of the mall, comfortably far from the beating rays of the sun, especially those buff lads from that dreary *Lord of the Rings* trilogy, who were paid tens of thousands of pounds to sit there and be starry, though it is impossible to feel glamorous in a shopping mall in Milton Keynes, whatever the pay. There were also many *Star Wars* actors. *Star Wars* actors could be spotted a mile off: if a person was extremely small or extremely tall, twenty to one he was a *Star Wars* actor. Oh, look over there! said an excited, fleshy child in a *Tomb Raider* t-shirt, there is the actor who played Sith Darth in the new instalment, or Sarth Dith, or whatever it was.

The signings were fun and interesting, but the real pleasure was the evenings, after the events were over.

In Birmingham, he spent an evening in an Asian restaurant with the lovely Nicola Bryant and Paul Darrow, who had played Avon in *Blake's 7*. For Matthew, this meeting with Paul was a reunion, because on half a dozen occasions he and Janet and Sarah had eaten lunch with him. Paul had not the slightest recollection of these lunches.

In one of those strange coincidences, Matthew had been talking about him only a few days earlier, at a convention in Massachusetts, the first time Paul had come up in conversation in thirty years. Matthew was eating dinner with a number of lady fans, including a striking woman, the kind of massive lesbian who takes up two seats on an aeroplane. This charming woman talked with unforgiving, if good-humoured, fury about Paul Darrow, who had apparently promised to come to a convention she had organized and then dropped out at the last moment. She was not the kind of person likely to forget such an outrage any time soon, and her portrait of Paul was withering.

With this gossip bouncing around in his head, Matthew expected Paul to be rather awful. This turned out not to be the case. He was funny, and the campest straight man on earth. He smoked like crazy, even while signing autographs. Signed photographs of Paul which do not have a burn hole in them are exceedingly scarce. Every moment between courses in the restaurant – which was very good, but went by the excruciating name of Beau Thai – was spent in the cramped attic smoking room. Paul Darrow made a good living doing voiceovers, including, shortly before Matthew met him in Birmingham, an advert plugging a Bryan Ferry album. "An awfully nice man," he said of Bryan Ferry.

He also had an extraordinary side-line, writing pseudonymous novels about the rock group Queen. Matthew was intrigued to hear that there was a market for novels about Queen, but Paul assured him the books did well. Paul pumped Matthew to admit that he was a huge Queen fan, but Matthew could not bring himself, even to please Paul, to pretend to care about that stadium group.

"No, I don't have a strong feeling in favour of Queen," said Matthew, "though I do love Queen novels." Certainly if he comes across a Queen novel, he will buy it.

Also at this event was Kate O'Mara, who had played a female version of the Master in a couple of stories. In her sixties, she was still very attractive. She was there to sign copies of her autobiography. She said to Matthew that she was delighted to meet him, having long admired his work. This pleased but baffled Matthew, as he didn't think she could have seen any of it, except perhaps for *Doctor Who*. (She had been the lover for many years of Richard Willis). Still, a compliment is a compliment. She was extremely charming.

Milton Keynes was amusing, because Matthew was put up in a very basic Holiday Inn which smelt of smoke and grease. Having lived for some years in New England where the distant sighting of a cigarette made people crease their faces critically, it was faintly nostalgic to stay in a hotel where the non-smoking rooms were smoking rooms with the ashtrays removed.

Matthew spent an evening with one of Patrick Troughton's *Doctor Who* girls, Deborah Watling. The weather was a pleasantly warm, so they sat outside, near a motorway. Deborah was what is known as 'a laugh,' and Matthew adored her. She reminded him of a slightly scandalous granny. Matthew said he had always loved her episodes.

"I was mad about all those Patrick Troughton stories."

She looked doubtful.

"You can't *possibly* have seen them! You're *far* too young!"

She was interested to hear that Matthew had a Green card.

"My ex, who was an actor, went off to America," she said, "and now he's a painter and decorator!"

They were joined by two *Doctor Who* fans, one of whom had just spent a year working for Disneyworld at Epcot, where every day he had stood outside The Rose and Crown – Disney's version of a British pub – holding up a colourful assortment of balloons and smiling, just as fit to burst as his balloons.

At another signing Matthew sat next to Caroline John, who was amused by the intensity with which he selected the right colour marker pen – gold, silver, blue, black – for a particular photograph. He had a deep frown, a tremendously serious look of concentration, she said.

She mentioned an unfortunate incident which had happened to her on an earlier occasion. A man approached her with a large poster which was smothered in the autographs of countless *Doctor Who* actors, living or dead.

"Yours is the very last I need," said the fan. Caroline picked up her pen and scrawled her signature in the small remaining space. When she had finished she saw that, unthinkingly, she had signed not her stage name, Caroline John, but her everyday signature, Caroline Beevers, the signature she put on cheques and letters. The fan turned a purple so deep it would have impressed a plum. Caroline corrected the autograph as best she could, but it is difficult to turn 'Beevers' into 'John'.

The morning after the grand signing at Milton Keynes, a taxi arrived to speed Matthew to Heathrow. The driver chatted away. I just had that new *Doctor Who* boy in my cab, he said, and he's incredibly nice, and you tell me you are the old *Doctor Who* boy and you seem incredibly nice too. What is it about *Doctor Who* boys that they are all so incredibly nice? It's a mystery, isn't it, said Matthew. Also incredibly nice, said the driver, was Nichelle Nichols from *Star Trek*. Driving through the countryside, Nichelle Nichols was in ecstasies about its green and pleasant beauty. She kept asking me to stop, said the driver, so she could photograph every tree and every sheep. Less nice, he went on, was an arrogant *Lord of the Rings* actor who kept me waiting for ages and never even gave me a tip. Mean git, said Matthew. That's not the worst, said the taxi driver. A *Star Wars* director called Irwin threw a tantrum when he was asked by an organiser if he'd mind sharing a cab to the airport. He demanded to be given his own private transportation *immediately*.

Some of those American actors, continued the taxi driver, are paid such crazy money for these appearances that they can't legally carry it on their person back home. So they split it into wads of a thousand dollars and fill up a pile of padded envelopes and I have to drive them to a post office where they buy loads of airmail stamps. But they don't post the envelopes at the post office: then I have to drive all over Milton Keynes, stopping at every letter box, and they drop one envelope into each. They hope most of them will find their way to the LA houses with bloody great swimming pools where these people live.

6

It was suggested that, when Matthew was in the UK, he might like to do some commentaries which would be added to the *Doctor Who* episodes for release on DVD.

Matthew shared Woody Allen's view that once a piece of work was completed, there was nothing to say about it and it should be left, unapologetically, to stand. He had only ever reluctantly done an interview for the *Doctor Who* comic, on the tenth request. Then he talked rubbish to get it over with. Woody Allen films appeared on DVD without any bonuses at all, except the trailer. Matthew thought this was the right approach. At the other extreme, DVDs of hugely commercial ventures came with bonus material running to many more hours than the original film. This was puzzling to Matthew. He could not get through the two hours of a *Star Wars* film without thinking how much more interesting it would be to do the laundry, but apparently enthusiasts were delighted to work through twenty hours of extras.

So Matthew thought that, even on the knockabout level of old *Doctor Who* serials, the episodes deserved to stand uncluttered. The episodes were all the mattered: everything else was white noise. The BBC were having none of this. And to be fair to them, there was a specific commercial problem: nearly all the buyers of the DVDs would be people who already owned the tapes. Owners of one hundred and sixty tapes had to be offered inducements to buy one hundred and sixty DVDs.

So, with or without him, the commentaries would be done. He agreed to do some. Dates were arranged, planes caught, limos sent. He saw actors and writers and directors he had not seen in years. Some he had not seen since the making of the programmes all those years ago.

There is a dramatic sub-genre, familiar to everyone, about reunions, the kind of play or movie in which school friends or college buddies or long-ago lovers meet again after twenty or thirty years, and the playwright unfolds their resentments, their failures, their disappointments, their guilt, all the detritus of the intervening years. The *Doctor Who* DVD commentary sessions were like mini versions of these plays, though happily without the darkness.

The meetings were very pleasant and often interesting. It may be significant that the single most memorable encounter was with the man who had left the world of TV the earliest, and had made an entirely different life for himself. This was Andrew Smith, the writer of *The Planet That Slept*, who had been only eighteen or nineteen when the script was produced. Andrew had given up writing for TV almost immediately after *Doctor Who*. This may have been because he wanted a more secure life than TV promised to offer him, and it may be, though he never said this, that his experience on *Doctor Who* was so awful he wanted nothing to do with media people ever again. He became a copper, and not just any copper. He spent large amounts of time flying between Britain and Washington. This life was completely outside Matthew's experience and was fascinating to hear about. Andrew was as friendly as he had always been, but very much in control of himself. He was very precise in his speech. He was used to giving away as little as possible, while listening for the line which gives someone else away.

The writers were always interesting. It was a pity that the BBC was unable to trace Christopher Bailey, who had written *Kinda* and its sequel. But Johnny Byrne and Terrance Dicks were, of course, easily enough found.

Matthew was bursting to ask Johnny Byrne a question. He knew that there was another writer, a novelist, called John Byrne, and of course there was also the comic book writer and artist of the same name, but he had occasionally come across the name Johnny Byrne in unexpected places: once as co-author a late sixties novel about the drug-fuelled edge of rock music, and also as a poet who cropped up in small roneoed poetry magazines during the sixties, alongside people like Lee Harwood. These were the British equivalents of the little journals which came out of the Lower East Side movement of the St. Mark's Poetry Project in huge numbers.

Was this poet a fourth John Byrne, or was he the man who wrote for *Doctor Who*?

Johnny mentioned during *The Keeper of Traken* commentary that he was interested in old Irish myth, which underlined Matthew's suspicions. Johnny said that one of the inspirations for *The Keeper of Traken* was the old myth of the collars that strangled judges who made unjust decisions. This revelation was a chilling moment for Matthew. If the myth had been mentioned to him as recently as a few days earlier, he would have been unfamiliar with it. But on the plane over to London he had been reading a book about Yeats by Kathleen Raine, who had devoted some space to discussing this very story. How strange is that?

But when lunch came and Terrance Dicks arrived, the opportunity to ask the question about whether or not he was the poet Johnny Byrne who had edited *Night Train* – which ran to only one issue – disappeared, so Matthew never found out.

Matthew suspected that the DVD producer, Paul Vanezis, was more impressed to meet Johnny Byrne than anyone else. His favourite childhood series had been *Space: 1999*. He seemed slightly in awe of this extremely gentle man, and rather moved to be working with him.

Terrance Dicks and Peter Moffatt had come to do the *State of Decay* commentary in the afternoon. They joined Matthew and Anthony and Sarah and Johnny in the canteen. Terrance talked about script writing with Johnny. "I prefer writing books," said Terrance, "because your time is your own." He had recently quit a soap opera, because the story had turned to incest, "which I just don't want to write about." Matthew had snatched the last mini bottle of white wine, so Terrance had to make do with a beer. Johnny left. "What a nice man," said Terrance.

Anthony Ainley left too. He disappeared through the canteen door, and then turned back and caught Matthew's eye and waved and blew him a kiss. It was the last time Matthew would ever see him, or Johnny.

Terry Dicks, a high-end *Doctor Who* icon, was cheerfully vengeful about

Christopher Bidmead's attempted improvements to his script, most of which were scrapped. Peter Moffatt had looked at the "improved' version and had said, I don't want to do *this!* Where's that nice Gothic drama I read earlier? *That's* what I want to direct! So poor Christopher's version was binned and Terrance's dusted off. Terrance talked fondly about the BBC of the late sixties, producers pouring their little glasses of whisky at eleven thirty.

Matthew had read all Terrance's *Doctor Who* books, now thirty-five years old. Terrance was not an expert on *Doctor Who* by any means. Having turned out an adaptation, he swiftly forgot the story.

"Did you do three years," he asked Matthew, "or two?"

"Four," said Matthew with a smile, "and they are all classics. Especially *State of Decay*."

"Your performance," said Terrance, who knew how to return a compliment, "was always *most able.*"

Christopher Bidmead still had his wonderful swagger. He had long before given up writing for TV and moved into journalism, where he wrote about the workings of computers. He and Andrew Smith got into an intense discussion about the fantasy series *Lost*, about which Matthew had no opinion at all. "It doesn't *work,*" said Chris with finality, "it just doesn't work." He had a basement, he said, with an enormous TV in it, though he rarely watched TV. He had shortly before done a commentary with Tom Baker and said that Tom had arrived late and lingered in the Green Room doorway, making Bakerish remarks to the generality of the room, without catching anyone's eye.

"He's basically *shy,*" said Christopher, "and frightened."

Chris had a talent for stating the obvious as if it was an amazing new discovery.

In his commentary with Matthew, Chris sang an aria of overwrought praise for virtually every moment of *Full Circle*. Every shot was brilliant, every set was stunning. Matthew did not need to compete with anyone over his love for *Doctor Who*, and he felt it was possible to be affectionate and generous while observing that the set wobbled and the boom was in shot. But Chris was such a lively man that he created a useful, constructive energy in the studio.

Janet Fielding had done another commentary with Chris and had also noticed his propensity for throwing buckets of praise at everything. Isn't that set absolutely brillyyant???? God, she said, *everything* was brillyyyant! It was exhausting.

* * *

Lots of actors showed up for commentaries too. They remembered less than the writers, but more, surprisingly, than the two directors who contributed, though these were both delightful, Peter Moffatt and John Black. The passing decades had made scarcely a change in either of them. Directors do not age, it seems, they stay the same and then die. Peter watched the programmes unfold with a kind of engrossed silence, a wry smile all over his face which looked like it might break into a giggle any moment. His hair was now white, but otherwise, in features and poise and speech manner he seemed exactly the same. When directing *Doctor Who*, John Black had been working as a director for only five years and now he had decided to call it a day and his career was over, and yet he seemed remarkably similar, though not at home in the modern TV world where everything was shinier.

"I got fed up with being called in only to salvage a mess made by some ambitious young whizz kid who didn't know what he was doing."

John Black was the subject of one of the most astounding rumours Matthew had ever heard. It was reported to him as cold fact that John had ceased to work in TV long ago and was now one of the senior company directors at Sainsbury's, a multi-millionaire who took helicopters everywhere. Matthew asked what it was like to be so rich and to fly about in helicopters. John told him that the nearest he had ever come to Sainsbury's was shopping in the one near his house in Chiswick. Another rumour bit the dust. Good food costs less at Sainsbury's.

The delightful Nerys Hughes turned up to do *Kinda*, looking fuller-figured but otherwise unchanged. Always an unassuming woman, she seemed to remember little about *Kinda*, which must have been a tiny footnote in her long career, and whatever she remembered was drowned out by Matthew and Peter and Janet, the self-described 'mouth on legs'. With three big mouths sucking up all the oxygen, Nerys got to say very little. She sat there with a small, puzzled smile on her face.

She said to Matthew,

"You used to be so virginal!" She looked somehow disappointed that he had grown up, though he had not been a virgin even then. She was a calming influence in a studio which was in danger of combusting from the combined egos of Peter and Janet and Matthew.

Also quiet at her commentaries was Sarah Sutton, but she attended to the episodes with great concentration. She said little even about *Black Orchid*, though it was something of a show-case for her. The others mocked every frame and she did not pipe up and say, as Matthew hoped she might, *Shut up, I happen to like this.*

She said one afternoon with a little sigh, as she got ready to leave the studio, that she was looking forward to getting back to her home in

Guildford, "where I will go into the garden and sit in the sun with a nice glass of white wine." She made it sound idyllic.

It was lovely to see Janet again too, as smart and self-contained as ever.

She was not an ironist: when Matthew made a remark during a commentary like, "of course, men have to do the heroic stuff while the girls scream in corners," she rolled her eyes, having managed to take the remark at face value.

Janet got into an intense discussion with Peter about the Iraq war. A peculiar few minutes followed. Peter was standing at one end of the room and Janet sitting at the other: the conversation took over. Yet neither Matthew nor Sarah, though lingering about, were included. It was as if Matthew and Sarah were children, left to play while the grown-ups indulged in a serious discussion about politics. Matthew hovered by the fruit bowl and peeled an orange. He felt himself pulled down a time corridor, swept back. Thirty years had not passed after all, relationships were the same, neither of the 'children' had really lived at all. The status of the four people in the room was unchanged: Peter was 'important', being a 'star'; Janet 'intelligent' and 'thoughtful' and full of 'opinions'; Matthew and Sarah unserious teenagers, as free of thoughts as Disney characters. It was an exciting, time-travel sensation.

The producers of the commentaries, Paul Vanezis and Richard Molesworth, were open to experiments. Halfway through an episode, no-one having anything much to say, Matthew demanded a cup of tea, which was speedily fetched, the cups brought into the studio, the hot tea slurped noisily into the mike so listeners could picture it in the way of radio drama.

Sometimes there was silence. For some reason Matthew found little to say about *State of Decay*, though it was possibly his favourite story. Sometimes there was chaotic noise, everyone speaking over everyone else, as when *Black Orchid* proved to be slightly less wonderful than Matthew had remembered. Sometimes there was a shriek: "My *hair!*" cried Janet, as though it had been set alight.

For many years, Matthew lived under the impression that the wife of Roger Delgado had been in the box for the recording of Anthony's transformation scene at the end of *The Keeper of Traken*, though he had not been introduced to Mrs Delgado. He wanted to mention this on the commentary. He was assured by the producer, Paul Vanezis, that if Mrs Delgado had been there, it was such a closely guarded secret that it had never been leaked to anyone except Matthew. So what must have happened was that John had extended the invitation, which had been declined. Certainly the invitation was discussed.

Matthew had never thought the idea, though considerate, was in the best possible taste. Why would any widow feel flattered to watch a villain played many years earlier by her long dead husband being transformed into another actor?

Peter and Matthew and Sarah and Janet sat in the Green Room after one of the recordings, talking about their lives.
"I've just written a novel," said Matthew. "I hope to write another one."
"You should write a science fiction novel," said Peter. "It would sell loads of copies."
"Actually," said Matthew, "I would like to try to write a book about *Doctor Who*."
"If you do," said Peter, "I will go through it with a red pencil, marking everything that's untrue."
"Marvellous! I can inscribe a copy to you – Peter Davison's copy! – and you can mark in red everything you don't remember or think is wrong and it will be unique."
Later that evening, Matthew remembered Peter once saying that his favourite movie was *National Lampoon's Animal House*. If I ever write the *Who* book, thought Matthew, I will say that Peter quoted so relentlessly from *Animal House* that everyone got to know it by heart. That will give him something to cross out.

Matthew was asked if he would be willing to do a commentary with Tom Baker. He would have been very interested in doing so and it was informally suggested that he might like to do *Logopolis*. This failed to happen for logistical reasons. He could not be in the UK at the right time. A pity. Tom had by now found a fascinating new kind of celebrity. 'Eccentric' was still the word used to describe him, but it was in danger of becoming attached to the term "much-loved," as a result of his voice-overs for that comic masterpiece *Little Britain*, where he had on more than one occasion been compelled to pronounce Matthew's own name in his round, warm vowels. In a Chinese restaurant on Gerrard Street, two drunken couples from the suburbs adventuring in London for the day invited Matthew to their table. Matthew, always game for an unusual experience, joined them. They regaled him with quotes from *Little Britain*. It's bleeding fantastic, they said, just like this bloody country really fucking is! Matthew did not say that he had a unique if marginal connection to their favourite programme. Instead, he laughed as they produced quote after quote. "The only gay in the village! HAHA*haaahaaahaaa!*" "Not in effing Soho you're not! *Yaaahahaha*!" Roars of laughter all round. Matthew gave them assorted bits of information about decadent central London, the subject of which, in between the laughter, hugely interested them. The men were butch and into boating, their wives superstitious and sentimental. "Do you have a boyfriend back in America? Aaah. Do you really love 'im?" Matthew was so successful with these blotto people, evermore roaring with laughter, eyes streaming, that they paid for his dinner, before somehow making their way back to Essex. The waiter watched them leave and then threw Matthew a huge grin.

Matthew would have been curious to see Tom again, this difficult man whom he had strangely liked.

7

Finally, in 2009, Matthew saw an hour from the new version of *Doctor Who*. For several years he had been unable to see this programme because it was not shown in his area, and on the one or two occasions he had had the chance to take a look while in Britain, he had avoided it. This was the reason: he had liked *Doctor Who* all his life, with different levels of intensity of course, but never with less than affection. By the mid-eighties it had become numbing, general chat that it was no good anymore, but when he dipped into it he always enjoyed it – it remained inventive, distinctive, completely unlike anything else on TV, including the other space series, to which it bore little resemblance. He did not mind if occasionally the acting was dubious, there had always been buckets of that, he had contributed some dubious acting himself. He did not mind if the writing was stiff and limited, he accepted its limitations, you looked elsewhere for airy brilliance or poetic truth. Crude? Of course. Variable? Of course. Doesn't quite work? Of course. But it had remained, it seemed to him, *unpasteurised*. More than anything he despised the idea of a vapid, *pasteurised Doctor Who* for obese internet kiddies.

He had hardly watched TV in his adult life. This was not by intention, he merely lost touch with it. As an actor, in and out of work and living a slightly bohemian life, his days were not structured in the ordinary way which TV assumes. When he was working, he was busy in the evening. When he was not, he was living in flat shares with other actors and found the TV – when there was a TV, which was not always the case – got switched on too easily. Actors were the only people he knew who could tell him what was on at both one in the afternoon and one in the morning and he found this intolerable. Instead, he sat in pubs and read too much. Bob Langley of *Saturday Night at the Mill* had said of Tom Baker, *he sat in a corner reading a book all evening.* God, thought Matthew, that's me. He had probably not seen a series in its entirety since *Blackadder*.

So *Doctor Who*, whatever its faults, which have been too often and too tediously spelt out, represented everything he liked about telly, even discounting his own involvement. Telly and *Doctor Who* were pretty much synonymous for him. He *hated* the idea that he might *hate* the new *Doctor Who*. One actor from the old series expressed to Matthew an unflinchingly unfavourable view of the new.

"It's bollocks. Slick, shiny, empty, through-scored, Americanized, computer-generated bollocks."

This was a perfect description of everything Matthew hated.

"And when those fans ask what I think about it, I bloody well tell them, and they go all pink and flustered."

There was also the matter of music. Matthew had great love for the music of the old series, both the thrumming theme and the incidental lines which filled up those moments, otherwise silent but for footsteps, when characters ran down corridors. He'd liked Dudley Simpson's spare drum rolls and was fond of the little curls of synthesiser sound which had supplanted Dudley, though he had occasional reservations when, in the mid-eighties, Sylvester was drowned out by dance riffs. A friend of his, a composer, told him in 2004 that the expensive new *Doctor Who* series had achieved the impossible.

"The new music is even worse than the old!" exclaimed his friend.

"You're kidding!" said Matthew, acting appalled but secretly delighted.

"The latest musical wheeze is to stuff every moment of every episode with the endless squeal of a *massive* orchestra playing great undigested *gobs* of cod Stravinsky! The kind of stuff anyone with a first in music can turn out while playing *video* games!"

"I blame that John Williams," said Matthew. "He started this method of using music to dictate the audience's response."

"You're not wrong, you're right, though you have a habit of blaming *Star Wars* for everything that's crap in pop culture. But at least Williams' music is good by its own lights. This isn't, it's awful, awful, and it's relentless. It never ever bloody stops! I said to my friend Floppy – Floppy's his nickname – I said, this new *Doctor Who* is really good fun, you should give it a watch, and Floppy said after ten minutes he'd had to switch off, 'I can't bear all that fucking terrible music,' he said, 'it makes the whole thing unwatchable'."

"Dear, dear."

"It drowns out the cast all the time. I had to rent the DVD and use the subtitles to work out what one girl was on about. And it's often badly performed, the music."

"Really?"

"They have this chorus which goes *aaaahhhh* at what are supposed to be atmospheric moments, and they're always flat."

"Cripes. How wonderful. I hope they release the soundtrack."

"What's odd is, it's the BBC Welsh Chorus, which is normally very good. Maybe they're taking the piss. Do you think they're taking the piss? Musos are like that."

"You mean they all sing flat because they think *Doctor Who* is such balls?"

"I've met musos who'd do worse."

Then an episode of the new *Doctor Who* turned up in 2009 on BBC America, a channel which had suddenly become available on Matthew's TV.

So, nervously, he decided to give it a chance.

He loved it. He thought it was great fun, hugely enjoyable. Even on BBC America, broken into six-minute chunks to make room for commercials, it was great fun. (It was, however, deeply depressing to see that a series which had, in the nineteen seventies, included a starkly anti-capitalist satire called *The Sun Makers* was now sponsored by Wal-Mart, ultimate symbol of unvarnished capitalism).

The episode he saw was called *Doctor Who: Planet of the Dead*. It was written by Russell T. Davies, who Matthew had not met, and a man he had met and liked called Gareth Roberts. In it, Doctor Who flew high over a desert landscape the colour of warm butterscotch in a London bus, like Ermintrude over the moon, with an honourable lady at his side who, though wealthy, was a thief, for the adventure of it. There were a lot of other characters, most of them of the distinctive small part mode, though God knows the actors were trying their damnedest.

An impression was made by a bespectacled Welsh UNIT scientist who repeatedly expressed his love for the person of the Doctor in one of those comic ideas which do not come off 100%. There was a wonderful black lady on the flying bus with a shopping bag. She was gifted with powers of prognostication. She kept warning *Doctor Who* that he was doomed. This poor actress was bestowed with lines which would have caused hoots of laughter around the Acton rehearsal rooms of the old programme. Indeed, the lady looked as though she was struggling to keep her giggles inside her, but with what grace she suppressed those titters and spoke those words! Matthew hoped she would get her own spin-off series. Perhaps the UNIT scientist could have his own series too. Tom Baker had always regarded *Doctor Who* as a sitcom – he often used the term – but there had never been a formal *Doctor Who* sitcom in the style of *Terry and June*, complete with canned laughter and applause, and the UNIT scientist in love with *Doctor Who* might be the very character to pull it off, frustrated love being of course a comic staple. The UNIT scientist's sitcom might prove extremely amusing.

Doctor Who: Planet of the Dead was delightful. Matthew was in every way enchanted. The music was every bit as rotundly orchestral as his friend had said.

He happened to know that Gareth Roberts was in thrall to the season of the old *Doctor Who* which included the Paris story by Douglas Adams and *The Creature from the Pit* and *The Horns of Nimon*. Matthew had also liked these programmes, but then he had more or less liked all of *Doctor Who*. Gareth had formed a theory that several episodes during that season had garnered the highest *Doctor Who* ratings ever because, though 'fans' hated it, the public were enthralled. He refused to accept that a strike which had blacked out ITV had anything to do with these freakish ratings...

Matthew noticed speedily that the tone of *Doctor Who: Planet of the Dead* was in part a pastiche of these old slapstick programmes. (Thus, the reference to the honourable...) Russell T. Davies and Gareth Roberts had filled their script with faux Bakerisms. Fakerisms, they might be called. In 1980, these would have been received coolly by the star. Listening to the dialogue, Matthew knew that had Tom been presented with Russell T. Davies and Gareth's scenes, not a single fakerism would have been allowed to get on air. Authentic Bakerisms would have taken their place.

Another dimension of strangeness was that these fakerisms were spoken not by the Fourth Doctor, but by a marvellous, gangly fellow called David Tennant, who looked more like the young Morrissey than Tom Baker, though he made his eyes wide and globular at every opportunity. David Tennant's sparkling *Doctor Who* had a contemporary 'classless' accent of the kind spoken by modern ministerial war-mongers. It was like listening to Tony Blair reciting the speeches of Winston Churchill.

Doctor Who: Planet of the Dead contained what must be the first shit joke ever in *Doctor Who*, by which is meant the first joke about shit, not, of course, the first bad joke. There have been plenty of those, many of them Bakerisms.

When *Doctor Who: Planet of the Dead* came to an end, Matthew was fantastically excited and relieved. *He liked it!* Thank *God!* Now he could watch more. Yet, the next week no new episode could be found, but instead an extremely aggressive commercial for the DVD version of *Doctor Who*: *Planet of the Dead*. In the early days, episodes were shown once and then disappeared. Many years later they became slim books. Now they were permanently to hand. Memory had no chance to transform them.

This was sad.

Someone leant him a DVD with a two-part serial about a library, then he saw a dark thriller directed by Graeme Harper called *The Waters of Mars*, which culminated in a suicide, and he saw finally the end of David Tennant. It was all very enjoyable. Matthew had never seen an episode of the old series he had not enjoyed and now it seemed to be the same with the new one.

He felt divided about one element of the new programmes, which was the character scenes, in which girls and boys and sometimes even the Doctor himself emoted. *How wonderful he is, what would the universe be like without him,* said one girl of the Doctor. *I'd be very proud if you were my son,* said Bernard Cribbins. *I would be very proud if you were my father,* said the Doctor, though he was a great deal older than Bernard Cribbins. Matthew knew that, if he had been handed scenes like these in 1980 he would have thought they were brilliant. *At last, character!* Watching them in the twenty-first century, he found he liked them and found them touching, but they left him wondering. They had a sentimental tinge which was absolutely new to *Doctor Who*: apart from the sense of excitement, viewers had not been asked to be *moved* by the series. Adric was often self-pitying in the way of a teenager but viewers were not being expected to admire it, to go *aaah, poor thing.* Now even the Doctor was allowed an occasional little glimmer of self-pity- *it's very lonely being a Time Lord, all your friends leave you in the end.* In the past, when he had saved a planet the aliens had said thanks and the Doctor had said bye and he'd buggered off to his next adventure. Now there were long, lingering moments of tears and joy. *How moved everybody was.* Matthew thought the benefit – a new warmth, perhaps, a new kindness, a richness to the backgrounds of the companions, who now had parents, lovers, jobs, houses, worries, a yearning for children – came at a loss. The old characters had been wooden, undoubtedly, but in this sheer woodenness there was something dry, something admirably unsentimental.

Accompanying these programmes – on BBC America, at any rate – were funny little self-congratulatory documentaries. Russell T. Davies praised his own scripts without looking the slightest bit embarrassed, though he wore strange green spectacles. (Perhaps they were ultramarine?) A lady called Julie, an Executive Producer, had a magnificent line in promotional guff. Every time she read a new script by Russell, she said, squinting dewily, it was a very *private* moment. Aaaah, she said of one scene, looking moved, it was such a very dramatically *human* scene, so *touching...*

But David Tennant answered questions pleasantly in his unexpected Scottish accent, appearing distracted and slightly unwell. This is the way it should be done.

Matthew wondered how the old crew would have dealt with such documentaries. John Nathan-Turner would have loved them, he supposed. He would have loved to have been an above-the-title producer like Russell T. Davies, feted by all. But had Tom Baker said that looking over a script by Christopher Hamilton Bidmead had been a very private moment, it could have meant only that he had read it sitting on the toilet.

Perhaps the big difference between the old series and the new one is that people actually like the new! Viewers who watch *EastEnders* and *Britain's Got Talent* and the Channel Four programme in which people in a house scratch each other's eyes out, also enjoy *Doctor Who*. On a recent visit to Britain, Matthew found himself in a library in Sussex on the day children from the special needs school came, each required to choose a book. They were about the age Matthew had been when he had tried to steal *Doctor Who and the Zarbi* from the library van at his school. All but one rushed into the room where the children's books were. The exception, a slow-moving child of maybe seven, was drawn like a magnet to the DVD shelves, from which he plucked an episode of the new *Doctor Who*. He stroked the colourful plastic case and took it to his teacher.

"*Doctor Whoooo*," he said, and again, "*Doctor Whoooo*...," stroking the box with his lumpy fingers all the while. Obviously, he loved the programme, its colour, its zip, its aura of fun.

"Yes, *Doctor Who*," said the teacher, "isn't he great? I love him too. But today you have to choose a *book*."

"*Doctor Whooooo*," said the boy, eyes glistening, looking at David Tennant's grinning face, thrusting the box to his teacher.

It was unimaginable in Matthew's youth that a teacher would admit to liking *Doctor Who*. What nonsense it is, they said. They liked only *Star Trek*, with its admirable messages, designed to make people nicer.

In those days, people came in on a Saturday afternoon after football or raking leaves and switched on the TV. They checked their Pools and the television stayed on, murmuring in the background.

"What's on now?"

"It's *Doctor Who*."

"Christ, what's on BBC2?"

There were no channel changers so someone had to walk across to the TV and press a button. Click.

"A documentary about insect life in the outback."

"Bloody hell. What's on ITV?"

Click.

"Dusty Bin."

"Crumbs. Well, turn it back to *Doctor Who* – it'll be *The Generation Game* in ten minutes anyway."

At that time, the BBC drama department was awesomely, perhaps insanely, ambitious, making the most artistically adventurous TV in the world. The most popular programmes usually came from another department, Light Entertainment, though Drama made plenty of widely watched programmes, including an awful hospital soap called *Angels*, and a historical romance serial set in 18th Century Cornwall called *Poldark*, itself something of a cult, and middle brow entertainments about vets. But many producers were interested in intensely demanding, intensely literary, material. There were lots of grittily political one-off plays, directed by people who might later work at the National Theatre. The link between TV and theatre was very strong – TV fiction had not yet come to mean pretend movies. BBC people came from the world of theatre, not from film. Some ITV directors had made movies. Charles Crichton, director of Ealing comedies, turned out many hours of the wondrous *Avengers* series, but then ITV was a whole other world. Here at the BBC were Dennis Potter serials which belonged to no genre but their own. Here were Alan Bennett's *Talking Heads*, half-hour plays featuring a single actor. Here were serials for the family drawn from old classics: Dickens, Jane Austen, H. G. Wells, *Little Lord Fauntleroy*, *The Prince and the Pauper*, *Anne of Green Gables*. In the 1970s, a dramatisation in twenty parts of *War and Peace* was made, though lord knows what it was like. Someone proposed *Crime and Punishment*. Okay, that'll fill up a few slow winter evenings.

Perhaps all this sprang from that old Fabian socialist ideal that, freed from labour, everyone would become a philosopher, a seeker after profound truths, a reader of dense tomes. Matthew once heard a potty old drunk woman who worked as a PUM say in her thick German accent,

"Americans are goot at *entertainment, yezzz,* but they don't understand *drama!*"

Much of the point of the BBC was saving Britain from America. No-one wanted a country run for the interests of commercial profiteers. Nobody wanted programmes sponsored by car companies and drug companies and Burger joints. *Doctor Who* was created in a public service environment – it had nothing to do with making a profit. It had nothing to do with Wal-Mart. It was not a product.

JNT didn't care about adapting Dostoevsky or Thomas Hardy, what he liked was *Dallas*. The theatre he liked most was light: pantomimes and American musicals. While making *Doctor Who* he wrote and produced a couple of pantomimes, including one featuring *Doctor Who* actors: Peter Davison as Buttons, Anthony Ainley as Baron Hardup. He talked about ratings, which he wanted to be enormous, though ratings were more the preoccupation of the commercial channel, with its need to sell advertising. More important in the BBC was the appreciation index, which measured not numbers but quality of enjoyment. Curiously, in all its years, *Doctor Who* never fared very well on the appreciation index.

John wanted a hit, but, strikingly, he presided over a series which was increasingly an acquired taste. Matthew could never square this contradiction. He did not mind the contradiction, in fact he liked it, it was interesting. Up until John, people knew roughly what they would get each week on *Doctor Who*, just as they knew what they would get each week on *Doctor Finlay's Casebook* or *Some Mothers Do 'Ave 'Em*. But when Matthew watched later *Doctor Who*, which he did occasionally, he found it impossible to predict even the tone, let alone the content, week by week. This was thrilling and exciting. One week, you got a Lost In Space style low-brow comedy, the next a peculiar little thing with old ladies in a Rolls Royce, then a breathtakingly fast dazzler in which a guy in sunglasses went up and down in an elevator in an old house. You got Georgina Hale, you got Martin Jarvis, you got Richard Briers, you got Ken Dodd. You got Hale and Pace. Perhaps it was not always scary any more and sometimes not especially suspenseful – the action scenes, the Cybermen stalking along a high gantry towards the Doctor's companion, Ace, went for less than ever – but it was exhilaratingly weird. More even than before, it was unlike anything else on TV. More even than before, if you didn't like it you *really* didn't like it, which is always a good sign: less David Bowie than Peter Hammill, not for everyone but *absolutely* for some. *Doctor Who*, groaned the newspapers, was in decline. If it was, it was a triumphant decline.

It was Stilton suffused with brandy. The revival was brilliantly tailored for a more mainstream taste. It was not a burger and fries, by any means, but something everybody could like: Shepherd's Pie, perhaps, topped with slices of melted, browned American Jack. Captain Jack, that is.

Victorian novels often end with quick summaries of the fates of the minor characters, their marriages or deaths. In the twenty-first century chatter had it that the part of *Doctor Who* guaranteed great stardom and even the *Doctor Who* girl will end up on telly in Hollywood. In the old days, stardom was never mooted and certainly never came, but marriages happened in fair numbers. Once Mark Strickson joined *Doctor Who*, the regular cast, for the first time in history – John told Matthew – consisted solely of married men and women, Janet having wed her journalist, Sarah having wed her doctor. After her work promoting Catholic theology, Lalla Ward gave up acting and married a scientist. Janet gave up acting too, working for a campaigning organisation called *Women In Film*, then successfully running an agency, with Paul McGann among her clients. Actors morphed into agents at a great rate. Wendy Padbury became one, managing Colin Baker, and Tom told Matthew that the secretary to his agent Jean Diamond had, long, long before in the very early years, been a *Doctor Who* girl. "They're everywhere!" said Tom.

Only Matthew lingered on, for years and years and years, somehow usually earning enough at the end of each year to pay his rent and buy wine and books.

The curse of *Doctor Who*, as far as there was a curse, applied only to careers: Doctors and companions lived on happily enough. They did not go crazy or die young. They led interesting lives and had interesting adventures. The only story for which the word tragedy might be appropriate was John Nathan-Turner's. Matthew had not seen him for twenty years when he died, but was upset to come across his obituary so unexpectedly. They had been in touch shortly before. Matthew had wanted the right to come and go from the US as often as he chose. He asked John to write a letter for his Green Card application, and John's response could not have been surpassed for flattery. Matthew was very grateful for his help. But, always a drinker, he had taken to spirits in such enormous quantities that this once large man shrank to scarcely a hundred pounds.

Having a temperament which naturally liked the programme, Matthew felt mainly pleasure when he thought of it, and it was nice to have an association with material for which he did not have to fake affection, an affection which never quite vanished, even when he wished it would.

The sentimental view is that the possibilities for people are infinite. This is not true. Children are the creatures they are, and will become the creatures they become. But children are scarcely aware of options anyway, and as they grow older and become more aware of them, the fewer there will be. So it goes on. They longer they live, the fewer the possibilities, and the more they will be aware of the lost ones, or what they imagine are the lost ones. Finally, of course, for everyone, there will be no options at all.

Of all the many possible lives Matthew might have lived, the one he has lived seems to him among the best. The decision the producer made in casting him in *Doctor Who* was, by any realistic standards, life-changing, in the stark and direct meaning that his life was changed by it. Without it, it would have been different.

Sometimes he found a job in a play which went down well. Occasionally a well-known actor would make a nice comment to him.

"I don't know why you aren't busier," said one household name. "You are the kind of character actor who should be working all the time." Matthew smiled and said thank you. But he knew why he was not working all the time. He was, forever, the boy from *Doctor Who*.

But Matthew was sceptical about the implication that it halted careers which would otherwise have been stratospheric. He did not think that, had he not been in *Doctor Who*, he would have been a movie star. He was happy enough as a jobbing actor, making a living of a sort doing interesting plays, meeting interesting, often exciting, people.

He did not believe that *that* actor would, but for *Doctor* bloody *Who*, have become a great interpreter of Chekhov, or that *that* one would have been lighting up movie screens, or that *that* one would have become a great light comedienne. And one thing was sure: *Doctor Who* was a better bloody job than most people had.

The subsequent years have been exciting, unexpected, dramatic. Not without darkness, and Matthew is aware that he has, by luck or by charm, been saved from disaster, more than once, by lovers, friends, circumstance, the falling of a card. There is a romantic idea, prevalent in our culture, of those who live on the edge. Most people feel themselves to be trapped, so they are romantically drawn to those who seem to be free: the figure of Doctor Who and his TARDIS represent an idea of this freedom, like Huckleberry Finn and Arthur Rimbaud. It has often been remarked that all the big science fiction cults are fictional worlds without money. Matthew has lived nearer the edge of things than most, emotionally, financially. He is glad to have seen over the cliff's edge, and glad not to have toppled over. But of course there is still time for that.

8

Matthew walks along the promenade towards Brighton Pier. The sea is grey. At the entrance to the pier, in the court flanked by two arcs of little booths selling fish and chips and burgers and slices of pizza, is a blue police box. A banner above the pier gates announces a *Doctor Who* exhibition down the end.

Matthew looks in wonder at the police box and reaches out and touches it.

He hears voices. Behind him a fattish man in his fifties with a Yorkshire accent is talking to his two adult sons.

"Gor!" says the father. "Look at that bloody thing!"

"Yeh," says one of the sons.

"Bloody rubbish. May as well get a bloody photo of it I suppose. Excuse me. Would you mind taking a picture of me and my kids by this bloody thing?"

"Certainly," says Matthew, and takes the digital camera. They stand in front of the box and grin like fools. Matthew presses the button, the picture is taken. They look at it.

"Great! Thanks!" says the father. "Bloody ridiculous thing." They cross the street to Harry Ramsden's.

Matthew touches his beloved box again. Dusk is falling. He goes down the steps to the beach, as swiftly and silently as a shadow.

February 2009 – February 2010
Montreal, Quebec / New Haven, CT

available from
whatnoise.co.uk

Matthew Waterhouse has worked extensively as an actor, in theatre and for the BBC. He is the author of three novels: *Fates, Flowers*, *Vanitas*, and *Precious Liars*, and one volume of memoirs, *Blue Box Boy*. He lives in New Haven, CT, visiting Europe frequently.

Also available from What Noise Productions

When Harry Met Sheila
The Autobiography of Sheila Steafel

When Harry Met Sheila is a powerful story about one woman's journey of self discovery, her marriage to Steptoe and Son actor Harry H. Corbett, and her struggle to let go of the demons of the past.

Sheila's autobiography is a brave and honest account by an actress who was once crowned 'The Queen of Comedy', in which she explores how the traumas of her childhood and growing up in a dysfunctional family in apartheid-torn South Africa in the 1930s and 40s have impacted her personal life and career.

The Devil Take Your Stereo by Anthony Keetch

Who is the mysterious intruder in the bedroom of socialite Marjorie Ashbrook?
Why are there Nazis in Hampstead?
Will playboy and dog-meat heir Simon Tubular-Wells succumb to an act of shame which could shatter his standing in society?
What diabolical and probably foreign mastermind is behind it all?
Can Charles, the tough but classy aristocrat rescue his friends and save the world from the dark satanic forces which threaten to engulf it… or will even he forfeit his soul in the War Against Beastliness?

Best-selling and globally-acclaimed author Sir Desmond Stirling brings you his 243rd novel - another of his insanely successful satanic chillers, specially designed to scare the living daylights out of you. Set in the glamorous jet-setting world which is out of reach for most of you, *The Devil Take Your Stereo* is a exciting and blood-curdling yarn which you won't be able to put down, provided you pick it up in the first place.

Fates, Flowers: A Comedy of New York
by Matthew Waterhouse

Sara Smith is one of the most monstrous characters you could hope not to meet. She lives in Greenwich Village - on life insurance courtesy of her late husband - but she has fallen into a dreary routine: work in a card shop by day - where she is the rudest sales clerk imaginable - and weary evenings passed in the same cellar bar, night after night, with the same old people. But when she meets, and seduces, a gorgeous boy called Steve, she has no idea what she is getting herself into.

Neither has he.

Neither will you.

Vanitas: A Comedy of New York
by Matthew Waterhouse

When you wish upon a star, your dreams come true...?

They did, at any rate, for Florinda Quenby, though not in the way she had planned. When she flew out to Hollywood to become a movie star, she could not imagine the terrible struggles ahead of her, from riches back to rags, or that fame and wealth would finally come from an entirely different quarter, her fantastical soup factory in Harlem modeled on the Taj Mahal...

Once she was famous, she became one of New York's grandest hostesses and one of America's most beloved celebrities. Her parties for the Christmas season in her huge, gold-lined apartment overlooking Central park were an unmissable part of Manhattan's social calendar. Those parties grew wilder and wilder every year, until finally she decided to throw one last party, designed to top all the others...

This is a tale of ambition and wealth and fame and vanity. This is Florinda's incredible story.

Wishhobbler by Francis O'Dowd

Somewhere in the damp, twisting alleyways of the Songwynd slums, there lives a hideous freak of nature. Driven by poverty, Spin and her family move to the Songwynds in search of work. There they share a tiny, rat-infested flat with a wishhobbler. An enormous toffee- and custard- guzzling fleabag, the wishhobbler's viciousness has caused fear and mayhem among the slum dwellers. Unable to hit back at the wishhobbler, her victims instead pick on Spin and her family. Friendless, haunted by thugs and bullies and struggling to cope with a bizarre illness, Spin isn't having much fun.

When the wishhobbler disrupts the carefully laid plans of the mysterious Television Racers, Spin finds herself at the centre of a deadly confrontation.

And then things take a turn for the worse...

Jaggy Splinters by Christopher Brookmyre

Everyone's favourite unorthodox journalist, Jack Parlabane, goes undercover to investigate the mysterious and lucrative world of alternative medicine - in particular, the practice of homeopathy. Are there unexplained forces that can be harnessed to heal us, or is it all a load of sugar?

Meanwhile, a sinister tale of restorative justice and the occult takes an even darker turn; two body-snatchers find more than they bargained for when raiding a morgue; and a contract killer finds that fatherhood has sent him on the straight and narrow... sort of.

Fast paced and wickedly entertaining, Jaggy Splinters is a dark, twisted and hilarious collection of short stories from bestselling author Christopher Brookmyre.

Star Cops by Chris Boucher

Arriving at the European space station *Charles de Gaulle*, Chief Superintendent Nathan Spring struggles to adapt to conditions in low gravity while working to mould his team into an effective force for law enforcement. Before he's even begun to adjust, he discovers that several crewmembers have recently died, following unforeseen spacesuit malfunction. Although these apparent accidents fall well within the limits of statistical acceptability, Spring's instincts again lead to him to suspect the work of a saboteur. He decides to expose the culprit by taking a desperate course of action - gambling with his own life...

Elsewhere, Spring's second-in-command David Theroux investigates an explosion on a distant space freighter that has knocked the craft off course and condemned its two pilots to death, the Star Cops are warned of terrorist attacks by a communications expert based on the Moon, a scientist disappears without trace from the American space station - with the crew denying his very existence - and rumours begin to grow of alien artefacts having been discovered on Mars...